DATE DUE

DE 21 '02			
8021 '03			

The State of the Nation

The State
OF THE
Nation

*Government
and the
Quest for a
Better Society*

DEREK BOK

Harvard University Press
Cambridge, Massachusetts
London, England
1996

Library of Congress Cataloging-in-Publication Data
Bok, Derek Curtis.
The state of the nation: government and the quest for a better
society / Derek Bok.
p. cm.
Includes index.
ISBN 0–674–29210–3 (alk. paper)
1. Quality of life—United States.   2. United States—Social
conditions—1945–   3. United States—Economic conditions—1945–
4. United States—Politics and government—1945–1989.   5. United
States—Politics and government—1989–   I. Title.
HN60.B65   1996
306′.0973—dc20   96–22881

Preface

This book began with a wholly unexpected visit from emissaries of three foundations during the last week of my twenty-year effort to preside over the unruly affairs of Harvard University. When I first learned of their coming, I assumed that my visitors wanted to discuss the possibility of a new grant to Harvard. To my surprise, they asked instead whether I would consider spending whatever time I needed to write about why the government of the United States seemed to be encountering so much difficulty and provoking so much dissatisfaction.

The offer could not have come at a better time. After wandering for a quarter of a century in the trackless desert of academic administration, I had resolved to spend my remaining active years doing what I first came to Harvard to do—reading, thinking, and writing about problems of abiding interest. Suddenly, here were three foundations offering me a chance to do exactly that.

From the beginning, however, I felt that I could not simply assume that government in the United States was performing badly. Despite the loud complaints directed at politicians and bureaucrats, the claim that they were failing the country was an assertion that deserved careful scrutiny, like any other important proposition.

After months of reading on the subject, I found that discussions of this issue were not as common as one might think, notwithstanding the flood of articles and books about our government and its problems. Some of these works—mostly those of a scholarly variety—did not purport to judge the effectiveness of the government as a whole but simply explored a puzzling question or tried to explain an interesting new development. Other books—more often written by journalists—described some important failing of government or some crisis allegedly brewing and tried to explain why the problem had arisen and how it might be overcome. But rarely did an author begin by making a careful, dispassionate effort to assess how well or badly our government was performing overall.

In these troubled times, many readers may assume that the failings of our political leaders are so obvious that they do not require demonstration. Yet the United States is still the most prosperous nation in the world, with a remarkable degree of personal freedom and an enviably stable, democratic government. Our public officials must have been doing *something* right. For this reason, it would surely be unwise to jump to conclusions by offering a diagnosis before giving the patient a thorough examination. Accordingly, I have decided to write an initial volume comparing the progress of our country with that of other leading democratic nations to determine whether Americans have reason to feel pessimistic about their society and, if so, whether the government has helped bring us to our present state. In the course of this inquiry, I will try to arrive at a fair and balanced account of the strengths and weaknesses of our government, before moving on in a second book to probe more deeply the question why our policies and programs so often fail to meet our expectations.

In reviewing the progress of our society and the role of government in it, I have had to explore many different facets of American life. Not all of these subjects were familiar to me when I began. Fortunately, I have been blessed to have friends who are experts in these fields and who were willing to read and criticize chapters. In particular I wish to thank Graham Allison, Francis Bator, Douglas Besharov, William G. Bowen, Gerald Bracey, Lewis Branscomb, Harvey Brooks, Bob Brustein, Paul DiMaggio, John Dunlop, David Ellwood, Ben Friedman, Nathan Glazer, Mary Ann Glendon, Peter Hall, Mark Moore, Lawrence Mead, Joe Newhouse, Paul Osterman, Diane Ravitch, Marc Roberts, Henry Rosovsky, Theda Skocpol, Robert Stavins, Abigail Thernstrom, Sid Verba, Paul Weiler, and Lloyd Weinreb. Any errors that survived the scrutiny of these colleagues are all of my own making.

I would also like to thank my editor, Michael Aronson, for his patience and many helpful suggestions, and Laurel Imig of the Brookings Institution, who gave invaluable help in preparing various tables and ensuring the accuracy of much information used in the study.

Many added thanks go to my assistant, Connie Higgins, who has loyally typed more drafts and retrieved more books than I care to remember.

As always, I owe a special debt of gratitude to my wife, Sissela, and my daughter, Hilary; they read the entire manuscript and gave me much good advice and encouragement. My son, Tomas, was exceptionally helpful with the technical aspects of presenting relevant data.

Last but not least, I would like to thank the Robert Wood Johnson, Rockefeller, and MacArthur foundations for giving me the chance to tackle such a challenging subject. They have been extraordinarily patient in allowing me to go about the task at my own pace and in my own way. I could not be more grateful.

Contents

V. VALUES

VI. WHAT IT ALL MEANS

The State of the Nation

Introduction

In the early 1990s, by all outward appearances, America's cup seemed to be running over with good fortune. The United States had finally won the Cold War after almost fifty years of unrelenting effort to halt the spread of Communism. For the first time in decades, people no longer lived in the shadow of an impending nuclear holocaust. Despite the burden of having long maintained the world's most expensive military force, the United States continued to enjoy the highest standard of living of any major country on earth. Unemployment levels were among the lowest in the West, while inflation was holding steady at a small fraction of what it had been only a dozen years before.

How did the public respond to these manifold blessings? In April 1995, 74 percent of Americans summed up their feelings by declaring themselves "dissatisfied with the way things are going in this country."[1] This verdict was hardly an isolated example. In 1994, more than 50 percent of the American people felt that their children would not have as good a life as they themselves had enjoyed.[2] A majority believed that the United States was no longer the leading economic power in the world.[3] The Harris alienation index, which measures how far the public feels estranged from the powers that be, reached its all-time high.[4] By every available measure, ordinary citizens had lost confidence in the major institutions of the country and in the leaders responsible for its welfare.

Such gloom is not characteristic of Americans. Throughout our history, we have always been noted for our optimism—our faith that every problem has a solution and that progress is the natural state of human affairs. Even in the Great Depression, most people saw the

1

nation's troubles as merely a temporary setback in a land exceptionally blessed by abundance and opportunity.

The pessimism of today stands in vivid contrast with the mood that prevailed in the United States beginning in 1953 when Dwight D. Eisenhower entered the White House. Eisenhower's election seemed to usher in the good times that most people had been waiting for since the end of World War II. Victory over Germany and Japan had not immediately produced the era of normalcy and domestic tranquillity that many had expected. Instead, the Communist takeover in eastern Europe, the fall of China, the news of a Soviet atomic bomb, and the invasion of South Korea made Americans realize that their triumph over fascism had not been the war to end all wars. Revelations that spies had given military secrets to the Russians and charges that Communists had infiltrated the higher reaches of government led to a campaign by Senator Joseph McCarthy of Wisconsin to expose individuals suspected of harboring Communist sympathies and connections. Eventually, however, McCarthy's influence waned and the Korean War came to an end. At last, the nation was ready to savor the fruits of peace and unprecedented prosperity.

To many eyes, the United States seemed remarkable indeed. As one ebullient British author wrote: "There never was a country more fabulous than America. She sits bestride the world like a Colossus; no other power at any time in the world's history has possessed so varied or so great an influence on other nations."[5] Added Vice-President Richard Nixon, "The United States, the world's largest capitalist country, . . . comes closest to the ideal of prosperity for all in a classless society."[6]

With only 7 percent of the world's population, Americans accounted for more than half of all the goods and services produced on the entire planet. Defeated, disorganized, and ravaged by war, Germany and Japan gave little sign as yet of the economic miracles they would perform in coming decades. Our victorious European allies were too depleted by the recent conflict to pose an economic threat. The few advanced nations that had been spared destruction, notably Switzerland and Sweden, hardly seemed large enough to count as major economic powers.

Favored by a growing economy, enterprising Americans quickly produced a burst of innovations promising untold benefits for consumers. William Levitt brought the methods of mass production to the housing industry, opening huge tracts of suburban homes at prices that ordinary Americans could afford (as low as $7,990). Betty Furness explained to countless housewives the wonders of new kitchen appliances and frozen vegetables. Automobiles rolled off assembly lines by the millions as new federal highways began to spread in a huge network across the country. Fast-food chains such as McDonald's, discount stores such as Korvette's, franchised motels such as Howard Johnson's and Holiday Inn were sprouting everywhere.

Above all, television came into its own, bringing *Ozzie and Harriet, Leave It to Beaver,* and other visions of the model suburban family for all Americans to emulate and enjoy. To be sure, the ideal American family did not leave much room for women yearning for a career of their own. According to Mrs. Dale Carnegie, "The two big steps that women must take are to help their husbands decide where they are going and use their pretty heads to help them get there."[7] In this atmosphere of cheerful domesticity, the proportion of women Ph.D.'s dropped below 10 percent, while women lawyers and doctors grew less common than they had been in the early years of the twentieth century.

As the 1950s wore on, stirrings of discontent could be detected here and there, harbingers of turbulence yet to come. The youthful rebelliousness of James Dean, Jack Kerouac, and Marlon Brando struck a responsive chord in many young people. Sloan Wilson's *Man in a Gray Flannel Suit* and David Riesman's *The Lonely Crowd* awakened fears of excessive conformity to the social norms of suburban neighborhoods and large corporations. At Smith College, Betty Friedan returned for her fifteenth reunion to find growing discontent among her housebound classmates. On a Birmingham bus, Rosa Parks refused to give up her seat, sparking a citywide bus boycott and a new career for a young minister named Martin Luther King, Jr. Almost unnoticed, an outspoken young Yale alumnus, William F. Buckley, Jr., launched a conservative magazine, *The National Review.* These early signs, however, were not fully understood at the time, nor could many people imagine just how far they would eventually lead. For the moment, in the words of Tennessee's governor, Frank Clement, Americans were content to relax and enjoy "looking down the long green fairways of indifference."[8]

The View from the Nineties

In retrospect, of course, we know that in the 1950s the country was hardly as robust as most Americans seemed to believe. Health care was primitive by current standards and certainly not available to all. Poverty was widespread, though much of it lay hidden on farms and in rural communities, out of the sight of most Americans. Much housing was still substandard, especially in rural areas. Black children in the South were relegated to segregated schools; their parents could not sleep in most hotels, eat in most restaurants, cast their ballots in elections, or enjoy the public parks and pools reserved for whites. Women had no rights in the workplace, let alone the right to equal treatment in applying to college. Factories polluted the air and water and buried their toxic wastes with little heed for the consequences.

Looking back, therefore, we are now better off in many ways than our forebears were four decades ago. Yet Americans today are far gloomier about their country than they were in the 1950s. No one would dream of describing voters in the 1990s as contentedly "looking down the long green fairways of indifference." In 1960, the vast majority of Americans believed that the nation was progressing nicely and that it would be even more successful in the future than it had been in the past.[9] By 1991, 64 percent of the public believed that the country was "headed in the wrong direction."[10]

What accounts for all this anger and pessimism? Is the country really going downhill? Or are Americans simply suffering from one of those inexplicable crises of morale that sometimes come over us, singly or collectively, for reasons even psychologists cannot explain?

Although many people claim to know what ails the country, ascertaining the true state of affairs is actually more difficult than one might think from reading the current commentaries on America. There is sharp disagreement over the state of almost every institution and field of endeavor in the United States. To President Bill Clinton, Americans are "choking on a health care system that isn't working."[11] To Republican lawmakers (echoing President George Bush before them), Americans have the finest health care system in the world. According to Jacques Attali, "Industry is the only lasting foundation of a nation's power, and it is in this sense that the signs of America's lasting decline are everywhere."[12] Yet the World Economic Forum, composed of leading business executives from many countries, recently pronounced

American business the most competitive in the world. To Richard Goodwin, "It is no secret to most parents and concerned citizens that our public school system is a disaster."[13] According to a recent survey, however, 70 percent of American parents would give the school their children attend a grade of either A or B.[14]

The list goes on. According to Vice-President Gore, "Modern industrial civilization, as presently organized, is colliding violently with our planet's ecological system. The ferocity of its assault on the earth is breathtaking and the horrific consequences are occurring so quickly as to defy our capacity to recognize them, comprehend their global implications, and organize an appropriate and timely response."[15] In striking contrast, Gregg Easterbrook, toward the end of his 700-page tome on the environment, concludes that "in the Western world the Age of Pollution is nearly over."[16] One last example: In 1988, 87 percent of white Americans affirmed that "in the past 25 years, the country has moved closer to equal opportunity among the races."[17] Yet at about the same time, only a minority of blacks agreed that racial equality was increasing.[18]

In addition to disagreements over the state of different facets of American life, there has also been much debate over whether the country as a whole is in decline. The controversy first sprang up in the late 1980s, in the wake of publicity over the sagging performance of American companies in world markets.[19] Soon, a flurry of statistics and arguments appeared in print on both sides of the issue.

Taking the somber view, Paul Kennedy, Edward Luttwak, and a number of other writers pointed to the fact that several countries have been outdistancing the United States in productivity growth, their companies have successfully invaded our markets, their health care is cheaper and more accessible, and their children spell and compute more proficiently than ours. To these authors, our huge deficits and trade imbalances signal an erosion of our economic strength, while the widespread resort to drugs and violence in America points to a moral and spiritual malaise of even more troubling proportions. According to Paul Kennedy, the most likely prognosis for America is not collapse but a future in which the country continues to "muddle through." Yet he added, "The long-term implication of muddling through is slow, steady, relative *decline*—in comparative living standards, educational levels, technical skills, social provisions, industrial leadership, and, ultimately, *national power*, just as in Britain."[20]

At Harvard University, an institution rarely noted for bullishness about America, scholars quickly took issue with the pessimists. According to Samuel Huntington and, in a separate book, Joseph Nye, America is much stronger than the prophets of gloom make out:[21] our military forces have never enjoyed such superiority, our universities are the envy of nations everywhere, our scientists are still preeminent in the world. Far from declining, say the optimists, the U.S. economy remains more productive than those of its rivals, and its share of world production has not diminished for at least the past decade or two. Although other countries grew faster than America did for many years, it was only natural that they should do so at a time when they were rebuilding after the ravages of World War II. Now that the reconstruction is over and differences in productivity rates and standards of living have narrowed throughout the industrialized world, the critical point is that America has retained its position of economic leadership. As a result, according to Professor Nye, "The United States remains the largest and richest power with the greatest capacity to shape the future."[22]

This debate has been muddled from the start by the fact that the participants are often talking about different things. For some, the issue is whether America's economic strength is eroding relative to that of other advanced, industrialized nations. Others are asking whether our influence and power in the world are on the wane. Still others inquire whether the United States is as well prepared as Europe and Japan to cope with the great challenges to come in the twenty-first century—population growth, technological change, and global environmental hazards. Since the authors are asking such different questions, it is not surprising that they arrive at different conclusions.

It is also clear that none of these writings speaks to all the issues that trouble the public today. Americans worry that our society may no longer be making progress toward a broad array of objectives that matter to many people. Responding to such wide-ranging concerns requires far more than simply asking whether the United States is preserving its power in the world or maintaining its capacity to meet specific global challenges, important though these questions may be. Even economic growth, with all the benefits it provides, is too narrow a focus. For growth has but a tenuous connection with other aspects of society that also matter to Americans—our personal freedoms, our moral standards, the quality of our natural environment, and the justice of our laws and institutions, to name just a few.

There is a compelling reason for a careful, objective look at the full range of problems that are troubling Americans. Heated discussions are currently in progress all across the United States about the condition of our society. More than at any time in recent memory, familiar premises are being questioned, established ways of conducting the nation's affairs are under attack, policies that would have seemed unthinkable in earlier periods are being actively considered. At such a moment, it is especially important to agree, insofar as possible, on what the true condition of our society is and whether the nation is indeed "headed in the wrong direction." If it is, we need to know exactly where America is losing ground so that we can concentrate our efforts on the problems that need to be solved. If the country is not in a state of decline, we ought to know that, too—not merely to preserve our peace of mind but to keep from searching needlessly for scapegoats and conjuring up exaggerated and unnecessary remedies.

This study will reveal that although America has made progress in many important respects over the past forty years, the record of this country often compares quite poorly with that of most other leading industrial democracies. From a position of unequaled strength and prosperity, the United States has fallen behind other advanced nations in achieving many of the goals that large majorities of Americans care most about. The individualism, initiative, and independence which seemed to serve this country admirably during its first 150 years no longer appear to be working so well in the face of a new array of challenges. There are reasons, therefore, to justify the pessimism about America so starkly revealed by current opinion polls.

What accounts for this disappointing record? Government and the politicians who control it are the culprits most frequently singled out for blame. Over the past thirty years, confidence in public officials has eroded drastically.[23] A plurality of Americans now believe that Washington poses the greatest threat to the welfare of the nation. A majority has even concluded that the federal government generally makes matters worse when it decides to take hold of a problem.[24]

These sentiments leave Americans in an awkward spot. By large majorities, we aspire to a kind of society that no country has yet approximated without the aid of a strong and active government. By equally large margins, however, we harbor the gravest possible distrust of government and those charged with making it work. This is not a healthy state of affairs, nor does it seem viable in the long run. Something needs to be done to bring our views about ends and means into closer alignment.

At present, more and more people are concluding that the answer to this dilemma is to shrink the government drastically and rely much more on private initiative to build the kind of society most people want. This solution would at least reduce the role of the state to a level more in keeping with the public's low regard for its capacities. Yet comparing America's experience with that of several other leading industrial democracies yields a rather different conclusion. In many instances, it is true, poorly conceived and badly executed public policies have a lot to do with our disappointing record. But there are grave dangers in responding to our problems by constantly denigrating public officials and undermining their authority. Like it or not, a careful look at the record will reveal that the skill with which a government defines its role, constructs its policies, and carries out its programs has now become the chief factor that determines which modern democracies succeed best in building the kind of society their citizens desire. The challenge for America, then, is not to dismember the government but to learn how to help it function more effectively.

To meet this challenge successfully, it is best to begin by trying to grasp as clearly as possible just what part the government has played in this country and how it has both helped and hindered efforts to move society forward. Only then can Americans understand the record of their government sufficiently well that they will neither ask the State to assume responsibilities it is ill-equipped to perform nor insist on ill-considered remedies that weaken it in carrying out its essential tasks.

Toward this end, the following study—the first of two volumes— will describe the development of the United States since the 1950s and compare it with that of several other leading industrial democracies. By examining many different aspects of American life, I will try to ascertain where our society has progressed, where it has lost ground, and whether the nation is indeed in a state of decline. Throughout, I will pay particular attention to the ways in which government—federal, state, and local—has contributed to our setbacks and our successes and how it has come to play such a central role in the affairs of this country and other advanced democratic nations. By the end of the inquiry, I hope to have laid the foundation for a second volume which will inquire more deeply into why our public officials and institutions often fail to achieve their goals and what, if anything, can be done to help them do better.

Assessing the Nation's Progress

How can one possibly hope to arrive at any firm conclusion about a question as amorphous as whether America is progressing or suffering a decline? With so much information to choose from, it is easy for advocates on either side to take almost any aspect of American life and argue that matters are either getting better or growing worse. Depending on one's conception of what an ideal society should be, different people can look at the same body of evidence and come away with radically different views of whether the nation has advanced or fallen back over the past thirty to forty years.

Fortunately, there is one firm rock on which to build. In order to evaluate the nation's progress, the surest way to proceed is not to argue endlessly over competing visions of the ideal society but to measure our record against the kind of society to which most Americans aspire. In a democracy, that is the most appropriate goal toward which a nation and its government should strive and the best yardstick for evaluating their performance.

Despite all the arguments that divide us, Americans remain surprisingly united on what the basic goals of the society ought to be. Five major aims enjoy especially broad support. They have consistently gained the approval of large majorities ever since polling organizations started to ask the public about its beliefs several decades ago. With these objectives as a guide, it is possible to determine how much progress the United States has made, not toward liberal goals or conservative goals but toward aims that Americans from every walk of life consider important.

The first of these objectives is a buoyant expanding economy. Economic growth, rising productivity, full employment, and stable prices are all vital to Americans because they make possible so much of what people want in order to live a satisfying life. When the economy ceases to expand, opportunities for advancement are fewer, and the struggle among interest groups for resources begins to intensify. Confidence erodes, America's influence in the world tends to diminish, and people are less inclined to sacrifice their interests for the common good. When unemployment rises, families suffer, breadwinners lose their sense of self-respect, and insecurity grows even for those who still have jobs. Year in and year out, therefore, voters judge politicians more heavily on the state of the economy than on any other factor.

The second important goal is a quality of life that includes elements transcending economic prosperity. For example, in addition to simply earning a good income, Americans want to preserve nature, breathe clean air, live in peaceful, pleasant neighborhoods, and enjoy a vibrant culture with art, music, literature and other forms of entertainment that appeal to every segment of a diverse population.

A third basic aim is a society that offers a chance for all people to achieve as much as they can in light of their talents, aspirations, and efforts. Americans may not care a great deal about equality of results; in fact, they have tolerated greater disparities in income and wealth than citizens of any other industrial democracy and have long been cool to proposals that would substantially redistribute income.[25] What they do believe in strongly, however, is equality of opportunity. Opportunity has been central to the American experience from the beginning. It has been nourished by successive waves of immigrants arriving here in search of a better life, and it continues to be a principle supported by more than 90 percent of the people.[26]

The fourth major goal for most Americans is to enjoy adequate personal security against the principal hazards of life—the risk of being victimized by crime, of being abandoned and destitute in old age, of being fired arbitrarily or injured on the job, of falling ill without being able to afford adequate health care. Left to their own devices, many people lack the resources to protect themselves against these dangers; they want some mechanism to give them the security they desire. That is why Social Security is among the most popular of all federal programs and why government outlays for crime prevention and health care enjoy more grass-roots support than almost any proposed public expenditures.

The fifth and last aspiration shared by large majorities of Americans is to preserve a set of fundamental values. One of these is individual freedom—the right to be safe from unjust or unnecessary interference, especially from the State, in the exercise of political and personal liberties. Every survey that asks people what they cherish most about being an American finds that personal freedom tops the list.[27] With individual freedom, however, comes a corresponding responsibility to respect the legitimate rights and interests of others. Polls that ask Americans what troubles them most about their country frequently show that one of their greatest concerns is that the sense of individual responsibility is eroding.[28] Beyond the desire for high ethical standards is a broader social concern—or compassion, if you will—toward the least fortunate members of society. Although there is much controversy over particular social welfare programs, most Americans want to help the poor, especially those who cannot help themselves. In fact, by the end of the 1980s, more than 60 percent of the public believed that the government was spending *too little* on the poor, whereas only 9 percent felt that it was spending too much.[29] Similar results have been recorded throughout the post war period.[30]

The five basic goals just described are not unique to the United States; they are shared by all leading industrial democracies. What is distinctive about this country is the way in which Americans choose to go about achieving these objectives. At the core of this approach is an abiding faith in the power of self-reliant individuals—an optimism about what this country can achieve by giving people ample freedom and abundant opportunities to succeed to the limit of their abilities and ambitions. In comparison with the citizens of most other industrialized nations, Americans have tended to place much less stock in modifying the economy or changing the fruits of private enterprise to bring about greater equality of results. Instead, they have continued to believe that the entire society will move ahead faster if talented people are allowed to succeed and reap the rewards of their success. Conversely, Americans have always been suspicious of big government and skeptical about national efforts to achieve social goals through centralized planning and elaborate state programs.

The faith in self-reliant individualism plainly served this nation well for many generations. Natural resources helped the economy grow, and surrounding oceans kept it relatively safe from the destructive wars that ravaged most other leading countries. Favored by these advantages, competitive individualism seemed to produce all of the captains of industry and entrepreneurs, the risk takers and inventors, the institution builders and community leaders that the nation needed to grow and prosper. Starting with nothing but a barren wilderness, enterprising Americans made the United States the wealthiest country in the world by the end of the nineteenth century.

In the midst of this remarkable growth, of course, social problems of all kinds abounded. But conditions were hardly any better in other industrializing nations. Nor did these problems cause much anguish among the country's leaders. While many people were aware of widespread suffering and want, few of them measured the progress of America or its place in the world by counting the number of poor people or comparing statistics on infant mortality.

With the Great Depression in the 1930s, followed immediately by the Second World War, conditions began to change. The goals of the United States grew more ambitious, as they did in all industrial democracies. Americans have long aspired to personal security, good health, individual freedom, and material comforts in their own lives. But only in the past sixty years has a broad consensus arisen that matters such as adequate housing, decent health care, proper nutrition, clean air and water, security in old age, and other benefits of life are conditions that all Americans should enjoy. Only in this period has the public begun to regard these conditions as objectives the country should try to reach and goals by which to measure our success as a nation.

At the very time when Americans were reformulating their aims, however, the circumstances of the country were beginning to change as well. No longer did the United States enjoy an abundance of open land. One by one, its natural resources ceased to be adequate for its needs. With its new industrial preeminence, America was no longer able to progress, as it did so often in the previous century, simply by copying innovations made in Europe. In addition, economic strength brought new and formidable global responsibilities. Increasingly, the United States felt compelled to assume a disproportionate share of the burden of maintaining international security, especially (until recently) against the threat of Communism.

In short, changing circumstances in the past half-century have presented America with a new challenge in trying to achieve the basic aspirations of the society. For more than 150 years, Americans demonstrated how well they could perform with abundant natural resources and limited national objectives. Since World War II, our task has been the more demanding one of trying to achieve much more ambitious goals under more constrained conditions. The question worth asking after a half-century of effort is how good a job the society has done of adapting its traditional style and institutions to a new and much more formidable set of challenges.

To answer this question, it is not possible to examine all of the innumerable events and activities throughout the society that bear upon the achievement of America's basic aims. For example, no effort will be made to consider the important subject of foreign policy.[31] Yet enough different aspects of American life will be included to give adequate attention to each of the country's principal objectives. By attending to fields that are important enough and broad enough in scope, the chapters that follow should succeed in constructing a reasonably accurate composite picture of what this country has achieved over the past forty years in its effort to reach the goals of greatest concern to Americans.

Which fields of domestic activity are best suited to these purposes? There is no answer that will suit everyone's taste precisely. Yet many areas of endeavor are so manifestly important that one would expect them to appear on almost anybody's list.

For example, under the broad rubric of "economic prosperity," one would certainly wish to know how much the economy has grown, how rapidly productivity has increased, how much unemployment has occurred, and what the rate of inflation has been. In addition, one might want to know how much progress has occurred in fields that bear most directly on the long-term prospects for a healthy, growing economy—the amount of savings and investment, the progress in scientific discovery and technology, the quality of education, and the training given the work force to prepare for an increasingly sophisticated economy. A careful look at all these areas should give a reasonable sense of how well the economy has performed and how firm a foundation has been laid for continuing prosperity.

Improving the quality of life is a much more amorphous aim which could include many items, such as personal safety and good health care, that are discussed here under other national objectives. In the end, one can only hope to select a small, representative sample from the many activities that might in some way fit under this rubric. Three topics, however, seem important enough yet sufficiently diverse to capture something of the breadth and scope of this category. The first involves the physical surroundings in which Americans live—the dwellings in which they reside and the neighborhoods in which they live, raise families, and make friendships. The second topic has to do with the environment and the programs devised to protect the air, soil, and water from pollutants that jeopardize health, interfere with recreation, and endanger plant and animal life. The last of the three subjects is the arts, especially the efforts made in the past thirty years to expand the number of arts organizations and enlarge their audiences.

Opportunity is another goal with many facets. Three aspects of the subject, however, seem especially important for the purposes of this study. The first has to do with efforts to give every child a good start in life—a chance to be born healthy, to receive adequate nutrition in infancy, to be protected against illness, to have good child care if the parents work, and to have the help required to begin school in a state of readiness to learn. A second topic of great concern to America is the handicap of race, particularly for blacks, who have experienced such special problems throughout our history. A third important aspect of the subject has to do with the possibilities for a successful and satisfying career and whether all Americans, women as well as men, can achieve as much as their efforts, ambitions, and talents allow.

The quest for personal security is an easier goal to explore because there is wide agreement on the kinds of security that matter most to Americans. Everyone wants protection from being victimized by crime, especially from violent attacks. (Fear of crime was actually the chief cause of concern among Americans in 1994.) Another form of security that matters to almost everyone is the assurance of affordable, good-quality health care in case of illness. Most people also want to be protected at work against the risks of accident and unfair treatment and the hardships of layoff and unemployment. The final need is for security in old age, chiefly protection against the risk of being forced into poverty due to long-term illness or the death of a spouse at a time when one is often vulnerable and unable to help oneself.

The last great objective shared by most Americans—to have a society that respects basic values—may seem the most amorphous of all America's basic goals. Even so, it is possible to throw some light on the nation's progress in combining individual freedom with personal and social responsibility. A plausible way to chart the growth of personal freedom over the past few decades is to examine the work of the courts in defining the scope of individual liberty under the Constitution. Calculating the ebb and flow of personal responsibility is a much more complicated process, but one can search for clues by looking at trends in various types of behavior that reveal how much Americans obey the law and respect the legitimate interests of others. With enough indices of this kind, it may be possible to draw some rough conclusions about how well people are living up to their personal obligations and whether they are taking these responsibilities more or less seriously than in the past. Finally, the much-discussed subject of poverty should throw valuable light on how compassionate the society has been in responding to the plight of others and how seriously Americans take their collective responsibility to care for needy strangers.

The many fields of activity just described overlap, and some could plausibly be included under more than one of our national objectives. Together, however, they touch upon each of America's basic social goals while being diverse enough to include all of the most important segments of society—rich and poor, rural and urban, young and old, employed and unemployed, blacks and whites. Some of the topics lend themselves more readily than others to precise description and measurement. For each of these areas of endeavor, however, it is possible to establish in a general way what Americans are trying as a society to achieve. (The disputes that divide the country occur mainly over the methods to pursue and the amounts of money to spend on the task.) In housing, for example, federal legislation defines what most people would accept as a goal in any case—to provide "a decent home and a suitable living environment for every American." Similarly, in the field of crime, liberals and conservatives can agree that their common objective is to minimize the incidence of violent crime within the limits set by the Constitution and by widely accepted norms of justice and fair play in the society.

Using such general definitions of our aims, we should be able to describe—often quite precisely—how much progress the United States has made over the past few decades. In almost every case, we can also compare our record with that of other advanced industrial democracies. Such comparisons should provide a clearer sense of how much progress modern democratic societies are capable of making and thus throw additional light on how successful America has been in achieving the goals that matter most to us.

In the end, of course, the fields we will explore are far too diverse to allow us to combine them in a precise overall index that will measure our progress as a society since the 1950s. At best, we can assemble important aspects of our experience into a mosaic that gives us a crude picture of how the society has fared over the past several decades. In the course of putting together these fragments, however, we should succeed in clarifying some of the sharp disagreements that have arisen over the nation's performance in a number of fields that are important to our future. More than that, we may be able to decide in the end whether America has truly been in decline and—if this is indeed the case—why we find ourselves in such a state and to what extent government has contributed to our predicament.

I

PROSPERITY

1

The Economy

In 1932, John Maynard Keynes wrote an essay prophesying the end of "the economic problem"—a time when scarcity would be banished and everyone would have all the material goods they desired.[1] If this were the only memorable statement Keynes had ever made, his reputation by this time would be wearing rather thin. Far from being vanquished, the appetite for possessions seems every bit as great today as it was when Keynes first published his prediction. And so it is that amid the facts and figures that flood our consciousness every day, the most popular index of the nation's progress continues to be the rise and fall of the Gross Domestic Product (GDP).*

To be sure, a growing GDP is not the only mark of a successful economy. Closely linked to growth is rising productivity, for greater productivity is the only sure way to increase per capita wealth over a long period. Minimizing unemployment is important too, not only be-

---

*"Gross Domestic Product" (GDP) includes all goods and services produced in the United States by U.S. or foreign companies. It replaced the term "Gross National Product" (GNP), which included all goods and services produced by *American* companies either in this country or abroad. Critics assail the GDP for indiscriminately lumping together every kind of good and service regardless of its nature. Increases in the production of safety locks brought on by the growth of crime and extra lawyers' fees attributable to higher divorce rates are counted just the same as additional food and the building of new homes. There is still no agreement, however, on how to construct better measures of "progress." This study tries to take account of this problem by looking at many indicators and activities other than changes in GDP. For a recent discussion of these issues, see Clifford Cobb, Ted Halstead, and Jonathan Rowe, "If the GDP Is Up, Why Is America Down?" *Atlantic Monthly,* 2 (October 1995).

cause putting more people to work adds to total output but because
jobs matter a lot to self-esteem and self-fulfillment. Finally, stable prices
are widely regarded as a vital goal—especially today, when international bond traders can punish a country that allows inflation to get
out of hand.

By most of these measures, American industry achieved a global
dominance in the late 1940s and 1950s that no nation has equaled
before or since. Much of this preeminence resulted from the effects of
World War II, which acted as a giant stimulus to the American economy while ravaging the factories and equipment of most of our chief
industrial rivals. As peace returned, Europe and Japan had a chance at
last to rebuild. Gradually, the gap between their economies and ours
began to narrow. Four decades later, how close have other nations
come to matching the wealth and productivity enjoyed in the United
States? Does America still retain the entrepreneurial skill, technological
virtuosity, and financial strength to keep our economy growing steadily
at rates equivalent to those of other highly developed industrial democracies? Or have Americans grown slack, unable to innovate
enough, save enough, and work enough to avoid sinking gradually to
a secondary position among the major economic powers of the world?

Economic Policy Here and Abroad

Improvements in the economies of democratic, capitalist nations owe
much to the work of the private sector, notwithstanding politicians'
efforts to take credit for new jobs and rising prosperity. The entrepreneurial and management abilities of business executives, the creativity
of scientists and engineers, the dedication and skills of the work force,
and the willingness of people to save and companies to invest all have
a bearing on the pace of economic growth. Yet government policies
also affect the progress of the economy in a variety of ways.

To begin with, the central bank has power to influence interest rates
and the supply of money and thus to affect the economy's rate of
growth and the level of inflation. In addition, the power to tax alters
incentives in ways that have an impact on the amount of work performed and the propensity to save and invest. Decisions by the government to run deficits or surpluses can alter aggregate demand and
thus influence inflation and employment. They can likewise encourage

or inhibit savings and hence affect capital formation, which in turn can stimulate or retard economic growth.

Governments also influence productivity and growth by deciding how much or how little to shelter sectors of the economy from the pressure of competition. In addition, by regulating companies for a wide variety of purposes, officials add to corporate costs and affect competitiveness in world markets. Conversely, through military spending, tariff policies, and a variety of other measures, lawmakers subsidize particular industries and thus help them either grow and prosper or become complacent and uncompetitive.

Finally, the government decides how much it will spend on activities that are widely regarded as important to long-term growth and productivity. Public funds can expand the school system and thus help build a more educated work force. They can improve vocational training. They can support research and pay for mechanisms to speed the transfer of new technology to businesses throughout the land.

All governments try to use these powers to increase economic growth, keep prices stable, and lower unemployment. But countries go about this task in markedly different ways. Some regimes are notably activist in seeking to develop and implement a plan of economic growth. Typically, they try to promote the expansion of certain industries and sectors while allowing others that are not considered competitive in the long run to decline and even die away. Japan and France are the leading examples of this strategy.

Both countries engage in national planning to set a strategic direction and establish goals for various sectors of the economy. In both countries, a strong consensus favoring activist methods helps the government bureaucracy act quietly through the financial system to implement its plans by giving priority in credit and other forms of assistance to companies and industries picked for expansion. For example, during the early postwar years in Japan, the government used its control over foreign currency and foreign technology licensing to implement its priorities.[2] In addition, an easy loan policy tended to force banks to reach their credit limits and to appeal to the Bank of Japan for permission to extend further loans. The latter typically assented, provided the banks involved agreed to follow the government's lending priorities. Since the 1960s, these levers of influence have become less potent, and the government has had to rely more on informal methods of persuasion coupled with strong measures to keep savings and investment at high levels. Whatever the means, the bureaucracy has tried to avoid having its economic policies politicized while encouraging a steady flow of resources away from labor-intensive goods into more sophisticated products that can capture growing shares of world markets and support higher wages and salaries.

Germany has taken a different course.[3] By and large, public officials have not tried to "pick winners" by favoring particular firms or sectors. Nor has the central government been able to use monetary policy as a tool, since the proudly autonomous Bundesbank has often pursued a determined course to keep prices stable even when it appeared to be acting at cross-purposes with the party in power. If any outside force has played an important role in developing German industry, it is the large commercial banks, which are immensely powerful not only as a source of funds but as a major owner of corporate stock with authority to vote by proxy the shares of other stockholders. Controlling a majority of the stock in Germany's largest corporations, banks use their seats on boards of directors to watch over the long-term growth of companies, help arrange useful mergers, and avoid harmful takeovers. Meanwhile, the government works with well-organized, powerful employers' associations and trade unions to train young people for skilled jobs and to implement labor market policies that improve productivity and help declining industries and sectors make way for more productive enterprises.

Sweden has followed a somewhat different path to guide the economy.[4] During four consecutive decades of Social Democratic rule, the Swedish government did not try to nationalize firms or even to interfere much with the business judgment of corporate leaders. But the government did participate in national wage negotiations between the powerful union movement and the confederation of employers. By virtue of the ruling party's close ties with the labor movement and the necessity for such a small country to compete effectively in world markets, these national negotiations produced a series of relatively noninflationary agreements. By favoring more equal wages throughout the economy, officials put pressure on inefficient firms and industries to use labor efficiently or go out of business. In addition, the government instituted the most active labor market policies in Europe, featuring extensive worker training, job placement assistance, and public works employment during recessions. These policies helped ease the phasing out of uncompetitive industries and keep unemployment at a bare minimum without producing excessive inflation.

In the late 1960s, as economic growth began to slow, the Social Democrats initiated an explicit policy of aiding emerging sectors and growth industries. But economic difficulties eventually derailed this plan. Ironically, it was a coalition of nonsocialist parties in the 1970s that turned industrial policy into a program of subsidies for floundering industries. Eventually, several large firms were nationalized in an effort to rescue them from bankruptcy. By the late 1980s, the original plan to stimulate growing industries had largely disappeared, and much of what passed for industrial policy consisted of local efforts to attract business or to shore up companies showing signs of weakness. All efforts to promote development were eventually neutralized by the growth of a welfare state so massive that incentives were skewed, productivity rose more slowly, and economic output actually declined in the early 1990s.[5]

The United States has followed a course quite different from any of those just described. By and large, the federal government has not made a practice of targeting industries and sectors deemed especially promising for growth. Nor have the banks played a role similar to the one pursued by their German counterparts. Instead, the job of allocating capital has been left almost entirely to the financial markets and to companies themselves through the use of retained earnings for internal investment and expansion. Individual firms have been quite free to follow their own business judgment (subject to antitrust laws that preserve competition and various forms of regulation that protect the public interest). Even the trade unions have not seriously challenged management's right to choose technologies, lay off workers, or expand and contract for business reasons.

There has been talk in recent years of a more deliberate industrial strategy for America. Yet government leaders have not been of one mind on this matter. Some have urged the government to follow the lead of Japan and actively encourage "sunrise industries" that have a bright future in an increasingly high-tech economy. Many economists and public officials, however, have questioned whether any government can make better choices than the market. More than a few skeptics have doubted whether Congress could mount an industrial policy that would not quickly degenerate into politically popular efforts to save jobs in declining sectors or to favor businesses in districts represented by powerful legislators. Lacking a consensus, the United States has continued to do less than most of the other leading economic powers to establish a centrally directed economic strategy.

Despite the national differences just described, common forces are at work that cause the practices in all advanced countries to converge. Increasing global competition, especially in financial markets, has narrowed the discretion of governments everywhere. The power of Keynesian economics has waned, causing officials in all industrial nations to rely less on fiscal policy to stimulate their economies. Sensing the need for large structural adjustments brought about by changes in technology and international competition, governments in Europe have begun to depend more on the market and to privatize nationalized industries. Finally, large sectors of the private economy are becoming less susceptible to influence from the State. In Japan, industry has grown more independent of the bureaucracy, while labor movements in countries such as Sweden and Germany are more fragmented than they once were and hence more difficult to coordinate. The forces just described have by no means eliminated all of the variations in the economic policies of leading industrial powers, but they have undoubtedly narrowed the differences.

Comparing National Performance

Regardless of their approach to economic planning, all advanced democratic governments have made great progress in using monetary and fiscal policy to avoid major depressions. Gone are the prolonged declines in national output that plagued America and Europe in the 1930s and at periodic intervals during previous generations. This achievement has prevented much suffering and is too little appreciated.

It is less clear how successful governments have been in crafting an industrial policy that can increase the rate of economic growth. Many observers believe that the task of maintaining industrial expansion, stable prices, and high employment is mysterious enough and subject so often to forces beyond any government's control that even the best-laid plans will not outperform a more laissez-faire approach over the long run. Although commentators often point to Japan as a model of what capable bureaucrats can accomplish, critics have questioned how much planning has truly helped the Japanese and whether its vaunted bureaucracy has actually been all that astute in choosing which industries to favor.[6]

In light of these doubts, it is interesting to examine the performance of the major industrial democracies with their varying approaches to economic policy and compare their record over the past several decades. Table 1.1 reveals how the growth of our GDP from 1960 to 1990 stands up to the record of other leading competitor nations. These figures show that our record is neither the best of the group nor the worst. Analysts debate whether matters are improving. Economic growth in America slowed perceptibly after 1974, but not as much as for our leading competitors. *Historically,* then, our record has deteriorated over time, yet *relatively speaking* we performed considerably better after 1974 than we did in the preceding fifteen years. That is why pessimists can look at our recent record and talk gloomily about

Table 1.1. **Annual rate of growth in real GDP,[a] in percent, 1960–1995. (In parentheses: average real GDP, in billions of dollars.)**

Country	1960–1969	1970–1979	1980–1989	1990–1995
United States	3.84	2.82	2.51	2.00
	(2,836)	(3,891)	(4,964)	(6,024)
Japan	9.10	4.13	3.62	1.16
	(581)	(1,201)	(1,784)	(2,356)
France	4.98	3.14	2.10	1.04
	(443)	(699)	(887)	(1,052)
West Germany	3.94	2.62	1.68	3.21[b]
	(580)	(838)	(1,021)	(1,365)
United Kingdom	2.60	2.15	2.63	1.13
	(504)	(653)	(787)	(930)
Canada	4.88	4.42	2.93	1.54
	(198)	(325)	(456)	(544)
Sweden	3.99	1.79	1.87	−0.09
	(78)	(108)	(130)	(143)

Source: OECD, *Economic Outlook,* Statistics on Microcomputer Diskette 56 (December 1994); and author's calculations.

a. Annual rate of growth is compounded annually for each period. Real GDP is calculated using the 1991 purchase power parity.

b. This figure may be inflated by the reunification of Germany and the addition of East Germans working in West Germany.

our declining performance while optimists study the same figures and report that we are doing better.

Comparisons of *per capita* growth (Table 1.2) tell a different story that is less flattering to the United States. The more discouraging picture revealed by these figures is easily explained. Throughout the entire period, the population of the United States has risen more rapidly than that of our principal competitors. Our increases in total output, therefore, are partly the result of population growth. When that factor is removed by looking at per capita growth, America's relative performance declines. Unfortunately, per capita GDP is probably a better gauge of well-being than total output, since individuals do not necessarily benefit from an expanding economy if the fruits must be divided among larger numbers of people.

America's sluggish per capita rate of growth reflects a failure to

Table 1.2. **Annual rate of growth of real per capita GDP,[a] in percent, 1960–1995. (In parentheses: average real per capita GDP, in dollars.)**

Country	1960–1969	1970–1979	1980–1989	1990–1995
United States	2.65 (14,688)	1.87 (18,070)	1.61 (20,808)	1.08 (23,464)
Japan	8.10 (5,919)	2.99 (10,867)	3.08 (14,820)	0.89 (18,927)
France	3.97 (9,161)	2.58 (13,326)	1.64 (16,078)	0.64 (18,316)
West Germany	3.14 (9,973)	2.50 (13,638)	1.60 (16,628)	2.56[b] (21,009)
United Kingdom	2.02 (9,327)	2.04 (11,642)	2.46 (13,900)	0.88 (16,055)
Canada	3.20 (10,168)	3.29 (14,416)	2.03 (18,135)	−0.25 (19,384)
Sweden	3.33 (10,107)	1.47 (13,298)	1.65 (15,577)	−0.53 (16,505)

Source: OECD, *Economic Outlook,* Statistics on Microcomputer Diskette 56 (December 1994); and author's calculations.

a. GDP is calculated using the 1991 purchase power parity.

b. This figure may be inflated by the presence of East German workers not counted in the West German population.

increase productivity rapidly. In the 1960s and 1970s, our rate of improvement lagged well behind that of most leading industrial nations. As Table 1.3 reveals, even in the 1980s, our record remained below average. Since 1982, however, only Britain and Japan have raised productivity at a rate significantly greater than ours, and even Japan has not performed particularly well since 1990.

Notwithstanding its sluggish record, the United States continues to have the highest rate of productivity in the world, by most careful measures. Other countries, notably Japan, have overtaken us in a number of important industries such as automobiles, auto parts, metalworking, steel, and consumer electronics.[7] In fact, if one measures productivity by GDP per hour worked, Germany and France may now have surpassed us in the economy as a whole.[8] But French and German employees take longer vacations and thus work fewer hours, so that their *annual* productivity (GDP per full-time worker) is considerably lower than ours. And Japan, for all its achievements in automobiles, television sets, cameras, and other export industries, still has remarkably low levels of efficiency in large areas of its economy—such as agriculture, food processing, and retailing—that have been sheltered from competition. Thus, if labor productivity (GDP per person employed) in the United States is assumed to be 100, then economy-wide productivity in France in 1990 stood at 95, Germany at 89, Japan at 77, and Britain at 75.[9]

Over the past twenty years, the benefits of growth and rising productivity in America have not been distributed evenly throughout the

Table 1.3. **Total factor productivity in the business sector**[a] **(average annual percentage changes), 1960–1994.**

Country	1960–1973	1973–1979	1979–1994
United States	1.6	−0.4	0.4
Japan	5.6	1.3	1.4
France	3.7	1.6	1.3
West Germany	2.6	1.8	0.4
United Kingdom	2.6	0.6	1.6
Canada	2.0	0.6	−0.1
Sweden	2.0	0.0	0.9

Source: OECD, *Economic Outlook*, A68 (December 1995).

a. Total factor productivity growth is equal to a weighted average of the growth in labor and capital productivity.

population. Rather, the pattern conforms more closely to what one would expect in a country that is unusually disposed to reward the successful, resist heavy government intervention, and allow individuals to fend for themselves. As the figures in Table 1.4 make clear, the economic gains in the United States since 1970 have gone disproportionately to the top half of the population, principally people with college and professional degrees. Families below the median derive most of their income from wages, and wages for the bottom half have grown very little, if at all, during the past twenty years. Real wages for workers with only a high school degree actually declined by roughly 15–20 percent from 1973 to 1990, while wages for high school dropouts fell by approximately 30 percent. Thus, the poorest 40 percent of American families were earning no more in 1990 than similarly situated families twenty years before, and the lowest 20 percent were actually earning less.

Fortunately, these figures do not mean that 40 percent of American households failed to increase their living standards from 1970 to 1990. Families that found themselves in the lowest income quintile in 1970 were unlikely to still be there in 1990. Most young couples starting out at the bottom of the heap managed to increase their earnings with age and experience over the next two decades. As they moved up in the earnings hierarchy, their places at the low end of the scale were taken by younger workers entering the labor force at lesser rates of pay. What the figures do suggest, however, is that families in the lower half of the scale in 1970 experienced much slower rates of income growth than similar families had enjoyed in the preceding decades, and

Table 1.4. **Mean family income for different quintiles, in constant 1992 dollars, 1967–1992.**

Income segment	1967	1972	1977	1982	1987	1992
Lowest fifth	9,380	10,769	10,591	9,535	10,157	9,708
Second fifth	21,227	23,725	23,554	22,441	24,591	23,337
Third fifth	30,510	34,847	35,521	34,375	38,185	36,777
Fourth fifth	40,919	47,588	49,021	48,757	54,650	53,365
Highest fifth	72,253	82,534	84,040	85,881	99,875	99,252
Top 5 percent	114,316	126,529	127,336	128,248	156,348	156,290

Source: Current Population Reports, *Money Income of Households, Families, and Persons in the United States, 1992,* B-13 (1993).

Table 1.5. Standardized unemployment, in percent, 1964–1994.

Country	1964–1969	1970–1979	1980–1989	1990–1994
United States	3.92	6.03	7.16	6.40
Japan	1.20	1.66	2.49	2.36
France	1.90	3.73	9.02	10.58
West Germany	0.78	2.28	5.93	5.32
United Kingdom	2.85	4.42	10.01	9.12
Canada	3.97	6.64	9.27	10.18
Sweden	1.77	2.05	2.47	5.04[a]

Source: OECD, *Economic Outlook*, A25 (December 1995).
a. Swedish figures do not include workers in training programs or temporarily employed in government-created jobs.

a substantial number of those with the lowest incomes may even have lost ground in absolute terms.[10]

The pattern just described differs from the experience of Europe and Japan. Earnings in these countries continued to rise in the 1980s even for the lowest-paid workers. In Britain, the only nation besides the United States to experience a marked increase in wage inequality, real wages for the bottom tenth of the labor force still managed to rise modestly from 1979 to 1989. In Japan, they rose by a full 40 percent.[11] These trends, however, may prove to be short-lived. In the 1990s, inequality seems to have started to increase in most European countries as well.

Although falling wages cramped the lifestyle of many Americans, the U.S. economy did succeed remarkably well in creating additional jobs. From 1970 to 1990, total employment rose by 40 percent in the United States, 25 percent in Japan, 10 percent in Germany, 8 percent in France, and only 3 percent in Britain. Although much of America's growth in jobs merely kept pace with the rising population, the effects on jobless rates were also substantial. Prior to 1970, unemployment levels in the United States were quite consistently above those of Western Europe. After 1980, our rates began to compare more favorably. In the 1990s, as recession struck Western economies, unemployment in Europe rose to double digits, while in the United States it gradually diminished to a level below 6 percent (Table 1.5).*

*Readers should be aware that official unemployment rates can be misleading and hard to compare. Some countries, such as Sweden, keep official rates quite low by placing large numbers

Table 1.6. Annual rates of inflation (Gross Domestic Product Deflator), in percent, 1960–1994.

Country	1960–1967	1968–1973	1974–1979	1980–1990	1991–1994
Canada	2.8	5.3	9.2	5.4	1.45
France	4.0	6.9	10.9	6.8	2.30
West Germany	3.2	6.2	4.7	3.1	3.88
Japan	5.4	7.0	8.1	1.9	1.10
Sweden	4.2	5.9	10.6	8.1	3.55
United Kingdom	3.6	7.5	16.1	7.4	4.10
United States	2.5	5.3	8.0	4.6	2.73

Source: OECD, *Historical Statistics / Statistiques Retrospectives, 1960–1990*, Table 8.1, 82 (1992); OECD, *Economic Outlook*, A16 (1995).

Just why European nations have had such persistent unemployment since 1980 is a matter of dispute. Some observers place most of the blame on generous unemployment benefits, high minimum wages and payroll taxes, low geographic mobility on the part of workers, and strict employment regulations that make companies reluctant to hire more permanent employees.[12] But economists as distinguished as Robert Solow and Olivier Blanchard argue that the factors just mentioned are overemphasized.[13] In their view, the sudden rise in unemployment around 1980 points to another cause—restrictive monetary policies—suggesting that lower interest rates might have kept unemployment to levels much closer to those in America.

Low and declining wages in the United States have had a restraining effect on inflation rates during the past twenty years, just as comparatively high unemployment rates helped curb them in earlier decades. Since 1960, therefore, the United States has had a relatively good record of maintaining stable prices. The figures in Table 1.6 make this clear. The remarkably high inflation rates of the 1970s, of course, were not primarily the result of wage trends or monetary policies in the most advanced economies of the world. Rather, they were the product of sudden, massive increases in the price of oil brought about by mounting global consumption, peaking levels of production in America and

---

of jobless workers in training programs or specially created government jobs. Nations also differ in how they determine who is in the work force, and no figures take accurate account of part-time workers who would like to have a full-time job, employees who have been encouraged to retire prematurely, or workers who are too discouraged to remain in the labor force.

the Soviet Union, and the rise of the Organization of Petroleum Exporting Countries (OPEC).

Interpreting the Record

By and large, federal efforts to encourage economic growth have continued to reflect the traditional values of this country. While using the methods of monetary and fiscal policy, the government has not intervened in the economy through planning, ownership of key industries, or credit policies to nearly the extent practiced by many other advanced industrial nations. It continues to rely primarily on the talents and energies of the individual. Thus, rewards for top business executives are greater in the United States than they are in any of our leading competitors, while earnings for the least-skilled workers tend to be lower. How well has this strategy served America over the past thirty to forty years?

By all of the relevant indices save for inflation, virtually every country discussed here did better than the United States until 1980. Whether one looks at overall growth, increases in per capita GDP, unemployment rates, or productivity gains, the record of these nations was superior to America's by a substantial margin.

During much of this period, however, the success of our competitors reflected a process of catching up after World War II. It was much easier for countries such as Japan and Germany to copy innovations from America than it was for us to make new technological breakthroughs. As capital flowed more plentifully, Europe and Japan could build modern factories with state-of-the-art equipment to replace what they had lost during the war. Meanwhile, to a greater extent than Europe, America was shifting its economy from manufacturing to services, where productivity gains have been traditionally harder to achieve.

By 1980, the period of catch-up was pretty well over. Productivity growth abroad slowed to levels much closer to those of the United States. Because the record of the earlier postwar period was so greatly influenced by atypical conditions, the years since 1980 offer a much better test of relative economic performance.

Since 1980, just as in preceding decades, the record of Japan stands out. By every relevant test, the economy of Japan performed substantially better than that of the United States or any other leading nation.

In the past few years, however, even the Japanese have encountered severe difficulties that have caused their economy to grow less rapidly than our own. Whether this slowdown is only temporary or the beginning of longer-lasting problems is still unclear at this point.

The experience in Europe has been altogether different. Since 1980, overall growth rates in America have exceeded those of most European countries. Our inflation rates have generally been lower. As for unemployment, England, France, Germany, and Sweden have all had deteriorating records, with the result that jobless rates in each of these countries have risen since 1990 to levels well above ours.

America's relatively low levels of unemployment, however, have been accompanied by declining wages for unskilled workers, leading to shrunken paychecks for many people. By the early 1990s, more than two million heads of families in America were working full time throughout the year and still falling below the official poverty line. Wage earners in the lowest-paid 10 percent of the work force were earning less than half of what their counterparts were paid in Germany, even though our total per capita wealth was greater. For most American families, incomes rose more slowly than they had in earlier decades, even though many people were working longer hours.

Also troubling is the large deficit in our international trade which has persisted to this day, notwithstanding much corporate restructuring and major declines in the value of the dollar. Thus far, other countries have been willing to tolerate the deficit and to accumulate large quantities of dollars. Eventually, however, their patience may wear thin and they may start selling dollars, driving the value of U.S. currency down to a point at which our exports and imports come into balance again, but only at the cost of substantial reductions in our standard of living and major shocks to the world economy.

At the root of these difficulties is a sluggish rate of growth in productivity. Despite the corporate restructuring and the sustained prosperity of the 1980s, output per worker throughout our economy continued to advance at a slow pace (approximately 1 percent per year).*

---

*There is some reason to believe that indications of a resurgence of productivity in recent years are overstated and reflect a statistical distortion rather than real change. Of the two most commonly cited sources of productivity growth—computers and corporate restructuring—investments in computers have not risen markedly while restructuring has not always led to greater productivity, even for the firms involved, and often does not produce economy-wide efficiency gains because laid-off workers do not obtain jobs that are as productive as the ones

Although other countries are also experiencing much lower rates of productivity growth, experts worry that our progress continues to lag behind the average rates historically achieved by the economy.

Does it matter if productivity rises by only 1 percent per year, instead of the higher rates traditionally achieved in the United States? More than one might think. In a six-trillion-dollar economy, even the addition of only 1 percent in economic growth for a single year produces an extra $60 billion in GDP. After a period of years, the cumulative effect of persistently sluggish growth becomes enormous. Over twenty years, the gain in GDP from a 1 percent higher growth rate will rise to well above one trillion dollars. In other words, a 1 percent addition to our growth rate over this period could wipe out the budget deficit, restore the viability of our Social Security program, increase the incomes of all families, and still leave enough money in additional tax revenues to extend health insurance to every American and fully pay for a host of other social programs that are now only partially funded or about to be cut back.

Despite this discouraging look at what might have been, not all economists are worried about America's record.[14] Some observers emphasize that there will always be a tendency for productivity to rise relatively slowly in the most efficient national economy, because it is invariably easier for other countries to copy the practices of the leader than it is for the leader to innovate and improve beyond what is currently known. Eventually, when other countries come closer to the productivity levels of the leader, their rate of progress will slow as the opportunities to copy diminish and the challenge of continued innovation grows more difficult. To analysts of this school, there is nothing surprising in the fact that other advanced economies increased their productivity more rapidly than we did for several decades after World War II. The decisive point for them is that since the mid-1980s other countries have not reduced the significant advantage that America still enjoys.

What accounts for America's continuing advantage in productivity so many years after the end of World War II? This was the subject of a massive recent study by the McKinsey Institute. Drawing upon the experience of many years of corporate consulting around the world,

---

they lost. For a recent discussion of these issues, see Stephen V. Oliner and William L. Wascher, "Is a Productivity Revolution Under Way in the United States?" *Challenge: The Magazine of Economic Affairs,* 18 (November–December 1995).

McKinsey investigators looked in detail at a large number of service
and manufacturing industries in the United States, Japan, Germany,
France, and, in a separate study, Sweden.[15] As expected, many factors
contributed to differences in productivity within the industries inves-
tigated. In some cases, variations in the organization of work made a
decisive difference; in others, product design allowed some companies
to manufacture more cheaply; in still others, variations in the amount
of capital invested and the types of equipment and technology used
were important.

For the most part, however, these differences were the result of
choices made by the companies involved. The root question, then, was
why some companies made better choices than others, leading to
greater levels of efficiency. For the McKinsey investigators, one explanation overshadowed all others. The most efficient industries tended
to be those most exposed to competition, domestic or foreign. Conversely, the least efficient industries were those least subject to commercial rivalry, either because they were nationalized or because they
were sheltered from competitors by trade barriers, cartel-like arrangements, or laws regulating prices, output, or hours of operation. In the
end, therefore, the relative productivity of advanced industrial economies turns out to depend primarily on the extent to which governments
are willing to expose their industries to rigorous competition at home
and abroad.

As growth rates have slowed among the leading industrial nations,
officials in all these countries have begun to lower existing barriers to
competition. Nationalized enterprises have been sold to private owners, import restrictions modified, anticompetitive regulations relaxed.
If this process continues, differences in productivity among the leading
economies should tend to narrow as companies everywhere are pressed
by competition to adopt more efficient practices.

Yet even the economists who subscribe most strongly to this "convergence theory" admit that productivity growth among leading national economies does not resemble the race between Achilles and the
tortoise. It is not at all certain that the United States will maintain its
current leadership position indefinitely.[16] Japan already has achieved
much higher rates of productivity than the United States in several
major industries (while lagging far behind us in others). Nor does convergence mean that differences in productivity will eventually become
too small to matter. Over a sufficiently long period of time, even mod-

est differences among nations in their rate of productivity growth can produce major differences in overall efficiency, which will in turn have substantial effects on living standards, influence in world affairs, and other matters of concern to the American people.

Apart from competition, what determines how well nations perform over the long run in raising productivity? One important factor is the level of investment, since it is through investment that a country maintains and expands its infrastructure and modernizes its plant and equipment. On this score, America's record does not compare well with that of its leading competitors. In 1990, total investment in the United States was significantly below the level in any of the countries on our list (as it has been fairly consistently for several decades) and was barely half the level achieved by Japan.* Not only did America rank last among the other nations in our sample in gross capital formation; it also ran behind all of the other twenty-three members of the Organization for Economic Cooperation and Development (OECD).[17]

The gap between the United States and other nations is not so large with respect to investment in plant and equipment, which is the form of investment most critical to productivity. Even so, America has tended to lag behind its leading competitors, at least until recently. Table 1.7 records the trends since 1972 in the United States and other advanced industrial countries. In explaining this record, most economists stress the anemic levels of private savings in the United States, together with the large government deficits since the mid-1980's that have pushed up the national debt and siphoned off savings from the private sector.[18]

As yet, higher rates of savings and investment in countries such as Germany and Japan have not hurt the United States, because American firms, under the pressure of competition, have learned to use their capital more efficiently than their counterparts in other leading industrial nations. Some firms abroad allow their facilities to lie unused or only partially used during periods of the day or year; others indulge in

---

*Some economists believe that these figures greatly overstate the differences in investment among different countries. They point out that the prices of capital assets are relatively cheap in the United States, so that an investment in America may buy more new machinery and equipment than an equivalent investment elsewhere. They also point out that foreign governments may "invest" more in mass transit while Americans "consume" more automobiles, thus making the United States seem to lag in investment even though it is spending as much as other countries on transportation. See, e.g., Robert E. Lipsey and Irving B. Kravis, *Saving and Economic Growth: Is the United States Really Falling Behind?* (1987).

Table 1.7. Private industry expenditure on plant and equipment as
        percent of GDP, 1975–1994.

Country	1975	1980	1985	1990	1994
United States	9.35	11.04	11.60	10.58	11.84
Canada	9.55	11.30	10.15	12.06	11.60
France	11.70	12.04	10.55	12.89	10.76
Japan	13.09	13.24	14.75	19.64	15.61
West Germany	10.89	12.16	11.50	13.26	12.99
United Kingdom	11.83	11.73	12.84	14.10	11.88

Source: Data obtained from the Council on Competitiveness, Washington, D.C.

"gold plating"—that is, using machines and equipment more sophisticated than the work to be done truly requires. For reasons such as these, although Germany and Japan both have invested much more capital per capita than the United States, their productivity continues to lag behind ours.[19] Eventually, of course, global competition may force their executives to utilize capital as effectively as American managers do. When that time comes, the United States will find it difficult to match the productivity gains in Germany and Japan or equal their growth in per capita income.

Vital as they are, savings and investment in plant and equipment are not the only determinants of rising productivity and growth. Other important elements are technological innovation and added know-how and skill on the part of the work force. In turn, innovation and labor skills are much influenced by trends in research and development and by programs of education and training. The chapters that follow take up these subjects, in order to throw more light on America's past economic record and its prospects for the future.

Scientific Research
and Technology

Since ancient times, advances in knowledge have had a transforming effect on the way in which people live. Discoveries such as the wheel, the plow, the pump, and the pulley have shaped entire civilizations, causing some societies to prosper and others to decline. Modern economies continue to depend on scientific and technological advances for new products and new methods of production. But science and technology are vastly different enterprises today from what they were in centuries past. The sums of money required for the process of discovery, the sophistication and complexity of modern research, the speed with which new advances appear and spread through the economy have all risen to levels unimagined only a few generations ago.

Economists estimate that advances in science and technology have accounted for up to half of all gains in productivity in the United States throughout much of this century.[1] Having such effects on growth and prosperity, science and technology are matters of high national importance. In every advanced country, public officials must concern themselves with the quality of research performed within their borders and the speed with which fresh advances in knowledge are made known and applied throughout the economy.

A government could allow private firms and other organizations to carry out research and development (R&D) by themselves. Certainly, corporations already spend considerable sums for these purposes, and economists have shown that such expenditures are highly profitable. But there are reasons private companies may not invest

enough in R&D to serve the nation's interests. When firms engage in
basic scientific inquiry, the practical applications are generally quite
unpredictable. As a result, business executives may decide that the
chances of reaping a reward from such research are simply too small
to make the investment worthwhile. In certain fields, such as nuclear
power or major weapons systems, the sums of money required for
research are so large and the payoff is so risky that private companies
may be reluctant to spend money even on projects for specific, practical
purposes. As for technology, there may be instances in which economies of scale are so great or the purposes sufficiently noncommercial
that it is sensible for some public entity to take responsibility. Even the
normal processes of industrial research and development may yield
private rewards that are well below the total returns to society, leading
to significant underinvestment. Finally, governments may need to take
positive action to ensure that small companies become aware of new
technological breakthroughs that could help them operate more efficiently.

For reasons such as these, lawmakers in all advanced industrial
states have chosen to invest heavily in research and development. Deciding how much the state should do, however, and how it can best
encourage good research and hasten its application throughout the
economy, remains a challenge that different countries have tried to
meet in different ways.

R&D Policy in America

Science policy in the United States began in earnest only after World
War II.[2] Attracted by the success of American scientists in making discoveries such as radar and the atomic bomb, a few federal agencies,
notably the Office of Naval Research, continued to fund research after
hostilities ceased. Persuaded of the growing importance of science,
President Harry Truman decided to embark upon a more comprehensive effort to support the highest quality of research. After much dispute over how to proceed, Congress authorized the National Science
Foundation to foster basic research primarily in the natural sciences.
The National Institutes of Health followed suit to support work in the
biomedical sciences. Other federal agencies, such as the Department of
Defense, built their own more focused programs to fund scientific investigation related to their mission.

Approximately 15 percent of the government's R&D support has gone directly to universities, chiefly for basic research (scientific inquiry carried on without explicit regard for its eventual usefulness or application).* Most of these funds are distributed to individual investigators after other scientists have evaluated the quality of the work proposed. In addition to supporting campus-based projects, Washington has performed large quantities of research in federally owned laboratories, chiefly for defense, energy, or other government programs. A third form of public funding has gone to industry, mainly to support applied research and development for military and other national purposes.

In 1994, $177 billion was spent in the United States for all forms of R&D. Over the years, the federal government's share has gradually declined, as it has in the other countries in our survey. By the 1990s, more than half of all R&D funds were coming from business, chiefly for applied research and development. The federal government contributed less than 45 percent of the total, including most of the money for basic research along with large sums for mission-oriented R&D in fields such as energy, space, and defense where Washington has a special interest. Recently, the Clinton administration has signaled a desire to orient more of its support, even in universities, toward projects related to a range of important national needs, including economic competitiveness.

In addition to funding science directly, the federal government has created incentives to encourage business to invest more in research. The oldest method of accomplishing this result is through issuing patents. More recently, Congress has provided tax credits for increased corporate investments in R&D. Still other measures, such as favorable tax treatment for capital gains, may likewise stimulate R&D by attracting more venture capital to support new high-tech companies.

Governments also support research by subsidizing the education of scientists. The National Science Foundation (NSF) has long offered scholarships to promising graduate students. Along with other agencies, the NSF provides traineeships and postdoctoral fellowships in many fields of research. In recent years, the NSF has grown concerned

*In fact, "basic research" is a much more imprecise category than this traditional formulation suggests. Much investigation classified as basic actually has fairly direct practical applications (for example, much agricultural genetics and clinical research involving patients), and much is undertaken with an understanding that it will probably be useful at some point in the future.

about the pool of scientifically inclined young people in America, especially women. Accordingly, the foundation has stepped up funding to upgrade science teaching in the nation's schools.

Promoting technology is a process quite unlike supporting research, and the United States has proceeded in a markedly different way. The centerpiece of the federal strategy has been a series of large, centrally planned and administered projects aimed at important national goals. Such initiatives date back to the Manhattan Project that produced the atomic bomb during World War II. Over the years, Washington has launched similar programs to place a man on the moon and to conduct other forms of space exploration, to tap new sources of energy such as synthetic fuels and solar power, and to develop supersonic transport and communications satellites.

If science is to benefit the economy, it is not enough to increase the rate of new discoveries or bring about great technical innovations. These advances must somehow find their way into the products that companies sell and the processes they use to manufacture goods.

In principle, every company should be alert to capitalize on any new technology that could lower its costs or boost its profits. In practice, however, thousands of small and medium-size firms lack the ability to scan developments in science and engineering that might be relevant to their needs. Governments everywhere look for ways to help overcome this problem.

More than a hundred years ago, Washington hit upon an imaginative solution. Concerned by the backwardness of agriculture, Congress established a system of land grant colleges in 1863 and a network of agricultural experiment stations in 1887 to demonstrate to farmers the latest discoveries and techniques from the research laboratories of the new public universities. Later, county agents were appointed to travel from farm to farm dispensing seed, fertilizer, and practical advice. The experiment proved to be a huge success, helping to raise productivity on American farms to levels unequaled throughout the world.

Despite these accomplishments, the federal government has only recently begun to take similar steps to speed the flow of technological knowledge to American industry. In part, the government's reluctance to move in this direction stemmed from a widely shared conviction that business decisions about technology were matters for the market alone to decide. In part, the inertia reflected a complacent belief that

America was technologically dominant and did not need special efforts by the government.

Within the last decade, as concern mounted over America's competitiveness in the world economy, Washington had a change of heart and launched a number of initiatives to hasten the spread of new technology. Congress relaxed the antitrust laws to permit firms to join together for research purposes. Public officials encouraged companies to join consortia and form business-government partnerships to move ahead faster in fields such as semiconductors. New efforts were made to establish mechanisms analogous to the county agent system, so that universities and independent technology centers could offer advice and training to small and medium-size companies.

In 1993, President Bill Clinton announced his intention to expand these initiatives and develop a full-blown technology policy.[3] Under the president's plan, new emphasis would be placed on collaborative efforts with private industry and on encouraging state programs to improve the transfer of technology from the laboratory to the shop floor. Federal officials were supposed to identify "critical technologies" that had the potential for a variety of useful applications and then work with industry to develop them more rapidly. Government agencies would also take the initiative to help develop an "information superhighway" to improve access to vast data bases for the benefit of business, universities, libraries, and government offices. At the same time, Washington would shift part of its R&D effort away from defense, space, and atomic energy toward activities aimed at making American business more competitive.

Policies of Other Countries

Research policies of other advanced nations are similar in some respects to those of the United States.[4] All of the countries compared in this study rely chiefly on government and industry to fund their research. The shares contributed by each do not vary much from one country to another (Table 2.1).

Although all nations spend heavily on research and development, their priorities differ significantly. For example, despite the preeminence of American science, the United States (as well as England and Japan) appears to devote a considerably smaller proportion of its R&D funds to basic research than do most other countries.[5] It is also signif-

Table 2.1. R&D expenditures by source of funding, in percent, 1991.

Country	Government	Business	Universities	Other
United States[a]	43.7	46.0	3.0	7.3
Canada	44.6	41.0	2.0	12.3
France	48.3	43.5	0.3	7.9
West Germany	37.2	59.9	0.0	2.9
Japan	18.5	72.7	8.1	0.8
Sweden	54	42.0	0.0	4.0
United Kingdom	34.5	50.1	0.8	14.6

Source: National Science Board, *Science and Engineering Indicators, 1993*, 377–378 (1993). The low shares that government spends on R&D in Germany and Japan reflects the comparatively small military budgets in those countries.

a. Figures are for 1990.

icant that despite our concern over economic competitiveness, America spends much less on promoting industrial development than any of its leading competitors, while allocating considerably more to health and defense.[6] This tendency reflects a traditional faith in the market as a means of raising and allocating funds for commercial, profit-making purposes.

Substantial differences also exist among the policies countries use to encourage technology.[7] England and France have generally followed a path similar to ours by emphasizing large, centrally directed projects while doing little to stimulate the rapid diffusion of technical knowledge throughout the economy. Germany and Sweden, on the other hand, have done precisely the opposite. Both governments have avoided large projects to develop new technologies. Instead, they have concentrated on promoting diffusion by training a highly skilled work force and by developing cooperatively run laboratories and other mechanisms to ensure a constant flow of new discoveries and technologies to industry, especially to small and medium-size firms that cannot afford to maintain a research capability of their own.

Japan has followed a mixed strategy, stressing diffusion but also launching a number of centrally planned, large-scale projects to develop new technology. The Japanese government has likewise organized a long-term planning process which tries to build an industry-wide consensus on which technologies to emphasize. In contrast, the Swedish and German governments have not engaged in centrally directed planning or development efforts, choosing to leave the uses of technology entirely to the market.

Scientific Research: A Comparative Evaluation

How do the results of our research-and-technology policies compare with those of our leading competitors? All of the nations in this survey allocate roughly similar shares of GDP to all forms of research and development. In 1991, for example, Japan devoted the largest share of GDP to these purposes (3 percent) while Germany devoted 2.8 percent; the United States, 2.6 percent; France, 2.4 percent; and Britain, 2.1 percent.[8]

Greater differences appear in the shares of total funding devoted to *civilian* or *nondefense* R&D (Table 2.2).

These figures suggest that America may suffer from a major disadvantage in global economic competition because so much of its research goes for military purposes. This practice might not have posed a problem two or three decades ago, when defense research was a fertile source for civilian applications, as in the case of electronics and materials science. More recently, however, such applications have been much less common, and our low levels of civilian R&D have become a greater cause for concern.

At the same time, comparing percentages of GDP devoted to research obscures the advantage America enjoys because of its absolute size. In funding civilian R&D, the United States may devote only two-thirds the share of GDP that Germany and Japan provide, but the total

Table 2.2. Nondefense R&D as percent of GDP, 1971–1991.

Country	1971	1981	1991
United States	1.7	1.8	1.9
Canada	1.2	1.2	1.4
Japan	1.9	2.3	3.0
West Germany	2.0	2.3	2.7
France	1.4	1.5	1.9
United Kingdom	1.5[a]	1.8	1.7

Source: National Science Board, *Science and Engineering Indicators*, 376 (1993).
a. Figure is for 1972.

number of dollars America spends is greater than the amount spent by both of the other countries put together. Although the United States has a larger, more complex economy that demands more civilian R&D, there are undoubtedly advantages of scale that make the small share of GDP allocated to civilian R&D a misleading index of America's true strength vis-à-vis our competitors.

Because of its great size, the United States also maintains a commanding position in terms of the total number of scientists and engineers it employs. Indeed, in 1990, there were more scientists and engineers engaged in R&D in the United States than in Germany, Japan, France, and Britain *combined.*[9] Once again, however, America's lead has steadily diminished. Relative to the size of the work force, the number of scientists and engineers in the United States is barely greater than it is in Japan, and our lead over other industrial nations has likewise narrowed (Table 2.3).

In research, the number of participants is not nearly as important as the quality of their work. A first approximation of a nation's international standing in science is its share of all scientific articles published in refereed journals throughout the world. On this score, the United States has a dominant position. With its great absolute advantage in research dollars and scientific manpower, America's share is much larger than that of any other nation (Table 2.4).

By themselves, of course, these figures do not accurately reflect the true quality of America's scientific research (beyond the fact that all

Table 2.3. **Scientists and engineers per 10,000 in labor force, 1965–1991.**

Year	United States	Japan	West Germany	France	United Kingdom
1965	64.7	24.6	22.6	20.9	19.6
1970	64.1	33.4	30.8	27.3	—
1975	55.3	47.9	38.2	29.2	31.1
1980	60.0	53.6	43.2	32.1	35.7[a]
1985	68.4	63.9	49.7	42.8	35.3
1991	75.7	75.5	59.2[b]	52.5	45.0

Source: National Science Foundation, *National Patterns of R&D Resources, 1992,* 67 (1992). National Science Foundation, *National Patterns of R&D Resources, 1994,* 49, 76 (1995).

a. Figure is for 1981.
b. Figure is for 1989.

Table 2.4. Share of world scientific literature in refereed journals, in percent, 1975–1991.

Year	United States	Japan	West Germany	France	United Kingdom
1975–1979	37.1	6.0	6.4	5.5	8.9
1980–1986	35.7	7.2	6.1	4.9	8.3
1989–1991	35.1	8.1	6.8	4.8	7.7

Source: National Science Foundation, *International Science and Technology Update, 1992*, 91 (1992). Ibid., 423–424 (1993).

articles published in refereed journals must satisfy some basic scholarly standard). More helpful indications come from observing how often articles published by scientists of different countries are cited by other investigators. Efforts have been made to compare the number of citations of all published articles with the number of citations one would expect in light of the volume of articles published by researchers in each country. (A number greater than one indicates a larger number of citations than would have been anticipated.) Using this criterion, data from the mid-1980s suggest that articles by Americans are cited more frequently than expected in every major field of knowledge and that the United States enjoys the highest citation ratios in all of these fields except mathematics (where we rank second to Great Britain). In contrast to so many other fields of endeavor, America's lead in research does not seem to be diminishing. In fact, the number of citations per paper written by Americans grew slightly, from 1.39 in 1973 to 1.41 in 1984 (Table 2.5).

Whether one looks at the number of Nobel Prize winners, the share of articles in scientific journals, or the frequency with which scientific results are cited, the United States has plainly had great success in promoting the discovery of new knowledge. Much of the explanation lies in several natural advantages enjoyed by this country. America's great size ensures that scientists can usually achieve an appropriate scale of effort and that several competing teams will almost always be at work on any important problem. Another strength has been a system of higher education composed of a large number of public and private institutions, all vying with one another for students, faculty, and intellectual distinction. Such a network, with its many independent centers of initiative, tends to exhibit greater adaptability, greater creativity,

Table 2.5. Citations of scientific literature, per paper, 1984.

Field	France	West Germany	Japan	United Kingdom	United States
All fields	0.89	1.01	0.88	1.12	1.41
Clinical medicine	0.71	0.68	0.84	1.08	1.31
Biomedical research	0.85	0.90	0.87	1.12	1.42
Biology	0.86	1.02	0.90	1.22	1.18
Chemistry	0.98	1.01	1.12	1.32	1.69
Physics	1.02	1.34	0.87	1.07	1.80
Earth and space sciences	0.91	1.01	1.08	1.07	1.42
Engineering	0.99	1.10	1.16	1.01	1.17
Mathematics	0.98	1.06	0.78	1.45	1.29

Source: National Science Foundation, *International Science and Technology Data Update, 1991,* 97 (1991).

and greater energy than the monolithic public university systems common in Europe. Finally, America has profited from its tradition of welcoming strangers from abroad, especially now that English has become the *lingua franca* of the scientific world. From 1950 to 1990, fourteen Nobel prizes in medicine and twelve in physics went to foreigners who had settled in this country. Because the United States remains an inviting place to do research, it continues to attract a remarkable influx of talented scientists from all parts of the globe.

The federal government also deserves part of the credit for the nation's scientific achievements. Certain key decisions just after World War II were especially important. Relying on universities as the primary source of basic research helped America capitalize on its strengths and ensured a continuing stream of new talent by encouraging the best scientists to work in settings where they could train their successors. The use of peer review for research grants put the emphasis on intellectual quality, in contrast to politically tempting alternatives such as dividing up research funds by state or by region. Finally, the decision to rely primarily on grants to individual investigators made it easier to allocate funds according to merit than it would have been had Washington simply distributed sums of money to universities. If Congress had handed out block grants, strong pressures would have arisen to spread the funds among many institutions on the basis of political rather than scientific considerations. Universities themselves would have encountered political difficulties of their own if they had been forced to draw distinctions of quality among different departments and faculty members on their own campuses.

To be sure, Washington's record in promoting basic research is not unblemished. According to many observers, the government has not provided adequate sums to build and renovate university research facilities since the early 1970s.[10] Worse yet, recent efforts to distribute more money for this purpose have suffered, as individual legislators have insisted on treating such appropriations as pork-barrel funds to favor their own constituencies. For example, within the 1992 R&D appropriations approved by Congress were 566 allocations earmarked for specific facilities and research, amounting to a total of $993 million.[11] Critics also claim that the peer review process has become bureaucratic and cumbersome: smaller grants often cost a dollar in administration for every dollar distributed for research. Other scientists complain that the government has allowed megaprojects, such as the late supercollider or the human genome program, to crowd out smaller, potentially more valuable research.

These difficulties, however, cannot negate the government's achievement in helping to build the strongest national research program in the world. Aided by federal funding, American scientists still capture a disproportionate share of the Nobel prizes in science, and American universities remain the institutions of choice for the best young scientists around the world seeking advanced training abroad.[12] The Japanese, who rival the United States in so many fields, are much less successful in basic science. Repeated surveys of the state of Japanese and American research place Japan ahead in only a handful of important fields.[13]

The Applications of New Knowledge

Although research is vital to progress in medicine and industry, preeminence in science does not give a nation as much of a commercial advantage as some enthusiasts suggest. In a world of easy travel and instant communication, new research findings can be quickly learned and put to productive use by companies in other countries. Thus, Japan has long compensated for its weaknesses in basic science by excelling at staying abreast of new knowledge and applying it rapidly. To prosper in the global economy, therefore, a country must not only do well

Table 2.6. U.S. patents granted, by nationality of inventor, 1970–1990.

Country	1970	1975	1980	1985	1990
United States	47,077	46,715	37,356	39,554	47,283
Japan	2,625	6,352	7,124	12,746	19,477
West Germany	4,435	6,036	5,747	6,665	7,590
France	1,731	2,367	2,088	2,400	2,860
Canada	1,066	1,296	1,081	1,342	1,854
Sweden	NA[a]	914	822	857	767
United Kingdom	2,954	3,043	2,406	2,495	2,783
Total (all countries)	64,429	72,000	61,819	71,661	90,158

Source: National Science Foundation, *International Science and Technology Data Update, 1991*, 101 (1991). Figures for 1990 are from *Science and Engineering Indicators, 1993*, 455 (1993).

a. Not available.

in research; even more important is the capacity to adapt new discoveries swiftly and effectively for commercial uses.

Unfortunately, America has not fared quite so well in applying science and technology. One indication, as shown in Table 2.6, is the share of U.S. patents received by inventors from different nations. (Most countries try to patent their inventions in the United States because of the size and importance of its market.)

Although America retains a dominant position, its share of all U.S. patents granted has shrunk since the mid-1970s, from over 70 percent to only a little over 50 percent. Whereas the number of U.S. patents granted to Americans was almost exactly the same in 1990 as it was in 1970, the numbers of patents granted to Europeans and, even more dramatically, to Japanese have risen substantially.

What about the quality or importance of the patented discoveries made in the United States? As with scientific articles, one can make a rough estimate of the value of patents by observing how often they are cited by others. By this measure, America does well but lags somewhat behind Japan (Table 2.7). A breakdown of these figures into sixteen separate industries shows that Japanese patents are cited most often in six industries, American patents in five, English patents in three, and German and French patents in one industry each. Although these measures are admittedly crude, they suggest that the commercial importance of American patents may now rank below that of Japanese patents.[14]

Table 2.7. Average citations per patent by year patent was granted, all industries, 1980–1991.

Country	1980	1987	1991
United States	3.58	1.01	1.05
West Germany	2.86	0.75	0.72
Japan	3.79	1.30	1.35
United Kingdom	3.12	0.82	0.91
France	2.82	0.77	0.75
All countries outside the U.S.	3.09	0.97	—

Source: National Science Board, *Science and Engineering Indicators, 1991* (1992).

There is more disturbing evidence suggesting that new technology is not finding its way into common usage in the American economy as rapidly as it does in some other countries. This is exactly what one would expect from the low levels of investment in new plant and equipment that have been characteristic of the United States. Table 2.8 offers a revealing comparison of the use of new technology in manufacturing enterprises in America and Japan. Not only do these figures show that American firms are lagging behind Japanese firms in using new technology; they reveal an especially sluggish perfor-

Table 2.8. Technology users in Japan and the United States, as percent of small and large manufacturing firms, 1988.

Types of technology	Japan		United States	
	Small firms	Large firms	Small firms	Large firms
1. Numerically controlled machine tools	57.4	79.4	39.6	69.8
2. Machining centers	39.4	67.4	9.1	35.9
3. Computer-aided design	39.1	75.2	36.3	82.6
4. Handling robots	22.6	62.2	5.5	43.3
5. Automatic warehouse equipment	10.9	44.9	1.9	24.4
6. Assembly robots	8.3	41.4	3.9	35.0

Source: National Academy of Sciences, *Mastering a New Role: Shaping Technology Policy for National Economic Performance*, 39 (1993).

Table 2.9. Share of global market for high-tech products, in percent, 1965–1985.

Country	1965	1975	1985	1990
United States	27.5	24.5	24.2	23.1
Japan	7.2	11.6	19.4	17.1
West Germany	16.9	16.8	14.8	15.3
France	7.3	8.4	7.9	8.4
United Kingdom	12.0	9.6	9.2	9.1

Source: National Science Foundation, *International Science and Technology Data Update,* *1991*, 125 (1991). Figures for 1990 supplied privately by the National Science Foundation.

mance by small firms relative to the record of their Japanese counterparts.

One last rough index of our success in applying research for commercial purposes is America's share of the world market for high-technology products. By this yardstick, the United States still occupies a leading position (Table 2.9). Even so, our margin over Japan has been gradually eroding, although there is evidence that we have regained some lost ground in the past decade.[15]

Overall, the record suggests that the United States has held its own reasonably well against Europe but has not matched the gains achieved by the Japanese in transferring scientific knowledge to industry. Certainly, we have not maintained our commanding lead nearly as well in developing and applying technology as we have in scientific research. In particular, we have lost significant ground to the Japanese in developing new patents, applying new technology, and competing in the global market for high-tech products.

Rethinking Technology Policy

America's record in exploiting technology reveals a need to examine and adapt traditional policies. As indicated earlier, the government's strategy until quite recently has emphasized a series of large, centrally planned, mission-oriented projects. These ventures have had a mixed record. The Manhattan Project in World War II and the placing of a man on the moon in the 1960s were national triumphs of a high order.

The communications satellite can probably be ranked as a success. But there is an ample list of failures as well: the synthetic-fuels program, the Clinch River breeder reactor, and the supersonic transport, to name but a few.[16]

Many of these cases exhibit a similar pattern. In order to obtain congressional approval, administration experts have often made extravagant estimates of what new projects can accomplish. Political pressures for quick dramatic results have then distorted priorities. As funding continues, and local firms and communities come to depend on federal support, new pressures have developed not to terminate the projects even when prospects for success have become remote. In the end, much money has been wasted.

Efforts to speed the commercial application of technical knowledge have also had a mixed record. They have worked well in agriculture, where county agents forged a link between farmers and universities, and also in medicine, where teaching hospitals fostered close connections between the health sciences and medical practice. These successes, however, have not yet been duplicated in industry. In contrast to the governments of other industrial democracies, Washington has allocated almost none of its extensive R&D budget to industrial development. Until recently, the government has not even made a systematic effort to foster closer cooperation between universities and corporations.

Because American scientists and engineers change jobs often and carry their knowledge with them, and because ample supplies of venture capital have been available for high-tech firms just starting out, many new ideas have quickly found their way to the marketplace without the government's help. As competition from abroad has intensified, however, critics have increasingly pointed to weaknesses in the private sector that retard the diffusion of scientific knowledge.[17] There is general agreement that U.S. corporations have a shorter time-horizon in planning R&D investments than their competitors in other countries, apparently because so much of their stock is held by institutional investors seeking a quick return. Inadequate technical training has occasionally slowed the adoption of new technology on the shop floor. Traditions of independence, buttressed until recently by antitrust laws, have inhibited cooperative R&D among competing firms that are not large enough to mount separate research efforts.

In addition to these problems, there appear to be flaws in the research strategies preferred by American companies. Too little effort has gone into looking at new developments elsewhere and too much into making innovations "in-house." In particular, American firms have not been able to borrow new ideas from foreign sources as easily as foreign companies borrow from them. In addition, corporate executives, with encouragement from their scientists and engineers, have tended to use the bulk of their applied-research budgets to develop new products instead of seeking improvements in the processes and methods of production. Thus, an estimated two-thirds of all applied research funds in America have gone to product innovation and only one-third for process improvements.[18] In Japan and Germany, exactly the reverse is true. These contrasting priorities may help explain why American companies are so often the leaders in developing new products, only to lose market share to foreign competitors at the stage when goods must be mass-produced and sold all over the world.

The end of the Cold War has created an opportunity to reexamine some basic questions about America's research-and-technology policy. The passing of the arms race and the rise of global competition invite a reconsideration of national priorities, especially the proper balance to be struck between military and civilian R&D. The massive expenditure cuts required to balance the budget underscore the need to set clear priorities and to utilize R&D funds more efficiently. Meanwhile, mounting competition and corporate restructuring have led large companies such as IBM, Kodak, and AT&T to cut back their laboratories, forcing these firms to look for ties with other sources of scientific research. How these challenges are met will have profound effects on America's ability to compete effectively in the world market.

Efforts by the government to address these issues have brought into sharp relief long-standing differences about the proper role of government in promoting research and technology. Everyone agrees in principle that federal funds should support activities, such as basic research, which the private sector cannot perform adequately by itself. But disagreements have arisen over just how much the market can do and whether public officials are capable of implementing active programs to enhance and accelerate private efforts to develop needed technology. Four questions illustrate these tensions.

If federal funds must be cut, it is especially important to move money freely to those programs that promise to achieve the best results. No one disputes that principle. But developing clear priorities and living up to them in practice are difficult tasks indeed when R&D programs are split among so many agencies and departments in the executive branch and are then reviewed by an equally scattered array of separate committees and subcommittees in the House and Senate. Outside commissions have repeatedly called for better means of coordination, but neither Congress nor the executive branch has been able to arrive at a satisfactory solution.

Another long-standing issue is what to do with government-owned laboratories, which currently consume more than $20 billion per year. With the end of the Cold War, some of these laboratories are outmoded. All of them suffer from what one recent report described as an "unfortunate environment that the federal government provides for research and development, through excessive and inflexible rules governing personnel, supplies, equipment, and facilities."[19] Should outmoded laboratories be closed, with all the conflict and anguish that accompany efforts to shut down major facilities, or can they be "reinvented" and given a new mission to support industry? In the case of those laboratories that continue to exist, should they remain under government control, with all the red tape and micromanagement that public management has traditionally entailed, or should they be placed under corporate management with limited federal oversight?

Still another question grows out of the need for industry to establish closer ties with universities, especially now that their own laboratories are being reoriented to focus more on the practical needs of the company. How actively should the government seek to encourage such cooperation through offering public subsidies or creating special institutional structures? To some lawmakers, such interventions promise to speed the transmission of good ideas from academic laboratories to corporate offices. To others, initiatives of this kind threaten to encroach upon the independence of universities and tempt them into arrangements that may distort their priorities and deflect them from their true mission.

The last important issue of technology policy is whether the government should use federal funds to try to encourage the development of innovations that are risky but may turn out to have high commercial value. This question has arisen most clearly in connection with the Clinton administration's effort to expand the Advanced Technology Program, which offers matching funds to develop "precompetitive" technologies of great commercial promise. To proponents, government money is needed in these cases, because the uncertainties at such an early precompetitive stage are often sufficient to deter private firms from investing. Conservative critics tend to dismiss these arguments and to regard the Advanced Technology Program as "corporate welfare." In their view, when discoveries have genuine potential, the market will fund them. If the government tries to improve upon the market by "picking winners" itself, much waste will arguably ensue. With a welter of interest groups clamoring for special assistance, it is not even clear that federal officials will be able to make decisions in a thoroughly impartial manner. As former Senator William Proxmire once said: "Anyone who thinks that government funds will go to firms according to merit has not served in Washington very long."[20]

These issues reveal how far apart federal policymakers remain in considering the role that government should play in encouraging technology. The result is that America has not managed to create programs for speeding the development and application of technology that are as successful as its efforts to encourage first-rate scientific research. In retrospect, the strategy of promoting large specific projects while doing little to speed the diffusion of technology seems to have been ill-advised on both counts. Many megaprojects have been expensive failures. At the same time, left to its own devices, the private market has not done especially well at technology transfer: on the whole, small and medium-size businesses have been slow to adopt such basic innovations as numerically controlled machines, computer-assisted design, and simple robots.

Even if the United States develops more effective policies, however, speeding the transfer of technology will not be enough to ensure America's long-term economic prosperity. Equally important is the need to develop a work force sufficiently educated and skilled to perform well in an advanced, technologically sophisticated economy. Although the challenge of building an effective technology policy is difficult enough, greater problems have arisen in trying to develop educational and training programs that equal those of countries such as Germany and Japan.

3

Education

One of the great transformations sweeping over America and the industrialized world is the shift from an economy based on muscle to an economy founded on knowledge. As Peter Drucker put it, "In this society, knowledge is *the* primary resource for individuals and for the economy overall. Land, labor, and capital—the economist's traditional factors of production—do not disappear, but they become secondary."[1] According to most students of the subject, each additional year of schooling brings a 5–10 percent increase in earnings.[2] Government officials, business executives, and opinion leaders of all kinds now look upon education as more important than ever, not only for students but for the progress of the economy and the welfare of society as a whole.

The United States was the first country to proclaim the ideal of universal public education. In the nineteenth century, education for all meant attending primary school; later, access to high school became increasingly important. As late as 1940, however, less than half of all Americans aged twenty-five to twenty-nine had actually graduated from high school. By 1960, the proportion had climbed above 60 percent. By 1975, it exceeded 83 percent and has stayed at about that level ever since.[3]

Americans have traditionally had high hopes for what education could accomplish and have tried to achieve a variety of goals through the schools. An early concern was to use education to build loyalty toward a new nation in the minds of a geographically dispersed population accustomed to thinking of themselves as citizens of separate

states. Toward the end of the nineteenth century, schools took on a
different role as places for integrating large numbers of new immigrants into American society by teaching them a common culture.
Starting in the Depression years, educators began to emphasize the
need to teach students to adjust to society (perhaps because it appeared
that society was not adjusting much to them). In the 1950s, after the
launching of Sputnik, a brief period ensued of intense national concern
over whether our schools were graduating enough students with
enough proficiency in science to enable America to keep up militarily
with the Soviet Union. The 1960s brought a new and challenging mission of seeking to integrate the races and overcome the handicaps imposed by generations of inequality for black Americans.

Since the 1970s, policymakers and business leaders have begun to
worry increasingly about American competitiveness in world markets.
Corporate executives have expressed great concern over whether our
high schools are graduating students equipped to function well in a
global economy. In the words of one executive, "Blow up the current
education system. No more tinkering at the margins."[4] According to
another, "Band-Aids won't work anymore; we need a total restructuring."[5] Explained still another, "American companies are being forced
to adapt to these low skills by organizing their businesses around people with seventh-grade skills and a day and a half of training. Then,
to remain competitive, they must lower wages and increase hours."[6]
With corporate leaders complaining and economists emphasizing the
close connection between education and rising productivity, educators
and policymakers have begun to focus more and more on what Mortimer Adler describes as "the skills of reading, writing, speaking, listening, observing, measuring, estimating, and calculating."[7]

One may well wonder whether economic competitiveness has come
to play too large a role in our thinking about the public schools, to the
detriment of other traditional purposes of education. Be that as it may,
intellectual competence has clearly become the chief preoccupation of
debates about American public education, far overshadowing other
important concerns such as integrating the races or building civic responsibility. Among the national goals adopted in 1989 by the president and the governors of the fifty states, one objective is to have American students rank first in the world in math and science by the year
2000. Another stipulates that all children should be competent in core
academic subjects. Still other goals seek to improve the knowledge and

skills of the entire population by asking that all young children begin school in a state of readiness to learn and that high school graduation rates reach 90 percent by the end of the century.[8]

With the nation's attention focusing more and more on intellectual skills, reports of college board scores and results of achievement tests in basic subjects have now become front-page news. Featured stories describe how the performance of American students compares with that of other young people around the world. Thus far, all this data has failed to produce much agreement about the state of public education. Critics regularly assail the schools for failing to improve, and school boards and state officials struggle to make changes. Yet large majorities of the public profess to be quite content with the schools their children attend, and a few commentators even insist that American public education has never been better.[9] What can we make of these differences? Now that we have had more than a decade of debate and reform, it is reasonable to ask how well our students are performing and whether the flurry of recent innovations has had any impact.

The Competence of American Students

Elaborate efforts have been made to measure the abilities and achievements of American students in such basic subjects as science, mathematics, reading, and writing. The results, alas, are often ambiguous and easily misused. Every year, newspaper reporters and assorted critics seize upon students' scores on the College Board exam, or Scholastic Assessment Test (SAT), as evidence of how well our schools are teaching America's youth, even though officials responsible for these exams regularly protest that they are not a test of academic achievement. To add to the confusion, the percentages of high school seniors taking the exam change significantly over time, so that trends in SAT scores may reflect differences in the background of the test takers rather than changes in the overall abilities of American students or in the quality of the schools that teach them.

Other tests provide a more reliable index of trends in the knowledge and competence of American youth. The best of these is the National Assessment of Educational Progress (NAEP) which has tested nine-, thirteen-, and seventeen-year-olds nationwide since 1969. The oldest are the Iowa Test of Basic Skills and the Iowa Test of Educational

Development, which have been given to students in grades three to twelve since the mid-1950s.

None of these instruments tells us everything we would like to know about the educational progress of our students. Composed of standardized, short-answer questions, they do not give a reliable indication of the depth of students' understanding, their creativity, or their ability to integrate a body of knowledge. Nevertheless, they do provide a rough measure of a student's mastery of basic skills.

What do these tests reveal about the competence of young people today? Are American schoolchildren performing less well than they did in years past? After reviewing the results of many tests, the Congressional Budget Office concluded that beginning in the late 1960s, scores in science and math for students above the third grade declined until the late 1970s.[10] After the late 1970s, however, scores began to improve steadily. Results from the Iowa tests suggest that students in every grade but the eighth and twelfth are now performing at all-time highs, and that the eighth and twelfth grades are very close to their peak levels.[11]

NAEP scores extend over a shorter period than the Iowa results, but have the advantage of covering the entire population rather than only a segment. The results are mixed. The NAEP tests do show a gradual rise in math and science skills since the early 1980s.[12] Although the increases were large enough to return nine- and thirteen-year-olds to the levels of 1970, seventeen-year-olds in 1990 still performed less well in science than their counterparts had twenty years before.* Over the same period, however, reading skills rose slightly for seventeen-year-olds while staying virtually unchanged for nine- and thirteen-year-olds.

In sum, although there are plenty of reasons to worry about the intellectual competence of young people, no reliable evidence exists that students as a whole are performing less well than they did twenty-

*One troubling charge was recently leveled by Richard Herrnstein and Charles Murray, who examined SAT scores for white students and found a substantial decline especially in the verbal scores from 1963 through 1991, with little improvement since the low point in 1980. On the other hand, NAEP tests appear to show that the upper quartile of students at ages nine, thirteen, and seventeen all surpassed 1971 levels of reading comprehension by 1990. In light of these conflicting results, there appear to be no clear trends as yet in the proficiency of high-scoring students. Herrnstein and Murray, "What's Really Behind the SAT-Score Decline?" 106 *The Public Interest*, 32 (Winter 1992).

five years ago. One often hears laments alleging declines in educational achievement from some earlier golden age. But there is no convincing way to test such assertions. Moreover, historians of education can cite speeches and editorials from every era in our past decrying the illiteracy and incompetence of American schoolchildren. In 1912, Ella Francis Lynch of the *Ladies Home Journal* denounced an educational system that "throws every year ninety-three out of every one-hundred children into the world of action absolutely unfitted for even the simplest tasks of life."[13] In 1927, the chairman of the National Association of Manufacturers' Education Committee complained: "Forty percent of high school graduates haven't a command of simple arithmetic, cannot multiply, subtract, or divide correctly in simple numbers and fractions. Over forty percent of them cannot accurately express themselves in the English language or cannot write in the mother tongue."[14] Remember that these words were written to describe the abilities of high school graduates at a time when only a small, privileged minority of our youth even reached such an advanced level of education.

Wading through a long series of similar comments, one comes away suspecting that sweeping assertions about declines in student performance are probably false and certainly unsubstantiated. That is the conclusion reached by one of the few scholars who have made a careful attempt to measure student achievement over many decades.[15] Comparing the answers given to similar questions of American history asked in tests over a long period of time, the author found no evidence of decline.

Contrary to all the alarmist talk, there are even some recent signs of modest improvement. Results on the Iowa tests for almost all grades are higher than they have ever been. By 1992, graduating seniors averaged 49 percent more courses in algebra and 33 percent more courses in science than their counterparts ten years earlier. The proportion of thirteen-year-olds who reported that they had no homework or had failed to carry out their assignments fell from 38 percent in 1980 to 25 percent in 1992. The numbers taking Advanced Placement tests have also grown, from 93,313 in 1978 to 504,823 in 1995. The proportion of schools with computers rose from 18 percent in 1981 to 99 percent in 1993, and the number of students per computer fell from 125 to 14. Finally, scores for minority students have climbed appreciably while dropout rates have fallen. In fact, educational achievement is one of the few cases in which the position of minorities and poor people seems to have improved relative to middle-class whites during the 1980s.

It is important to keep these positive signs in perspective. Although test scores for American students as a whole may not have declined, the fact remains that they have increased only slightly at best since the 1960s, while real expenditures per student have risen more than three-fold (from roughly $1,500 in 1960 to $4,622 in 1990).[16] Observing this record, skeptics question whether the country has received full value for its mounting investments.[17] In addition, critics point out that even if student performance has edged up slightly, the demands of a more complex society and a more technologically sophisticated economy have probably been rising faster. If so, our schools may be doing as good a job as they ever did, but the gap between student accomplishment and the needs of the society will have widened nonetheless.

International Comparisons

In a competitive global economy, Americans are no longer merely interested in asking whether students are learning as much today as they did in the past. There is increasing concern with how our levels of proficiency and achievement compare with those of other leading industrial countries.

As a pioneer in developing universal public education, the United States for a long time graduated higher proportions of young people from high school than any other country. In recent years, however, other nations have overtaken the United States in this respect (Table 3.1).

In the realm of higher education, Canada has now moved ahead of the United States in the proportion of young people graduating from college. Other countries have also increased their university enrollments greatly in recent decades. Nevertheless, America still leads the world in the average total number of years of education (Table 3.2).

More important than the years students spend in school is the amount they actually learn and the levels of proficiency they achieve. Those who take an interest in these matters have increasingly looked to the results from international tests of basic cognitive skills. Unfortunately, many people who publicize these comparisons do not make clear just how treacherous they can be. Many tests are of no use at all

Table 3.1. Comparative high school graduation rates, 1992.

Country	Percent of population graduating high school at normal age
Japan	92.2
France	78.2
Canada	68.4
United Kingdom	80.1
West Germany	109.6[a]
United States	75.7

Source: Centre for Educational Research and Innovation, *Education at a Glance: OECD Indicators*, 214 (1995).

a. Includes students enrolled in apprenticeship programs as well as students in high school, and many are enrolled in both.

Table 3.2. Comparative university graduation rates (in 1992) and average years of education (in 1990).

Country	Percent of population graduating college or university at normal age	Average years of education
Canada	32.2	12.1
Japan	23.4	10.7
France	14.5	11.6
West Germany	13.0	11.1
Sweden	11.4	11.1
United Kingdom	20.4	11.5
United States	27.4	12.3

Source: OECD, *Education at a Glance*, 218 (1992); United Nations Development Programme, *Human Development Report, 1993*, 194 (1993).

because the student populations they measure vary so widely. For example, one cannot validly compare high school seniors in the United States, where 80 percent of all young people graduate, with seniors in developing countries where less than half of all young people even reach the twelfth grade. Nor is it useful to make comparisons with China if it turns out that the Chinese administered the tests only to students able to speak Mandarin. Still less can be learned from comparing the algebra skills of ninth-graders in the United States and Japan if most American students do not study algebra before the tenth grade while most of their Japanese counterparts do.

One international study that makes a serious effort to avoid these pitfalls is the 1991 assessment of reading conducted by the International Association for the Evaluation of Educational Achievement (commonly referred to as IEA). The results, using comparable samples of nine- and fourteen-year-old students from more than thirty countries, give a much more positive account of American education than the picture commonly found in the media (Table 3.3).

Unfortunately, recent evidence casts doubt on whether the reading achievements of our nine-year-olds are representative of the state of literacy in the adult population. This at least is the clear implication of the First International Adult Literacy Survey, conducted in 1994 by the OECD.[18] Samples of individuals aged sixteen to sixty-five from

Table 3.3. Results of IEA international reading test, children aged nine and fourteen, 1991.

Nine-year-olds		Fourteen-year-olds	
Country	Mean scores	Country	Mean scores
Finland	569	Finland	560
United States	547	France	549
Sweden	539	Sweden	546
France	531	Hungary	536
Italy	529	Iceland	536
Norway	524	Switzerland	536
Iceland	518	*United States*	535
Switzerland	511	East Germany	526
Ireland	509	Denmark	525
Belgium (French)	507	Portugal	523
Greece	504	Canada (British Columbia)	522
Spain	504	West Germany	522
West Germany	503	Norway	516
Canada (British Columbia)	500	Italy	515
East Germany	499	Netherlands	514
Hungary	498	Ireland	511
Netherlands	485	Greece	509
Portugal	478	Spain	490
Denmark	475	Belgium (French)	481

Source: Warwick B. Elley, *How in the World Do Students Read? IEA Study of Reading Literacy,* 14, 24 (International Association for the Evaluation of Educational Achievement, 1992).

several countries—including Canada, Germany, Sweden, and the United States—were tested on their ability to understand information in a text and to comprehend material in documents, such as maps, charts, graphs, job application forms, and transportation schedules. Participants were then ranked in five categories according to the level of their ability.

In reading texts, 20.7 percent of American adults ranked in the lowest category, somewhat more than West Germany (14.4 percent) or Canada (16.6 percent), and much more than in Sweden (7.5 percent). Conversely, only 21.1 percent of Americans ranked in the top two categories—considerably better than West Germany (13.4 percent), but slightly below Canada (22.7 percent) and far below Sweden (32.5 percent). In comprehending documents, 23.7 percent of Americans fell into the lowest category—more than Canada (18.2 percent), Germany (9.0 percent), or Sweden (6.2 percent). Only 19 percent of Americans performed at the top two levels, approximately the same as Germany (18.9 percent), but well below Canada (25.0 percent) and Sweden (35.5 percent).

Adult literacy scores are sobering, but they are not the scores that have produced the doleful tales of American performance so widely publicized over the last decade. Those accounts have to do with the competence of students in math and science. For these subjects, the two most reliable tests are the Second International Mathematics Study in 1982 and the tests of math and science administered by the International Assessment of Educational Progress (IAEP) in 1988 and 1991.

The Second International Mathematics Study covered eighth-graders in twenty countries.[19] When the results were tabulated, American students finished sixteenth in geometry, eighteenth in measurement, twelfth in algebra, and tenth in arithmetic. Additional tests were given to twelfth-grade college preparatory students in advanced algebra, geometry, and elementary functions/calculus. Although the cohort of young people taking these tests varied from country to country, the 15 percent of American high school seniors taking college preparatory math was a more select group than that of most other countries in the sample. Even so, among students from fifteen countries, American students ranked twelfth in geometry, twelfth in elementary functions/calculus, and fourteenth in advanced algebra.

Only six countries participated in the 1988 IAEP examinations—the United States, Ireland, South Korea, Spain, Great Britain, and Can-

Table 3.4. Results of IAEP tests in math and science, thirteen-year-olds, 1988.

Subject	U.S. rank (measured by mean score)	Number of participating countries doing significantly better than U.S. (of 12 participating systems)	Number of participating countries doing significantly worse than U.S.
Mathematics	12	10	0
Science	9	8	0

Source: Elliot A. Medrich and Jeanne E. Griffith, *International Math and Science Assessments: What Have We Learned?* 26 (National Center for Education Statistics, 1992).

ada—although seven Canadian provinces, each with a separate school system, were included. The results for thirteen-year-olds are shown in Table 3.4.

The 1991 IAEP tests covered a much larger group of countries, twenty in all, but participation in several was too low to be reliable.[20] Of the ten nations with adequate coverage for nine-year-olds, American students ranked third from the top in science. In math, however, they performed much less well, relatively speaking, finishing next to last. The significance of these tests is limited by the fact that in both cases the average scores of participating nations were quite closely bunched, so that the differences *within* each country were much greater than the differences *among* the countries.

The results were less encouraging for American thirteen-year-olds. Compared with students in fourteen other nations with sufficiently high levels of participation, American youngsters scored thirteenth out of fifteen in science, and tied for thirteenth in math.[21]

Many people assume that our poor showing in most international tests of math and science must be due chiefly to low scores in inner-city schools, especially those heavily populated by minority students. The facts do not support this supposition. Among thirteen-year-olds in math and in science, Americans in the tenth (the lowest) percentile did score below their counterparts in virtually all European and Asian countries—China, Korea, Taiwan, Britain, France, Italy, Canada, Hungary, and Switzerland. But so did American students in the fortieth percentile, the seventieth percentile, even the ninetieth percentile. In fact, American students at the fortieth and seventieth percentiles were further behind their counterparts from other countries than American youngsters in the tenth percentile. The same results occurred for nine-year-olds in math, where students at the fortieth and seventieth percentiles were again further behind their counterparts in other countries than Americans in the bottom 10 percent. Only among students in the top 1 percent were the scores of Americans approximately equal to those of comparable students from the other countries. All in all, therefore, the results suggest that the problems of American education are not confined to special categories of students or schools, but permeate the entire educational system.[22]

Searching for Causes

In sum, American students do not seem to be improving their knowledge and skills to keep pace with an advancing economy, nor do they compare particularly well in science and math with their counterparts in other countries. Although the differences between the scores in this country and those in other nations are not always large, and even though American students perform quite well in tests of reading, the overall results are not especially encouraging. The ultimate question is who or what is responsible for this modest showing.

A natural response is to blame the schools. After all, they are the institutions officially charged with educating children. With this in mind, some observers point to such problems as the "dumbing down" of high school texts and a shallow, repetitive curriculum that does not pursue questions of science and mathematics in the same depth as teachers do in countries such as Japan. Another common claim is that American students do not spend as much classroom time studying science and math as students abroad. As Table 3.5 points out, however, this assertion does not appear to be valid.

Before blaming public education too severely, we must remember that schools are not the only influences that affect how much young people learn. Other factors, such as families, friends, health, nutrition, and neighborhood influences all have an impact as well. Many researchers confirm this impression, but different investigators stress different aspects of the environment in trying to account for our poor showing on international tests of math and science. One writer analyzing the results has concluded that much of the difference between

Table 3.5. Average amount of time spent on science and math
            instruction, per student, 1992.

Country	Mathematics (minutes per week)	Science (minutes per week)	Science and math (hours per year)
Korea	179	144	977
Taiwan	204	245	1,177
Switzerland	251	152	1,052
Hungary	186	207	658
France	230	174	1,073
United States	228	233	1,003

Source: National Education Goals Panel, *National Education Goals Report: Building a Nation of Learners*, 8–9 (1992).

the records of our students and those from other countries can be explained by the higher rates of poverty in America and, to a lesser extent, by the greater number of single-parent families.[23] Another investigator has suggested that results seem to be related to the average amount of time per week that children in each country devote to watching television. Table 3.6 bears this out.

Still another study comparing Japanese and American schools emphasizes differences in the support that children from each country

Table 3.6. Comparison of the time that teenagers devoted to homework
            and television, 1992.

Country	Percent of thirteen-year-olds who:		
	Spent 4 hours or more on science homework each week	Spent 4 hours or more on math homework each week	Watched 5 hours or more of TV every day
Hungary	13	11	13
Taiwan	10	24	10
Korea	9	33	11
France	1	17	5
Switzerland	1	15	7
United States	7	15	20

Source: National Education Goals Panel, *National Education Goals Report: Building a Nation of Learners*, 102–103 (1992).

receive from sources outside the school.[24] In Japan, families regularly help their children with their homework and communicate with teachers about the work of their offspring. In the United States, parental involvement is much less common. Many schools in the United States do not even assign substantial amounts of homework, because they cannot expect parents to help make sure that the work gets done. Moreover, American students are permitted to spend much more time watching television or working at paid jobs than most Japanese families allow.

Beyond these parental influences, competition to enter universities in Japan is keen. Those who do not go to college also have an incentive to excel, since Japanese corporations regularly ask teachers for their recommendations of which graduating seniors to employ. The combination of parental involvement, university admission procedures, and corporate hiring practices gives Japanese students motivations to learn that are considerably stronger than anything the average American student experiences. Indeed, if most of our public schools suffer from a lack of incentives to excel, the problem in Japan is the reverse.

These contrasting explanations point up the difficulty of trying to decide how much responsibility we should assign to schools in accounting for the performance of American students. Many different forces help determine the amount that children learn, and it is no simple matter to pull them apart to measure just how much any single factor is responsible. The most sophisticated recent research suggests that the quality of schools may account for up to 15 percent of the differences in achievement by students from comparable socioeconomic backgrounds, and that the quality of teaching may account for another 10 percent.[25] These findings are still only tentative. Nevertheless, they are consistent with a widely shared opinion that variations in intelligence, family background, and parental upbringing account for most of the differences in student performance but that schools are sufficiently important to rank among the more significant influences— enough so, surely, to warrant a determined effort to make them as effective as possible.

The Effort to Reform

Acting on this premise, public officials at all levels of government have been working hard for more than a decade to improve the nation's schools. This is not the first time in our history that reformers have tried to introduce large-scale changes. Over the years, successive attempts have been made to introduce such innovations as shifting from a teacher-centered to a student-centered form of instruction, consolidating smaller high schools into larger ones, or revising science curricula with the aid of university faculty. By and large, reformers have been most successful in persuading schools to add new functions, such as bilingual instruction, special education for learning-disabled children, and driver training. They have also been able to implement administrative changes, such as centralizing or decentralizing authority and consolidating or breaking up school districts. What they have rarely managed to do is change traditional methods of classroom teaching—dividing students by grades, teaching them in hour-long classes, using textbooks, and having teachers control the course of instruction by lecturing or questioning their students. Having to teach potentially unruly students several hours each day and with precious little time to prepare, teachers have naturally opposed new ideas that seemed too difficult to implement or too threatening to their ability to maintain order in the classroom. When teachers have resisted on these grounds, few administrators have succeeded in forcing them to change their ways.

Over the years, school reform has also suffered from the mistaken notion that lasting improvement can come from a single transforming idea, generally imposed from above. In fact, the process of changing teaching and learning in the schools is much more complicated, because so many different things need to happen in a coordinated fashion in order to bring about lasting progress. Raising salaries to attract better teachers will accomplish nothing if school systems do not improve their hiring practices, which are often remarkably slipshod. Hiring better teachers will not make much of an impact unless they receive enough time and encouragement to work together to build better curricula and try new methods of instruction. Such opportunities are not likely to come unless there are principals willing and able to offer academic leadership rather than merely administer their schools. Useful innovations will not endure without clear objectives and reliable feedback for gauging progress. And none of the above is likely to happen if state and local officials do not provide the funds, the direction, and the political leadership to guide the process properly.

The United States has constructed an educational system that is not at all easy to change in such a comprehensive way. It is highly decentralized, much more so than the systems of the other six nations we have been considering. Even in Britain, which gives broad discretion to its local authorities, schools receive 60 percent of their money from the central government, which sets the curriculum and conducts national examinations.[26] In the United States, the federal government supplies only 6 percent of the funding and has not yet established national standards for what students are expected to learn or how they should be taught. Real power over education still rests in local communities and increasingly in the state capitals. Inducing fifty states and thousands of separate school districts to reform their educational systems in a coordinated way is a formidable task indeed.

One advantage of our highly fragmented system, with all of its independent school districts, is that innovators find it relatively easy to experiment. In Richard Elmore's words, "It has been possible to do almost anything in American education, as long as one didn't try to do it on a large scale, over a long period of time, or in a way that threatened the basic patterns of practice in most schools."[27] During the past dozen years, educators and public officials have made the most of these opportunities. Rarely have so many new initiatives been tried in such a brief span of years.

During the first wave of reform, in the mid-1980s, most of the changes took the form of tightening the rules to improve student learning.[28] Many school systems and state legislatures lengthened the school year, required students to take more basic academic subjects, and introduced merit pay, career ladders, evaluation systems, and other devices to strengthen the motivation of teachers. By forcing students to take more demanding courses and encouraging instructors to work harder, authorities believed that results would soon improve.

Rightly or wrongly, the idea gained ground after a few years that "top-down" changes were not accomplishing enough and that new strategies were needed. In particular, evaluations seemed to reveal that few of the early reforms had much of an effect on what teachers did in the classroom. Some way needed to be found to engage teachers more fully in the reform effort. Accordingly, states and localities began to make more comprehensive "bottom-up" efforts to restructure the schools. Under the newer approaches, districts or even states could establish goals and standards, but individual schools would have more power to decide how to achieve these objectives. There was much talk not only of "school-based management" but of giving greater authority to teachers and parents to work together and decide on appropriate curricula and teaching methods.

Along with these two waves of reform has come a third approach, which sees inertia and bureaucratic indifference as the critical obstacles to meaningful change. This strategy looks to the private market for inspiration and seeks to introduce more competition into the schools as a means of motivating teachers and officials to work harder at improving quality and adapting their programs to serve the needs of students. In search of competition, experiments have been launched in many cities and towns to allow students to choose which public school to attend, or to invite groups of teachers or even outsiders to establish model "charter" schools.[29] Occasionally, local officials have actually contracted out a few schools or even entire municipal school systems for private companies to manage.

With all the new initiatives being tried, there is still no indication that a successful, comprehensive system of reform is under way in more than a few states. Nor is there much sign that some long-standing weaknesses are being corrected. The move toward educational standards—so important for feedback and accountability—has run into trouble over what the content should be, how results should be measured, and whether government officials should prescribe to local communities what their schools should try to teach. More than a decade after the new era of reform began, most teachers are still receiving relatively low salaries, their morale is generally poor, and the profession continues to draw most of its new recruits from the bottom third of American college classes.[30] Current methods of teacher education leave much to be desired, but little evidence exists that fundamental reforms are taking place in the faculties where most of the nation's teachers are trained. Despite a firm consensus on the importance of strong academic leadership in building successful schools, the manner of choosing principals continues to be haphazard, and the quality of their preparation remains unsatisfactory. Finally, with all the effort being made to change curricula and improve teaching, there is still very little success in enlisting the help of parents and employers to increase students' motivation to work hard at their studies.

Looked at as a whole, the debate over educational reform has proved to be a curiously compartmentalized affair in which every interested group knows what the problem is but none seems to be listening to the others. Parents are convinced that the critical problems to be solved are disorderly conduct in the classrooms, physical violence in the halls, and drugs in the playgrounds and adjoining streets. Teachers feel that progress could be made if only parents would take an interest in their children, put them to bed at a reasonable hour, and insist that they do their homework instead of listening to music and watching television. Educators talk of enriched curricula, smaller classrooms, cooperative learning, and more computers. Conservatives feel that nothing of much value will occur until some way is found to break the hold of the teachers' unions and loosen the grip of the administrative hierarchy. Probably, all sides have some valid points to make, but that only underscores how formidable the agenda for reform has become.

Amid the welter of promising experiments and persistent problems, it is difficult to assess in any rigorous fashion how much progress has been made since serious reform began more than a decade ago. In the early 1990s, the federal government developed a set of national goals for education in an effort to focus reform efforts more sharply and measure results more accurately. Although the goals are meant to be achieved by the year 2000, the methods of measurement have been so slow to emerge that there is no clear indication yet of how much improvement has occurred. But there is enough evidence in hand to make some intelligent guesses about the prospects for success. A few of the goals—especially becoming first in the world in math and science— seem wildly unrealistic and were probably never intended seriously. More worrisome are initial findings on how many students are currently performing at the levels deemed necessary for all our children by the National Education Goals Panel.[31] According to a panel report in 1995, only 25 percent or fewer of all pupils in the fourth, eighth, or twelfth grade met the prescribed standard in mathematics, and only 30 percent of fourth-graders and eighth-graders and 36 percent of twelfth-graders reached the standard in reading. Fewer than 20 percent of our students in these three grades met the standards set for history, and 28 percent or fewer satisfied them in geography. Although miracles do happen, it would be truly remarkable if anything close to 100 percent of our students could achieve the designated levels of proficiency before the decade is out.

In the end, therefore, the balance sheet for educational reform continues to be mixed. One must certainly applaud the sustained effort underway to find effective ways of improving public education. Nothing this far-reaching has been tried in American education for many decades. After all of the experiments, however, there is still no agreement on what a successful school looks like and no assurance that such schools, if they do appear, will spread widely and eventually become the predominant model. In the case of scientific research and technological innovation, important breakthroughs soon become known and are quickly disseminated and widely used. In the case of school reform, it is much less clear what constitutes a successful innovation or how quickly it will be copied. As a result, after more than a decade of reform, one sees much creative ferment but still no convincing evidence that overall results will improve substantially anytime soon.

4

Labor Market Policies

For years, vocational education and training were dull pursuits reserved for those not bright enough or ambitious enough to engage in serious study. Suddenly, within the past decade, such preparation has become a matter of real concern to policymakers. Job training has come to be perceived as an important part of American competitiveness in the global economy and a key to better jobs and greater prosperity for American workers.[1]

This new-found prominence is largely a result of changes that have occurred on the shop floor. During the era of mass production made famous by Henry Ford, the needs of industry were relatively simple. A small segment of the work force, mostly college-educated managers and professionals, performed all of the functions requiring judgment, analysis, and other problem-solving skills. The rest of the labor pool consisted of production workers who carried out routine, repetitive tasks. In them, management looked for qualities of obedience, attention, perseverance, and loyalty rather than technical skills and intellectual ability.

Today, the assembly line has given way to new forms of production that require many workers to have better problem-solving skills and greater technical mastery than their predecessors. Better-paid jobs increasingly call for an ability to perform several tasks, to shift from one job to another, to learn new methods when changing circumstances require. In the service sector, more and more positions call for an ability to use computers and other information technology. In manufacturing, workers are viewed less and less as faceless automatons and more and more as active members of a team trying not only to carry on efficiently in accustomed ways but to help figure out how to make the firm function better. The Japanese, in particular, have shown how much a company can benefit from having its blue-collar workers contribute by suggesting ways to improve methods of production and adapt them to meet changing markets.

Employees, too, have a vital stake in good training. If the United States can produce a larger supply of well-trained workers, it can sustain an economy with greater numbers of challenging, well-paid jobs. If not, other countries are more likely to capture the markets served by firms requiring highly skilled employees, leaving Americans to perform less demanding, less remunerative work. It is therefore important to everyone to know how well our labor force is currently being trained and whether it could be prepared more effectively.

What can a nation do to help its work force gain the added skills required for a modern industrial economy? Of prime importance is a network of primary and secondary schools that not only teach basic competencies, such as reading, writing, and mathematics, but develop more demanding problem-solving abilities as well. Next comes a system to ensure a smooth transition from school to work—one that gives young people the initial skills they need to find a satisfying job. In a dynamic economy, however, initial training cannot suffice; most people will change jobs several times in their career. As a result, opportunities must exist both to retrain employees at strategic points in their working lives and to reach out to those who have not managed to find steady jobs and prepare them for positions with a future. Finally, to help link employees and training programs to the actual needs of the economy, a mechanism is required to gather and disseminate information about current job vacancies and economic trends that may affect work opportunities in the future.

As in so many other fields of endeavor, public officials must decide how much to rely on the private market to perform these functions and how much to leave to the State. All industrial nations have used a combination of company training and government programs. But each country has found its own distinctive way of combining public and private initiatives to prepare its work force.

Foreign Approaches

Sweden has developed an exceptionally elaborate and expensive series of training and job placement programs.[2] At the center of this effort is the National Labor Market Board. All employers are obliged to list their open positions with the board, which actively counsels job seekers with the aid of computerized lists of all open positions throughout the country. In addition, the board manages an elaborate set of training programs to equip young people as well as older workers for a wide range of jobs. During recessions, the board sponsors public works programs and subsidizes employers who create jobs for those in need of work. No one who will not accept an offer of a temporary job or enroll in a suitable training program is entitled to receive unemployment benefits.

Because Sweden is a trading nation, exposed to the vagaries of the world market, the government has made great efforts to help employees move from declining industries to new jobs in expanding fields through the use of special training programs, relocation allowances, early retirement, and counseling by the Labor Market Board. Such programs, of course, are expensive, as are the training courses and public works programs. In return, however, Sweden had unusual success for several decades in avoiding long-term unemployment and limiting the amounts it had to pay in jobless benefits. Throughout the postwar period, unemployment stayed below 2 or 3 percent until the early 1990s. At that point, a worldwide recession overwhelmed the system and pushed jobless rates above 7 percent (more than 10 percent if one includes all those in training programs or public works jobs). With unemployment persisting at high levels, critics are beginning to question whether such heavy outlays for training and temporary jobs are actually worth the cost and whether they truly help reduce the number of people out of work.

Like Sweden, Germany has a national body that administers an elaborate series of programs for counselling, training, placement assistance, and incentives for employers to create jobs.[3] But Germany is best known for its distinctive way of preparing teenagers for employment. Almost all young people who do not go to college enroll at age fifteen in some form of apprenticeship program encouraged by the State but operated by employers. During their apprenticeship, young people continue to attend classes for a part of each week but spend most of their time working for an employer at approximately half the prevailing wage. After a stipulated period of years, apprentices take exams and earn certificates attesting to the fact that they have mastered an industry-approved set of skill requirements. Thereafter, they can continue working for their employer at full wages if they wish. In fact, a large majority elect to do so, though many of them leave their post within a year and find jobs with other firms.

The government plays only a limited role in the apprenticeship system, establishing national standards for job skills and training in consultation with employers' associations and unions. Industry-wide associations to which all employers must belong actually administer the apprenticeship program by giving examinations, awarding certificates of completion, and designating employers who can participate in the program.

The German approach does not work perfectly. It tends to track students at an early age and press them into choosing a career before they have had time to experiment with different kinds of work. It is weighted toward traditional jobs rather than emerging opportunities. More recently, it has been threatened by levels of unemployment so high that there may not be jobs for those who complete their training. As in Sweden, there is little indication that job training can reduce unemployment. What the system does do is to enable almost all German youth to begin their working lives with some generally recognized marketable skill.[4]

Japan differs from Sweden and Germany in relying much more on the private economy to take care of initial job preparation and subsequent training.[5] Most employers seem to prefer students with a broad education and a sound command of basic skills. As a result, only a quarter of Japanese students attend vocational high schools.

The process of hiring young people for their first job is marked by close cooperation between companies and schools. Corporations rank different schools and try to recruit their new employees from the best institutions. Teachers in turn rank different companies in terms of their attractiveness as places to work and advise their students where to accept employment. In this way, companies and schools exert gentle pressure on one another to achieve the highest standards, and both create strong incentives for young people to do well in their classwork.

In the process, students are guided to jobs commensurate with their interests and abilities.

Once the initial hiring takes place, larger Japanese firms generally commit themselves, after an initial trial period, to employ individuals throughout their working lives. The training and retraining of these workers becomes a matter of considerable importance to the companies, since firms must keep their regular employees productive and capable of adapting to several different jobs over a long period of years. In Japan, therefore, managers specializing in human development and training have higher status than personnel officers in the United States. As Ronald Dore and David Cairncross point out, "Personnel Departments . . . are seen as key departments, likely to be manned, not by a company's more sluggish and unimaginative elements, but by some of its brightest and most imaginative spirits."[6] Even among Japanese firms with only twenty to ninety-nine employees, more than two-thirds appoint a training manager—a figure well above the level in the United States.

The American Experience

The United States has followed an intermediate course in its labor market policies. Officials look to private employers to carry on much of the needed job training. At the same time, public schools and community colleges offer vocational courses, while the government pays for programs to help displaced workers and hard-to-employ individuals gain the skills they need to find a steady job.

As in all industrial nations, the federal government operates an employment service to assist in guiding job seekers to employers needing workers. In contrast to firms in Sweden, however, companies in the United States are not obliged to list employment openings with the service. As a result, employers seldom do so, and skilled workers rarely use the service. Instead, the employment service largely confines itself to referring unskilled workers to firms with appropriate job openings.[7]

Unlike Sweden, America has not relied to any great extent on state-created jobs to help reduce unemployment and develop skills. Twice in modern times the federal government has mounted large-scale jobs programs—in the Depression, with the Works Progress Administration and the Civilian Conservation Corps, and again in the 1970s, with

the Comprehensive Education and Training Act (CETA). On both occasions, the programs proved controversial and were eventually
stopped.[8]

In the high schools, vocational education has enjoyed continuing
federal support since 1917 to supplement local resources. Until 1963,
however, most of the courses were devoted to home economics and
agriculture. In that year, Congress encouraged schools to broaden their
vocational programs to meet the needs of the industrial economy and
to link them more closely to employers. In 1976 and again in 1984,
Congress renewed its effort to bring vocational training into closer
alignment with industry. Today, more than 5 million students throughout the country take courses in word processing, automobile repair,
elementary accounting, and similar subjects.[9]

Since the 1970s, community colleges have played a growing role
in vocational education, not only for young high school graduates but
for people of all ages.[10] By 1993, more than 6 million students were
attending community colleges, and almost two-thirds were enrolled in
vocational courses. In recent years, many of these colleges have built
close ties with employers to create joint, "customized" training courses.
Today, nearly 75 percent of all community colleges and technical
schools have some sort of cooperative program with local employers.

Beyond the schools and colleges lies a battery of special training
programs sponsored by the federal government.[11] Unlike similar efforts
abroad, these federal initiatives are not designed primarily to help employers meet their manpower needs. Instead, they arise from Congress'
desire to aid particular groups that have difficulty finding jobs—the
chronically unemployed, older employees, young people unable to obtain steady jobs, and workers displaced by economic change, among
others. The sheer volume of programs is staggering: one survey in 1994
counted 154 at a total cost of more than $24 billion per year.[12]

Assessing the Record

Few knowledgeable observers would rank our labor market programs
and institutions among the brighter achievements of American public
policy. The employment service has a particularly poor reputation, although its quality varies considerably from one state to another. Studies show that workers registering with the agency often have no better

record of finding jobs than those who do not register at all.[13] Most workers looking for jobs do not even bother to register, while employers repeatedly complain that the service sends them unqualified people. In contrast to Sweden, where the Labor Market Board works closely with unions, schools, and employers in matching workers to the employment needs of the economy, America's employment service is isolated, passive, and generally looked down upon as an enterprise trafficking in unskilled and largely unwanted employees.

The history of high school vocational education in America is scarcely more successful.[14] Although several million students are enrolled in such programs, the courses have long failed to have much connection with real work. "Voke Ed." instructors are typically professional teachers with little practical experience or record of cooperation with employers. Frequently, programs train students for jobs for which there are no openings. Fewer than three participants in ten find jobs that require the skills they learned in school. In one study, Voke Ed. graduates turned out to be no more likely to obtain work in their chosen field or to receive higher pay than students who had not received any special training at all.[15] Other surveys show little or no wage advantage from the completion of vocational courses.[16] Even studies that find initial gains from such instruction report that these benefits disappear within a few years. All in all, as one commentator put it, "vocational education has acquired a pretty dismal reputation as an irrelevant corner of the high school curriculum—over-the-hill instructors teaching unnecessary skills on outmoded equipment—that frequently has been used as a dumping ground for dim, unwanted or troublesome students."*

Vocational courses in community colleges are often more effective, although the quality varies greatly. Many of the colleges that have developed close connections with local employers seem to have considerable success in training and placing students. Some have developed truly innovative programs. Along with these successes, however,

---

*Rochelle Stanfield, "Ugly Duckling," 25 *National Journal*, 335 (1993). Approximately three-quarters of a million students also enroll each year in for-profit proprietary schools that teach vocational skills. The practical value of this training appears to be comparable to that of the average community college. But three-quarters of all proprietary school students without a high school diploma and half of all enrollees who have graduated from high school drop out before completing their programs.

are numerous examples of other institutions that are no more successful at placing their students in jobs than colleges with no vocational
training programs at all.[17]

When one evaluates the efforts of schools and colleges to prepare
young people for jobs, it is only fair to point out that creating school-
to-work programs is a much more difficult task in America than it is
in many European countries. In the United States, there are few strong
industry associations that develop uniform standards and skill requirements to which vocational teachers can direct their training. There is
no central labor board where educators can join with employers and
union representatives to match training programs to emerging needs.
Because most large companies prefer to hire people who are several
years beyond high school, employers have little incentive to work
closely with principals and teachers to develop better vocational programs. In short, if schools and colleges seem remote from the world of
work, it is partly because the labor market is much more amorphous,
fragmented, and difficult to approach than is the case in much of Europe.

Federally sponsored job training also earns little applause. No one
has much good to say about the extraordinary proliferation of overlapping programs created by Congress. Trainees, employers, and providers are often baffled by the tangle of differing standards, eligibility
criteria, and administrative requirements. Many programs are too brief
to change the skills and the earnings of participants to any substantial
degree. Administrative costs are needlessly inflated. Job seekers frequently enter inappropriate programs. And still the confusion persists.[18]

The Job Training Partnership Act (JTPA) is the largest of the government's training efforts and reflects some of the problems that have
bedeviled programs of this kind. Congress deliberately designed the act
to depart from prior models with reputations for excessive bureaucracy, petty corruption, and inefficiency. Instead of trying to carry out
training itself, the government sought to proceed by relying primarily
on for-profit providers. Rather than micromanage these organizations,
Washington established targets and performance criteria and left it to
the states, localities, and providers to decide how best to achieve the
government's goals. Instead of measuring success by "input" criteria,
such as how many people were trained and how much money was
spent, local agencies would be judged by "output" measures—how

many trainees were placed in real jobs, at what cost per placement, and with what increase in wages. No longer content to monitor expenses after the fact, Congress announced guidelines and spending limits in advance, to avoid the extravagances widely imputed to CETA.

These methods reflected the new philosophy of "reinventing government," with its emphasis on having public officials steer the ship of state rather than rowing themselves or even prescribing in detail how the rowing should be done. In theory, this approach would allow the government to harness the energies of the private sector to achieve public goals. In practice, the new techniques turned out to have consequences that Congress did not anticipate.[19]

Since the government judged training organizations by the percentage of their trainees who found unsubsidized jobs, providers tended to choose participants who were easy to teach and place rather than those who most needed help. Because programs were also evaluated on the basis of their costs, they often concentrated on forms of training that were simple to execute even though they might not lead to challenging jobs with a future. Further muddying the waters, federal guidelines emphasized immediate results, although independent studies tended to show that initial placement was not a reliable measure of whether a program could achieve lasting positive effects. To top matters off, the Reagan administration insisted on doing away with stipends for participants undergoing training, for fear that stipends would turn the federal programs into boondoggles for individuals without real motivation to better themselves. Since few low-skilled workers can afford to go for very long without payment, the result was to discourage longer-term training, the type of training most likely to produce substantial improvements in the skills and earnings of the participants.

By now, studies evaluating training programs lie thick upon the ground. The results range from ineffective to modestly helpful. Some initiatives have had little or no positive impact in improving the employment prospects of their graduates or in leading them to better-paying jobs. A few actually carry a stigma, so that those who finish the course are *less* likely to find a job than members of the control group. By and large, programs for high school dropouts are most likely to disappoint in this way. In contrast, programs for single mothers on welfare typically produce modest increases in earnings of up to $2,000 per year—significant, but rarely enough to lift such women out of poverty. Programs for disadvantaged adults also tend to bring positive results. A recent summary of existing program evaluations found that, after thirty months, men with training earned 10 percent more than a control group while women enjoyed an earnings advantage of 15 percent.[20] Perhaps the best-known success story is the Job Corps—a program that lasts approximately one year, costs $15,000 per participant, and yields a handsome return if one counts not only increased earnings but reduced crime and public assistance payments.[21]

Overall, the federal job training effort is only moderately encouraging. Some programs are clearly helpful to participants. But modest investments predictably yield modest returns. Only rarely do current programs succeed in changing the lives of individual workers by giving them the skills to move substantially higher in the occupational hierarchy or achieve a significantly higher standard of living. Worse yet, the most successful providers do not necessarily get rewarded with increased funds. Instead, political considerations at the local level often lead to continued funding for programs of little real value. As a result, the public receives considerably less for its investment than a well-run system could provide.

International Comparisons

How do America's labor market programs compare with those achieved by other countries? By all accounts, the United States government appears to devote less money to training workers than almost any other leading industrialized nation. Table 4.1 confirms that the United States government spends much less than other countries (save Japan) on every category of training except programs for the disabled.

The meager amounts that governments in Japan and America spend on labor market programs reflect the decision of policymakers in both countries to look primarily to the private economy for job training. One advantage of this strategy is that on-the-job training appears to be considerably more effective than vocational courses in school or government-sponsored training programs. Nevertheless, the strategy works much better in Japan than it does in the United States. Scattered evidence suggests that Japanese employers spend far more preparing their workers than their American counterparts do. For example, a study of automobile companies carried out by the U.S. Office of Technology Assessment revealed that Japanese firms spend three

Table 4.1. Breakdown of public expenditures on active labor market programs, as a percentage of GDP, 1991–1992.

Country	Total	Public employment services	Training adults	Training youth	Subsidized employment	Measures for disabled
United States	0.25	0.08	0.09	0.03	0.01	0.05
United Kingdom	0.56	0.15	0.17	0.18	0.03	0.03
Japan[a]	0.13	0.02	0.03	—	0.07	0.01
West Germany	1.21	0.22	0.47	0.05	0.24	0.22
France[b]	0.80	0.13	0.33	0.21	0.07	0.06
Canada	0.62	0.22	0.36	0.02	0.02	—
Sweden	2.15	0.21	0.80	0.12	0.16	0.78

Source: OECD, *Employment Outlook,* 92–103 (July 1992).
a. Figures are for 1990–1991.
b. Figures are for 1990.

times as much on training as American companies, and six times as much during the first few months after a new employee comes to work.[22]

The same conclusion seems to hold for other advanced nations as well. Another study by the Office of Technology Assessment found that German companies of all kinds spent twice as much on training their workers as employers in the United States—and a remarkable seventeen times as much training the average apprentice as American firms spent training their typical young worker.[23] Similarly, OECD reports that Sweden trains a substantially greater percentage of its work force each year than the United States, and spends $12,000 per worker enrolled, compared to $1,800 in the United States.[24]

Overall, American companies train approximately 17 percent of their work force, compared to 8 percent in Canada, 26 percent in Sweden, 30 percent in Japan, 32 percent in France, and 75 percent in Germany (including apprentices).[25] Moreover, training in the United States is often diluted by the need to make up for the inadequacies of our public schools. Thus, a study of the nuclear industry revealed that American companies spent half of their training on remedial math and literacy skills, whereas European firms were able to use the available time for advanced study of nuclear engineering and plant administration.[26]

If training can improve productivity, why don't American employers provide more of it? There are two reasons. Since wages for low-skilled employees have been allowed to sink to levels well below those of our principal competitors, American companies do not feel such an acute need to assemble a highly skilled work force. Moreover, firms in the United States hesitate to spend heavily on training because they suspect that many of their employees will soon leave them and that the company's investment will be wasted. In contrast, because most large Japanese firms give lifetime jobs, they expect little turnover and hence have less reason to fear that they will lose the benefit of their training expenditures.

The United States also lags behind several other countries in preparing its youth and providing them with suitable credentials to help them find a job and begin their careers. In Germany, more than 80 percent of all young people either attend college or enter an apprentice program from which they can emerge with a recognized certificate of accomplishment. Much the same is true of Sweden, although most Swedish youth who do not go on to college prepare themselves for jobs by vocational training courses rather than apprenticeship programs.

The situation is quite different in the United States. It is true that close to 60 percent of young people enroll in some form of college, a percentage substantially higher than in Europe. Yet half of these students do not graduate. Apprenticeship programs reach only 2 or 3 percent of the noncollege population, at most, and proprietary schools and vocational courses rarely offer training that ends with any generally accepted certificate of accomplishment.[27] One study in the late 1980s involving young employees who had not graduated from college revealed that only 14.7 percent had been enrolled in a formal off-the-job training program, 4.2 percent had received company training, and 1.8 percent had been in some sort of apprenticeship program.[28] Overall, therefore, despite higher rates of college attendance, roughly half of all American youth start looking for work without any widely recognized degree or training credential. Because of poor high school preparation, many in the remaining half lack not only job training credentials but basic reading, writing, and computational skills as well.

Without a more effective system to ready young people for work, over 30 percent of all high school graduates in the United States and well over one-third of all high school dropouts have not found stable employment by the time they reach thirty years of age.[29] In Germany, on the other hand, fewer than 10 percent of men and women between the ages of twenty-nine and thirty-one report having held their current job for less than a year.[30] Youth unemployment has also been unusually high in America, despite the fact that employers can hire young people at a much lower cost than companies in Europe. As late as 1991, jobless rates for youth fifteen to nineteen years of age were more than twice as high in the United States as in Sweden, Germany, and Japan.[31] Only recently, after Europe fell into severe recession, have youth unemployment rates in countries with strong labor market policies risen to levels close to ours.

America's Policies in Perspective

In theory, at least, the United States has followed a definite strategy for preparing its labor force for productive work. The government is chiefly responsible for giving young people a sound educational foundation for their careers. All children can attend public schools. Some go on to college and universities to prepare for managerial, professional, and more demanding technical jobs; and the others take vocational courses in high schools and community colleges for less intellectually challenging work. Once schooling ends, employers bear the primary burden of providing specific job training, since they know best what skills their businesses require. Finally, the government steps in again to organize and finance remedial training programs for those who fall between the cracks, such as school dropouts, the chronically unemployed, and workers displaced from their jobs.

On the surface, this division of labor seems sensible enough. In practice, almost every element seems to work badly. The sole exception is the system of higher education, which probably does a better job than most universities abroad both in equipping students for management and professional careers and in offering continuing education for older students wishing to acquire new skills. In contrast, vocational education is the least effective form of instruction in our high schools; teachers are out of touch with the world of work, and use outmoded equipment to instruct students who often lack basic intellectual skills. As for job training, most companies underinvest because they fear, in this mobile society, that too many of their employees will leave and join other firms after an expensive course of preparation. The government's remedial programs deliver a meager return on their investment because the courses are often too brief and too poorly conceived and executed, and because participants are frequently too hard to train and deficient not only in their basic education but in their attitudes toward work itself.

In part, these results reflect the distinctive way in which funds for training have been allocated in America. Resources in the United States flow predominantly toward the preparation of the college-educated segment of the population. The government invests a cumulative sum averaging $25,000 in the education and training of young people between the ages of sixteen and twenty-four who complete college. In contrast, only $5,000 is spent to prepare those in the same age group who drop out of high school.[32] Employers likewise channel most of their training funds into programs for college-educated managers and professionals. Even high schools favor the college-bound, since local control over education means that prosperous communities tend to have more to spend on education than poorer neighborhoods where few children plan to go beyond high school.

The money available for those who do not attend college is in much shorter supply and is often used ineffectively. Preventive efforts, such as early child nutrition, preschool programs, and compensatory education in the early grades are chronically underfunded. Vocational education has been notably ineffective, while programs to keep students from dropping out of school have been neglected. For those already in the labor force, in-service training seems to work best, but the government has not yet found an effective way to overcome the persistent tendency on the part of employers to underinvest in preparing their lower-paid workers. Government training programs exist, but they reach only a tiny proportion (approximately 3 percent) of the eligible population. Moreover, since these programs are typically quite brief and are concentrated on the neediest people (who are usually the hardest to train), the benefits tend to be limited at best.

The strategy just described has produced what one analyst describes as "an emerging consensus that U.S. workers' skills are not on a par with those of workers in Europe and Japan."[33] If this verdict is correct, what consequences follow? American employers do not necessarily lose out to Japanese and European competitors, since they can compensate for poorer training by taking advantage of the lower wages paid to unskilled workers in the United States. But America's productivity presumably suffers to the extent that employees with better training could have performed more efficiently. And unskilled workers receive lower wages than they would if they were well prepared and able to be more productive.

How did we work ourselves into this position? Part of the answer has to do with a complex of social problems that produces a large number of poorly educated, poorly motivated young people by the time that training programs even begin. But part of the explanation probably lies in the fact that no important group in the society, at least until recently, has had much interest in having America develop a strong labor market policy. In an economy traditionally marked by low minimum wages and less than full employment, employers have not felt pressed to have a highly skilled work force in order to find employees productive enough to justify the pay they receive. Most economists and policymakers have tended to stress macroeconomic measures to guide the economy, and have regarded job training as a relatively unimportant matter that the economy can take care of by itself. Labor unions interested in job skills have typically created their own apprenticeship programs or bargained for training with employers. Conservative politicians have looked upon training as a task that the private sector should perform, whereas liberal lawmakers have been more interested in remedial efforts to try to rescue unskilled minorities, displaced workers, or high school dropouts after they have experienced difficulty finding a job. The only groups with a vested interest in training—the vocational education teachers and the proprietary schools—have expended most of their efforts trying to maintain the status quo from which they gain their livelihoods.

Only in recent years—after mounting competition from abroad, sluggish growth in productivity, and declining wages for millions of low-skilled workers—have labor market policies become an important topic of conversation in influential circles. Today, one hears much talk about the need to prepare for global competition by upgrading the skills of the labor force. High-level advisory groups deplore the quality of our work force and describe the challenge before us as "America's Choice: High Skills or Low Wages."[34]

If we are to do better in the future, it will not be simply by emphasizing the kind of remedial efforts favored in the past. Even if every government training program could produce results equal to the most successful initiatives yet devised, Washington would have to spend hundreds of billions of dollars simply to bring the earnings of noncollege workers back to the levels of 1979.[35] There is no sign whatsoever that American taxpayers would be willing to make this investment. Moreover, it is far from clear that the government could implement such a massive effort effectively or find a way of significantly improving the skills of chronically unemployed or hard-to-employ Americans. Nor is there much assurance that, if such a program did succeed, employers would upgrade jobs and earnings to take full advantage of the larger supply of trained workers.*

In view of these difficulties, there are many signs around the country of renewed interest in earlier interventions that seek to improve the work of schools and community colleges to prepare students for productive jobs. Many states have mounted ambitious experiments to improve vocational training, hoping to attract businesses and enhance productivity. Some schools are creating apprenticeship programs in close cooperation with employers and local schools and universities. Federal officials are making fresh efforts to combine vocational education with on-the-job training in cooperating companies. One popular innovation is the "Tech-Prep" model, which joins high schools and community colleges in a cooperative effort with local businesses to integrate their programs and link them closely with actual job opportunities.[36] More and more companies are working with community colleges to develop "customized" training programs to fit their special needs.[37]

These initiatives seem promising. Nevertheless, it is still too early to tell whether they will ever come together in a comprehensive system or merely add to the ample list of experiments that already choke the vast untidy garden of American labor market policy. The United States has a long record of producing imaginative projects at the local level to cope with pressing social problems, only to founder in trying to build on these initiatives to form successful national programs.

*In 1994, the Clinton administration announced a new plan to consolidate large numbers of existing programs into a single scheme that will give vouchers to individuals and allow them to choose which training program to enter. While consolidation would be welcome, the administration's approach raises at least two questions. Will the vouchers be good for only short-term training of the type favored in so many existing programs? If so, it is likely that the new initiative will yield very modest results, since experience strongly suggests that long-term training is usually needed to prepare people to increase their earnings significantly. The second question is what kind of help individuals will receive to enable them to make intelligent choices. The record of proprietary schools, featuring heavy dropout rates and indifferent rates of successful job placement, clearly reveals the hazards of simply turning people loose to enter whatever training program they choose. Without guidance and careful monitoring, the voucher approach is very likely to lead to new levels of waste and frustration.

In response to this challenge, the Labor Department is now encouraging schools, community colleges, and employers to collaborate in comprehensive school-to-work programs. Washington has begun to offer grants to states willing to engage in planning efforts of this kind. The prospects for this strategy, however, are uncertain. In a country not accustomed to tight labor markets or high minimum wages, companies have little incentive to work closely with schools in costly programs to develop a more highly skilled work force. With their tradition of independence, keen competition, and weak industry-wide associations, employers are not as well positioned as their European counterparts to help organize and administer comprehensive school-to-work training efforts. Here and there, one can find promising examples of communities that are coming together to connect their schools more closely to the world of work. But there is no clear evidence yet that Washington has found a way to build on these scattered local initiatives to create a viable national system. For the time being, then, we seem fated to continue with a patchwork of public and private training that leaves American workers less prepared than employees in several of our principal competitors.

Meeting the Challenge of Global Competition

The introduction to this volume referred to America's traditional formula for achieving national prosperity—our emphasis on self-reliant individualism stimulated by high rewards for the successful and relatively modest interference from the State. How well has this strategy served the country in trying to achieve continued growth and economic leadership under the conditions of a new global economy.

Fifty years after World War II, America remains the wealthiest industrial nation on earth. For the moment, at least, the United States has managed to retain and largely stabilize its lead in productivity over other major economic powers. Decades after the vast destruction of World War II, countries such as Germany and Japan have still not managed to use their capital investments as effectively as America, although they have been investing significantly more than we in new plant and equipment. Major restructuring in the 1980s helped increase efficiency in many large American corporations, while strong universities continue to give us an advantage in scientific research.

Even more important to productivity has been our long-standing inclination to expose all sectors of the economy to competition, both domestic and international. Japan, for all its accomplishments in many important industries, still protects its markets from the entry of foreign goods and leaves major areas of its economy so insulated from competition that levels of productivity continue to fall far below those of the United States. Sweden, France, and Germany have not only maintained inefficient state-run industries but have sheltered agriculture and other sectors behind tariff barriers and protective regulations. As a result, they, too, are much less efficient than America in many important fields.

At the same time, our traditional formula has not been wholly successful. Growth rates have been so slow that incomes for half of all American families have barely risen during the past twenty years. Moreover, our practice of maximizing incentives by allowing high rewards for the successful has not managed to lift all Americans to levels of prosperity above those of citizens in other economies. Such evidence as we have suggests that people at the low end of the scale are better off in several other industrialized countries than they are in the United States. As many as 25 percent of Americans may have lower incomes than their counterparts in countries such as Germany, Sweden, Belgium, or Switzerland. Poor schools and ineffective job training programs perpetuate this problem, giving little prospect for improving the lot of our least successful citizens.

Even our present advantage in productivity may not last indefinitely. As long as other countries continue to shield so much of their economy from competition, the United States should be able to retain its lead. But current practices are changing. Governments in Europe are beginning to privatize their state-owned industries and reduce tariff barriers with the aid of the General Agreement on Tariffs and Trade (GATT) and the European Economic Community. Japan, too, may eventually stop protecting agriculture and retailing and turn its energies and resources to modernizing these backward areas of its economy.

If and when these reforms occur, levels of productivity throughout the industrialized world will come to depend more and more on the basic ingredients of investment, education, and training. It is here that the United States lags behind in ways that our traditional approach cannot readily overcome. The incentives of the private market have not proved sufficient to achieve high savings rates, rapid diffusion of technology to small and medium firms, or effective job training and labor market policies. Nor can the private economy alone give us a high quality of education for our young people or provide urban neighborhoods conducive to good schooling. In all these domains, government intervention is essential, yet government policies have not yet been able to master the problems they are called upon to solve. For this reason, as a new century beckons, America's position as the most productive economy in the world seems more precarious than the record of the last few years might suggest.

II

QUALITY OF LIFE

5

Living Conditions

Much that makes life worth living transcends the level of prosperity in the nation. Friends, family, and personal relationships of all kinds are the most obvious illustrations. Religious faith and other beliefs that give meaning to our lives provide further examples. More tangible than these are all the aspects of our environment that enrich our experience and help make up our "quality of life." Among these elements are the homes we live in and the neighborhoods and communities in which we reside.

Next to food and health care, housing matters more to most people than anything else they buy. Since the Housing Act of 1949, the official goal of the United States has been to provide "a decent home and a suitable living environment for every American." Most people believe that a "decent home" should be a dwelling owned by its occupant. That is and long has been the preference of more than 80 percent of all adult Americans. As Herbert Hoover put it, "The sentiment for home ownership is so embedded in the American heart that millions of people who dwell in tenements, apartments, and rented rooms . . . have the aspiration for wider opportunity in ownership of their own homes."[1]

What kind of a dwelling do we have in mind "for every American"? Not everyone, of course, can be expected to own a comfortable, detached, single-family home. But whether one's residence be a free-standing house or a rented apartment, it should at least meet certain standards. In the view of government agencies responsible for such matters, a decent home requires indoor plumbing, electricity, proper heating, a watertight roof, and floors and walls without gaping holes. "Decent" also implies a suitable uncrowded environment—no more than one person per room, and no more than two to a bedroom.

If such housing is to be enjoyed by all, it must be within financial reach of the entire population. A decent home, in other words, must be affordable. Like "decency," "affordability" has taken on a more exact meaning through a long series of official deliberations and reports. Today, it means a dwelling that individuals and families can rent or buy without spending more than 30 percent of their gross monthly income.

Finally, it is a goal of national policy to secure not only good housing but "a suitable living environment for every American family." The Housing Act did not describe exactly what "a suitable living environment" might mean. Presumably, however, Congress had in mind a pleasant neighborhood with good schools, safe streets, and reasonable access to jobs, shops, playgrounds, and theaters.

A clear consensus exists, therefore, on what the aims of our housing policies should be. As various federal laws have repeated, everyone should enjoy "a decent home" in "a suitable living environment" at "affordable" prices. Now that approximately half a century has elapsed since Congress first proclaimed these goals, how close have we come to achieving them?

Increasing Homeownership and Housing Quality

Americans have always done well in securing a home of their own.[2] Even in 1890, almost half of all heads of households in the United States owned their own abode. Compared to Europe, America enjoyed a much more favorable environment for home building. Land was abundant and cheap. In addition, the development of the balloon frame house made construction much easier and less expensive; for at least a century, 90 percent of all new homes would be constructed by this method regardless of whether their exterior was built of wood, brick, or stone. As the nineteenth century wore on, trolleys, trains, and other forms of mass transport brought new tracts of land within commuting distance and made more home building possible.

These developments enabled the United States to keep the level of homeownership at approximately 45 percent from 1890 to 1940, even as the population doubled and redoubled and urbanization steadily increased. After World War II, the ownership rate began to rise. From 1940 to 1980, the percentage of families owning a house of their own grew from 44 to 64 percent before leveling off in the 1980s.[3] One reason for this postwar boom was the stimulus given by the government through Federal Housing Administration (FHA) mortgage guarantees and mortgage interest deductions from federal taxes. Even more important was a growing economy that lifted millions of Americans into the middle class.

As home building surged, overcrowding gradually disappeared. In 1940, over 20 percent of all housing units had more than one occupant per room. By 1960 the proportion had fallen to 11.5 percent, and by 1990 it had diminished to less than 3 percent.[4]

The United States has made even greater progress in reducing the fraction of the population living in dilapidated conditions. In 1940, more than half of the nation's homes either had serious plumbing deficiencies or needed major repair. Today the proportion of all housing units that lack plumbing facilities or are dilapidated and in need of major repair has dropped below 5 percent. Table 5.1 records in greater detail the progress made since 1973.

Even the least affluent segments of the population have shared in the improvements. By the late 1980s among the poorest 10 percent of American families, only 1.7 percent still lacked a sewer or septic system, only 2.5 percent did not have a complete bathroom, and only 7

Table 5.1. Incidence of selected deficiencies, as percent of all housing units, 1973–1991.

Deficiency	1973	1983	1991[a]
Leaking roof	7.9	7.4	6.7
Holes in floor	2.0	2.2	1.2
Open cracks in ceiling or walls	6.0	6.2	5.1
Unusable toilets	3.3	2.8	5.0
Heating system breakdowns	8.5	4.9	2.0
Some rooms lacking outlets	5.3	3.0	1.8
Exposed wiring	4.0	2.7	1.6

Source: *American Housing Survey*, selected years.

a. In 1985, the American Housing Survey chose a new national sample, designed a new questionnaire, and developed new weighting procedures. As a result, several items in the 1991 survey are not strictly comparable to data from 1973–1983.

percent had holes in their floor. Less than 12 percent had a leaking roof, while 19.9 percent had open cracks in their walls or ceilings.[5]

While the United States relied heavily on the private market for home building, European governments took a more active part in meeting the housing needs of their citizens. In fact, they could hardly have done otherwise in view of the devastation that existed at the close of World War II.[6] For most of these nations, the first stage in their evolving strategy featured massive subsidies to builders, especially for apartment units. By constructing units themselves (England) or by creating nonprofit organizations to build subsidized dwellings (Germany, France, Sweden), European governments managed to avoid some of the problems that America encountered in trying to create inducements for private developers to construct low-income housing. Like the United States, however, France, Germany, Sweden, and other European countries went through a phase of building huge complexes for poor and moderate-income families, only to find that the buildings were ugly, lacking in social amenities, poorly served by transportation, and dispiriting to live in.

As economies revived and standards of living rose, officials in Europe began to move toward encouraging single-family homes, rather than apartments, in response to the changing tastes of a more affluent population. When hastily built postwar apartment houses started to deteriorate, rehabilitation assumed greater importance. Eventually, the cost of helping to finance construction and rehabilitation for a large fraction of the population forced officials to seek ways to restrict public subsidies.[7] Once housing shortages eased, therefore, more and more governments changed from subsidizing construction to giving rent supplements to needy families.[8]

By the 1990s, most other leading democracies had progressed to such an extent that the United States no longer had a significantly higher level of homeownership. In 1970, 63 percent of American household heads owned their own home, a proportion far larger than that in any country of Western Europe. By the late 1980s, our rate had barely increased to 64 percent, but Canada, Sweden, Britain, and Japan had all reached approximately the same level.[9]

Europe also made rapid progress in improving the quality of its housing stock. Table 5.2 compares America's record with that of four other nations.

In sum, other industrialized countries have largely closed the gap

Table 5.2. Comparison of housing amenities, 1989–1991.

Country	Percent of units with water piped inside	Percent of units with fixed bath or shower	Percent of units with central heating	Average number of persons per room
Canada	96.0	94.0	94.6	0.45
France	99.7	92.4	94.9	0.67
United Kingdom	100.0	99.5	80.0	0.50
Denmark	97.5	90.0	95.7	—
United States	99.7	97.6	88.1	0.68

Source: United Nations, Economic Commission for Europe, *Annual Bulletin of Housing and Building Statistics for Europe*, 92, 101 (1991, 1992, and 1993).

in homeownership and basic amenities that seemed so large in the early decades after World War II. The same appears to be true of crowding. What still distinguishes the United States is the amount of space available for housing. Not only is the average size of rooms in America considerably greater; the lots on which most suburban homes stand are much bigger, with front lawns and backyards more spacious than those commonly found in Europe.

Making Housing Affordable

Because of cheap land and efficient design, Americans have long been accustomed to inexpensive housing. After World War II, as the economy grew briskly, new homes became increasingly affordable for young families. Spurred by William Levitt and other pioneers in large-scale, low-cost construction, developers began opening huge tracts in suburban locations, and homeownership rates rose rapidly.

By the end of the 1960s, however, the pace of economic growth was beginning to slacken, and the earnings of working people were stagnating or actually declining. After 1972, therefore, the cost of buying a home increased more rapidly than the average income of first-time home buyers. By 1982, typical first-time buyers had to pay 44 percent of their average income to purchase a house, rather than the 22 percent which they were paying only a decade before. Accordingly, from 1973 to 1982 the rates of homeownership for family heads under twenty-five declined, after decades of steady growth.

During the 1980s, rates of homeownership continued to fall, not only for young families under twenty-five but for all household heads under forty. The reasons for the decline are not entirely clear, since the burden of acquiring a new home (that is, the monthly costs relative to average income) stopped rising after 1982 and began to drop steadily. Part of the explanation may have to do with falling earnings for low-skilled workers without a college education. For them, the burdens of buying a home must have continued to seem prohibitive during the 1980s. Part of the trend may also be explained by the fact that more young people are staying single longer and hence do not want to buy a house. Whatever the reason, two million fewer American families with heads under the age of 45 own homes today than would be the case if the ownership rates of 1980 still prevailed.

A more formidable challenge is to keep rental housing affordable for poor families. The federal government has taken several steps to address this problem. An early method was to pay for the construction of low-income apartments that could be rented to needy families at a cost they could afford. When this strategy was proposed in the Housing Act of 1949, it encountered determined opposition from conservative lawmakers who resisted such a direct intrusion by the federal government into the housing market. In the compromise that followed, a public housing effort was approved, but it received far less money than was needed to achieve its ambitious goals, and local governments were given an effective veto power over the siting of projects. As administrators tried to stretch the available funds, the quality of construction often suffered and there was too little money to maintain the buildings properly. In addition, because the supply of public housing was so limited and the rents were so low, entry was restricted more and more to the poorest families. The all-but-inevitable result was run-down buildings, crime, drugs, and widespread unemployment in many projects. Before long, public housing had acquired a bad name, leading to charges by critics that the government was incapable of administering such a program effectively.

As public housing fell into disrepute, the government turned increasingly to granting subsidies, tax breaks, and other incentives to induce private developers to build new units that poor and moderate-income families could afford. Most of the time, however, opponents in Congress kept the subsidies low enough that the desired amount of new housing was not built. Only in the late 1960s did a Democratic

Congress enact new laws with high enough subsidies and sufficient appropriations to finance much larger numbers of new units. Developers responded with massive amounts of new construction. In the pressure to increase production, however, government monitoring proved to be haphazard. Some developers engaged in graft to get accepted into the lucrative new programs. Others took advantage of government guarantees by selling homes for inflated amounts to families that couldn't afford them, so that the government had to step in and pay the price when purchasers defaulted. As news of such scandals spread, opponents claimed that federal agencies were incapable of managing programs of this kind.

A third approach to affordable housing was simply to give subsidies directly to owners and renters. This technique had been used successfully in the 1930s through the use of FHA guaranteed mortgages with tax deductions for mortgage interest payments. In the 1970s, in order to help the poor cope with escalating rents, conservatives who opposed more grandiose federal programs advocated housing vouchers, provided that the program was kept small and restricted to the neediest families. Once introduced, such programs succeeded in enabling poor families to rent apartments of reasonable quality using the vouchers to keep the rents affordable. But the funds that Congress appropriated for this purpose were so limited that only a minority of those officially classified as poor were able to participate.

Over the years, therefore, the mix of federal housing programs has shifted back and forth on several occasions: liberals have favored large-scale efforts to build new units for moderate-income and low-income families, whereas conservatives have tried to hold down new construction as much as possible and to confine federal subsidies to the neediest families. Until 1970, subsidized housing was limited to less than 10 percent of all new housing starts. In the 1970s, subsidized units rose in number to make up 20 to 40 percent of all new starts. By 1983, at President Reagan's urging, the share of assisted units again fell back below the 10 percent level.

As earnings have declined for workers with only a high school education, the burdens of paying rent have grown greater for renters toward the bottom of the income scale (Table 5.3).

Whereas in Europe housing allowances typically go to all families of low and moderate income, the experience in America is entirely different. Although the number of poor people assisted by the federal

Table 5.3. The burden of paying rent, 1960–1987.

| Year | Percent of low-income renters paying more than: | |
	25% of reported income	35% of reported income
1960[a]	84.6	68.2
1970[a]	91.1	77.5
1980[b]	86.9	75.1
1987[b]	92.5	77.4

Source: American Housing Survey; HUD, *National Housing Production Report*, Table 7, 49 (February 1980).

a. Figures are for lowest income quartile.

b. Figures are based on lowest 31–32 percent of renters, in terms of income.

government through public housing, subsidized housing, and rent supplements has steadily risen from 100,000 in 1940 to 4.6 million in 1990, the percentage of eligible families who receive such aid had barely reached 30 percent by the early 1990s (up from 18 percent in 1974). The problem is not simply one of cost. The United States in 1992 provided almost $90 billion in housing subsidies. But $70 billion of this sum took the form of a mortgage interest deduction for homeowners. Because this tax advantage increases with the cost of a home, more than half of the total subsidy goes to families with incomes in the highest 20 percent. If these benefits were directed instead to poor renters, there would be more than enough to pay for housing vouchers for all families below the poverty line.

Many poor families who do not have direct subsidies are on welfare and obtain allowances to cover housing. Nevertheless, these allowances vary widely among the states and are typically set well below the prevailing rents for modest apartments.[10] For those families *not* receiving a housing voucher or living in a housing project, the percentage having to pay more than *half* of their reported income in rent rose from 57 percent in 1974 to 70 percent in 1985 and then to 77.2 percent in 1989.[11]

Poor renters could hardly pay such large fractions of their income in rent and still have enough left over to buy their food and other necessities. How do they manage? The answer is that reported incomes are not a very reliable way of measuring the actual circumstances of families in poverty. For example, government figures suggest that in the period 1988–1990 families with children in the bottom income quintile actually spent 73 percent more than their official income.[12] Some of their added resources consist of food stamps; some may come from friends, savings, and charitable donations. Many of the officially poor undoubtedly earn money they do not report. Taking these resources into account, the best available estimate suggests that the 20 percent of American households reporting the lowest expenditures devote approximately 25–30 percent of their income to paying their rent.[13]

If that were all there were to say, one might conclude that the plight of the poor renter is not particularly serious. Nevertheless, the figures just presented undoubtedly conceal great variations. A fortunate minority of poor tenants have housing vouchers or live in public projects with restricted rents, so that their housing costs make up only a small fraction of their total expenditures. But the majority of poor families must normally pay much higher rents, and presumably there are many in this group who do not have extensive outside incomes. For them, the goal of affordable housing is still unfulfilled, and the cost of keeping a roof over their heads must be a heavy drain on their resources.

The most seriously afflicted category, of course, is made up of those who are actually homeless, living in shelters or sleeping on sidewalks, on park benches, or in railway stations.[14] No one knows precisely how many people are homeless on an average night. Estimates vary from a few hundred thousand to several million, with the lower figure probably being closer to the truth on any given night but with a considerably higher figure reflecting the total number of persons who slip in and out of homelessness during the course of a year.

Perhaps one-third of the homeless are mentally disturbed individuals who would have been institutionalized twenty-five years ago; others have severe drug and alcohol problems that place them beyond the reach of any regular housing program. But a considerable fraction are people—including increasing numbers of women and children—who cannot find a place to stay at a price they can afford. For the poorest renters, declining incomes after 1973 and the destruction of many low-income one-room rental units made it increasingly difficult to find a place to live. Ironically, among the reasons for their predicament were building codes established according to middle-class notions of proper housing, which pushed the price of apartments so high that poor people could not afford them. Arguments continue over the extent to which such individuals are homeless because of their own lack of initiative or because of a combination of low welfare payments, high housing costs, and an eroding minimum wage. Whatever the reason, their predicament offers a poignant reminder that adequate housing is not yet affordable for all Americans.

The Quest for Pleasant Neighborhoods

In building a vast network of neighborhoods across the nation, Americans followed a distinctive path. Throughout most industrializing countries, well-to-do residents claimed much of the residential space in central cities for themselves, leaving poorer families to find cheaper housing in less desirable areas further away from the downtown area. Increasingly throughout this century, the pattern in the United States has been exactly the reverse.[15] With every improvement in transportation, wealthier residents pushed outward in search of privacy and space, while still commuting daily to their work in the law firms, hospitals, banks, and companies that remained in the heart of the city. Meanwhile, poorer families rented apartments in high-density neighborhoods, many of them close to the downtown business district.

Early in the century, only affluent families could build a residence in the suburbs. After World War II, rising prosperity brought home-ownership well within reach of the middle class. To families, the suburbs brought many benefits—space, a backyard for the children, cleaner air, safer streets, better schools. For those who came of age in the 1950s and 1960s, the lush green lawn, the picket fence, the tree-lined streets of suburbia symbolized the good life in America, the embodiment of the American Dream.[16] In 1950, only 41 million families lived in the suburbs. By 1970 the figure had jumped to 74 million, and surged to 115 million by 1990.

There were disadvantages, of course. To city planners, the steady growth of new tracts for development meant urban sprawl and the loss of beautiful countryside. Housing densities were insufficient in most suburbs to make mass transit feasible. As a result, suburban living led to long commutes and frequent traffic jams. By 1990 the typical suburbanite averaged 20 minutes getting to work each day, and over 30 percent spent more than half an hour.[17] Owning two cars became a necessity for many families, since shops, theaters, restaurants, and schools were rarely within walking distance. Elderly couples led limited lives if they could not drive, while children had to be constantly transported to schools, to friends, to music lessons, and to the movies.

Commentators often criticized the suburbs as isolating, lonely places lacking the close community feelings that enthusiasts recalled in traditional urban ethnic neighborhoods. As Lewis Mumford put it in the 1950s, the new suburban developments consisted of "a multitude of uniform, unidentifiable houses, lined up inflexibly at uniform distances, on uniform roads, in treeless communal waste, inhabited by people in the same class, the same income, the same age group, witnessing the same TV performances, eating the same prefabricated foods from the same freezers . . ."[18]

Distasteful as suburbs may seem to some people, however, there is a danger in looking at these communities only through the lens of sociologists and city planners. Our sprawling metropolitan areas may appear to be impersonal and uneconomical, but that is the way many Americans want to live. In a 1991 NBC-Newsweek survey, only 13 percent of the respondents preferred to live in the city. At least 25 percent of the public indicated they wished to reside in a suburb, 24 percent opted for life on a farm, and 37 percent replied that they would like to be in a small town.[19] The fastest-growing counties today are "exurban" areas beyond the suburbs, and the principal reason people give for moving there is that they want bigger lots and larger houses. Apparently, then, Americans would prefer even *more* sprawl and *less* density than they have at present.

In any event, the most serious neighborhood problems in the United States exist not in the suburbs but in the central cities.[20] As urban residents moved outward in the 1950s and in subsequent decades, successive waves of immigrants, blacks from the South, and other poor rural families took over vacated homes and apartments or moved into public housing projects built with government funds. Of course, there were exceptions to this pattern. Some suburbs in the less desirable "inner ring" became home to relatively poor families. Conversely, young white professionals often carved out fashionable urban enclaves where they could live close to the office buildings, banks, and hospitals in which they worked. Still, the dominant trends were clear. City residents had once been wealthier, on average, than the rest of the metropolitan area population. Increasingly, the reverse came to be true. Cities had once been populated almost entirely by whites. Now, the populations of the largest cities were more and more composed of minorities and immigrants. By 1990, in New York, 57 percent of the inhabitants were minority; in Chicago, 62 percent; in Los Angeles, 63 percent; in Detroit, 70 percent; in Miami, 88 percent. As the numbers of immigrants reached record postwar levels, more than half were settling in just ten major cities.[21]

During the 1970s and 1980s, employment in the suburbs increased rapidly. Vast shopping malls attracted large retail chains, and more and more companies shifted their offices and manufacturing operations to outlying areas. "Edge cities" began to spring up; these were no longer "bedroom communities" for the old metropolitan center but self-contained towns with their own light industry, restaurants, theaters, and other amenities. Meanwhile, the prospects for many central-city residents worsened as more and more factories began to move from urban locations, causing hundreds of thousands of manufacturing jobs to be lost either to the suburbs or to automation or overseas locations. From 1967 to 1987, Detroit lost 51 percent of its manufacturing jobs; New York City, 58 percent; Chicago, 60 percent; and Philadelphia, 64 percent. New urban jobs were also created, especially in the service sector, but many of them did not pay as much as factory positions, nor did they always involve the type of work that blue-collar workers were trained to perform.

Thus, as the century nears its end, the typical metropolitan area in the United States has come to consist of a central city encircled by a necklace of suburbs, most of them middle class, some distinctly prosperous, and some predominantly poor. The city, in turn, is composed of a cluster of new office towers and public buildings, often surrounded by neighborhoods filled with the least advantaged members of the society—minorities, immigrants, and the unemployed.

The Role of Public Policy

The massive movement to the suburbs began as a search for bigger homes, larger yards, and a cleaner environment. Later on, fear of crime and a desire to escape inferior schools played a more important part. But the exodus from the cities did not come about simply by the choices of individual citizens. For half a century, government policy has helped bring our current living patterns into being.

Official efforts to encourage suburban living picked up momentum after World War II.[22] Federal highway programs and low gasoline taxes made it easier to live in the suburbs and commute every day to city jobs. Sewage plants, telecommunication costs, and other needed infrastructure were subsidized by general tax revenues.

National policies also worked in several ways to ease the cost of buying a home in the suburbs. The Federal Housing Administration was much more inclined to approve government guaranteed mortgages for homes in the suburbs than it was to give mortgages for multifamily dwellings of the kind commonly found within cities. The FHA was also unwilling to extend its help to homeowners in "unstable neighborhoods," which often meant inner-city areas heavily populated by poor people and minorities. Federal tax laws seemed to be skewed in favor of homeownership, since they allowed buyers to deduct mortgage interest while offering no deduction for rental payments.[23]

While federal programs helped families move to the suburbs, city governments made it harder to create more attractive urban neighborhoods that could retain people and provide nearby employment. High wages granted to municipal employees put heavy pressure on city budgets and inflated the costs of city services. Local bureaucracies were frequently bloated and inefficient, adding further to municipal costs and impairing the quality of schools and other services. Outmoded zoning rules and building code restrictions hindered redevelopment and kept potentially valuable property vacant, while inadequate transportation systems and decaying infrastructure impeded the growth of new businesses.

Federal policies created further burdens.[24] Requirements established by the Department of Housing and Urban Development (HUD) made it needlessly complicated to find willing lenders under its urban building programs. Lead-paint laws pushed up the cost of renovation. Environmental requirements inflated costs and created risks of prohibitively costly cleanup operations that kept firms from developing urban vacant land. Together, these policies and practices helped keep normal market forces from working to renew inner-city areas and create jobs to replace the factories that had abandoned urban sites for new locations in the suburbs or overseas.

Another way in which public policy contributed to the distinctive pattern of American metropolitan growth was the practice of home rule. To a much greater extent than in Europe, states in this country have delegated power to individual cities and towns to operate their own schools, provide their own municipal services, and raise their own

revenues, chiefly from property taxes. Such decentralization has allowed separate municipalities to be more responsive to the needs of
their residents. But it has also aggravated the problems of central cities,
especially in the East and Midwest, by leaving them to meet the needs
of a burgeoning poor population without being able to tax the more
prosperous residents of the metropolitan area who work downtown
but live predominantly in the suburbs.

Not only has local self-government shielded wealthier suburbs
from having to pay for the social problems of the poorer central cities;
it has also allowed suburbs to impose zoning restrictions, bans on
multifamily dwellings and mobile homes, and stringent building codes
that kept their property beyond the financial reach of poor families.
Local authorities have had obvious reasons to make full use of these
powers. Poor people burden a town by adding to local social service
costs while contributing little in new taxes. They also threaten the
property values of existing residents. Hence, "snob zoning" and restrictive building codes have proliferated. For added protection, Congress has made sure that local authorities could veto public housing
developments. The result of these policies has been to keep poor people
in the urban centers at the very time when these cities have been losing
jobs and sources of industrial revenue. Increasingly, then, urban neighborhoods have deteriorated as large municipalities find themselves fis-
cally squeezed by rising social service needs and an eroding tax base.[25]

Federal Programs for the Cities

Recognizing this problem, the federal government has launched a series
of programs over the past forty years to try to ameliorate the plight of
inner-city neighborhoods.[26] An early federal effort was the urban renewal program, which subsidized the clearing of blighted areas to induce private developers to build anew in the central city. Although the
program did help cities rebuild their downtown business districts, for
years it displaced poor families without making adequate provision for
relocating them.

Urban renewal eventually gave way to the War on Poverty and its
Community Action Program, which sought to empower local residents
in poor neighborhoods to plan improvements and enlist the support
of local officials. Before long, however, the new community groups
began criticizing City Hall, demanding immediate aid and provoking

strong complaints to Congress from big-city mayors.[27] Scantily funded and subject to increasing attacks, the program soon stalled and eventually died, to be replaced a few years later by a program of federal block grants that sought again to attract private money to rebuild downtown areas. Although the grants did succeed in leveraging large amounts of private funding, most of the projects were commercial in nature and did little to improve the quality of residential areas.[28]

As repeated attempts to revitalize urban neighborhoods came to naught, Congress began authorizing more and more money to help defray the mounting costs of assisting the swelling ranks of urban poor. Through Title I of the National Defense Education Act, Congress gave billions of dollars to supplement the education of disadvantaged children. More and more federal money was devoted to paying a share of burgeoning welfare costs. Medicaid provided funds to help with health care expenses. Housing vouchers enabled a fortunate minority of poor families to pay their rent without unduly straining their resources. A massive job creation program sprang up to offer employment to the poor. At the peak of national spending in 1978, more than 18 percent of city budgets came from federal support of one kind or another. By 1981, central cities were receiving 63 percent more federal aid for each inhabitant than suburban communities, even though per capita assistance had been approximately equal only a quarter of a century before.

Much of the federal assistance was sufficiently fragmented that its effectiveness was limited. While HUD delivered funds for housing assistance and other forms of community development, the Department of Education aided the schools, the Small Business Administration gave grants to inner-city companies, the Department of Health and Human Services administered welfare and other social programs, and the Department of Justice worked with local police. Not only did these federal agencies fail to coordinate programs among themselves; they often had difficulty working harmoniously with municipal officials and organizations, which usually had political agendas of their own. The problems of the inner city were highly interrelated and needed a tightly integrated comprehensive approach. Instead, they received a welter of assistance programs that were hard to comprehend, cumbersome to deal with, and sometimes at cross-purposes with one another.

In the wake of these difficulties, HUD issued a report in 1980 which concluded that the outlook for housing and jobs in the inner city had actually deteriorated in the preceding decade, notwithstanding all the federal assistance.[29] Such findings lent credence to President Reagan's claim that the federal government was not well suited to dealing with urban problems and that responsibility should shift to states and municipalities. To accomplish this purpose, Reagan persuaded Congress to reduce federal funding while giving local officials greater discretion over the use of block grant funds. This initiative was only one of a series of efforts by the president to slash federal funding for the cities. Despite Democratic control of the House of Representatives, Reagan was remarkably successful. By 1990, the share of city revenues accounted for by federal outlays had shrunk from 15 percent to barely 6 percent. State governments did not fully make up the shortfall, and local governments had to learn to live on leaner rations.[30]

Faced with adversity, a number of neighborhoods displayed great resourcefulness in trying to improve their condition. In particular, community development corporations (CDCs), partly funded by churches and foundations, managed to develop several hundred thousand units of new and rehabilitated housing during the 1980s. But CDCs were too small and too scantily funded to make a major dent in the vast array of problems that had accumulated in poor urban neighborhoods.[31] The burden of crime, drugs, chronic unemployment, and poverty continued to grow during the Reagan administration.

Eventually the Bush administration announced a new plan—the enterprise zone—to address the urban crisis. This concept, borrowed from the British (who in turn were inspired by the success of Hong Kong), amounted to another attempt to adjust economic incentives to attract private enterprise into blighted communities. This time, the lure to mobilize the private sector was an offer of tax advantages to companies willing to locate in designated depressed areas. Never enacted during Bush's tenure, the idea was resurrected in adapted form by President Clinton as the centerpiece of his urban policy.[32] The fate of this experiment is still unclear. Based on experience in states that have experimented with enterprise zones, however, there is reason to doubt whether tax incentives of the kind envisaged by such plans will succeed in attracting many businesses to deteriorating inner-city locations.

Perhaps the most hopeful signs in this bleak picture are the local initiatives that have sprung up in cities across the nation to try to revitalize blighted urban neighborhoods.[33] These efforts are characterized by a resolve to recognize the links among all the community's problems by addressing them together rather than piecemeal. The new programs emphasize grassroots organizing in order to keep control in the hands of residents rather than giving it to outside professionals and activists. In contrast to what took place under the poverty program, leaders seem eager to approach government officials and local businesses not as adversaries but as necessary allies. Several of these community ventures have made promising beginnings.[34] It is still too soon to tell however, whether they represent a model of self-help that can transform urban neighborhoods or only the latest in a long, disappointing series of failed experiments.

Experience Abroad

The desire to flee the urban core for a home with a garden is no longer unique to the United States. In the last twenty to thirty years, most large central cities in Europe and Canada have also experienced a loss of population resulting from a movement to the suburbs on the part of middle-class and prosperous families. More recently, the exodus has slowed, and there has even been a modest counterflow of families back from the suburbs into the central cities. Just as in the United States, however, the "gentrification" movement has been small, and urban renewal efforts aimed at attracting middle-income families have had only limited success.[35]

Yet there are noticeable differences between the experience in the United States and trends in Canada and Europe.[36] American cities have developed a much more pronounced municipal sprawl, with population densities in the urban core and in the suburbs that are typically only half as great as those in other advanced countries.[37] The reasons are many. For one thing, the principal urban problems driving people out of central cities in the United States—poor schools and crime— are not nearly so severe in Europe and Canada. For another, governments abroad generally own or control much of the land surrounding the cities and are more inclined to insist on ample green zones, while concentrating suburbs in more restricted areas clustered near public transport. Governments abroad also do much less to subsidize suburban living, gasoline is heavily taxed in Europe, and several countries, such as Canada, do not provide tax deductions for mortgage interest payments.

Another major difference between the United States and other advanced nations is that residential areas abroad are not so divided by income and by race. In the words of Loic Wacquant, one of the most perceptive writers on urban poverty in Europe and America,

> The American inner city is not simply much poorer and much meaner than the French *banlieu:* It is a different urban form altogether, specific to the United States, in which race functions as the primary template of social and spatial division. Thus, while it may be proper to speak of "pockets of immigrant poverty" or "ethnic concentrations" in France (and in other European countries such as the Netherlands or even England), it is misleading—or to say the least very premature—to announce the formation of ghettos there in the sense that this term takes by reference to the situation of blacks in the American city.[38]

Although chronic unemployment and rising levels of immigration have awakened fears of an emerging underclass, European governments work in various ways to avoid excessive segregation.[39] Public officials have more room to maneuver, because they can control much larger fractions of the housing stock and can influence the living arrangements of many more renters, so as to avoid projects with heavy concentrations of poor and minority families. In addition, local communities in Europe have much less power than American towns either to use zoning restrictions to exclude the poor or to refuse to have public housing within their boundaries.

The limited authority given to municipal governments in Europe and Canada also helps avoid the inequalities found in the United States.[40] Although some countries, notably France, have decentralized power and given more responsibility to local officials, even they do not allow the amount of local autonomy commonly found in America. As a result, there are no large differences in school funding or the fiscal health of towns and cities such as those that exist in many American states. Planning commonly takes place on a regional basis, and most countries require that regional plans be approved by the national government.[41] Competition to attract new companies has begun, but its effects are much more controlled. Either municipalities are prohibited from granting concessions to attract firms, or the types and amounts of concessions are strictly limited, or the national government weakens the incentive to compete by automatically adjusting allocations to cities to offset differences in tax revenues.[42]

In sum, most of the other nations discussed here have succeeded through government policy in mitigating the worst residential problem of the United Sates—the segregation of the poor, with the attendant growth in crime, dropout rates, and other ghetto afflictions. To be sure, most cities abroad do not lack problems of their own. For example, Japanese officials have not been particularly successful in limiting urban sprawl. The huge size of Tokyo and the crowded conditions along the Tokaido Corridor have clogged the highways, seriously inflated land values, and confined Japanese families to dwellings of a size most Americans would find intolerable. Traffic congestion in many old European cities that were not made for automobiles is likewise a serious problem.

It is also worth noting that governments in Europe have managed to avoid the worst of our urban ills only by interfering more directly with the choices individuals make about their living arrangements. Compared with American cities, European governments own much more municipal land, place clearer, tighter boundaries around cities to limit urban growth, and exercise closer supervision over the design of buildings. In return for greater regimentation, citizens abroad have received a more efficient transport system, shorter commutes, and relief from the worst pathologies of the American urban ghetto.[43] Whether the bargain is a good one must be more a matter of opinion than a subject for empirical demonstration.

In the long evolution of housing policy in the United States, the chief problem has been that certain segments of the population have not shared fully in the benefits of residential life. Although the quality of American housing may be unsurpassed, even for the least affluent families, many poor and near-poor families in the United States have to pay a greater share of their incomes for rent than federal officials consider appropriate. Moreover, many inner-city neighborhoods are highly segregated by income and race, far removed from areas of growing employment and plagued by all manner of social pathologies. As a group of European experts reported after a tour of American cities, the conditions they found were "to be expected in a poverty-stricken Third World country, not in one of the earth's richest nations."[44]

Liberals and conservatives are deeply divided over the reasons for these conditions. Liberals emphasize persistent racial discrimination in housing and employment, the siting of public housing projects, the disappearance of urban manufacturing, and the erosion of the municipal tax base. They point to the highway subsidies and tax preferences that have helped the well-to-do flee the cities, and to the zoning laws that have helped them keep less affluent families at bay. Conservatives put the blame on a declining work ethic and eroding moral standards among the poor.[45] They particularly criticize welfare policies that encourage illegitimacy and idleness, along with ineffective city bureaucracies and law enforcement practices that frighten away businesses, waste money, and tolerate crime.

These sharply differing opinions have given rise to periodic changes in policy, as liberal and conservative fortunes have alternately waxed and waned. Ambitious Democrat-sponsored programs to construct more public housing and rebuild the inner cities have given way to Republican efforts to delegate authority to state and local governments, reduce government spending, and rely on housing vouchers, enterprise zones, and other market-oriented policies. Despite these differences, neither side ever manages to win a clear-cut victory and implement its program fully. Democrats announce large programs of public housing, but actual appropriations permit construction of only a fraction of the projected units and leave too little money to maintain the buildings adequately. Republicans slash housing appropriations drastically, but discover that funds already in the pipeline keep the number of new units from decreasing. In the end, sharply different policy positions result too often in awkward compromises that do not do justice to either of the contesting urban philosophies.

Whichever side one takes in the debate among liberals and conservatives, the practical results are clear. Residential segregation by race and income is higher in the United States than in any of the other countries surveyed here. Differences in living standards between the inner cities and the suburbs are also greater. Although the causes of these conditions are in dispute, both sides would probably agree that government practices and policies have failed to solve the problem, and in a variety of ways have actually made it worse.

Whatever the reasons, the racial and income segregation that pervades our metropolitan areas hides the full extent of our urban problems from those with the most influence to resolve them. It limits the social interactions that help unify a healthy democratic society. Meanwhile, the violence, the troubled schools, the inadequate health care, and the peer pressures of neighborhoods without strong role models eat away at the life chances of ghetto children and rob them even of the freedom to come and go as they choose.

In fairness, it should be pointed out that the size of the urban underclass in America is often exaggerated. According to most careful estimates, fewer than 10 million poor people live in central cities, and the number living in neighborhoods with concentrations of poverty of 40 percent or more is probably less than 3 million. Still, the growing segregation of the poor in blighted urban neighborhoods creates an awkward reality for a nation that has prided itself on having a classless society. So long as such conditions persist in our inner cities, the quality of life in America will be seriously flawed, and the United States will continue to fall short of its announced desire to create "a suitable living environment for every American family."

6

The Environment

Federal efforts to control pollution go back at least to the laws of the last century that limited smoke from locomotives and furnaces and stopped people from throwing refuse into public waterways. But concern over the environment did not become truly widespread and intense until the 1960s. Rachel Carson struck a major blow in 1962 with the publication of her book *Silent Spring.*[1] Within a few years, a series of dramatic events helped focus even more public attention on the problem. The lower Cuyahoga River in Ohio exploded into flame when industrial wastes caught fire; scientists reported that Lake Erie was "dead" from pollution; and newspapers carried pictures of West Coast beaches coated with oil from tanker spills. Against this backdrop, environmental issues quickly assumed unprecedented urgency.

As in many other industrial countries, popular concern sprang up so quickly and with such force that lawmakers scrambled to respond. The result was a flurry of legislation aimed at curbing activities that polluted the air and water and endangered plant and animal life. At the national level, no less than seventeen separate pieces of environmental legislation were passed between 1969 and 1976, even though control over the executive and legislative branches was divided throughout between Republicans and Democrats. To carry out its programs, Congress created a separate institution, the Environmental Protection Agency (EPA), and began appropriating billions of dollars each year to create a cleaner, safer environment.

The aim of environmental policy is to reduce pollution and waste to a point at which they do not impair the enjoyment of nature or pose a significant threat to the lives and health of human beings and other living species. Many Americans speak of such goals in uncompromising terms. For example, in 1988 two-thirds of the public agreed that improvements in the environment should be made "regardless of cost."[2] In enacting environmental laws, Congress itself has repeatedly ruled out efforts to weigh the expense of fighting pollutants against the gains to be achieved, fearing even to suggest putting a price on preserving nature, let alone human lives.

It is clear, however, that environmental protection, like all public undertakings, has its limits and that lowering pollution beyond a certain level causes expenditures out of proportion to any likely benefits achieved. Whatever individuals may say to a pollster, they would balk at the prospect of paying large tax increases for tiny increments of added purity in the air or water. After the Clean Air Act of 1970 set strict standards for reducing pollutants, citizens rebelled as soon as several cities proposed gas rationing, highway tolls, and other stern measures to comply with the goals. More recently, voters in California, New York, and other states have turned down proposals that would impose higher taxes to improve the environment. Any sensible policy, therefore, must take account of costs while also respecting the public's strong desire to reduce pollution to a point that will minimize threats to health, the enjoyment of nature, and the survival of other species. Finally, regardless of the position one takes on the proper cost of environmental programs, almost everyone would agree that such programs should be carried out as efficiently as possible to produce the greatest achievable environmental gains with the resources available.

In little more than twenty years, the United States has come to spend an enormous amount of money on protecting the environment. In 1993, the country devoted approximately $115 billion to this purpose. Roughly 20 percent was spent by government and 80 percent by private institutions complying with government regulations. Together, these sources have paid more than one trillion dollars to clean up the environment during the past quarter-century. With such large amounts at stake, it is fair to ask what the nation has received for its money, and whether all the funds have been wisely spent.

The Impact of Environmental Policies

In the case of air pollution, there are six principal pollutants that the government has tried to curb: carbon monoxide, sulfur dioxide, nitro-

Table 6.1. Changes in air pollution in the United States, in percent, 1970–1993.

Pollutant	Change in emissions
Sulfur dioxide	− 30
Nitrogen oxides	+ 14
Suspended particulates	− 78
Volatile organic compounds	− 24
Carbon monoxide	− 24
Lead	− 98

Source: U.S. Environmental Protection Agency, *National Air Quality and Emissions Trends Report*, 26 (1994).

gen oxides, suspended particulates, volatile organic compounds, and lead.* From 1970 to 1993, progress occurred in curbing emissions of almost all these substances (Table 6.1).

Despite these advances, the battle is far from over. In 1992, 54 million people were still living in areas of the country that had failed to meet at least one of the EPA's National Ambient Air Quality Standards.[3] Imposing as this figure seems, however, it is approximately half the number of people who had been living in substandard areas only a decade earlier.

It is much more difficult to find reliable data measuring progress in improving water quality. According to the Senate report accompanying the passage of the Clean Water Act of 1972, "much of the information on which the present water quality program is based is inadequate and incomplete."[4] Twenty years later, after the government had spent many billions of dollars trying to clean up rivers and lakes, data on water quality were still in short supply. As a result, neither Congress nor anyone else could be sure how much had been accomplished for the vast sums already spent. Nor could they determine what future measures would produce the greatest benefits for the least cost. Only recently have monitoring programs been put in place to gather the information needed to answer these questions.

The limited data available suggest that some gains have been made.

---

*I do not take up two pollutants with predominantly global environmental implications, carbon dioxide and chlorofluorocarbons, since international programs to reduce these substances have only recent begun. For reasons of space, I will also pass over such topics as biodiversity and preserving wetlands.

The percentage of the United States population served by waste-water treatment plants rose from 42 percent in 1970 to 74 percent in the early 1990s.[5] Thanks to improved sewage disposal and water treatment, the total volume of suspended solids has declined by 80 percent since 1975.[6] The Fish and Wildlife Service reports that levels of arsenic, cadmium, and lead in fish decreased by 50–63 percent between 1976 and 1986 and that toxic chemicals such as DDT-related compounds and PCBs likewise diminished by more than 60 percent between 1970 and 1986.[7]

By the early 1990s, approximately 60 percent of all assessed rivers were reportedly meeting their water quality standards and supporting their declared uses, such as fishing and swimming; 25 percent were partially meeting their designated uses; and the remaining 15 percent failed to support their designated uses.[8] (Unfortunately, less than half of all river miles had been assessed, and no one knows to what degree the assessed rivers are representative of those waterways not evaluated.) Similar success was reported in cleaning up lakes; by the early 1990s, 56 percent of these waters fully met their intended uses, 35 percent succeeded partially, and only 10 percent failed entirely to do so.[9] (Once again, however, roughly half of all lake areas were not assessed, so that the overall record of achievement is still uncertain.)

Not all the news about water quality is positive. Up to half of all pollution comes not from factories or other fixed facilities but from so-called nonpoint sources, much of it in the form of runoff from farmlands laden with chemical fertilizers. Congress has been unwilling to enact strong (that is, mandatory) controls to reduce such pollution, with the result that the problem remains unresolved. In 1989, agricultural runoff alone impaired or threatened more than 100,000 river miles and almost two million acres of lakes.

In addition, Congress has often attacked water pollution by setting impossible targets and deadlines. As a result, in an effort to show tangible progress, the EPA has concentrated on pollutants that are familiar and easy to work with, while neglecting others that are less well known but potentially more dangerous. Even with these priorities, deadlines have been repeatedly extended, and progress has often fallen woefully short of meeting Congress' expectations. In the case of toxic substances, for example, Congress passed legislation in 1979 requiring the EPA to promulgate regulations as soon as possible for 126 "priority" pollutants. Deadlines for completing this task had to be extended repeatedly—in 1979, 1982, 1983, 1985, 1986, and 1987. By 1994, the EPA had addressed only 109 of the 126 pollutants, and had managed to do next to nothing about other toxic substances which many experts believed to be more dangerous than the items on the priority list.[10]

All in all, the fairest appraisal of our campaign against water pollution is that—with some notable exceptions—water quality was apparently not as bad as many people thought at the time the critical legislation was passed. Since the advent of federal rules, further improvement seems to have occurred and some pollutants have declined greatly. Even so, important sources of pollution are still not effectively regulated, and many substances that may well be dangerous are still uncontrolled. Until the EPA's monitoring efforts improve, however, no one can be sure just how much progress has been made.

With respect to solid-waste disposal, America's problems are substantial and growing larger. From 1960 to 1990, total waste generated by Americans doubled, while the total amount of municipal waste per year, net of recovered material, rose from 81 million tons to 177.5 million tons in the early 1990s.[11] Disposing of this mountain of refuse is itself an expensive process, costing some $25 billion nationwide in 1992.

Ed Koch, former mayor of New York City, is reported to have said, "You can do four things with garbage. You can burn it. You can bury it. You can recycle it. Or you can send it on a Caribbean cruise." Traditionally, our cities have chosen the burial route: America still deposits more than 70 percent of its solid waste in landfills. As open space grows scarcer in many parts of the country, however, especially in the Northeast, costs have shot up. More than one-third of the nation's landfills have reached their capacity, and municipal officials are encountering more and more resistance from local residents in searching for new sites.

Recycling is often touted as the preferred way to cope with mounting problems of waste. But America still does not recycle enough to offset the steady growth in the volume of discarded material. Although efforts have intensified, recovery rates remain well below the levels achieved in most other advanced industrialized countries.[12]

The existence of hazardous or toxic wastes has created special problems. The issue heated up politically after the highly publicized accounts of leaking poisons at Love Canal in New York State, followed by reports of hundreds of hazardous waste sites, many created decades earlier, which could pose a threat to human beings. The resulting outcry prompted Congress to enact legislation to clean up these areas with the aid of a "Superfund," which would pay the cost when it was impossible to find any companies directly or even remotely responsible.

The Superfund program is run by the Environmental Protection Agency. The program requires parties in any way responsible for contaminated sites to clean them up or reimburse the EPA for doing so. But progress has been extremely slow, in large part because of the long delays occasioned by lawsuits to apportion liability among the numerous firms and organizations that are linked to each site. Appropriations to the Superfund in the first thirteen years topped $12 billion, with only $728 million in costs having been recovered from offending firms.[13] In 1993, of the 1,320 sites that had ever been listed on the government's priority list, only 4 percent (fifty-two sites) had been fully cleaned up.[14] Although no one knows for sure how many sites will eventually have to be dealt with, the Office of Technology Assessment has predicted that the total cost will run to $100 billion or more, and other estimates place the amount much higher. At the current rate, efforts to clean up hazardous waste promise to last several decades.

International Comparisons

How does our record of environmental protection compare with that of other industrial nations? At present, all of the countries discussed here have active environmental programs. By the early 1990s, public and private sources in the United States were devoting a slightly higher share of GDP to improving the environment (1.8 percent, 1993) than Japan (1.65 percent, 1990), Germany (1.6 percent, 1990), Britain (1.5 percent, 1990), or Canada (1.1 percent, 1981).[15] It would be unwise, however, to read much into these variations. Two countries equally committed to achieving the same environmental goals could end up spending widely varying amounts because of differences in their population density, industrial makeup, and regulatory methods.

More revealing are comparisons of the rates of progress made by different countries in reducing various forms of pollution. Air quality offers the clearest information of this kind. The seven countries under review have each identified the same major pollutants, and each has established standards for reducing them. By and large, the United States has tended to set targets of more-than-average stringency. But the record of achievement in controlling pollutants tells a somewhat different story. Although the United States has a higher amount of emissions per capita than any of the other countries for virtually every pollutant, it has rarely accomplished as much in reducing pollution.[16]

From 1970 to the late 1980s, the United States reduced sulphur oxide emissions by approximately 35 percent.[17] Over the same period, France, the United Kingdom, and Canada managed to bring about reductions of almost 50 percent, while Japan and Germany lowered their emissions by at least 60 percent (substantially more in the case of Japan).[18] With respect to sulphur dioxide, the United States again trailed most of the other countries by the late 1980s, having achieved reductions roughly equivalent to those of Canada but markedly lower than those in Germany, England, France, Sweden, and Japan.[19] Carbon dioxide emissions in the United States rose by 19 percent from the early 1970s to the late 1980s—not as much as the growth in Canada and Japan but much less impressive than the results in England, France, Sweden, and Germany, where carbon dioxide emissions actually declined.[20] In the case of nitrogen oxides, America's record is somewhat better. From 1970 to the late 1980s, no country save Japan seems to have succeeded in reducing nitrogen oxides. The United States and Britain have kept their nitrogen oxide emissions at close to the 1970 level.[21] None of the other countries has been able to avoid significant increases.

Comparisons of the sort just made should be taken with a generous grain of salt because of differences in the methods and reliability of measuring air quality from one nation to another. On the basis of existing evidence, however, the United States does not seem to have performed better than the other countries in improving its air quality, and has almost certainly done less well than Japan.

International comparisons in the field of water pollution are not particularly helpful, since the waterways of one country are so different from those of another. One can only compare the percentages of the population served by waste-water treatment plants. Table 6.2 indicates the progress made in all seven countries from 1970 to 1990.

With respect to waste disposal, it is possible to make at least some crude comparisons. The United States generates more municipal waste

Table 6.2. Percent of population served by waste-water treatment, 1970–1991.

Country	1970	1980	1985	1991	Primary[a] (late 1980s)	Secondary[b] (late 1980s)	Tertiary[c] (late 1980s)
Canada	—	56	57	70	13	53	0
France	19	43	50	68	—	—	—
West Germany	62	82	88	86	2	13	75
Japan	16	30	36	44	—	—	—
Sweden	63	82	94	95	1	10	84
United Kingdom	—	82	83	87	6	53	25
United States	42	70	74	74	15	59	0

Source: OECD, *The State of the Environment*, 58 (1991); *Environmental Performance Reviews: Japan*, 72 (1994).

a. Primary treatment removes 60 percent of suspended solids, 20 percent of nitrogen compounds, and 30 percent of oxygen-demanding wastes.

b. Secondary treatment removes up to 90 percent of oxygen-demanding wastes and an additional 30 percent of suspended solids and nitrogen compounds.

c. Tertiary treatment brings water close to or above drinking standards. But compared with secondary-treatment facilities, tertiary-treatment facilities are four times as expensive to operate and twice as expensive to build.

per capita than any of the other countries, and more industrial waste than any nation save Japan. Our rate of growth of solid waste per capita has also been virtually the highest in the group (on a par with the rate in France). At the same time, Japan and most countries in Europe have made much greater progress in moving from landfill to recycling (Table 6.3).

These figures do not necessarily mean that Europe and Japan have been more far-sighted than the United States in perceiving the problems of waste disposal or more decisive in doing something about them. The greater density of population in these countries presumably forced their governments to find alternatives to landfills at an earlier point than was necessary in Canada or the United States. Moreover, the optimum pattern of waste disposal varies according to the circumstances of each country. Although enthusiasts talk as though recycling is always desirable, it can sometimes cost more than any benefits it yields. Similarly, incineration is often more expensive than landfill and can have potential toxic effects that require even more money to remove. For this reason, programs to recycle or incinerate more extensively do not necessarily imply a superior job of waste management.[22]

Table 6.3. **Percent of waste products recycled, 1992 and 1993.**

Country	Percent of waste paper recycled (1993)	Percent of glass recycled (1992)
Canada	32	12[a]
France	42	44
West Germany	45	65
Japan	51	56
Sweden	43[b]	44
United Kingdom	32	26
United States	34	20

Source: OECD, *Environmental Performance Reviews: Canada,* 83 (1995); OECD, *Environmental Performance Reviews: United Kingdom,* 76 (1994).
  a. Figure is for 1985.
  b. Figure is for 1990.

Cost Effectiveness

Experts seem to agree that America could accomplish just as much in reducing pollution at far less than the current cost. In the case of air pollution, Richard Stewart, who served under President Bush as assistant attorney general in charge of environmental issues, estimated in 1985 that expenditures using prevailing methods were at least twice as high as they would be under a least-cost system.[23] Even more troubling conclusions have emerged from studies of efforts to control particular pollutants in specific locations. These inquiries suggest that air quality projects have often cost *several times* more than was theoretically necessary.[24] More reassuring conclusions have emerged from studies of various projects to improve water quality. Even here, however, several studies from the 1980s reveal costs for specific projects that exceed optimal levels by 20 to 50 percent or more.[25]

There are several reasons for the inefficiency of our environmental programs. Political considerations have often distorted environmental regulations and inflated their costs. For example, to avoid burdening existing firms, laws are often drafted to apply only to new facilities. Framed in this way, environmental rules achieve the paradoxical result of favoring the repair of older, inefficient, more highly polluting plants over construction of modern, cleaner facilities. Political pressures have also led Congress and the EPA to shape the rules in ways that benefit one region over another. Thus, in passing the Clean Air Act of 1977, legislators from the eastern part of the country managed to protect producers of high-sulfur coal by requiring that *all* coal-fired power plants install expensive scrubbers, even though plants in the West using low-sulfur coal did not need scrubbers to meet environmental standards.[26]

Lawmakers have likewise avoided political controversy by refusing to order unpopular controls even when they promise to yield important environmental benefits. For example, Congress has repeatedly refused to encourage conservation and diminish air pollution by raising taxes on gasoline, even though gas taxes (and prices) in the United States are far below those of other advanced countries and consumption per capita is two to three times higher. Rather than increase taxes, Congress has imposed fuel efficiency standards that are more costly to consumers, apparently because they are less visible and controversial. Congress has likewise hesitated to limit pollution by farmers, or even to stop subsidizing the cost of fertilizers and sprays that represent a major cause of water pollution.[27] Similarly, municipalities have been reluctant to charge for garbage disposal according to how much refuse residents produce, thus failing to encourage frugal habits on the part of the public.

The continued use of traditional methods of regulation contributes further to unnecessary costs. Conventional rules limiting the amount of pollution that plants can emit or specifying the technology that all firms must install force each company to spend whatever it takes to reach the prescribed goal. This is a costly way of achieving the desired objective.[28] Because some plants can lower their emissions much more easily than others, the government could achieve compliance most efficiently by encouraging firms that can reduce emissions cheaply to move below the required level, while requiring less of firms that would have to spend much more to meet the official standard. It could obtain this result by placing a tax on effluents. Alternatively, officials could issue permits allowing firms to discharge specified amounts of pollutants so that companies that can limit pollution cheaply will find it profitable to do so aggressively and sell their unused permits to companies that find it harder to reduce emissions. Experts claim that such techniques could cut the costs of compliance in half—although such estimates may be optimistic, since proponents of tradable permits often underestimate the costs of establishing a market and of monitoring firms to make sure they do not exceed their emission limits.

In recent years, the EPA has begun to introduce more efficient methods, first by authorizing "bubbles" (schemes that allow firms with several plants to use unusually low pollution levels at one plant to offset higher levels in other plants), and then by authorizing a full-blown tradable-permit scheme under the Clean Air Act amendments of 1990. By and large, however, the government has been slow to substitute economic measures for conventional regulation. Many environmentalists and lawmakers have felt uncomfortable treating pollution not as an evil to be proscribed but simply as a product that can be traded like a commodity on the market.[29] In the case of effluent taxes, officials find it difficult to estimate how high the levy should be to ensure the desired reduction in pollution, or how to monitor every firm to determine the amount of "pollution tax" that it should pay. Bedeviled by imperfect information and a highly contentious atmosphere, regulators often find it easier simply to order the use of state-of-the-art antipollution technology than to employ more sophisticated regulatory methods that call for controversial judgments and complicated methods of implementation.

While resisting some of the most efficient instruments of regulation, the United States spends exceptional amounts of money and time implementing the rules that it does employ. The causes are rooted in the distinctive methods commonly used in this country to regulate business. Bills introduced in Congress almost never reflect a consensus achieved through prior negotiation among the parties involved. Instead, interest groups appear separately before congressional committees to argue their case or talk individually to legislators and their staffs. If all goes well, a law eventually emerges, but its provisions almost always bear the scars of intense lobbying and horse trading among legislators.

In the case of environmental legislation, Congress has tried to satisfy all major groups but in ways calculated to produce an extremely cumbersome result. To show their commitment to the environment, lawmakers have set specific goals and timetables for reducing pollution that are often ambitious to the point of being unrealistic. To satisfy local interests, Congress has directed the EPA to ask the states to submit environmental plans specifying how they can meet the standards required by Washington. To protect business from the threat of arbitrary action, companies have been given the right to appeal adverse rulings to the federal courts. At the same time, to convince environmental groups that the EPA would not be "captured" by commercial interests, lawmakers have allowed private organizations and citizens to sue agency officials in order to force them to act fast enough to meet Congress' deadlines. On top of all these safeguards, the White House may have concerns of its own that it tries to impose on federal agencies. For example, President Reagan initiated the practice of reviewing all regulations proposed by the EPA to make sure that they did not impose undue burdens on industry.

The result of this process is to expose the EPA to constant pressure from different sources that have conflicting interests. Litigation is especially common, particularly by regulated firms—which have every reason to appeal orders against them, since they normally do not have to comply with costly regulations while a lawsuit is in process. In the years following the promulgation of water quality standards, companies and trade associations brought suit against 140 standards. The announcement of a single set of regulations for industrial waste led immediately to fifty-two separate notices of intent to bring suit by industry and environmental groups.

Many months or even years have passed while the process of litigation works its way through the courts. Meanwhile, interested parties frequently complain to Congress or the White House in a further attempt to modify or rescind objectionable rules. At every stage, the process is marked by adversary methods, heavy reliance on expert witnesses and technical reports, and liberal use of time, money, and lawyers to exhaust every possible avenue of redress. Amid constant controversy, environmental regulation has had a seesaw existence, as first environmentalists and then corporations gain the upper hand in Washington. Periods of reaction and counter-reaction have only added to the EPA's problems, without resulting in a thoughtful debate that would enable Congress to learn from the past and set a stable regulatory course for the future.

The process in most of the other countries considered in this study is quite different.[30] The executive branch, rather than the legislature, is typically the forum for considering the views of interested parties. Such consultation takes place before a bill is drafted and presented to the legislature. Officials generally allow ample time for discussion to facilitate consensus, often through official advisory committees composed of representatives from employers' associations, unions, and other recognized interest groups. The appropriate ministry then drafts a bill and introduces it in the legislature. In parliamentary systems, such bills usually pass with little change, as legislators dutifully vote the party line.

Since the officials who propose legislation also control the bureaucracy, the government in power can be confident of implementing the laws pretty much as it wishes. Without having to worry about legal challenges, lawmakers can draft the regulatory standards in general terms, leaving the ministry to apply the provisions to specific cases through a process of consultation with interested parties. In Germany, the bureaucracy usually formulates precise rules following consultation. In England, inspectors will often forgo specific rules in favor of negotiating separate understandings ad hoc with the management of each company. In either case, regulation is far less adversarial. The government guides the discussions with interested parties to arrive at conclusions compatible with the public interest.

In carrying out their work, officials in other countries speak with more authority than the EPA because they cannot be overruled by so many different agencies of government. Appeals to the regular courts are either nonexistent or strictly limited, and the bureaucracy receives little supervision or interference from either the judiciary or the legislature. At best, aggrieved parties can appeal to a special administrative tribunal, which is likely to show much greater deference to the judgment of agency officials than judges are inclined to do in this country. Because the regulations are created by consensus, however, these restrictions on the right of appeal do not seem to have caused intense conflict or resentment.

The European style of regulation is not without problems. It is much less open to public scrutiny than procedures in this country, and much less accessible to arguments from environmental organizations and other citizens' groups. It puts much more faith in the bureaucracy and is more likely to allow mistakes to go uncorrected. In technical fields, such as the environment, where lightly staffed legislatures are ill-equipped to judge what regulators are doing, the European system leaves the bureaucracy largely unaccountable to anyone.[31]

At the same time, the American style of regulation has glaring problems of its own. It is very time consuming and expensive. It breeds antagonism, rather than compromise and agreement. Short on negotiation and consensus building, it creates winners and losers rather than leaving the parties feeling committed to carrying through a mutually agreed-upon solution. With its multiple safeguards and opportunities for everyone to challenge authority, it perpetuates a distrust of bureaucracy and a dissatisfaction with its work unparalleled in other industrial nations. In the end, there may be no sure way of proving which system is better. What does seem clear, however, is that regulation in the United States generates greater resentment, operates more slowly and more expensively, and produces no better results than the methods commonly used abroad.

Fortunately, there are signs that the EPA is experimenting with more consensual ways of protecting the environment. In working to reduce chlorofluorocarbons in order to protect the ozone layer, the agency has negotiated successfully with each of the industries that use these compounds to agree on efficient ways of meeting Congress' deadlines. The agency has also been successful in disseminating information about lighting to small and medium-size firms and offering them inducements to speed the adoption of energy-saving devices. Even more intriguing are efforts to have individual firms negotiate with their communities in setting overall pollution limits and timetables, and then to give firms discretion in figuring out the best way of reaching their goals. What distinguishes all of these ventures is their reliance on negotiation rather than command-and-control regulation. Although the experiments are promising, it is still too early to tell how successful they will be and whether they will gradually come to replace the more contentious regulatory methods of the past.

Balancing Benefits and Costs

The final question in evaluating our environmental programs is whether the gains achieved through all this regulation have been worth the billions of dollars expended. Although much effort has gone into trying to resolve this question, the answers are hard to come by. The costs of environmental programs can be estimated with tolerable accuracy, but the same is not true of the benefits. How to calculate the number of lives saved or the illnesses avoided through cleaner air and purer water? How to place a value on human life and health? What is it worth to swim again in Boston Harbor or to fish for salmon once more in the Penobscot River?

Experts have done their best to grapple with these questions in order to weigh the costs and benefits of environmental programs. Although various methods have been used, a broad consensus seems to have emerged. Almost all of the studies conclude that the benefits of the clean air programs have substantially exceeded the costs to date (although there are doubts whether this is still true, especially after the passage of the Clean Air Act of 1990).[32] With respect to water pollution, the conclusions are quite different. Annual costs placed at $25–30 billion have yielded estimated benefits of $5.7–27.7 billion per year, so that the net effect can be positive only if the most optimistic assumptions prove correct.[33] Since this is highly unlikely, most experts agree that water pollution efforts have probably cost considerably more than they are worth in monetary terms.

In order to keep the costs of environmental programs from outrunning the benefits, the government needs to focus its efforts on the highest risks where the potential benefits of intervention are greatest. Only within the past few years, however, has the EPA begun to seek an expert consensus on comparing environmental risks to provide a firmer basis for setting priorities.[34] Beyond the intellectual problems of trying to rank environmental hazards with limited knowledge, the EPA is further hampered by the fact that different agencies use different methods of assessing risks so that even the findings accepted by the government are not always easy to compare.

By far the greatest difficulty in trying to focus resources on the greatest risks is that the public and Congress often view environmental hazards very differently from the experts. The Superfund program provides a particularly vivid example. According to the public, hazardous waste represents the gravest of all environmental threats to human health. The experts strongly disagree, at least on most types of waste. Faced with such a conflict, Congress has sided with the people, often resoundingly so. In Senator Robert Stafford's words, "We are dealing with human lives that are devastated by the impacts of these chemicals; children born with permanent defects, adults stricken with crippling diseases, entire communities with their supplies of drinking water contaminated beyond use."[35]

Having described the environmental risks in such apocalyptic terms, Congress must feel that devoting one-third of the EPA's budget to cleaning up toxic-waste dumps is a modest price to pay. Yet experts examining the record are well-nigh unanimous that the bulk of Superfund dollars could be spent for other purposes with far greater effect.[36]

This is by no means an isolated example. At the EPA's request, scientists have assessed the environmental risks under the agency's purview. They have ranked these hazards in a manner markedly at variance with the public's priorities. Granted, scientific risk is not the only factor that is relevant in assigning priorities, but it is surely one of the most important. Failing to take it into account can be expensive. According to a careful recent study, federal agencies, including the EPA, could cut their spending on reducing human risks by $30 billion per year and still save as many lives as they do today. In the alternative, they could spend the same amount they currently spend and save 60,000 additional lives per year if they allocated their funds according to what is now known about relative risks.[37]

Evaluating the Record

In judging the accomplishments of the EPA, one must remember what a difficult challenge environmental pollution poses for government officials. Our air, water, and soil are being permeated with thousands of different substances that could adversely affect human health or the environment. Little or nothing is known about the effects of many of these items, and scientific tests often conflict with one another. Countless firms, individuals, and organizations contribute in all kinds of ways to the steady accumulation of pollutants and waste. Many have a high stake in avoiding regulation. Somehow, operating with imperfect knowledge in an atmosphere of high emotional intensity and partisan conflict, government officials must develop effective ways of restoring nature and protecting the public from toxins.

Faced with these difficulties, the United States has clearly done much to improve the environment over the past twenty-five years. Our air is much freer of pollutants. Our waterways are cleaner. And the country has made a modest but significant start on recycling waste and cleaning up hazardous-waste dumps.

In approaching environmental problems, the United States has also been unusually innovative. Sophisticated forms of risk assessment and cost-benefit analysis have flowered here to a greater extent than abroad. Tradable permits, "bubbles," and other efficient new economic tools of regulation had their origin in this country. Requirements that firms publish their emissions of toxic wastes proved to be an imaginative way of bringing about substantial voluntary reductions for very little cost and no coercive regulation.

Finally, those who worry about the power of corporate lobbyists in America can take some comfort from the record of environmental regulation. Although business has opposed much environmental regulation, the standards adopted by Congress are at least as stringent as those of most other countries. Many substances that the EPA has labeled potentially injurious to human health have not been outlawed in Europe, and officials here have frequently pursued polluters with a zeal unmatched abroad.

Despite these signs of regulatory vigor, our record overall leaves much to be desired. Congress has repeatedly passed legislation with highly ambitious goals, wildly improbable deadlines, and insufficient resources to carry out the assigned tasks. Instead of pursuing a set of realistic goals in a consistent fashion, policies and programs have veered back and forth as proenvironmental or antienvironmental forces gained the upper hand. In the words of William D. Ruckelshaus, twice director of the EPA, "The anti-environmental push of the nineties is prompted by the pro-environmental excess of the late eighties, which was prompted by the anti-environmental excess of the early eighties, which was prompted by the pro-environmental excess of the seventies, which was prompted . . . but why go on?"[38] Along this zigzag course, there has been far too little serious dialogue between the two camps. Rather, committed advocates have pushed their positions with uncompromising zeal so that policies have seldom evolved by trial and error to become truly effective but have continued to be buffeted by partisan struggles in unproductive ways.

In terms of specific results, the government has pressed hard to control emissions from factories and other large stationary sources, but has done little to address the politically sensitive areas of consumer behavior, farm practices, and small-business activity that account for large and growing shares of pollution. At the same time, almost all students of environmental regulation feel that a great deal of money has been wasted, partly because America's regulatory methods have been badly designed and partly because the government has often been unwise in assigning priorities and overly zealous in prescribing the level of safety to be reached. The net result is that several major programs have probably cost considerably more than any benefits they have achieved, while other, more promising opportunities have been neglected. Finally, our methods of regulation have proved to be much more contentious, costly, legalistic, and time consuming than is typically the case in other countries, yet they have not produced greater results. All in all, therefore, despite commendable accomplishments, the government still has far to go in translating ecological concerns into sound priorities, well-designed rules, and efficient means of implementation.

7

Encouraging the Arts

Another activity that has traditionally influenced a nation's quality of life consists of those creative pursuits referred to collectively as "the arts." Although America was a new country carved out of wilderness, there were painters, musicians, architects, poets, and writers in the colonies long before the Revolution. By the middle of the nineteenth century, American authors such as Edgar Allen Poe, Ralph Waldo Emerson, and Herman Melville were attracting considerable attention abroad.

Throughout most of its history, however, the artistic achievements of America have been overshadowed in almost every field by those of Europe. When the New York Philharmonic was founded in 1842, it was staffed almost exclusively by musicians from Europe. The "Swedish nightingale," Jenny Lind, sang to larger, more enthusiastic audiences than any American performer. In 1913, when New York City staged a massive exhibition of American and European paintings, artists in this country were chagrined to find that wealthy collectors were interested almost entirely in purchasing pictures from Europe. Many of our best artists and writers—Mary Cassatt, James McNeill Whistler, Henry James—went abroad to work, just as John Singleton Copley had done almost one hundred years before, to escape a land that offered him "neither precept, example, nor models."

This pattern continued well into the twentieth century. Americans went to the ballet, but almost always to watch a touring company from Europe. Leading American orchestras were largely conducted by Europeans and featured European soloists. In a major international exhibit of architecture at the Museum of Modern Art in 1932, "there were few buildings in America that [Alfred H.] Barr, Philip Johnson and Henry-Russell Hitchcock, who collaborated on the show, thought worth including."[1] The best-known American writers, such as Eugene O'Neill, T. S. Eliot, Gertrude Stein, and Ernest Hemingway, continued to spend much of their working lives abroad. Prior to World War II, it was primarily in the newer art forms—film, musical comedy, and especially jazz—that Americans won international acclaim.

The Role of the Government

For centuries, the flowering of the arts in Europe was supported by the generosity of kings, nobles, princes of the Church, and other powerful patrons. Many of the most creative artists owed their livelihood to the commissions they received from persons in positions of authority. In slightly altered form, this tradition still continues. Although painters and musicians no longer depend for their livelihood on dukes and bishops, all forms of art receive substantial support from the public treasury.

What accounts for all this help over such a long period from persons in high places? A desire to provide enjoyment and entertainment, perhaps, but there is more to it than that. Some heads of state have suspected that posterity would judge their regime by the treasures of art and literature that it left to the world. Other leaders have looked upon famous works of art as marks of greatness to impress other nations. More recently, persons in authority have believed that levels of civility and culture will be enhanced by great music, painting, and poetry.

A different pattern emerged in the United States. In the early days of the republic, Americans were of two minds about art. On the one hand, there were citizens of the world such as Thomas Jefferson, who proclaimed: "You see that I am an enthusiast on the subject of the arts. But it is an enthusiasm of which I am not ashamed, as its object is to improve the taste of my countrymen, to increase their reputation, to reconcile them to the respect of the world and to procure them its praise."[2] On the other hand, representatives of a more austere line of thought based on Calvinist teachings looked askance at sensual pleasure even of the most elevated sort. Reflecting these sentiments, the Continental Congress issued a resolution calling for the suspension of "horseracing, gambling, cockfighting, exhibition of shows, plays, and other expensive diversions and entertainments."[3]

The first forays of the new national government into the domain of art amply demonstrated the hazards of official patronage. In 1817, John Trumbull was commissioned to paint four monumental paintings to commemorate the American Revolution. On seeing the artist's rendition of the Declaration of Independence, John Quincy Adams grew deeply distressed, finding it "immeasurably below the dignity of the subject."[4] Even greater disappointment ensued when Horatio Greenough was enlisted to sculpt a statue of George Washington. When the completed work was unveiled in 1841, startled viewers saw the Father of His Country in the form of a deity naked to the waist with only a flowing drapery to cover the rest of his body. While a few observers with classical tastes may have applauded this effort to glorify our first president, the finished work was "unsparingly denounced by the less refined multitude."[5]

Apart from founding the Smithsonian Museum in 1846, the federal government did little for the arts until the early twentieth century. During the 1930s, however, as part of a national effort to put people to work, the New Deal reached out to artists in new and promising ways. At their peak, federal employment programs put 40,000 writers and artists on the government's payroll. The impact was substantial. According to one member of Congress:

> During the last few years, a cultural transformation has occurred in our national life. Theater, music, painting, sculpture, literature, and the other arts have become the possession of millions of people in every section of the country who never before had the means or opportunity to enjoy the benefits of culture. Twenty-five million people in 22 States have witnessed the Federal Theater productions; 65 percent of them had never witnessed a play before. Federal musicians have played to aggregate audiences of 92,000,000 persons in 273 cities in 42 States. Eleven million people have witnessed art exhibitions or have been taught in art classes . . .[6]

Still, an aura of criticism surrounded these triumphs. Congressional committees declared disapprovingly that some of the artists employed by the government were either Communists or harbored Communist sympathies. The chairman of the House Appropriations Committee launched an investigation of the Works Progress Administration in an effort "to get the government out of the theater business."[7] Within a few years, the New Deal initiatives to nurture the arts had all been brought to an end.

Without much encouragement from the government, however, changes were occurring that would lift the arts in America to new levels of importance in the society. In the 1920s and 1930s, symphony orchestras and art museums began to appear in significant numbers across the United States. Fleeing the persecution of the Nazis and the destruction caused by a new world war, many prominent writers, painters, musicians, architects, and artists of all kinds began to enter the United States to take up permanent residence. After the war, dance companies started to multiply, several new opera companies were founded, and summer stock companies and regional theaters were springing up everywhere. Beginning in the 1950s, a series of large grants from the Ford Foundation gave much-needed impetus to the development of symphony orchestras, dance companies, and other arts organizations.

During the 1950s, sentiment grew for establishing a permanent government program of support for the arts. By then, the Cold War had propelled America into a position of global leadership that caused prominent officials to think more consciously about the stature of the country in the eyes of other nations. According to an enthusiastic Congressman, "One of the major ways in which we might turn reluctant and uneasy military allies and the millions of uncommitted peoples into friends is to earn their respect for our culture."[8]

Once again, however, government efforts to promote the arts incurred the displeasure of other legislators. As the Department of State began sending cultural missions abroad, the House Un-American Activities Committee announced its disapproval. In Congressman George Dondero's opinion, an unholy mixture of Communist intellectuals and modern art was undermining the nation's culture. "Through the aid of Marxist evaluators in the cultural sphere," Dondero protested, "leftists in art are attempting to break down the standard to which artists of the past adhered."[9]

As time went on, enthusiasm for a federal role in the arts gradually overcame the skepticism of anti-Communist critics. Although Congress ultimately failed to go along, President Dwight Eisenhower gave his approval to a plan to create a federal advisory council on the arts. Senator Jacob Javits proposed a federally funded foundation to offer grants to artists and cultural institutions. Support for such a program of aid was implicit in the 1960 report of the Commission on National Goals: "In the eyes of posterity, the success of the United States as a civilized society will be largely judged by the creative activities of its citizens in art, architecture, literature, music and the sciences."[10]

As the 1960s began, two new political leaders occupied important offices—one in the White House, the other as the governor of the nation's most populous state. John F. Kennedy and Nelson Rockefeller were ideally suited by temperament and conviction to bring the power of government to bear on behalf of the arts. Both soon acted on their convictions, Rockefeller by creating a statewide council on the arts in New York, and Kennedy by introducing legislation to establish national endowments to support the arts and the humanities.

While virtually no one in the 1960s was prepared to deny the importance of the arts, there were still those who disputed the need for *government* support. A common criticism was that public subsidies would take tax money from working people to benefit the well-to-do, who were assumed to be the principal beneficiaries of high culture. Although at least one careful study has refuted this claim, the argument persists to this day.[11] Other opponents of federal funding argued that the arts were primarily a local responsibility. This point had already been made more than a century earlier, but its force seemed largely spent by 1960, after Washington had assumed so many powers previously reserved to the states. Probably the most powerful argument against government funding was that it would inhibit free expression and bring about conformity with official standards of quality and taste. The record of congressional investigations of federal arts programs during the New Deal and the early 1950s lent credence to this objection by showing that lawmakers were not reluctant to intervene whenever government assistance seemed to them to undermine basic American values.

The National Endowment for the Arts

Despite lingering opposition, Lyndon Johnson pressed ahead after the death of President Kennedy to secure legislative approval for a permanent organization to support cultural activities. In 1965, Congress agreed to create a National Endowment for the Arts (NEA) and a National Endowment for the Humanities, each with an initial funding of $2.5 million. In establishing the NEA, Congress had several objectives in mind.

1. To encourage more artistic endeavor.
2. To expand participation in and appreciation of the arts by increasing the audiences of museums, theaters, and other organizations for the display of art of all kinds.
3. To enhance the quality and excellence of the arts in the United States.
4. To preserve and transmit America's diverse cultural heritage.
5. To accomplish the preceding objectives without diminishing private support for the arts and without imposing any official censorship or cultural orthodoxy.

These objectives found wide popular approval. In 1990, the latest in a series of NEA-sponsored Harris polls revealed that 60 percent of the public favored government aid for the arts (including 78 percent of Americans between the ages of eighteen and twenty-nine and 64 percent of those aged thirty to forty).[12] A still higher proportion, 70 percent, approved of support for individual artists. Almost the same number of respondents (69 percent) even affirmed that they would be willing to pay an additional five dollars in taxes to support the arts.* (Such a sum from every adult taxpayer would double the total government funding for the arts.)

Armed with this evidence of public approval, the NEA has pushed ahead to achieve a variety of goals. It has followed Congress' wishes in supporting a wide range of art forms: "music (instrumental and vocal), dance, drama, folk art, creative writing, architecture and allied fields, painting, sculpture, photography, graphic and craft arts, industrial design, costume and fashion design, motion pictures, television, radio, tape and sound recordings, the arts related to the presentation, execution, and exhibition of such major art forms, and the study and application of the arts to the human environment." In distributing its funds, the NEA has aided both institutions and (to a lesser extent)

---

*Although there is no question that the American public looks favorably on the arts, differently worded surveys cast doubt on whether a majority actually supports *federal funding* for the arts. Thus, a 1990 Gallup survey commissioned by *Newsweek* revealed that 50 percent of the public opposed the use of federal funds to encourage and support the arts, while only 42 percent approved. See Joseph Zeigler, *Arts in Crisis: The National Endowment for the Arts versus America*, 121 (1994).

individual artists, long-standing organizations as well as new groups, innovative work along with traditional art.

The NEA has also gone to considerable lengths to encourage private support. In an effort to stimulate private donations, it has made extensive use of matching grants, often requiring institutions to raise three times the amount given by the government in order to obtain NEA funds. The favoring presence of a tax exemption for charitable gifts has provided a further incentive for private giving to the arts.

More elaborate methods have been used to avoid censorship. Seeking to distance itself from official judgments on questions of quality and taste, the NEA has relied heavily on advisory panels of artists and professionals to decide which individuals and institutions to support. A substantial fraction of the agency's funds has gone directly to state arts councils, further diversifying the groups making judgments about the allocation of money to artists and arts organizations. Finally, the use of limited government funds to leverage private support for the arts further diminishes the threat of censorship by creating multiple sources of aid to which artists and institutions can appeal.

The Record

How well has the NEA succeeded in achieving its objectives? Unfortunately, there is no way of measuring how much the arts in America have improved as a result of the agency's programs. Nor is it obvious how far any government entity can increase the number of truly gifted artists or lift the quality of poetry, drama, and painting. Impressionistic accounts, however, suggest that the stature of American artists and performers has risen appreciably during the postwar boom in culture. In the words of two seasoned observers, "Before World War II, high art and culture in the United States was dominated by European practitioners and traditions. (Theater and modern dance were the principal exceptions.)"[13] Such a statement could hardly be made today, when American artists perform around the globe and many Europeans consider New York the premier arts center of the world. How much credit the government can claim for the emergence of American artists and performers of international rank is impossible to say; other factors were undoubtedly more important. Still, it remains true that the stature of the arts in America has improved enormously during the life of the Endowment.

Table 7.1. Number of arts organizations in the United States, 1965 and 1990.

Type of organization	1965	1990
Symphony orchestras	110	230
Choruses	10	80
Small-press book publishers	650	3743
Dance companies	37	250+
State folk-art programs	1	46
Nonprofit theater companies	56	420+
Opera companies	27	120
State and territorial arts councils	5	56

Source: National Endowment for the Arts, *Arts in America, 1990,* 38 (1990).

More precise evidence is available to help evaluate the Endowment's success in achieving most of its other goals. For example, Table 7.1 clearly shows how impressively the amount of serious activity in the arts has increased since the NEA's founding.

In addition to the growth of arts organizations, the number of practicing artists in America has increased from 560,000 to well over 1.5 million during the same period.[14] Live audiences for artistic exhibitions and performances have likewise risen several-fold since 1965, a particularly impressive trend in light of the growing competition from television during this period (Table 7.2). More recent studies reveal that steady increases have continued into the 1990s.[15] These analyses show that different segments of the population participate to a markedly different extent. Education is the strongest factor in predicting

Table 7.2. Size of audience for selected types of arts performances, 1965 and 1988.

Type of performance	Total audience (in millions)	
	1965	1988
Symphony concerts	9	24
Professional operas	3	18
Nonpro fit theater	1	15
Dance performances	1	16

Source: National Endowment for the Arts, *"Press Release,"* (September 1990).

attendance at arts performances and events: fewer than 8 percent of persons with only a grade school education attend arts performances in the course of a year, compared with 77 percent of those holding a graduate degree.[16] Education is likewise the principal factor in determining the likelihood that a person will perform or actively participate in arts activities.

Another indication of the long-term growth in interest in the arts is the fact that, since the founding of the NEA, total consumer spending on the arts has risen almost twice as fast as the growth of disposable income. Remarkably, as Table 7.3 makes clear, Americans now spend more on the performing arts than they do even for motion pictures and spectator sports.

Table 7.3. Percent of disposable personal income spent on admission to various forms of spectator entertainment, 1947–1990.

Form of entertainment	1947	1970	1980	1990
Performing arts	0.111	0.074	0.092	0.123
Motion pictures	0.944	0.226	0.132	0.096
Spectator sports	0.132	0.157	0.117	0.112

Source: James Heilbrun and Charles M. Gray, *The Economics of Art and Culture: An American Perspective,* 14–15 (1993).

Of course, it is conceivable that the rapid increases in arts organizations, audiences, and total receipts after 1965 did not owe much to the NEA; they may have simply been a product of the forces of cultural expansion already under way in the United States. In fact, prior to the creation of the NEA several commentators declared that America was already experiencing a cultural boom.[17] More careful analysts, however, such as William Baumol and William Bowen, have concluded that the evidence for a boom was decidedly mixed.[18] Although resident professional theaters, Off-Broadway productions, and opera companies all increased after World War II, consumers spent a smaller proportion of their disposable income on the arts in 1963 than they had in 1929 and did not even exceed the level achieved in 1947. Moreover, much of the postwar growth in arts activities had slowed or stopped entirely by 1960. The number of opera companies of all kinds actually dropped from 1960 to 1964, as did the number of Off-Broadway productions. Real consumer expenditures on the performing arts (and on books as well) fell slightly as a percentage of disposable income. All in all, therefore, it is doubtful that developments after 1965 can be considered merely a continuation of trends already under way.

In all probability, the growth of the arts, beginning in the 1960s, was a product of several forces. Private endowments, notably the Ford and Rockefeller foundations, certainly helped through their ample donations, especially to particular endeavors such as the nonprofit stage. At the same time, the steady increase in the number of college graduates enlarged the audience for the arts. In any list of contributing factors, however, the NEA undoubtedly deserves an honored place.

Funding for the arts has grown dramatically since the creation of the Endowment. Its budget has risen from $2.5 million in 1965 to $167 million in 1994.[19] Since one of its aims was not to discourage but to stimulate other sources of funding, it is even more significant to note what has happened to state and local support and to private giving. State funding has increased from $1.3 million in 1965 to $277 million in 1990.[20] Local agencies, which also started from a low base in the 1960s, were contributing $328 million by 1990.[21] And private gifts to the arts, humanities, and culture increased more than threefold, from $2 billion in 1964 to $8.8 billion in 1991.[22]

No one can prove just how much of this increase in private support is due directly or indirectly to the NEA. But it is interesting that during the decade immediately preceding the creation of the agency, private philanthropy rose by only 6 percent, even though the economy was growing robustly and high marginal tax rates made philanthropy very attractive. There is every reason to suppose, therefore, that far from inhibiting private support, the NEA has contributed in some measure to increasing it.

The record of the agency in avoiding government standards of taste and artistic quality is much more problematic. Despite the attempt it made to insulate itself by relying on state agencies and advisory committees to make artistic judgments, the Endowment has not succeeded in avoiding responsibility in the eyes of Congress for controversial decisions regarding artistic content. In 1990, for example, it became embroiled in a heated controversy when the public learned that Endowment funds had supported an exhibit of photographs by Robert Mapplethorpe that were of a homoerotic nature, and another exhibit that included a photograph by Andres Serrano depicting a cross submerged in urine.

Led by Senator Jesse Helms, members of Congress objected vehemently to the use of public funds for such offensive works. In Patrick

Buchanan's words, "Conservatives and the religious community . . .
should choose to withdraw support and funding from the modernist
culture they profess to despise . . . The hour is late, America needs a
cultural revolution in the '90s as sweeping as its political revolution in
the '80s."[23] Eventually, Congress enacted the so-called Helms Amendment forbidding NEA support for material which could be considered
"obscene, including, but not limited to depictions of sadomasochism,
homoeroticism, the sexual exploitation of children, or individuals engaged in sex acts and which, taken as a whole, do not have serious
literary, artistic, political or scientific value."[24] The chairman of the
Endowment subsequently issued a directive requiring all grantees to
sign a statement acknowledging that none of its funds could be used
to promote, disseminate or produce materials that the agency deemed
obscene.

This episode touched off a national debate over the appropriate
role of the Endowment and Congress in supporting the arts. The controversy laid bare the dilemma created by the laudable desire not to
set official standards of artistic merit and propriety, coupled with the
understandable reluctance to use taxpayers' money to support works
of art deeply offensive to most Americans. Eventually, a federal judge
held the NEA stipulation unconstitutional, and the Endowment continued to leave judgments of obscenity to the courts.[25]

The Mapplethorpe and Serrano episodes did not succeed in laying
this problem to rest. In 1994, members of Congress were again upset
by the use of federal funds to support controversial works of art. Although the NEA had not itself made the funding decisions that gave
rise to the dispute, both houses of Congress threatened to cut its appropriations by several millions of dollars as a reprimand for allowing
such practices to continue.

Notwithstanding these controversies, there is little reason to suppose that Congress' behavior can impose some sort of official standard
of propriety on the visual arts in America. Despite the impressive
growth in the NEA budget, federal funds still make up only one-third
of all government support for the arts, the rest coming from state and
local assistance. In all, government funds of every kind constitute only
15 percent of the total amount of public and private support combined.

Of course, all outside funding—public or private—threatens to
influence artists by causing them, however subtly or unconsciously, to
adapt their work to satisfy potential donors and ensure continued sup-

port. Even a dependence on ticket sales tends to diminish innovation in favor of safe presentations that are sure to have broad audience appeal. Given this state of affairs, the best protection against stultifying conformity is probably a system like America's, with its many sources of support both public and private. Such a system has the added advantage of providing much more stable funding than one could expect from relying entirely on a government whose generosity is bound to wax and wane depending on the state of the economy and the priorities of the party in power. The only price to be paid—and it is substantial—is that artists and especially arts organizations must often spend inordinate amounts of time going from one potential donor to another seeking the money they need to continue functioning.

There is also a danger that NEA support will become a sort of Good Housekeeping Seal of Approval, a prerequisite to gaining assistance from corporations and foundations too uncertain of their own taste to render a judgment of their own. If private funding sources relinquish their independence in this way, the Endowment may well come to exercise an influence out of proportion to the minor share of funding it provides. Until now, however, the tremendous growth of arts organizations of every kind strongly suggests that NEA policies, with all their accompanying risks, have done more to stimulate than to discourage diversity in the cultural activities of America. As corporations and foundations become increasingly experienced and professional in their charitable activities, there is reason to hope that the risk of undue influence by the Endowment will diminish even further.

International Comparisons

Other advanced nations vary widely in their approach to supporting the arts.[26] On the continent of Europe, countries such as France and Germany have continued to rely primarily on public patronage. Government support in both nations is far greater than in the United States, while private philanthropy contributes very little even where the government has provided ample tax incentives. In France, for example, the government budget for the arts stood at roughly $7 billion in 1990, while private funding amounted to only $170 million, barely 2.5 percent of all State support.[27]

England and Canada have had a more austere tradition characterized by less direct government support than in France, Germany, and

Sweden.[28] Since World War II, however, Canada has taken a new tack and begun to support the arts at levels comparable to those of continental Europe. Britain, in contrast, still lags far behind in government funding, though it contributes more in direct public support than the United States. Private philanthropy, while greater than in continental Europe, continues to be a relatively minor factor both in Canada and in Britain.

Japan presents yet another model, with levels of government aid that are even lower than in the United States. Philanthropic support is also modest. As a result, the arts are largely dependent for their existence on ticket sales and other forms of earned income.[29]

Over the years, there has been a noticeable tendency for national patterns of funding to converge. Governments at all levels in the United States now support the arts, and the growth in public funding has been substantial. Even Japan has a government agency to promote the arts, with a modest budget to support cultural organizations. At the same time, arts organizations in Europe are showing more and more interest in looking to private philanthropy, especially from corporations. Eventually, then, the practices of all advanced nations may come to resemble one another more closely than they have in the past.

For the time being, however, as Table 7.4 makes clear, the countries discussed here continue to differ widely in their pattern of support for the arts.

Even with the addition of private giving (both corporate and in-

Table 7.4. Dollars per capita spent in public support for the arts, 1981–1984.

Country	Direct government funding	Indirect funding (forgone revenues from tax deductions)	Total
Canada (1981–1982)	32.00	Small	32.00+
France (1983)	32.00	Very small	32.00+
West Germany (1982)	27.00	Small	27.00+
Sweden (1983–1984)	35.00	0.00	35.00
United Kingdom (1983–1984)	9.60	0.40	10.00
United States (1983–1984)	3.00	10.00	13.00

Source: James Heilbrun and Charles M. Gray, *The Economics of Art and Culture: An American Perspective*, 232 (1993).

Table 7.5. **Percent of total budget from earned income, 1985.**

Arts organization	United States	France, West Germany, and Sweden	United Kingdom
Nonprofit theaters	72	10–20	45
Ballet companies	68	20–40	40
Symphony orchestras	77	18–25	52

Source: J. Mark Schuster, *Supporting the Arts: An International Comparative Study*, 63–65 (1985).

dividual), total support per capita for the arts in the United States falls below the levels of every country listed except for Britain. But this does not mean that the arts must get along with leaner budgets in America. According to the best available survey, arts organizations in the United States receive much larger amounts of earned income than their counterparts abroad (Table 7.5).

One weakness of the American system is that greater reliance on ticket sales requires higher ticket prices and hence may deter people from attending artistic events and performances. Whether for this reason or for others, total audiences in America do tend to be smaller than those in Europe and Canada (Table 7.6). Interestingly, an earlier study from the late 1960s shows the United States lagging even further behind in the size of its audiences.[30] It may well be, then, that attendance

Table 7.6. **Percent of population attending various arts exhibitions and performances within preceding year, 1980s.**

Country	Classical music concert	Theater	Ballet	Opera	Art museum[a]
Canada (Province of Quebec only; 1989)	16	39	8	—	28
France (1988–1989)	9	14	6	3	30
Sweden (1982–1983)	—	33	—	—	33
United Kingdom (1981)	10	24	4	3	19
United States (1982)	13	12	4	3	22

Source: James Heilbrun and Charles M. Gray, *The Economics of Art and Culture: An American Perspective*, 40 (1993).

a. Figures are not strictly comparable, since the British include only exhibitions whereas the French include all types of museums.

in the United States has begun to catch up with that of other countries after the cultural boom of the 1970s and 1980s. Since audiences in the United States continued to increase in the late 1980s and early 1990s, the audience gap may now be narrower still.

The Price of Success

All in all, therefore, the NEA gives every appearance of having succeeded impressively in accomplishing what Congress had in mind in 1965. The success of the Endowment closely resembles that of federal efforts to promote scientific research. By seeking to distribute public funds to talented individuals and enterprising institutions, both the National Science Foundation and the Endowment have managed to tap the wealth of creative talent in America for the benefit of large numbers of people.

As the NEA has matured, however, it has attracted far more criticism than the National Science Foundation. Many critics have attacked it for becoming cumbersome, bureaucratic, and unresponsive.[31] Long gone are the heady, informal days of the 1960s when Twyla Tharp could appeal for funds with her classic one-liner to the New York Arts Council: "I write dances, not applications. Send money. Love, Twyla."[32] Application forms have grown longer, the application process more formal and complicated. Strong ties have been forged between different programs in the Endowment and established arts organizations in the field. In the words of Phil Kadis, a *Washington Post* writer, "The NEA became no different from most government agencies . . . Instead of seeing itself as serving the public it had become the representative of the arts in Washington."[33]

In its grant-making policies, some have found the Endowment too conservative and too safe; others have complained that it is elitist; still others have charged it with being trendy and multicultural at some cost to quality.[34] There have been widespread complaints that it lacked a plan, a bold strategy, a clear set of priorities to maximize its impact and give its work coherence.[35] At the same time, cries have arisen that it has played politics at the expense of helping the most deserving applicants. According to Agnes de Mille, "Most of the money is being thrown away. It's being used for political purposes. They're spreading it around geographically, like Kiwanis, because every state has its Senators and Congressmen."[36]

Reading these complaints makes one realize that the task of the Endowment is much more complicated than that of the National Science Foundation. In contrast to basic science, the arts have no widely accepted standards of excellence; judgments conflict to such a point that one person's provocative originality is another's obscenity, while a single work of art can be simultaneously praised for its beauty and dismissed as banal. In addition, an agency to support the arts has a more varied set of goals than a science foundation, and there is much less agreement about the proper priorities among them. While some would press for artistic excellence, others would emphasize expanding and diversifying audiences, and still others would favor a strategy of building greater appreciation by supporting arts education or celebrating different cultures.

The NEA has to live with many such conflicts and contradictions. To avoid the risk of imposing conformity, it may diversify and delegate decision-making power to consultants and expert groups, but this only adds to the procedural complexities and delays of grant making. To escape the charge of censorship, it may rely on panels of artists to make professional judgments, but such a practice increases the risk of offering NEA support to works that powerful Congressmen find obscene. To sidestep charges of elitism, it will give generously to grassroots organizations all over the United States, only to provoke a complaint that it is no longer interested in artistic excellence. To win the appropriations it needs to satisfy the voracious appetites of its beneficiaries, it spreads its largesse widely and is especially solicitous of the interests expressed by key members of Congress. For its pains, it is pilloried for sacrificing aesthetic standards on the altar of political expediency.

An arts czar in a more authoritarian country could conceivably balance these competing pressures and emerge with a reasonably coherent program. In a society where NEA officials are subject to close press scrutiny, constant congressional supervision, and unrelenting pressure from arts organizations adept at grassroots lobbying, the Endowment in its maturity faces an all-but-impossible task.

Of all the problems facing the NEA, the most threatening is the continuing struggle over whether subsidizing the arts is an appropriate function of government. Long taken for granted in Europe, public support remains a matter of active controversy in the United States. In part, the issue reflects a persistent fear on the part of many legislators and officials that government funds are subsidizing blasphemous or obscene works of art. Artistic controversies are not unique to the United States, as anyone can attest who has witnessed the debate over whether to place 152 black-and-white striped columns in Paris' Palais Royal courtyard or the dispute over the Canadian National Gallery's exhibit *Veritas: Flesh Dress for an Albino Anorectic*. But the issue of propriety in the United States is not merely a recurrent subject of debate. Nor is it simply a matter of aesthetic disagreement. It is an issue of public morality forever primed to explode with special intensity, calling in question the very legitimacy of subsidizing art with taxpayers' money.

In addition to these disputes, the NEA has experienced further pressure from a related quarter. Many conservatives do not look upon the arts as a proper object of government support, but regard them as activities to be left to the private sector. The federal government's current budget difficulties have only served to strengthen this point of view.

As a result of these controversies, the NEA budget has suffered a steady erosion since 1980 that has sapped the agency's ability to inspirit the arts and expand their reach throughout the country. In 1994, a conservative triumph at the polls brought these pressures to bear with renewed intensity. A newly elected Republican Congress announced that it would cut NEA appropriations drastically or even end the agency entirely. This threat was spearheaded by a coalition of fiscal conservatives anxious to cut the budget and lawmakers angry about the use of public funds to support controversial works of art. Once again, therefore, arguments first expressed centuries ago reappeared in full force to imperil the existence of the Endowment.

Following this partisan assault, the NEA has had its 1996 budget cut by 40 percent, and its ultimate fate is still a matter of hot dispute. The Endowment has not offered a convincing picture of what its role should be, now that private support for the arts has grown so far beyond its 1965 levels and artists and arts organizations have multiplied so rapidly throughout the land. Nor would it be easy to decide on such a role amid the current financial and political uncertainty. Whatever the NEA's future may be, however, the agency's past record will remain as a signal success in achieving the goal that brought it into being in the first place—acting as a catalyst to help lift the quality, diversity, and public enjoyment of the arts in America to new levels.

How Fares Our Quality of Life?

With this description of the progress made in improving the arts, our homes and neighborhoods, and the purity of the environment, is it possible to compare the quality of life in America with that of other countries? Unfortunately, no. The term "quality of life" turns out to have an elastic nature that allows it to expand or contract according to the purposes of the user. In comparing *cities,* writers approach the subject much as these chapters have done—by looking at a variety of factors, most of them having to do with the vibrancy and diversity of cultural life, the quality of the air, water, and natural surroundings, and the condition of houses and other buildings. But writers comparing *countries* have looked at a much wider variety of conditions. If anything, they attempt to measure the full sweep of aims and activities that nations take seriously. In this respect, international comparisons are more relevant to this entire study than to just one of America's national goals.

As it happens, none of the comparative studies of quality of life ranks the United States close to the top. For example, after considering some forty economic, social, cultural, and political factors, *The Economist* (December 25, 1993–January 7, 1994) placed America eighth in a list of twenty-two first-, second-, and third-world countries:

1. Switzerland	9. Great Britain	16. Mexico
2. West Germany	10. Hong Kong	17. Bahamas
3. Spain	11. France	18. South Korea
4. Sweden	12. New Zealand	19. Russia
5. Italy	13. Israel	20. China
6. Japan	14. Canada	21. Brazil
7. Australia	15. Hungary	22. India
8. United States		

A similar survey limited to twelve developed nations again rated America eighth.[37] Of course, one should not place a great deal of weight on either of these ratings. Even viewed as broad rankings of national progress, both compilations are suspect, since the weightings given to the different factors are highly subjective and the factors themselves arbitrarily chosen.

Another intriguing set of inquiries has surveyed national populations to determine how they compare in their subjective well-being or
their satisfaction with life. One might think that the level of satisfaction
expressed by a people would throw some light on the objective conditions that make up the quality of their lives. For those who do not
lack the basic necessities of life, however, happiness seems to depend
much less on objective circumstances than on family, friends, religion,
and other intangible matters. Thus, according to one survey, 37 percent
of the wealthiest Americans (listed in *Forbes* magazine) were *less* satisfied than the average person; even lottery winners regularly turn out
to be happier only for a brief time.[38]

In short, there is no sure relationship between the external conditions of a society and the happiness of its people. It is true that several
western European countries—notably Denmark, West Germany, the
Netherlands, Norway, Sweden, and Switzerland—regularly show up
near the top in subjective surveys of satisfaction with life, as well as
in comparisons based on objective criteria. Other countries such as
France and Japan, however, tend to score well on objective evaluations
while falling far down the list in surveys of subjective well-being. Consider, for example, these combined results of numerous surveys ranking
38 countries according to the satisfaction of their inhabitants:[39]

1. Sweden,	14. New Zealand	27. Hungary
Iceland	15. Belgium	28. Italy
3. Denmark	16. Austria	29. Japan
4. Netherlands	17. South Africa	30. Portugal
5. Switzerland	18. Malaysia	31. South Korea
6. Finland	19. Thailand	32. Greece
7. Australia	20. Brazil	33. Egypt
8. Canada	21. Spain	34. Poland
9. Norway	22. Cuba	35. Panama,
10. Singapore	23. Philippines	Nigeria
11. United States	24. Israel	37. India
12. Great Britain	25. France	38. Dominican
13. Ireland	26. Mexico	Republic

We are left, then, with only a vague idea of how our quality of life
compares with that of other advanced nations. Whether one looks to
objective conditions or to subjective measures, the United States tends

to fall a considerable distance from the top of the list and a considerable distance from the bottom. With such an amorphous goal to work with, however, and such arbitrary measures to guide us, it is undoubtedly wise to take international comparisons of this kind with a heavy dose of salt.

Is it more helpful to ask whether the quality of life in America has improved or declined over the past thirty to forty years? Even if "quality of life" were not such a vague concept, answering this question definitively would require taking stock of many things in addition to changes in the arts, the environment, and housing—more by far than can possibly be covered in these pages. Among the obvious ingredients, however, most seem to have improved or increased in amount, variety, and accessibility since the 1950s. Rising prosperity has brought more choices, more possibilities, more comforts and diversions of every kind to enrich the lives of the great majority of Americans. Opportunities for travel have multiplied. Many more people are enjoying skiing, tennis, golf, running, hiking, and other recreational pursuits. Cable television, video cassette recorders, and portable tape players have vastly expanded the range of popular entertainment.

Have any important aspects of the quality of life deteriorated? Almost certainly yes. Commuting times have increased for many families. Although it is hard to measure changes in human relationships, membership in social organizations has dropped substantially since the 1960s (although many people may have forsaken the Elks or the Kiwanis or the Rotary for pursuits they value more). Fear for one's personal safety has unfortunately increased, to the point that over 40 percent of Americans currently acknowledge that there are places within a mile of their homes where they fear to walk alone at night.

What all of this means for the quality of life will depend very much on who is rendering the judgment. A visiting British aristocrat once observed that life in America had obviously declined over the past fifty years, since so few people could still afford to employ servants. A connoisseur of fine arts might deliver a negative verdict simply because of the vulgarity of our popular culture. For the purposes of this volume, however, the judgments of any single person must count for much less than the opinions of the public as a whole.

Fortunately, good data exist on whether Americans *feel* happier today than they did in 1960. By this yardstick, the verdict is clear: there has been no significant change in people's reported happiness over the past thirty to forty years.[40] On the other hand, if one could somehow force every American to choose whether to live in 1960 or to continue in the present, the vast majority would probably decide to remain in the world as it now exists, with all the conveniences, medical advances, and cultural advantages that were not widely available four decades ago.

Which of these verdicts is more suited to our purposes? Probably the latter comes closer to answering our initial question. When commentators speak of the quality of life in Pittsburgh, they refer to the physical surroundings, recreational opportunities, cultural amenities, and other external conditions that people value and consider important to their sense of well-being. On balance, despite some contrary examples, most of these ingredients have improved in quality and abundance for most Americans over the past several decades. Happiness, on the other hand, is more a matter of how one responds to what one has than a reflection of one's possessions and physical surroundings. As a result, except for those who are poor, improvements in the conditions of life often fail to produce equivalent gains in happiness, because new wants and expectations spring up, while experiences that once gave pleasure grow commonplace and lose their savor. In the end, therefore, if Americans are acquiring more and more of what they think they want while achieving no greater lasting satisfaction, that is not a failing of the society, still less of its government, but a personal challenge that must be met in the mind of each individual.

III

OPPORTUNITY

8

Child Policies

Americans, it is said, care little about equalizing the fortunes of rich and poor but feel very strongly that everyone should have an opportunity to achieve as much as they can according to their ability, effort, and aspiration. Opinion polls strongly confirm this impression. Only 29 percent of Americans believe that "it is the responsibility of government to reduce the differences in income between people" (compared with 61 percent of West Germans, 64 percent of Britons, and 81 percent of Italians).[1] But 94 percent of Americans affirm that "our society should do what is necessary to make sure that everyone has an equal opportunity to succeed."[2] Even President Clinton and Speaker Newt Gingrich agree that opportunity should be increased and made a centerpiece of American society.

In no small degree, this near-unanimity of opinion comes about because the words "opportunity" and "equality of opportunity" mean different things to different people. Almost everyone approves of the kind of opportunity that results from economic growth, since growth expands the total supply of attractive possibilities and thus leaves almost everyone in a position that is as good as, or better than, the one occupied before. There is also wide agreement on the need to expand opportunity by doing away with discrimination and other artificial restrictions that unfairly narrow the chances of particular groups, such as Jews, Catholics, and blacks. Forbidding restrictions of this kind expands the options of disfavored groups without depriving others of opportunities they had a legitimate right to expect. The disagreement occurs over efforts to increase opportunities in ways that cost taxpayers money or impose other burdens on people who bear no obvious responsibility for the plight of those whose options stand to be enlarged.

In cases of the latter kind, reasonable people often differ over who does have responsibility for handicaps imposed by past discrimination or by deprivations caused by growing up in blighted neighborhoods or neglectful families. Some people feel that burdens of this sort are part of the normal vicissitudes of life and that individuals can surmount them if they have the will and self-discipline to do so. Others concede that the handicaps are serious but still do not consider them the responsibility of ordinary citizens and taxpayers. Still others feel that society does bear a responsibility and should take active steps to ensure that all individuals have a reasonable chance to get ahead.

The case for intervening "to make sure that everyone has an equal opportunity to succeed" applies most forcefully to the youngest members of society. Because small children are unable to help themselves, there are compelling reasons to try to protect them from serious threats to their health, well-being, and future opportunities. A society such as ours, moreover, which bases its rewards so heavily on achievement, should consider it only fair to do what it can to give all young people a decent chance to compete and succeed. Even in the most practical terms, a nation has much to gain from aiding its children, since the more opportunity they have to learn and develop, the more productive the economy is likely to be. Such help can yield the greatest benefits in the earliest years, when good health, adequate nutrition, and continuous care and stimulation are most likely to affect emotional stability and intellectual development in later life. Funds spent to assist children in these ways often yield sufficient benefits to society that they do not impose a burden on taxpayers, at least in the long run.

The needs of children have become more acute in recent decades, as growing strains on the family have brought new risks to young people. Child abuse, drug use, and severe neglect have increased substantially over the past twenty-five years.[3] High divorce rates and growing numbers of out-of-wedlock births have caused greater numbers of children to spend all or part of their childhood with only a single parent in the home.* Almost half of all the offspring of married

---

*Divorces have risen from an annual level of 9.2 per thousand married women in 1960 to

parents will see their mother and father divorce, while the number of children in single-parent homes has tripled.

Even in traditional families, more and more wives have taken a job, with the result that two-thirds of all married women are currently employed. Many working mothers find themselves worn out by the end of the day, and a growing number of youngsters return from school to find no parent at home. Contact with other relatives or adults of any kind has also diminished: only 5 percent of children see a grand-parent regularly. As a result of these trends, small children receive less close attention and stimulation. According to the Department of Education, only half of all parents with small children tell them a story as often as three times a week, and less than 60 percent read to them every day.[4]

There are limits to what public officials can do to counter these trends and ensure everyone a reasonable start in life. To a large extent, the future prospects of children depend on their natural endowments and on behavior within their family, over which the government can exert little influence. But there is much that the State *can* do. It can take a variety of steps to avoid privations such as hunger and malnu-trition, which can stunt a child's life. It can improve the health of children by ensuring access to medical care and by taking preventive steps such as immunizing infants against disease. It can help young people gain a readiness to learn by establishing preschool programs. It can even encourage closer parental care during the earliest weeks of life by requiring employers to give periods of leave to one or both working parents.

Interventions of this kind may be costly. Nevertheless, according to a recent Louis Harris poll, two-thirds of the American people believe that "as a society, we spend too little on the problems of children."[5] Sixty percent of the public agree that they would be more disposed to vote for candidates who favored children's programs, and the same decisive majority express support for early childhood programs in ed-ucation and health.[6] The question remains how successful America has been in translating these convictions into practical results.

20.7 in 1990. Single-parent families have increased from 9.1 percent of all families to 26.7 percent over the same period. Births to unmarried mothers have jumped from 5.3 percent to 28 percent (64.5 percent of all births to black mothers).

Nutrition and Health Care

The first threat to children's opportunities in life occurs before they are born. Inadequate nutrition prior to birth and during the first years of life can lead to poor health and development and possibly cause neurological and behavioral disorders, such as learning disabilities and mental retardation. Malnutrition is most likely to occur among low-income families, and it is not rare: more than 20 percent of all American children live in families with incomes below the official poverty line, which is set to provide just enough money to sustain a minimally adequate diet. Although reliable data are hard to come by, the president of the Carnegie Corporation reports that "30 percent of blacks and 15 percent of whites in the United States are malnourished in a variety of ways."[7]

To avoid the risks of malnutrition for small children, the federal government in the early 1970s created the Special Supplemental Food Program for Women, Infants, and Children (WIC). This program supplies highly nutritious food to low-income women who are pregnant or breast-feeding an infant, as well as to children up to the age of five. According to the 1991 report of the National Commission on Children, participation in WIC reduces by 15 to 25 percent the chance that high-risk pregnant women will deliver a premature or low-birthweight child.[8] By saving the heavy costs of taking care of such babies, the program is said to return far more than it costs. Yet WIC has never been fully funded and currently serves only about 60 percent of the eligible population of women and children. Although available funds are channeled quite well to serve the neediest families, many mothers and children below the poverty line are still excluded from the program.

Timely, competent medical care can likewise increase the chances of a healthy birth and reduce the risk that infants will suffer debilitating illnesses in their early years. As a result, such care is an important element in a comprehensive program to give all children a good start in life. Although there are no perfect measures to gauge the quality of health care available to children, enough information exists to form at least some tentative impressions.

America has had substantial success in reducing the rate of infant mortality. In 1940, 47 children out of every thousand live births died within one year. By 1965 this figure was virtually cut in half, to 24.7.

By 1980 the number of infant deaths was 12.6, and by 1993 it had dropped to 8.3[9]

Over the past thirty years, however, many other nations have made even faster progress. In 1960, the United States ranked twelfth in infant mortality. By 1990 it had slipped to twentieth.[10]

America's record in reducing the number of low-birthweight babies leaves even more to be desired. In 1950, 7.5 percent of all babies born weighed less than 5.5 pounds. By 1970 the figure had risen to 7.9 percent, and then declined to 6.8 percent by 1980. Since that time, the percentage of low-birthweight babies has not decreased and has even risen slightly.[11]

Once again, comparisons with other nations do not favor the United States. By 1990, with the proportion of low-birthweight babies remaining at 7.0 percent in this country, the corresponding rate for Sweden was 5 percent; for France, 5 percent; for Japan, 6 percent; for Canada, 6 percent; and for Great Britain, 7 percent.[12] In 1990, thirty other nations had records equal to or better than America's.[13]

Prenatal care is one way of helping to ensure a healthy birth. In addition to lowering infant mortality, such care can reduce the risk of having a low-birthweight child by 25 to 50 percent. Moreover—according to Dr. David Hamburg, president of the Carnegie Corporation and an authority on children—of the 11 percent of American children who are born with a handicap, up to one-third could have avoided this fate or had a lesser disability if their mothers had had timely prenatal care.[14]

For more than two decades, a very high percentage of expectant mothers have visited a doctor at some point prior to the birth of a child. A greater challenge for public policy is to have such visits begin during the first few months of pregnancy. The United States has made some headway in this respect during the past twenty-five years. But progress has been slow and has even been reversed slightly since 1980 (Table 8.1).

Although comparative data are not extensive, studies carried out for the Institute of Medicine suggest that most European countries are more successful than the United States in reaching out into the community to enroll expectant mothers in programs of early prenatal care.[15] In Scandinavia, attendance levels approach 100 percent, and the rates of infant mortality and low-birthweight babies are virtually

Table 8.1. **Percent of babies born with prenatal care, by race, 1970–1992.**

	Some care			Care in first trimester		
Year	Total	White	Black	Total	White	Black
1970	92.1	93.7	83.4	68.0	72.3	44.2
1975	94.0	95.0	89.5	72.4	75.8	55.5
1980	94.9	95.7	91.1	76.3	79.2	62.4
1985	94.3	95.2	89.8	76.2	79.3	61.5
1989	93.9	95.1	88.7	75.8	79.2	60.6
1992	94.8	95.8	90.1	77.7	80.8	63.9

Source: National Center for Health Statistics, *Health, United States,* 1994 (1995).

the lowest in the world.[16] In France, prenatal care tends to begin earlier than in the United States, and fewer expectant mothers fail to receive such care.[17]

Programs in the United States are not always well designed to reach expectant mothers, especially in poor communities. Studies show that many women cannot find a doctor who will see them, while others are uninsured and cannot afford to pay the fees.[18] Still others must wait precious weeks while their eligibility is being determined. To be sure, the most effectively administered programs can accomplish only so much. Some poor mothers will not participate, no matter how cheap or convenient the services. Moreover, even the most conscientious doctors and social workers may be unable to persuade pregnant women to give up smoking, drinking, or the use of drugs, despite the threat such habits pose to the birth of a normal child. Still, the evidence suggests that lowering the financial barriers and further improving the accessibility of prenatal care would have beneficial effects in helping more mothers give birth to healthy babies.[19]

Another risk that threatens young children is infectious disease. In 1979, therefore, the Public Health Service announced two goals for America to achieve by 1990 in inoculating youngsters against such common diseases as measles, rubella, DTP (diphtheria-tetanus-pertussis), polio, and mumps. The first was to vaccinate 95 percent of all children attending school. This objective was reached in the mid-1980s. The second was to have 90 percent of all children receive the full basic immunization series before the age of two (when they are especially vulnerable). That objective is far from being achieved. By

1993, the proportion of two-year-olds vaccinated was still below 90 percent for each of the five most common childhood diseases and above 85 percent for only one.[20] The lack of coverage, especially prevalent among the poor, is all the more troubling in light of studies showing that timely vaccinations can bring savings of ten dollars for each dollar spent.[21]

On the whole, other industrial countries have done somewhat better in immunizing their children. What the figures listed in Table 8.2 do not show is that many other less developed countries, such as Singapore, Spain, Costa Rica, Hungary, Czechoslovakia, Poland, and Argentina, report higher immunization rates than those of the United States.

Just why America has had trouble achieving its goal is not altogether clear. Some critics blame the drug companies for the high cost of vaccines, but states that distribute shots free of charge have attained rates of immunization only a few percentage points above the levels elsewhere. Others have argued that fees for giving vaccinations under the Medicaid program are set so low that many doctors serving poor communities will not participate. Still others point out that public health clinics, which may be the only place for poor children to be vaccinated, are often inconveniently located. Finally, if the United States had national computerized records, as Britain and some other countries do, nurses could routinely remind all families who are behind in their shots.

Whatever the reason, recent efforts to improve America's record seem to be bearing some fruit. In 1995, the Center for Disease Control announced that vaccination rates had moved up sharply. Even so, the percentage of small children who had received all the recommended shots was still only 75 percent, well below the 90 percent goal.[22]

In addition to vaccinations and prenatal care, children need con-

Table 8.2. Percent of children immunized against three major diseases, 1990–1994.

Disease	United States	Canada	France	Japan	Sweden	West Germany	United Kingdom
Diphtheria	88	93	89	87	99	70	91
Polio	79	89	92	94	99	90	93
Measles	84	98	76	69	95	75	92

Source: UNICEF, *The State of the World's Children, 1996,* 85 (1996).

venient, affordable medical services. Over the past thirty years, access to health care has improved significantly.[23] Thanks to Medicaid, boys and girls from poor families are now much more likely to visit a physician. By 1980, they were actually seeing a doctor as often as well-to-do children. In the late 1980s, Congress took steps to expand the coverage afforded by Medicaid. States were required to give protection to all pregnant women and children up to age six in families with incomes below 133 percent of the official poverty level. Eventually, protection will extend to all children aged eighteen and under with family incomes below the poverty line.

The proportion of children covered by health insurance has also risen substantially since 1960. Nevertheless, in contrast to the universal coverage long since achieved abroad, 9.6 million (or 13.7 percent) of all American children under eighteen were still without insurance coverage in 1993, even though studies show that the uninsured receive substantially less medical care than those that are covered.[24] More serious still, some 8 million children (or more than 11 percent) were neither covered by insurance nor enrolled in Medicaid.[25]

Parental Leave

Everyone agrees that it is important for a child to have abundant love, care, and attention from one or both parents during the first months of its life. Most experts believe that mothers should have at least six to eight weeks to recover fully from giving birth, and four to six months to help ensure healthy development of the child.[26] Now that so many mothers have entered the work force, this goal is hard to achieve unless one or both parents can stop work for a time to care for a new child and be assured that their jobs will still be there when they return.

All of the other industrial countries surveyed here have passed laws requiring employers to grant stipulated amounts of leave to one or both parents when a child is born. In fact, every one of these nations provides that parents be paid during all or most of the prescribed leave (Table 8.3).

Until recently, the United States was the only industrial country that did *not* have legislation requiring employers to grant parental leave. President Bush vetoed such a law enacted by Congress, on the ground that leave requirements might burden employers unduly and

Table 8.3. Parental-leave legislation, as of January 1995.

Country	Maximum leave	Maximum duration of benefit	Type of benefit	Level of benefit
United States	12 weeks	—	None	None
Japan	Until child is age 1[a]	52 weeks	Proportional to earnings	25% of earnings
West Germany	Until child is age 3[a]	104 weeks	Flat-rate, income-tested	600 DM per month
France	Until child is age 3[a]	Until child is age 3	Flat-rate payment	2,929 FF per month
United Kingdom	26 weeks[b]	18 weeks	Two-tier system: Flat-rate benefit; proportional to earnings for the first 6 weeks	Two-tier system: flat-rate benefit of £52.50 per week; 90% of earnings
Canada	24 weeks[c]	10 weeks	Proportional to earnings[d]	57% of average weekly insurable earnings
Sweden	Until child reaches 18 months	65 weeks	Proportional to earnings for the first 12 months; flat-rate payment for the remaining 3 months	80% of earnings for 10 months[d]; 90% of earnings for 2 months; flat-rate payment for 3 months

Source: OECD, *Employment Outlook*, 175–178 (July 1995).
a. Including maternity leave period.
b. In addition to the fourteen-week basic period of maternity leave.
c. In addition to maternity leave period.
d. The benefit has a maximum ceiling.

thus endanger jobs. With the advent of a new Democratic administration in 1993, a parental leave law was finally passed by Congress and signed by President Clinton. The terms of the new legislation, however, fall far short of those in force in other nations. The statute applies only to enterprises employing more than fifty people. It guarantees only twelve weeks of leave, and even this period need not be with pay. (As of 1993, five states had required temporary disability for most employees, allowing partial compensation for wage loss during the period in which a mother is recovering from childbirth.)

Of course, employers can introduce their own leave policies if they choose, and many have elected to do so. Still, a 1990 report by the Small Business Administration showed that only 14 to 19 percent of firms employing more than fifty workers offered guaranteed leave, while only 5 percent of firms with fifteen or fewer employees had such a policy.[27] As a result, the United States still lags far behind other industrial nations in helping parents to remain with their children during the first months of life.

Child Care

In all industrial democracies, women have entered the labor force in rapidly growing numbers over the past few decades. The United States is no exception. In 1965, only 17 percent of all mothers with children under one year of age were working. By the early 1990s, the figure had risen to more than 50 percent. This flood of women into the work force has led to a growing need to find ways to take care of small children, especially those not yet of school age. Mothers cope with this problem in various ways. Some call upon relatives; others leave their children with friends. But the preferred solution for many parents, the solution currently used in the case of almost a fourth of all small children under the age of three, is some form of daycare or family child care.[28]

In contrast to most fields of public policy, Americans are ambivalent about the use of child care. Many people, especially parents, would like some form of affordable quality child care for all, a policy that would require substantial government support. Others oppose this solution, because they believe that mothers should stay at home with their small children or at least should not be encouraged by government subsidies to leave their offspring with others in order to work. Still others are indifferent to whether mothers work or not, but feel that the decision is a private matter that should not become a burden for the taxpayer.

Regardless of one's view on this question, everyone will agree that parents who choose to leave their children in daycare centers should be able to find centers with reasonable levels of quality. Investigators have discovered that adult relationships during the first three years of life are important in helping infants, especially those from poor families, to develop emotional stability, a sense of personal security, and sound intellectual and linguistic capabilities.[29] To help give every child a decent start, therefore, as well as to minimize disorders that can create problems for society later on, everyone has a stake in achieving reasonable standards of quality in child care. What "quality" means, essentially, is adequately trained caregivers, each responsible for only a small number of children, providing care in a clean and safe environment.

At present, states have the responsibility for maintaining adequate standards of child care. Unfortunately, few states have carried out this task effectively. According to the Carnegie Task Force on Meeting the Needs of Young Children, existing standards of care are "varied, weak, or even non-existent."[30] As the task force described the situation in 1993: "One state allows one adult to care for three infants and another allows one adult to care for twelve infants; twenty-three states do not set any standards for group size. Virtually all states allow infants and toddlers to be cared for by providers who have not completed high school, have no training specific to infant and toddler development, and have received less than five hours of annual in-service training."[31] Salaries for child-care providers are very low, averaging less than $11,000 in 1990. In regulated family child-care homes, half of all caregivers earned less than $8,000 per year. Turnover among staff is high, as one would expect, reaching 26 percent in 1991–1992. In such circumstances, it is hardly surprising that one study of a large sample of daycare centers found that "infants and young toddlers spent over half their time wandering aimlessly; older toddlers were unoccupied a third of the time."[32]

There is room for argument over how much the state should try to regulate minimum standards of child care and to what extent parents should decide for themselves what kind of care they want. But leaving the decision to parents works only if quality care is available at prices families can afford. At present, that situation does not exist. Although the government does pay subsidies to parents of modest means, the programs that do so have only limited coverage, and their eligibility requirements are often arbitrary and unsuited to the needs of poor mothers.[33] As a result, in 1990, among families who paid for their own daycare, those earning less than $15,000 spent 23 percent of their income for this purpose, while those earning from $15,000 to $25,000 devoted 12 percent.[34] Under these conditions, the pressures are enormous to settle for inexpensive child care even though the quality is poor.

The United States is not alone in facing a child-care dilemma, nor is our government the least successful in trying to achieve affordable child care of acceptable quality.[35] Several nations, however, notably Sweden and France, have chosen the much more ambitious route of trying to provide affordable child care of high quality to all working mothers who desire it. In Sweden, for example, parents using public child care pay a fee which is set at levels affordable to all. State and local subsidies cover the rest of the costs. In public child-care centers, every caregiver must take extensive training. And Swedish regulations stipulate that there must be at least two full-time adults for every five children under three years of age and one full-time adult for every five children aged three to five.[36]

One can argue, of course, that the French and Swedish systems are utopian and excessively costly, and that the State should not encourage mothers to abandon their children at such a young age even to daycare of exemplary quality. But these reservations hardly justify the prevailing policies in America. Welfare rules increasingly force mothers with small children to go to work. Declining wages for husbands with only a high school education or less have put great pressure on many wives to take a job in order to maintain the family income. Under these conditions, working mothers are a reality. The question is how their children will be looked after early in their lives, when the nature and quality of their adult relationships may have significant effects on their subsequent emotional and cognitive development. Only a minority of all child-care settings in America currently achieve standards of quality that allow a reassuring answer to this question.

Preschool Programs

To strengthen public education and help all young people get a decent start, the president of the United States and the fifty governors agreed in 1989 on a national goal: that every child arrive at school by the year 2000 in a state of readiness to learn. A key component of the nation's effort to achieve this goal is providing all children with the opportunity to attend some form of preschool.

For almost thirty years, the U.S. government has sought to increase the opportunities of low-income families to send their children to pre-school. The principal way to achieve this goal is through Head Start programs specially designed for poor families. Such programs not only include classes to help small children prepare for school; they offer comprehensive services including nutrition, health care, psychiatric counseling, and efforts to involve parents more closely in the education and development of their children.

Although such programs are popular, their value continues to be a matter of dispute.[37] Most experts agree that an effective preschool program can improve the academic skills of children for a time, although these gains appear to fade after a few years. Most also believe that comprehensive efforts such as Head Start can prepare children from disadvantaged backgrounds to accept the discipline of formal schooling and relate better to teachers. Quite possibly, Head Start teachers succeed in making some parents more involved in the education of their children. The most dramatic possibilities, however, involve the longer-term effects of preschool on the participants. These effects were reported in the so-called Perry Pre-School project, surely one of the most influential social science studies ever conducted. Much of the subsequent popularity of Head Start is traceable to this single piece of research.

The Perry Pre-School study did not actually involve a Head Start program but reported on the results of a much more expensive preschool enrolling more than 120 disadvantaged children and offering elaborate services to help students and their parents. The authors of the study followed the lives of the participants for almost three decades and compared them with the experience of other children of similar background. While cognitive differences faded over time, other differences proved to be striking.[38] Sixty-six percent of the Perry children went on to graduate from college, compared with 45 percent of the control group. Through age nineteen, only 31 percent of the Perry children had ever been arrested, compared with 51 percent of the control group. At twenty-seven, 71 percent of the Perry group were employed, as opposed to only 59 percent of the control children, and the teenage pregnancy rate for the Perry participants was almost one-third lower than the rate for the controls.

Experts remain somewhat puzzled by these findings, since no one yet understands just how a preschool experience could have such a marked influence on behavior many years later. Nevertheless, impressed by the Perry results, the federal government has gradually increased funding for Head Start and other preschool programs under Republican and Democratic administrations. Current federal appropriations for Head Start are above $3 billion per year, and presidents of both parties have announced the goal of making such programs available to all low-income children in America.

Despite the aura of success that has surrounded Head Start, limited funding allowed only 36 percent of all eligible children to be enrolled by 1996. But this was far from the most difficult problem. As more and more mothers have entered the work force, they have come to require some form of child-care setting in which to leave their children for nine hours per day, twelve months per year. For them, preschool programs are rarely suitable, since they continue for only nine months and rarely last all day. As a result, Head Start is increasingly used by welfare mothers who need more help as parents because they tend to have the most severe behavioral problems and the greatest emotional difficulties.[39]

At the same time, federal funding has risen much more slowly than enrollments, so that many of the programs have been cut to half-day and are staffed by underpaid teachers with doubtful qualifications. Average costs per child enrolled in Head Start programs in the early 1990s were little more than half the amount expended on each child in the Perry Pre-School study. Although Congress has recently taken steps to raise the standards for federally funded programs, the quality still appears to be well below that of the program on which so many proponents of Head Start have relied, even as the needs of participating families have increased. With inadequate funds and a clientele with exceptional needs, it is far from clear that the current Head Start program can produce anything like the benefits achieved in the Perry Pre-School experiment.

Other countries have also been expanding their early-education programs. Although the United States is not at the bottom of the list of advanced nations in the percentage of children enrolled in preprimary education, it is certainly below average (Table 8.4).

Whatever view one takes about the problems and potential of preschool, the federal government is looking to Head Start, along with programs for better nutrition and decent health care, to meet its announced goal of enabling every American child by the year 2000 to arrive at school in a state of readiness to learn. For reasons previously

Table 8.4. Percent of children enrolled in pre-primary education, 1992.ᵃ

Country	Age three	Age four
Canada	NA	45.9
France	98.8	100.0
West Germany	30.8	68.5
Japan	23.1	57.6
Sweden	45.2	50.8
United Kingdom	37.0	12.6
United States	28.5	53.0

Source: OECD, *Education at a Glance: OECD Indicators,* 131 (1995).

a. The numbers include full- and part-time enrollment in nursery school, kindergarten, and similar educational programs but exclude child care.

mentioned, however, America is still far from achieving this objective. According to a 1991 Carnegie Foundation survey of 7,000 kindergarten teachers, approximately 35 percent of the nation's children are currently arriving at school unprepared to learn.[40] According to one teacher, "Too many of my children come to school hungry. They are tired or in need of much love and attention. More and more students are coming with deep emotional problems that interfere with their learning." In the words of another teacher, "It's terribly discouraging to see children coming to school who don't know where they live, can't identify colors, and are unable to recite their full and proper name."[41]

In view of these problems, the chances are slim that the United States will come close to reaching its goal by the end of the decade. Although the reasons are numerous and not all within the government's control, the unwillingness to fund federal programs sufficiently to reach all potential beneficiaries or to maintain adequate standards of quality has doubtless contributed to the problem.

The Gap between Belief and Reality

Americans profess a firm belief in giving everyone an opportunity to succeed to the full limit of their abilities and ambitions. Translating this belief into policy, however, has proved to be exceptionally difficult in the case of small children. Part of the problem lies in basic differences of opinion over where the responsibility lies. In a nation that has traditionally set great store by the self-reliance and responsibility of private individuals, what role should the State attempt to play in trying to expand the opportunities of the young? To what extent is this task a responsibility of the family and to what extent is it a matter for the government?

At times, the United States has seemed to answer this question by making the government the ultimate guarantor of universal opportunity. Although Americans have never been keen on plans to redistribute income or limit the rewards of those who manage to succeed, they have strongly supported public schools as a means of enabling everyone to prepare to accomplish as much as their talents and ambitions would allow. The United States was the first nation to provide universal public education. In the past few decades, not only has America invested increasing amounts in its schools; it has also funded preschool programs, subsidized child care, and instituted a variety of other programs to enhance the health, nutrition, and care available to its youngest citizens.

When one looks at other advanced industrial democracies, however, the ambivalence in America's policies toward children becomes immediately clear. Most of these countries have long since instituted universal public education; several now have better high school graduation rates than those of the United States and spend larger shares of their gross domestic product on primary and secondary education. The contrasts become even sharper when one looks at measures to help small children before they arrive at school. Far from doing more than other nations to improve opportunities for the very young, the United States does considerably *less*. Whether one looks at child care, parental leave, immunization rates, access to medical care, or virtually any other measure, America finds itself in the awkward position of falling behind most or all of the other countries discussed here. Although the United States is still the wealthiest of all industrial democracies, poor children in America—that is, children in the poorest 20 percent—grow up in families with incomes that are lower (in purchasing-power parity) than those of comparable families in any other advanced industrialized country.[42] According to one recent study, families of poor children in the United States have *less than two-thirds* the income of comparable families in Sweden, Switzerland, Belgium, and Norway.[43]

It is only fair to point out that the United States has an exceptional number of poor mothers with problems stemming from drug use, illegitimacy, and family breakdown. Helping these parents—whether by prenatal counseling, Head Start programs, immunizations, or day-care—presents difficulties greater than those faced by Europe or Japan. With the handicaps that disadvantaged children face in America, however, and the long-term costs imposed on the entire society, one might have thought that the situation called for exceptional effort to devise effective policies. Instead, many programs for children in the United States are underfunded, poorly organized, and of indifferent quality.

Interestingly, at the grassroots level, one often comes across promising initiatives offering every kind of service to children and families.[44] Local governments, churches, schools, charitable organizations, and neighborhood groups can all be found in one community or another making vigorous efforts of this kind. Some of the programs are outstanding and rival any undertaking of their kind in the world. Where America falters is in pulling these initiatives together to form a comprehensive system capable of reaching all or nearly all children in the society. Exemplary programs, such as the Perry Pre-School, turn into shoddy underfinanced efforts when carried to a national level. Programs of widely acknowledged value are funded for only a fraction of eligible children and are often administered in ways that leave many families unaware of the benefits or confused about how to apply.

With its array of weak and partially funded programs, the United States gives its children less support than any of the countries considered in this study. It is odd that the United States should find itself in this position in view of the strong public approval of programs for children, the many creative initiatives in communities around the country, and the risk that neglect in the earliest years can have costly adverse consequences later on. The net result is that millions of children in America continue to labor under avoidable handicaps that threaten to limit their prospects for a full and productive life.

Race

The plight of black people in this country poses a uniquely vexing problem for Americans today, as it has throughout our history. The root of our concern lies in the fact that blacks did not come to the United States as other immigrants did; they arrived in chains to work as slaves, chiefly as field hands for white plantation-owners. Even after the Civil War had put an end to the practice of slavery, whites continued to discriminate against blacks by denying them the right to vote, to live where they chose, to enter public restaurants and theaters, to compete equally for jobs, and to attend the same schools as other children. This history of oppression has transformed the predicament of blacks into a moral problem, as well as an economic and political question. Although the stakes involved have included such tangible matters as houses, jobs, and college diplomas, the principal battlegrounds on which the issues have been fought have been the hearts and minds of human beings, both black and white.

No period in our history, save perhaps the Civil War, has been marked by such a determined struggle to improve the opportunities for blacks as the years since 1960. From 1965 to 1975, in particular, Washington produced a stream of civil rights legislation, fair-housing laws, affirmative action programs, and busing decrees in an effort to ensure more equal opportunities for all races. What progress has come from all these efforts, and has the government done everything it could and should to advance the cause?

Answering these questions fully would require an investigation of all manner of venues in which the struggle over race has waxed and waned—from places of public accommodation to real estate companies, from employment offices to college admissions committees. This discussion will focus on only three areas of opportunity: the right to vote, the right to live in the neighborhood of one's choice, and the right to attend an integrated school. The following chapter will deal with the opportunities available to blacks and other historically disadvantaged groups to earn a livelihood and pursue their chosen careers.

The Right to Political Participation

Of all the aspects of race, the question of voting has proved the simplest to address.[1] The right of all citizens to go to the polls is broadly understood and accepted. Compared with many forms of racial discrimination, the opportunity to vote is relatively easy to secure. After World War II, at least, opposition was not widespread throughout the land but concentrated in a minority of states in the South.

Throughout the first half of the twentieth century, southern white officials resorted to various means to keep blacks from casting a ballot: intimidation, poll taxes, all-white primary elections, literacy tests. One by one, these methods were declared illegal or unconstitutional. But laws on the books were worth little at the polls without some means of enforcement. Although Congress passed voting rights legislation in 1957 and 1960, these statutes relied on case-by-case litigation before judges who were often unsympathetic. From 1957 to 1962, despite the federal legislation, registration of black voters throughout the United States increased by only 4 percent. Plainly, stronger medicine was required to cure the discriminatory practices.

In 1965, Congress passed a Voting Rights Act with much sharper teeth. The new legislation suspended literacy tests and other exclusionary requirements wherever fewer than half the eligible voters had registered or voted; it authorized the U.S. attorney general to dispatch federal examiners and observers who would prevent intimidation; it required states and counties with low levels of registration or voting to submit all changes in voting procedures for clearance in advance; and it prescribed criminal penalties for violations. The effects were immediately apparent (Table 9.1). The impact on several states in the Deep South was especially noteworthy. Registration of blacks in Alabama rose from 11.0 percent in 1956 to 77.1 percent in 1992. In Lou-

Table 9.1. Reported registration rates in the U.S. South, by race, as percent of population, 1946–1992.

Year	Whites	Blacks
1946	—	3.1
1960	—	28.7
1964	61	41.9
1968	71	58.7
1972	70	55.8
1976	67	59.9
1980	66	55.1
1984	68	66.9
1988	67	63.7
1992	68	65.0

Source: U.S. Bureau of the Census, *Current Population Reports*, P20-466 (1992), and other editions.

isiana, over the same period, it jumped from 3 percent to 77 percent, while in Mississippi it climbed from 5 percent to 74.6 percent.

The effects on voting have been less dramatic, but still significant (Table 9.2). Much of the remaining gap between blacks and whites can probably be explained by socioeconomic differences, since research has shown that such differences, especially in levels of education, significantly affect levels of registration and voting among Americans of all races.[2]

The Voting Rights Act has also had a noticeable effect on the rep-

Table 9.2. Percent of population that reported voting in presidential elections in the U.S. South, by race, 1964–1992.

Year	Whites	Blacks
1964	59.5	44.0
1968	61.9	51.6
1972	57.0	47.8
1976	57.1	45.7
1980	57.4	48.2
1984	58.1	53.2
1988	56.4	48.0
1992	60.8	54.3

Source: U.S. Bureau of the Census, *Current Population Reports*, Series P20-466, v. (1992).

Table 9.3. Number of black elected officials nationwide, 1970–1993.

Year	Federal officials	State officials	County officials	Municipal officials
1970	10	169	92	623
1975	18	281	305	1,573
1980	17	323	451	2,356
1985	20	396	611	2,898
1990	24	423	810	3,671
1993	39	533	913	3,903

Source: Joint Center for Political and Economic Studies, *Black Elected Officials: A National Register* (1993).

resentation of blacks in elected positions. In eleven southern states, the total number of blacks serving in state legislatures and the U.S. Congress jumped from three in 1965 to 176 in 1985.[3] In the South, the percentage of blacks elected to state and local offices rose to higher levels than those achieved in any other section of the country. The same dramatic improvement has occurred in the election of officials nationwide (Table 9.3).

Despite these gains, African Americans are still underrepresented among elected officials, even in the South. By 1985, they made up less than 11 percent of the legislatures in southern states, although they accounted for almost 20 percent of the electorate. By 1993, though blacks made up roughly 12 percent of the total population, they occupied only thirty-eight of the 435 seats in the House of Representatives and only one of the 100 seats in the Senate.[4] In large part, these gaps reflect the fact that blacks are a distinct minority in almost all electoral districts, while candidates normally require a majority to win elections. Under such conditions, access to the ballot box cannot ensure the victory of black candidates, especially where prejudice and suspicion still linger in the minds of the white majority.

Because of this problem, after 1970 the battleground in political participation shifted from removing barriers to registration and voting toward attempting to influence districting to favor or discourage black candidates.[5] As the Voting Rights Act began to affect election turnouts, some states and localities tried to dilute the minority vote by changing from single-member districting to at-large elections or by dividing predominantly black areas among several white districts. Civil rights activists fought back by asking federal judges to protect their voting rights against efforts to dissipate their effects.

Not only did judges strike down the changes sought by southern white officials; they began ordering the creation of electoral districts with a majority or a large minority of black voters. Oddly shaped districts have emerged as a result, reflecting determined efforts to gather together the desired proportion of black voters. These gerry-mandered districts have brought about the election of many black representatives who otherwise might not have prevailed. The frequent result, however, has been to leave control of legislative bodies in the hands of majorities composed of white lawmakers from overwhelmingly white districts who feel little constituent pressure to respond to minority interests. Under these circumstances, just how much blacks have gained from their legal remedies is unclear. Further clouding the outlook for minority representation are recent Supreme Court rulings severely limiting the use of race as a factor in drawing up voting districts.[6]

Whatever the outcome of these districting disputes, the government has clearly made great strides over the years in securing for blacks the right to register and vote on relatively equal terms with whites. The remaining differences in the registration rates of blacks and whites may narrow further as a result of the 1993 Motor-Voter Act, under which states must give all eligible citizens the opportunity to register when they apply for a driver's license and must supply mail-in registration forms to certain agencies that provide welfare services. But giving a minority group the right to vote is not the same as making sure that its interests receive due weight in the councils of government. This dilemma has led some civil rights advocates to propose rules of voting and decision making that will give minorities more power over policy than they can achieve through ordinary electoral means.[7] For the time being, however, such suggestions seem to go well beyond what a majority of Americans are prepared to accept.

Residential Segregation

More than the struggle to vote, the desire to reside in a neighborhood of one's choice has provoked continued controversy in the United States. Blacks, of course, are quick to affirm such a right, and impressions to the contrary notwithstanding, large majorities of them would prefer to live in integrated neighborhoods.[8]

Attitudes among whites have changed substantially over the years on the question of having blacks as neighbors. For a long time, while recognizing that individuals should be able to live where they choose, whites also felt that residents had a strong and legitimate interest in preserving the kind of community they desired. In 1962, therefore, 61 percent of the population agreed that "white people have a right to keep blacks out of their neighborhood if they want to, and blacks should respect that right."[9] Only in 1970 did a slim majority (53 percent) begin to disagree with that statement.[10] By 1994, this majority had climbed to 83 percent, and the right of blacks to live in any community of their choosing free of interference by neighbors or by others seemed widely accepted as a proper goal of public policy.[11]

Despite its apparent support, however, the goal is far from being achieved in practice. Indeed, the nation is much more segregated now than it was at the beginning of the century. Prior to 1900, there was little racial division, even in southern cities. Either there were too few blacks to attract much attention, or they were integrated only in the sense of occupying servants' quarters in prosperous white neighborhoods. Whatever the reason, the most highly segregated city in the United States in 1890 was Indianapolis, where the average black lived in a neighborhood in which only 13 percent of the residents were of his own race.[12]

Residential segregation gradually increased, however, especially after 1930. By 1970 the average black, even in northern cities, lived in a far more segregated community than Indianapolis had been eighty years before (Table 9.4). Since 1970, segregation in most American

Table 9.4. Percent of black residents in neighborhood where average black resides, 1930 and 1970.

City	1930	1970
Boston	19.2	66.1
Chicago	70.4	89.2
Los Angeles	25.6	73.9
Philadelphia	27.3	75.6
New York	41.8	60.2

Source: Douglas S. Massey and Nancy A. Denton, *American Apartheid*, 48 (1993).

cities has diminished moderately. By and large, however, it has dropped significantly only in smaller, newer cities, especially in the South and West. In the largest and oldest cities, where most urban blacks reside, the situation has changed only slightly over the past quarter of a century.[13]

Of course, not all blacks are trapped in large cities. From 1970 to 1990, blacks living in the suburbs increased by 125 percent, while the number of white suburbanites grew by only 46 percent. By 1990, 32 percent of blacks living in metropolitan areas had managed to move to the suburbs.[14] Still, suburban living has not brought an end to segregation. In the 1980s, the average black in a northern suburb lived in a neighborhood that was 70 percent black. Even the well-to-do did not escape these trends. By 1980, the neighborhoods of blacks making more than $50,000 per year were almost as segregated as those occupied by African Americans of much more modest means.[15]

The patterns of segregation that exist today are the product of countless decisions by private citizens about where to live and whom to choose as neighbors. But public officials are implicated as well. Over the years, government policy has repeatedly played a crucial role in helping whites create the neighborhoods they wanted at the expense of blacks.

In 1934, Congress created the Federal Housing Administration to guarantee home mortgages. As an instrument to stimulate housing construction, the FHA was a great success. Nevertheless, it discriminated blatantly against blacks in issuing mortgages and even recommended the use of exclusionary racial covenants in white areas in order to safeguard land values. From 1945 to 1960, the FHA granted only 2 percent of its mortgages to blacks.[16] Even when President Kennedy issued orders to stop discrimination in lending, FHA administrators dragged their feet. Not until 1980 was the final regulation passed to put a halt to racially biased practices.

Mortgage rates were not the only means of keeping blacks out of the suburbs. Federal highway construction programs in the 1950s also contributed to this result. The new freeways facilitated the movement of whites to the suburbs, and were frequently sited in ways that divided black communities from other parts of the city, increasing their isolation. Zoning policies and building codes offered still other ways of keeping suburbs segregated. With these devices, suburban officials could push the cost of housing beyond the reach of all but a very few blacks and thus effectively exclude them.

Local control over the siting of public housing projects guaranteed that public projects would not become a vehicle for moving blacks en masse into a suburb against its will. Although officials in some states tried periodically to place low-income projects in middle-income communities, fierce resistance almost always ensued. In the 1950s and 1960s, therefore, virtually all housing projects for the poor ended up in inner-city areas. When it became clear after 1970 that such practices could not continue, local officials stopped making applications for public housing.

The federal government has gradually come to recognize an obligation to protect the right of blacks to live where they choose. But officials have moved far more cautiously and halfheartedly than they did in the case of voting. When Congress passed the Fair Housing Act of 1968, which prohibited discrimination in the sale or rental of housing, it provided methods of implementation so weak that the law had little impact. Enforcement was largely left to private suits, and even for those hardy enough to try to prove discrimination in court, the statute of limitations was limited to 180 days, and punitive damages were capped at $1,000. The Department of Justice was not permitted to sue unless it could prove a pattern or practice of discrimination, while the Department of Housing and Urban Development (HUD) was allowed only to investigate complaints and offer to conciliate. In the ensuing years, HUD referred no more than 10 percent of its investigations to the Department of Justice for further action, and only a small fraction ever ended in litigation. Thus, as a mechanism to help blacks live where they chose, the Fair Housing Act was ineffective.[17]

In 1989, a HUD study revealed that black renters encountered discrimination 53 percent of the time and black home buyers 59 percent of the time.[18] In that same year, Congress passed a new Fair Housing Act, which remedied the deficiencies in the earlier law. The statute of limitations was extended. The limit on punitive damages was raised to $10,000. HUD could now investigate on its own initiative, and the Department of Justice was empowered to sue on behalf of aggrieved individuals.

These new provisions will doubtless help discourage real estate agents from discriminating in their sales and rentals. After all, the next black client they refuse to help may turn out to be a government agent in disguise, ready to turn them in for violating the law. Nevertheless, some discrimination will continue undetected. Moreover, suburbs in most states retain their power to uphold zoning restrictions and to resist efforts to place low-income housing projects in their midst. More important, even if legal measures succeed in helping black families purchase or rent where they wish, they cannot force their white neighbors to remain.

The best hope for integrated neighborhoods resides in the gradually improving attitudes of whites toward the right of blacks to live where they choose. For the moment, however, the neighborhood preferences of blacks and whites are still incompatible. Although 88 percent of whites believe that blacks have a right to live wherever they want, 57 percent said they would feel uncomfortable in a neighborhood that was one-third black.[19] For their part, African Americans overwhelmingly prefer to live in integrated neighborhoods, but the neighborhood most of them seek would be 50 percent black, far above the comfort level for the great majority of whites.[20]

So long as these conflicting preferences persist, efforts to integrate neighborhoods are likely to produce white flight. Moreover, with heightened concern over the growth of crime and drugs and violence in black communities, white neighborhoods may continue to fight successfully to block official efforts to bring poor minorities into their midst. In the end, therefore, persistent segregation in housing is linked to all the other social ills of poor and blighted neighborhoods in ways that dim the prospect of conquering residential segregation by housing laws alone.

Education

By any measure, the education of black Americans was in a dismal state in 1950.[21] Fewer than 25 percent of all blacks graduated from high school. More than half did not remain in school beyond the eighth grade. Only 3 percent of blacks had completed college, less than a third of the proportion of whites who had done so. Black schools in the South tended to have much shorter academic years, much larger classes, and much lower salaries for teachers.

Four years later, the Supreme Court finally overturned the generations-old doctrine holding that segregated schools could be equal, and therefore lawful, under the Constitution.[22] For more than a decade, the federal government did little to enforce the decision, as southern politicians talked of elaborate schemes to keep schools as they were. Eventually, however, the Supreme Court's ruling began to be enforced, and rural areas and small towns in the South were compelled to desegregate their schools. In short order, black children and white children began to sit together in the same classrooms.

The cities, however, were quite a different matter. Patterns of residential separation soon revealed that merely reassigning students to the nearest school would do little to alter the racial makeup of student bodies. Blacks would continue to attend their neighborhood schools, and whites would do the same, with very little mixing of the races.

In 1968, the Supreme Court launched a vigorous attack on this problem by declaring that wherever residential segregation was partly the result of government policies, it would not be enough simply to cease requiring that black students and white students be separately educated.[23] Instead, authorities would have an affirmative duty to integrate their schools according to clear timetables. Three years later, the Court upheld the busing of children as an appropriate judicial remedy to achieve this goal.[24] In the same year, the Justices moved on northern cities by permitting complainants to attack de facto segregation by simply proving that government policies such as zoning had contributed to racial separation.[25]

These decisions inspired the courts to make much more determined efforts to end segregation in schools. Over the protest of crowds of angry residents, schoolbuses drove into all-white communities carrying black children. Cries of anguish, official requests for delays, riots, and bloodshed all failed to deter federal judges from shaking up accustomed patterns of schooling. Even the doubts and reservations of Richard Nixon did not stop the Department of Justice from bringing suit against many metropolitan school districts in the late 1960s and early 1970s.

As the furor continued, however, federal judges began to falter in their efforts to achieve racial balance in the schools. They stopped short of moving beyond city limits, refusing to require entire metropolitan areas to accept a comprehensive integration plan. As a result, all-white suburbs avoided the desegregation orders entirely, and whites within large cities had only to leave and take up residence in a nearby town in order to escape from busing requirements. As time went on, courts stopped ordering busing and instead became more receptive to voluntary plans, featuring incentives such as magnet schools with expensive facilities and attractive curricula, to lure white students into predominantly black areas. By 1990, the era of forced integration seemed to have come to an end. Even black mayors began to express opposition to mandatory busing.

Now that the tumult over desegregation and busing seems to have subsided, how much change has actually occurred over the past thirty years? Table 9.5 gives a summary. Similar trends have occurred in the percentages of whites enrolled in schools attended by a typical black student. After rising from 32 percent to more than 36 percent during the 1970s, the proportion gradually declined to 34.4 percent in 1991.[26]

Table 9.5. **Percent of black students in heavily minority schools, 1968–1992.**

Year	Predominantly (more than half) minority schools	Intensely (90–100 percent) minority schools
1968–1969	76.6	64.3
1972–1973	63.6	38.7
1980–1981	62.9	33.2
1986–1987	63.3	32.5
1991–1992	66.0	33.9

Source: Gary Orfield, *The Growth of Segregation in American Schools: Changing Patterns of Separation and Poverty since 1968,* 7 (1993).

A clear pattern emerges from these figures. Prior to 1968, segregation diminished very little in the nation's schools. Only after the Supreme Court began to insist on affirmative efforts to desegregate did progress occur. Interestingly, the greatest change took place in the South, where the percentage of black students attending predominantly segregated schools dropped from almost 80 percent in 1968 to just over 20 percent in 1976. Nationwide, although integration increased substantially for a few years, it slowed by the early 1970s and stopped completely after 1980. In the ensuing decade, the percentage of black students attending predominantly segregated schools continued to fall only in the West.[27]

Desegregation and busing were not the only actions taken by the government to improve the education of blacks. In the 1960s, Congress began to fund Head Start and similar forms of preschool education for low-income children. The proportion of black children enrolled in preschool has grown to more than 50 percent, with participation rates virtually equal to those of whites.[28]

Under Title I of the National Defense Education Act, Congress also began in the 1960s to give funds for compensatory education to schools with large concentrations of disadvantaged students. By and large, these moneys were used to provide more individualized and small-group instruction emphasizing basic skills. By the mid-1990s, spending under what is now termed Chapter 1 was nearing $7 billion per year and reaching more than 6 million students, many of whom were black.

What has been the impact of these government policies on the academic achievement of black students? With respect to desegregation, much depends on how schools were integrated and what kind of racial climate exists. But the great majority of researchers seem to agree that integrated schools do not have adverse effects on either black or white students.[29] Although the results are divided, most investigators have also found that blacks gain in math and reading, especially if desegregation begins in the early grades and occurs in schools that are predominantly white but have a critical mass of minority students.[30] In addition, several longer-term studies suggest that black graduates of desegregated schools, at least in the North, are more likely to attend desegregated colleges, live in integrated neighborhoods, find jobs in occupations heavily populated by whites, and send their children to integrated schools.[31] In short, school integration does seem to help somewhat in bringing about a desegregated society.

Studies on the effects of preschool programs, such as Head Start, indicate that these experiences can improve academic performance but only temporarily.[32] There is some evidence, however, that properly administered programs may give rise to other kinds of long-term gains, such as lower dropout rates and fewer instances in which students have to repeat a grade. Compensatory education under so-called Chapter 1 programs has led to even more evaluation studies. The largest of these, involving 120,000 students, showed significant gains in mathematics for grades one to six and significant reading gains for students in grades one to three, though not for grades four, five, and six.[33] But a later study commissioned by Congress showed no beneficial effects from the program. According to some critics, Congress diluted the potential benefits of Chapter 1 by opening eligibility for funding so widely that

90 percent of the nation's school districts could qualify. Others claimed that disadvantaged students were often stigmatized by being singled out for special instruction.

Whatever the merits of Title I and Head Start, black Americans have made greater progress in education over the past forty years than most people appreciate. They currently spend almost as many years in school as whites. Among students with the same economic background, dropout rates for blacks are now no higher than they are for whites. From the 1970s to 1990, thirteen-year-old blacks closed almost 50 percent of the gap separating them from white students in reading, 20.8 percent of the gap in science, and 35.7 percent of the gap in math.[34] Seventeen-year-olds have raised their scores to cut the racial gap by more than 40 percent in reading and almost 45 percent in math.[35]

Government programs have probably contributed to this progress. Yet other forces have doubtless played a larger role, especially the great migration that took blacks from farms and rural poverty in the South and brought them to cities where they could acquire more education and better jobs. Now that this movement is largely complete, the outlook for further progress seems less certain. Blacks still lag well behind whites according to most indices of achievement. Closing this gap cannot be accomplished by schools alone; it will depend on a host of other influences—family structure, nutrition, employment opportunities, housing, and the prevalence of drugs—that shape the environment in which young people grow and develop and acquire their ambitions for the future.

The Bottom Line

What verdict can we pass upon this record of social policy over the past thirty years? According to a recent study by Jennifer Hochschild, blacks and whites tend to disagree on this question.[36] Since the 1960s, whites have generally become more optimistic that progress toward equality has occurred and that racial discrimination has significantly declined. Although there are wide variations in the polls, blacks seem to have moved in the opposite direction, becoming increasingly discouraged about race relations and discrimination. Curiously, college-educated, middle-class blacks, who would seem to have benefited most from changes in racial policies, have become more pessimistic than less educated blacks. What accounts for these differences of opinion, and which group is closest to the truth?

On the optimistic side, one can hardly deny the progress that has been made in enacting laws to promote equality. Over the past few decades, strong legislation has been passed to ensure voting rights, entry to places of public accommodation, nondiscrimination in housing and employment, and equal access to college. Regulations have been implemented that grant favorable treatment to minorities in employment, admission to colleges and universities, even contracts to do business with the government. Although one can debate just how effective each of these measures has been, most blacks would acknowledge that they have been at least somewhat helpful and that they should definitely not be repealed.

In addition to these legal developments, major changes have also taken place in the attitudes of Americans toward racial issues.[37] The percentage of people who feel that whites should automatically have the first chance at any kind of job fell from 52 in 1944 to only 3 in 1972, when the question was dropped from opinion surveys. The percentage who object to having their child go to a school that is half black fell from 49 in 1958 to 10 in 1990. The percentage of whites who said that they would definitely move or might decide to move if blacks came to live next door dropped from 45 in 1963 to only 5 in 1990. One can always question the sincerity of answers to such surveys. Still, only a hardened cynic would deny that a genuine change has taken place in the minds of many Americans.

A skeptic might reply that surveys of this kind simply display a new, "politically correct" hypocrisy. White Americans may now understand that they must accept equality among the races as a matter of principle. Yet they continue to oppose government efforts to put the principle into practice through busing, affirmative action, or fair-housing legislation. Though superficially plausible, this argument is a bit extreme. Whites are not against *all* practical measures to achieve equality. They do support antidiscrimination legislation and laws guaranteeing blacks the right to vote. The laws they oppose are ones that grant minorities a preference in getting jobs and applying to college or that impose remedies, such as busing, which disrupt the lives of families and children.[38] One can disagree with such measures and still not harbor prejudice toward minorities or deny their right to equal treatment.

Blacks themselves are much less likely to support busing or affirmative action than to affirm the principle of equal access to jobs and schools.[39]

In the end, therefore, although one can argue the point forever, it seems hard to deny that real advances have been made over the past several decades both in legislation and in people's attitudes toward racial equality. It is equally clear that progress has occurred in the place of blacks in the society. The percentage of African Americans in colleges and professional schools has plainly risen, housing segregation has diminished at least slightly in many cities, voting has increased, and the black middle class has grown substantially. Even the percentage of African Americans living in poverty has decreased since the early 1960s.

Why, then, should blacks be more discouraged and disillusioned about the prospects for equal treatment? One obvious reason is that after hopes were raised and expectations aroused, the pace of progress toward full equality has clearly slowed over the past twenty years. Public schools are no more integrated now than they were in the mid-1970s. The wage gap between blacks and whites has not narrowed in the past fifteen years. College graduation rates for blacks have not risen significantly since 1970. And the worst big-city ghettos are, if anything, even more segregated and filled with poor families than they were a quarter-century ago.

But why should middle-class blacks, who have gained the most from racial progress, feel especially pessimistic about the prospects for equality? Even in the 1980s, their incomes rose faster than those of most white families. They moved to the suburbs in unprecedented numbers. They attended leading universities and gained jobs in the best corporations, hospitals, and law firms. Why, then, all the disappointment and despair?

One can only speculate about the reasons. It is likely, however, that many educated blacks in the 1960s saw racial inequality as primarily a southern problem—and a problem that could be largely overcome by legal means. What the past thirty years have brought is the disheartening realization that racial issues cannot be solved by laws alone and that they are rooted in feelings of prejudice and distrust that are by no means confined to the South. It is a bitter lesson indeed to discover that laws to desegregate the schools are enough to lead white parents to enroll their children in private schools, that fair-housing ordinances can cause white families to sell their homes and move to other communities, and that preferential admissions policies and affirmative action laws quickly provoke humiliating debates questioning the native intelligence and intellectual competence of one's race. In a very real sense, therefore, the end of discrimination in law has brought educated blacks more directly in contact with prejudice and racial stereotypes that are highly personal and hence even harder to bear. Worst of all, contemporary America has placed educated blacks in a confusing shadow world where it is hard for them to know whether the setbacks they experience are due to their own shortcomings or to racial discrimination, and equally hard to tell whether, when they advance, they have truly excelled or only been moved ahead as a grudging concession to comply with some legal requirement.[40]

In contrast, poor blacks are less likely to mix daily with whites or to feel the weight of discrimination and racial stereotyping. As they watch other blacks succeeding not only in entertainment and athletics but in politics, business, and the professions, they can more easily believe—as most poor whites have traditionally believed—that their bad fortune is due not to their race but to some personal failing of their own.

How can one evaluate the government's role in contributing to this mixed record of racial progress? Certainly, public policies have had a major impact on the opportunities for black Americans. Many of the disadvantages that still keep blacks from enjoying equal opportunities first arose through barriers that governments had a hand in making, from the earliest segregation laws and racial covenants to the subtler influence of mortgage guarantees and zoning requirements. Conversely, voting rights legislation, preferential admissions policies in public universities, and desegregation decrees had powerful effects in expanding the civic and educational opportunities of blacks in the 1960s and 1970s.

In recent years, the federal government has fought for racial equality with much less intensity than it did during the decade beginning in the early 1960s. In those years, courts, Congress, and administrative agencies joined in an unprecedented attack on the principal forms of discrimination. Had judges, legislators, and administrators continued this effort by instituting metropolitan area busing, enforcing fair-housing laws vigorously, and building low-income housing in middle-class communities, more of the momentum built up in the early 1970s might have been sustained.

Yet this conclusion is far from certain. The gains to be made by legal compulsion are often limited, as resourceful citizens of means find ways to circumvent the law's requirements. How much added progress would have occurred by pressing harder for the civil rights agenda must therefore remain conjectural. The subtler costs to race relations of perpetuating the intense controversy of the early 1970s are equally hard to gauge. In a democracy, public opinion must eventually count heavily in shaping the direction of policy. And in the case of busing and racial preferences, public opinion has been consistently opposed to government policy by a wide margin.

The United States is not unique in finding it difficult to eradicate prejudice. No nation and certainly no government has yet succeeded in changing popular feelings to a point sufficient to guarantee full equality for all racial groups. Over the past three decades, although minorities and other immigrants have arrived in substantial numbers in France and England, neither government appears to have done any more than officials in the United States to overcome discrimination. Indeed, with all the equivocation and delay, it is hard to think of any advanced industrial nation that has worked harder to tear down racial barriers and promote equality, or any that has persevered as strongly in the face of such angry resistance from large segments of its people. Unfortunately, the results of this labor are thus far limited. Like the proverbial half-filled glass of water, the verdict on the record of the past thirty years must remain very much in the eye of the beholder.

10

Career Opportunities

America has always radiated a sense of unlimited opportunity. The vision of land, individual freedom, and a new start in life has drawn millions of immigrants to these shores since the Pilgrims first arrived in 1620. From the Horatio Alger stories to autobiographies such as *The Americanization of Edward Bok,* the dream of rising from rags to riches in the New World kindled ambitions in minds and hearts both here and overseas.

Hopes of personal advancement continue to attract large numbers of people to this country. To what extent, however, is America's reputation truly deserved? Are career opportunities for the able and energetic more abundant here than in other industrial democracies and more equally distributed throughout the entire population? Have they been increasing or dwindling in recent years? How much can government do to break down barriers and expand opportunities, and has it accomplished as much as it could along these lines?

Social Mobility

In the past few decades, many scholars have sought to measure the extent of social mobility and opportunity in various societies. Most of them have proceeded by trying to ascertain how much success sons have had in moving to jobs with higher status or higher rates of pay than their fathers achieved.

Mobility of this kind can come about for either of two very different reasons. Sons may surpass the achievements of their fathers because the economy has evolved in ways that substantially increase the number of high-status positions. For example, the industrial revolution caused a massive shift in employment from the agricultural to the manufacturing sector. This transformation led to large increases in the number of better-paying factory jobs, along with growing opportunities in management and the professions. More recently, the manufacturing sector has receded in importance, while the service sector has greatly expanded. This shift has had the effect of increasing the number of jobs both in challenging, highly paid fields, such as information processing, financial management, and law, and in low-paid, low-status positions in restaurants, hotels, stenographic pools, and the like. Thus, the move from manufacturing to services has meant desirable new opportunities for better-educated men and women but limited pay and status for many people with no more than a high school education.

In addition to changes brought about by shifts in the mix of occupations, mobility can also increase because barriers of class, gender, and color have diminished, thus making it easier for disadvantaged groups to move into desirable jobs from which they were previously excluded. These changes in what scholars refer to as circulation mobility are chiefly responsible for the growth of black lawyers from 1 percent of the profession to more than 3 percent since 1960. Unlike structural mobility, which is usually a product of economic growth and thus involves an increase in the total supply of opportunities, circulation mobility is chiefly a matter of how fairly society distributes the opportunities that already exist. From a policy standpoint, however, circulation mobility is important, because artificial barriers of race, gender, and social class are unjust as well as harmful to economic efficiency and hence should be removed with the help of government. It is this kind of mobility that forms the principal subject of the discussion which follows.

Much controversy has arisen over whether individuals can improve their status more readily in the United States than in other industrialized countries. For a long time, many people assumed that mobility was greater in America because ours was a classless society and the quintessential "land of opportunity." In the 1950s, however, Seymour Martin Lipset and Reinhard Bendix looked at the evidence and found that there was nothing exceptional about mobility rates in the United

States.[1] If opportunities were greater in America, it was only because its economy had grown faster than that of most other countries.

This conclusion has been repeated more recently by other investigators, especially John Goldthorpe of Oxford, using more sophisticated statistical techniques.[2] One recent study even concluded that Germans in the 1970s and 1980s were somewhat *more* likely than Americans to make major advances up the income scale.[3] In view of these findings, one cannot say with confidence that mobility is higher in the United States than in other advanced nations or that America is an exceptionally open society. Still, not all scholars agree with Goldthorpe, and no one seems to be arguing that other societies are substantially *more* open than the United States.[4]

Most traditional studies of social mobility try to measure the total amount of movement up or down the status hierarchy from one generation to another. But research of this kind may not tell us much about the extent to which individuals have been hampered in their careers by reason of their race, gender, or socioeconomic origin. To get at this question, one must move beyond traditional studies of mobility and look at each of the principal social barriers to opportunity in our society—those that affect minorities, women, and persons growing up in poverty.*

Racial Discrimination

For generations, blacks have fared much worse than whites in finding jobs and earning money. Their wages have always been substantially below the average for whites, and they have long had rates of unemployment at least twice as high. Over the past half-century, however, their earnings have improved substantially relative to those of white

---

*Conventional studies of social mobility do not tell us much about the extent of artificial socioeconomic barriers to career advancement, because a lack of circulation mobility can result either from the existence of class-based barriers or simply from the influence of heredity and family upbringing on children's later careers. In other words, mobility may be low not only because of prejudice and discrimination but because a society with occupations distributed entirely according to merit could conceivably reproduce much the same pattern of achievement generation after generation merely because successful parents tend to have successful children. Until we prove that achievement does not tend to reproduce itself in this fashion, we cannot know what to make of a given rate of social mobility or to what extent enlightened policy can change it. See Christopher Jencks, *What Is the True Rate of Social Mobility?* in Ronald Breiger (ed.), *Social Mobility and Social Structure,* 103 (1990).

workers.[5] In 1939, the hourly wages of black men were only 45.5 percent of whites' wages. The proportion rose to 62 percent by 1949, 63 percent by 1959, 68 percent by 1969, and 79.3 percent by 1979, before declining somewhat in the 1980s.[6]

The earnings gap between black women and white women has narrowed even more rapidly. In 1940, black women were apparently more disadvantaged than black men compared with whites of the same sex. Over the intervening years, however, they moved ahead at a faster rate. By 1991, median earnings of black women were 90 percent of those of white women.[7]

Not all of these differences are the result of racial discrimination by employers. Some of the explanation lies in differences in education. Fortunately, the gap in years of schooling between blacks and whites has shrunk over the past half-century from four years to less than one.[8] If we compare students of similar family structure and social background, blacks and whites today have approximately the same likelihood of dropping out of high school or attending college.[9]

These gains have helped narrow the earnings gap separating black workers and white workers. After correcting for the remaining differences in education, however, significant disparities in earnings still appear to exist (Table 10.1). Some of the remaining differential may be due to the fact that blacks tend to do less well than whites of equivalent education on standardized tests of cognitive skills. But it is highly unlikely that these differences can explain as much as one-half of the earnings gap currently separating black and white high school and college graduates. Christopher Jencks points out that the existing nine-to twelve-point difference in standardized test scores between blacks

Table 10.1. Wage gap for full-time, year-round black male workers, by level of schooling, 1992.

Amount of schooling	Percent of whites' earnings received by blacks
High school dropout	79
High school graduate	78
College graduate	76
Master's degree	87

Source: U.S. Bureau of the Census, *Current Population Reports*, Series P60-184, *Money Income of Households, Families and Persons in the United States, 1992,* 119, 123 (1993).

and whites ordinarily translates into differences of only 6 to 9 percent in pay. Although subtle differences of motivation and work habits might account for some of the remaining differential, it seems unlikely that they could account for all of it.[10]

Black women have fared much better in closing the gap separating them from white women. In 1992, black female high school graduates were earning 97.4 percent of their white counterparts, while blacks who held a bachelor's or master's degree were earning more than 100 percent.[11] Apparently, then, the problem of racial discrimination in employment has virtually disappeared for black women. This is not to say that their employment problems have vanished. They still share the disadvantages of all women, who continue to earn less than men, even after correcting for education. Thus, although black women have narrowed the gap between their wages and those of white men, the latter still earned approximately 30 percent more than black women in 1990, even after controlling for education and hours and weeks of employment.

Blacks, both men and women, also made impressive advances up to 1980 in securing better-paying, higher-status jobs. Table 10.2 re-

Table 10.2. Black men and women in selected occupations, as percent of all workers, 1939–1984.

Occupation	1939	1949	1959	1969	1979	1984
Black men						
Professionals	1.8	2.2	3.8	7.8	10.7	8.0
Proprietors, managers and officials	1.3	2.0	3.0	4.7	6.7	6.3
Skilled craftsmen	4.4	7.8	9.5	13.8	17.1	15.8
Black women						
Professionals	4.3	5.7	6.0	10.8	14.8	13.9
Proprietors, managers and officials	0.7	1.4	1.8	1.9	3.7	5.2
Skilled craftsmen	0.1	0.7	0.5	0.8	1.4	2.6

Source: Gerald D. Jaynes and Robin M. Williams, Jr., eds., *A Common Destiny: Blacks and American Society*, 273 (1989).

veals the progress made in several categories of employment requiring high skills. These trends have brought about a modest increase in the number and share of blacks whose earnings lift them into the middle class. From 1970 to 1990, the percentage of black households earning more than $75,000 (in 1990 dollars, unadjusted for the Consumer Price Index) grew from 1.5 percent to 3.8 percent, while the percentage earning $50,000–$75,000 rose from 7.0 to 8.1.[12] Underlying these figures are increasing numbers of black professionals who are now represented at least to a limited extent in the leading corporate hierarchies, hospital staffs, university faculties, law firms, and government offices throughout the country.

The economic progress of blacks has been accompanied by profound changes in the attitudes of Americans toward employment discrimination over the past fifty years. As late as 1944, a majority of whites believed that if an opportunity for promotion came along, a white worker should be preferred over a black worker even if the latter were more qualified. By 1972, the prevailing opinion had changed so completely that 96 percent of whites believed the opposite, and surveys stopped asking the question.[13] Americans now affirm overwhelmingly that all workers should have equal employment opportunities according to their abilities and effort.

If that were all there was to the matter, it would be simple to translate this principle into law by passing a statute prohibiting all forms of employment discrimination based on race. Indeed, such legislation has been on the books for many years. Though plagued with huge backlogs of cases and chronically long delays, antidiscrimination laws appear to have had at least some effect in reducing racial bias in the workplace.[14] But some employers continue to discriminate, either because they are prejudiced themselves or because they fear that hiring blacks in certain positions will create frictions among co-workers or cause their customers to stay away. Such discrimination is often hard to detect, but few deny that it exists. Further obstacles arise because many employers engage, often unwittingly, in practices that subtly work against blacks. For example, a small-business owner seeking new workers will frequently ask his white workers to recommend a friend, or will call an employment agency that has no contacts in the black community.

The federal government has gone to considerable lengths to overcome such barriers through the device of affirmative action programs.

These programs require all organizations with more than fifteen employees who do business with the government to prepare a detailed plan comparing the level of their current employment of minorities (and women) to the available pool of potential employees with the requisite education and skills. Employers whose proportion of minority employees is lower than the percent of minority workers in the available labor pool must then set goals for themselves for the next few years along with specific steps to eliminate the gap as quickly as they deem possible.

The rules make clear that a company is not bound to achieve the goals it sets for itself; only a good-faith effort is required. Goals are intended as targets, not as quotas. Nevertheless, many critics have charged that affirmative action plans often turn subtly into something akin to a requirement to hire minority workers. Moreover, some court remedies for past discrimination do impose hiring quotas, while other government programs offer preferences to minorities in hiring public employees or awarding contracts to private firms. These methods have provoked great controversy and have consistently been opposed by large majorities of whites. The Supreme Court ruled in 1995 that programs of racial preference at all levels of government will be subject to strict scrutiny and upheld only if there is a "compelling interest" and if the preferences are "narrowly tailored" to address that interest and no more.[15] The federal government is reviewing programs of this kind to decide whether they should be continued.

What effects has affirmative action had on the employment of blacks? This question has given rise to prolonged controversy, and disagreements still abound. Nevertheless, the following conclusions seem reasonably secure.

First, most studies comparing firms subject to affirmative action with those that are not find that the former have hired somewhat larger numbers of black employees. For example, one investigator concluded that the employment of black men rose 0.62 percent faster per year in firms subject to affirmative action than in other firms of comparable size and location.[16] Another study found that black men were 8 percent *less* likely than white men in 1966 to work in firms subject to affirmative action but were 26 percent *more* likely to do so by 1980.[17]

Second, in cities in which local governments were found to have discriminated, courts imposed stringent remedies that imposed hiring quotas and protected minorities against layoffs. In these cities, the number of minority workers on municipal payrolls increased substantially in such traditionally all-white fields as fire fighting and police work. Minorities also made major employment gains in the federal government, although the most dramatic improvements for minority men occurred prior to 1960, suggesting that factors other than affirmative action were responsible.

Third, it is harder to estimate gains in wages due to affirmative action, since other factors, such as changing levels of education, also affect the relative pay of blacks and whites. According to a recent Rand Corporation study, affirmative action probably contributed strongly to the narrowing of black-white wage differentials from 1965 to 1975.[18] Since the late 1970s, however, wage differentials have not diminished, partly because the educational gap between blacks and whites began to narrow more slowly and partly because earnings declined for low-skilled and moderately skilled jobs in which blacks are disproportionately represented.

Fourth, although employers subject to affirmative action rules may have increased their employment of blacks, other employers appear to have hired *fewer* black men. In part, the decline may result from the disappearance of manufacturing jobs in cities where most blacks reside. In part, the problem may reflect the rising number of blacks with criminal records.[19] Whatever the reason, black men, especially high school dropouts, have had a diminishing ratio of weeks worked per year relative to whites.[20] By 1992, although employed blacks were earning 75 to 80 percent of the wages of comparably educated whites, *annual earnings* of black men were only 68 percent of the levels for white males, because blacks worked fewer weeks per year.[21]

Much disagreement persists over the net effects of affirmative action. Some analysts believe that it had a substantial role in accounting for the wage gains of blacks in the late 1960s and 1970s and that the downgrading of affirmative action helps explain the failure of blacks, especially college-educated blacks, to progress during the 1980s. Other writers disagree. In their view, rising levels of education among blacks, their massive migration from the rural South to the urban North, and the growth of the American economy explain the economic gains of blacks in the 1960s and 1970s, just as the disappearance of manufacturing jobs, the decline in wages paid for low-skilled work, and the rapid increase in the supply of black college graduates worked to reverse those gains in the 1980s.

It is even more difficult to agree about the net effect of affirmative action and other related measures on increasing black employment. Nevertheless, there is little doubt that other public policies not specifically directed at race have had an effect on the job prospects of minorities. Policies that favor full employment over stable prices tend to bring minority jobless rates closer to those of whites. Programs that expand the public sector are especially helpful to blacks, who have traditionally been more fortunate in finding jobs and receiving equal pay when working for the government. Efforts to rebuild the inner city tend to increase black employment because so many blacks reside in urban ghettos. By and large, policies that favor blacks tend to emerge more frequently from liberal rather than conservative administrations. That may well help explain why blacks made the greatest progress in overcoming their economic disadvantages during the 1940s, 1960s, and early 1970s, whereas they had little or no success in narrowing the wage gap during the relatively prosperous 1950s and 1980s.

Gender Discrimination

The civil rights revolution of the 1960s brought a heightened awareness of discrimination not only against racial minorities but also against other groups, especially women. Feminists organized, lobbied legislators, and wrote informative books and pamphlets. They dramatized injustices long taken for granted, and pointed out subtler inequities which few people had previously noticed. At the same time, more and more women began to enter the work force, including the higher-status professions. From 1970 to 1990, the numbers of women with bachelor's degrees in management rose more than tenfold. Female applicants to medical school grew by almost as much; and the proportion of women in graduating law classes increased to more than 40 percent.

Gradually, the gender mix in predominantly male professions began to change. During the 1970s, women registered large gains in thirty-three separate occupations, including administrators and public officials, financial managers, personnel specialists, pharmacists, designers, systems analysts, and education administrators.[22] The percentage of female physicians rose from 13.0 in 1975 to 20.4 in 1992. Over the same period, the percentage of women among lawyers and judges climbed from 7.1 to 21.4; among architects, from 4.3 to 15.3;

among economists, from 13.1 to 43.3.[23] In 1972, only 4.5 percent of working women occupied managerial or administrative posts, compared with 13.1 percent of all working men.[24] By 1989, the difference had narrowed substantially to 13.9 percent of the men and 11.1 percent of the women. Five years later, in 1994, women made up 43.0 of all executive management and administrative workers, although they were still heavily concentrated in the public sector and in certain professions, such as elementary school teaching and nursing, that have traditionally been largely female.[25]

As time went on, these changes began to have an effect on the difference in the pay of women and men. From 1939 to 1980, the wage gap hardly moved, fluctuating narrowly around 58 percent. Even during the 1970s, the ratio remained essentially the same.[26] Beneath the surface, however, major changes were taking place. Women were entering higher-paid callings in greater numbers, affirmative action laws were helping to break open predominantly male occupations, and antidiscrimination laws started to erode unjustified pay differentials.

Until the late 1970s, the effect of these changes on earnings was muffled by the fact that most of the increase in the number of working women consisted of young, recently arrived employees who naturally received less money than their older, more experienced male colleagues. By the 1980s, however, the new cohorts of women from the 1970s had accumulated more experience and had started to receive substantially higher wages and salaries, even as younger colleagues continued to enter the professions in large numbers. Gradually, the earnings gap began to diminish. From 1979 to the late 1980s, the female-male earnings ratio rose from 59 percent to 68 percent and climbed further to 72.4 percent in the early 1990s.[27]

Unlike minorities, the status of women in America can be compared with that of their counterparts in other advanced countries. Studies of developments abroad reveal that progress has been taking place in most industrial democracies just as it has in the United States.[28] Table 10.3 indicates that American women have made a comparatively strong showing in penetrating high-prestige occupations. More recent figures (Table 10.4) show a similar pattern in the conventional high-prestige occupational categories, though the gains have been somewhat less marked in the field of politics.

As the figures in Table 10.4 make clear, American women have

Table 10.3. **Percent of all full-time employees in high-prestige occupations, by sex, 1972.**

Occupation	Japan	Sweden	West Germany	United Kingdom	United States
High-prestige professions					
Men	5.4	8.5	7.5	4.8	11.1
Women	4.8	6.2	3.5	2.3	6.7
Administrative and managerial					
Men	8.4	5.2	2.7	6.1	10.4
Women	1.0	0.4	0.0	0.9	3.0
High-prestige sales positions					
Men	6.2	4.7	5.8	4.9	4.4
Women	6.3	1.1	4.3	3.5	1.5
High-prestige service jobs					
Men	2.0	3.8	5.0	5.5	5.0
Women	2.8	5.5	5.8	7.3	8.8
High-prestige production jobs					
Men	17.8	17.3	23.3	17.7	18.4
Women	7.3	2.2	5.3	4.7	4.5

Source: Patricia Roos, *Gender and Work: A Comparative Analysis of Industrial Societies,* 50–52 (1985).

Table 10.4. **Penetration of women into high-status occupations, early 1990s.**

Country	Percent of seats in national legislature (1994)	Percent of municipal council seats (1990–1994)	Percent of administrative and managerial positions (1992)	Percent of professional and technical positions (1992)
Canada	17.3	18	40.7	56.0
France	5.7	17	9.4	41.4
West Germany	20.0	20	—	—
Japan	6.7	3	7.9	42.0
Sweden	33.5	34	38.9	63.3
United Kingdom	7.4	25	22.7	39.6
United States	10.3	21	40.1	50.8

Source: United Nations Development Programme, *Human Development Report,* 60, 84 (1995).

moved into high-status occupations at least as successfully as most of their counterparts overseas. With respect to earnings, however, the United States has tended to lag somewhat in narrowing the gender gap. Table 10.5 makes it clear that women in the United States are still far from achieving the same earnings level as their male co-workers. Between 1979 and 1990, the average shortfall in women's wages declined only from 41 percent to 27.6 percent. What accounts for the remaining difference?

Much of the gap results from the fact that American women, on average, continue to have less education and training than their male counterparts. But some of the disparity reflects the unusually large differences in compensation between high- and low-paid occupations in the United States, since women in all of the countries surveyed are disproportionately represented in lower-skilled lines of work. If differences in pay were no greater in the United States than they are in western Europe, America's record would be much closer to that of France and Sweden.[29]

Even if one allows for differences in education and experience, however, disparities are still substantial in the United States. Granted, young women and men in the same type of job usually receive the same compensation. Nevertheless, although men and women may start off in the same job, they tend to have different career trajectories. According to one study, men change employers more frequently in the early

Table 10.5. **Ratios of hourly earnings (women's to men's), nonagricultural workers, in percent, 1970 and 1990.**

Country	1970	1990
France	78	80
West Germany	69	74
Japan	51	50
Sweden	80	89[a]
United Kingdom	60	70[b]
United States	62	72

Source: Francine D. Blau and Lawrence M. Kahn, *The Gender Earnings Gap: Some International Evidence*, National Bureau of Economic Research (November 1992).

a. Figure is for 1989.

b. Figure is for 1984.

years, and it is when they make such changes that they move ahead of
women of the same age and background in the same field of work.[30]
By this process, even in occupations that are now well populated by
both sexes, women tend to cluster in the job categories that are less
well compensated. Thus, women lawyers are overrepresented in the
low-paid public service and legal aid offices and underrepresented in
the large corporate law firms. Female physicians are heavily concentrated among general practitioners, family doctors, and pediatricians
but sparsely represented among the most highly paid specialists, notably surgeons.[31]

One is tempted to conclude that these differences must result from
discrimination. Having grudgingly allowed women to enter formerly
all-male occupations, men make sure that they are relegated to the least
remunerative jobs. But there is a problem with this hypothesis. Single
women, after controlling for education and experience, appear to be
earning only 5 to 10 percent less than men, undermining any simple
notion that employers discriminate heavily on the basis of gender per
se. The principal earnings gap is not for women but for mothers. In
the late 1980s, the birth of a first child appeared to depress earnings
by almost 10 percent, and the coming of a second child, by almost 20
percent.[32]

Can one say, then, that mothers suffer from widespread discrimination, presumably at the hands of bosses who suspect that they may
leave their job at any time to become full-time parents or stay away
from work unexpectedly because of emergencies at home? That is a
possible explanation. But it is also conceivable that mothers preoccupied with small children concentrate less single-mindedly on their
work. Or perhaps mothers choose jobs and career tracks that are somewhat less demanding (and less remunerative) so that they can be sure
of being able to devote sufficient time to their children. As yet, no study
has conclusively shown which of these theories is most nearly correct.
Probably, all of them have at least some validity.

How much has the government contributed over the past twenty-
five years to the progress of women and to the problems and obstacles
that still hamper their careers? Probably, cultural factors are chiefly
responsible for the progress. Women did not move forward until they
became more interested in working, more conscious of the effects of
discrimination, and more determined to obtain further education and

greater access to higher-paying occupations. But affirmative action and antidiscrimination laws undoubtedly played an important supporting role by reinforcing and legitimating women's demands for fair treatment by employers.

If public policy has contributed to women's successes, it is also implicated in the problems that mothers continue to encounter in trying to combine a family and a career. There are steps that the government could take to ease the conflicts between these two roles. One policy that seems to make a substantial difference is maternity leave. According to a recent estimate, an effective, universal program of paid maternity leave would reduce the current pay disadvantage of mothers by more than 40 percent.[33] Affordable child care could also help mothers pursue a career more easily. In Sweden, for example, mothers receive twelve months of paid parental leave, and quality child care is available to all families who want it. The options available to most American mothers are far less favorable.

Poverty

Many studies confirm that socioeconomic background is strongly related to career achievement.[34] Those who grow up in poor families with parents of limited education tend to be much less likely to attend college, enter a high-status occupation, or earn the same amount as persons of equal intelligence from better socioeconomic backgrounds. Apparently, according to one widely cited study, the effect of socioeconomic background declined by about one-third during the 1970s and 1980s, a decline almost entirely due to the growing numbers of young people attending college.[35] Apart from the effects of higher education, however, the handicaps of socioeconomic background have changed very little since 1970. What is less clear is exactly why these family circumstances have such marked and persistent effects.

We do know that children raised in poverty encounter greater risks than children who grow up in more comfortable circumstances and that many of the hazards they face threaten to close off opportunities to achieve a full and rewarding life. At the request of the Children's Defense Fund, a panel of economists recently tried to quantify these added dangers (Table 10.6). Although the figures are arresting, they do not tell how much of the added risk comes from poor neighborhoods and how much derives from the families in which poor children

Table 10.6. The risks of growing up in poverty, 1994.

Outcome	Ratio of risk of poor children to risk of average children (number of times as likely)
Death in infancy	1.3
Death in childhood	3.0
Victim of homicide	8.4
Suffering fatal accident	2.2
Subject to child abuse	4.5
Low birthweight	1.2
Only fair or poor health	3.0
Physical or mental disability	4.5

Source: Children's Defense Fund, *Wasting America's Future*, 62 (1994).

grow up. Even if the government could end the geographic segregation of poor and minority families and give them enough financial support to lift them all above the poverty line, it is still conceivable that their children would run above-average risks of being abused, murdered, and handicapped physically or mentally. Presumably, poverty and ghetto neighborhoods increase these dangers, but we do not know by how much.

There is much controversy over the effects of poor neighborhoods on the opportunities of ghetto residents. William Julius Wilson, along with other scholars, has emphasized the massive disappearance of manufacturing jobs from the cities and the exodus of successful middle-class blacks to homes in the suburbs.[36] In the urban neighborhoods that remain, he argues, positive role models are no longer present, and job opportunities have dried up, especially for black men. Such an environment destroys hope and self-respect and causes young people to turn increasingly to drugs and other criminal pursuits for want of suitable alternatives.

Other analysts disagree, believing that the problems of poor urban neighborhoods result from declining personal values.[37] Ghetto residents, conservatives contend, can lead decent lives if they have the determination to do so. As proof, they point to members of other disadvantaged groups, such as Vietnamese, Koreans, and Cubans, who have moved from urban poverty into thriving middle-class careers.[38]

In recent years, scholars have begun making serious efforts to resolve this dispute by determining more precisely what impact growing up in poor neighborhoods has on the lives of children.[39] The most intriguing indication of neighborhood effects emerged in Chicago, where several thousand poor black families were allowed to move from inner-city housing projects either to other inner-city residences or to the suburbs. Subsequent inquiries revealed that families who moved to the suburbs were 25 percent more likely to have jobs than the families remaining in the inner city, while their children performed better in school and were more than twice as likely as their inner-city counterparts to attend college.[40]

Unfortunately, the Chicago experience is not definitive, because the sample studied was small and there are questions about whether the two groups of families were entirely comparable. As a result, researchers continue to try to determine the effects of poor neighborhoods.

In a series of recent papers, investigators claim to have identified a number of important consequences resulting from growing up in urban ghettos, especially racially segregated communities with few successful fathers to serve as role models. According to these studies, such neighborhoods substantially increase the chances of slipping into behavior that prejudices future occupational success—behavior such as teenage pregnancy, dropping out of school, and committing crimes. As a result, some investigators have found that growing up in such surroundings can lower subsequent earnings by 20 percent or more.[41] Other papers suggest that inner-city schools may depress the performance of students, insofar as they attract less-qualified teachers, experience higher turnover, and have larger class sizes for younger children. One massive study of nine hundred school districts in Texas found that these factors accounted for 20 to 25 percent of the variation in performance between poor black children and their white counterparts.[42]

Although these writings seem plausible, they are not yet definitive. Most of them are contradicted by other work that has failed to find similar effects either from living in poor neighborhoods or from attending schools with less-qualified teachers and larger classes. As one recent study concluded, "We can no more expect to reduce teenage motherhood or (high school) drop out rates by dispersing 'at risk' families to less problem-ridden neighborhoods than we could expect to reduce illness and death by breaking up retirement communities."[43] At this stage, then, there are few conclusions one can safely draw. The effort to isolate neighborhood effects is still in its infancy, and much more work needs to be done before we can be reasonably sure of the results.

Access to Higher Education

One useful way to examine what has happened to opportunity for all groups in the United States is to observe the trends in access to colleges and universities. Higher education is particularly important to mobility, because a bachelor's degree seems to remove almost all the effects of socioeconomic background on students' subsequent careers while diminishing the force of gender discrimination as well.[44] For this reason, as access to college improves for women, minorities, and children from poor families, equality of opportunity increases throughout the society.

In the past thirty-five years, colleges and universities have made great progress in easing access for members of minority groups and women. In fact, controlling for socioeconomic background and parental education, black students were somewhat *more* likely to attend college in the 1970s.[45] Although the likelihood of graduating from college has since declined for blacks relative to whites of comparable socioeconomic background, the two groups continue to enroll at almost the same rate.

Women, too, have gained ground relative to men in their ability to attend college. In a retrospective study of Wisconsin students who were high school seniors in 1957, women with the same intellectual ability as men were far less likely to attend and graduate from college.[46] For example, among students in the top quarter both in ability and socioeconomic background, 91 percent of the men but only 55 percent of the women attended college. Since that time, especially in the 1970s and 1980s, the opportunity for women to go to college has steadily risen. Today, women of comparable ability and socioeconomic background, whether black or white, are *more* likely than men to attend college.[47]

Young people from families with low incomes and low occupational status have made less progress. Thirty-five years ago, according to one study, students of high intelligence from high socioeconomic backgrounds were almost twice as likely to attend college as students of similar intelligence from low socioeconomic backgrounds, and more than three times as likely to graduate.[48] During the 1960s, colleges expanded their enrollments, and high school graduates from all income groups entered in growing numbers. According to Michael Hout of the University of California, between 1972 and 1985 these changes were the principal factor in bringing about a decline of one-third in the impact of parental education and income on occupational achievement.[49] After the early 1970s, however, young people from low socioeconomic backgrounds stopped coming to college in greater numbers, despite the introduction of large federal scholarship programs for students of modest means.[50] By 1989, the chances that someone from a family in the lowest income quartile would earn a college degree were below what they had been in the early 1970s, and were *nine times* lower than the chances that young people in the top income quartile would do so.[51]

Clearly, part of this difference comes about because students from families with higher incomes are much more likely to possess above-average academic aptitude. Yet an analysis of the massive national survey of students graduating from high school in 1980 reveals that large disparities exist in college attendance rates even for students of comparable intelligence from different socioeconomic backgrounds (Table 10.7). Still greater differences must exist in the *graduation rates* of students from different socioeconomic groups, since students from poor families are much more likely than their wealthier classmates to drop out of school. These divergent outcomes show all too clearly what a handicap it still is to grow up in poverty, even for students of high ability.

Table 10.7. Percentages of students with different test scores and socioeconomic backgrounds attending college

Socioeconomic status of family (quartile)	Test score quartile				
	Bottom 25%	25–50%	50–75	Top 25%	Total
Bottom 25%	12.4	22.5	41.4	58.3	25.8
25–50%	12.1	24.8	43.0	68.2	35.7
50–75%	18.8	40.3	56.4	79.5	52.8
Top 25%	37.1	57.0	70.5	89.7	74.4

Source: Figures compiled specially from High School and Beyond Senior Cohort.

How Fares the American Dream?

All in all, the United States has made impressive progress over the last thirty-five years in breaking down barriers that have limited the opportunities of women, minorities, and persons from low socioeconomic backgrounds. All these groups face less discrimination today than they did in the 1950s and early 1960s. The record has been especially strong for young people with enough ability and ambition to graduate from college, since a bachelor's degree eliminates much of the impact of gender and socioeconomic background on later life success, and a graduate degree has some of the same effect for minorities. Since higher education expanded in the 1950s and 1960s, the effect of socioeconomic background on career achievement has declined by one-third, while opportunities have grown rapidly for women and minorities in management and the professions. Handicaps undoubtedly remain, and governments could doubtless do more to reduce them. Still, there has been no period in history when so much has been done to help all groups and classes gain access to higher education and thereby lower artificial obstacles to personal achievement.

Apart from opportunities created through higher education, there are signs of success throughout the economy in reducing discrimination and its effect on career opportunities. Granted, the gains have not been uniform for each group, and progress appears to have slowed significantly in recent years, especially for minorities.[52] Overall, however, both women and racial minorities unquestionably face less discrimination today than they did in the 1950s.

Curiously, despite these signs of improvement, there is a growing fear throughout America that opportunities in the society are shrinking and that children may not reach the levels of income and accomplishment that their parents achieved, let alone move forward in the classic American tradition to even higher pinnacles of attainment. Katherine Newman writes eloquently in *Declining Fortunes* about young adults who are no longer able to own homes of the kind they grew up in, or even to remain in the communities they lived in as a child.[53] Speaking of young people who graduated from high school in the 1970s and 1980s, she concludes that "the largest living generation of Americans is doing worse, enjoying less of the good life than those who came before, most notably its own parents . . . Only the most privileged . . . are likely to realize the promise of their suburban upbringing."[54]

Newman is not the only one to worry about the downward mobility of young Americans. In a 1995 poll, 58 percent of the respondents expressed the belief that "the future of the next generation will be . . . worse . . . than life today."[55] Eighty-five percent declared that the American Dream would be harder to achieve for future generations.[56]

Is there any basis for these beliefs? If the American economy has continued to grow more or less steadily over the past fifty years, why are people so gloomy about the prospects for coming generations? Several problems help explain the pessimism. One reason is that the economy has grown much more slowly over the past twenty years than it did from 1945 to 1970. As a result, opportunities for better jobs have not increased as rapidly as they did in earlier decades, especially for those not attending college. Among Americans with a high school diploma or less who turned twenty-one *after* 1980, the proportion earning twice the official poverty line income by the time they reached thirty years of age was only 32 percent, compared with almost half of those who turned twenty-one *before* 1980.[57] Worse yet, real wages have fallen for lower-skilled employees, so that many employees work full time all year round and still find themselves below the poverty line. In fact, median hourly wages for male workers today may be even lower than those that their fathers earned at comparable stages in their careers.*

Faced with these economic pressures, many households have maintained their standard of living only by having both parents take a job, often at the cost of considerable stress in taking care of home and family. With some expenses—such as housing, medical care, and college tuition—rising faster than the cost of living, families often find it harder to pay for food, clothing, vacations, and recreation. To many people, then, hard work no longer seems to be paying off in the old, familiar way.

In recent years, these economic strains have been augmented by fears of a different kind. As large companies restructure or relocate to distant places, thousands upon thousands of long-term employees lose

---

*Median wages for successive cohorts of male employees aged twenty-five to thirty-four who were born after World War II appear to be lower than those of the preceding generation at a similar age. Nevertheless, these calculations do not take account of higher benefits, or the fact that other family members may work, or the effects of smaller family size. Thus, such findings should not be taken to imply that the standard of living of young families today is lower than that of their parents.

their jobs. It is not simply unskilled workers who feel the pain. Displaced manufacturing workers find it difficult to obtain a new job with anything close to their old wages and benefits. Middle managers have been let go in large numbers. Even top executives and partners in large law firms have found themselves without employment. As stories of mass layoffs multiply, few people feel as secure as they once did.

Is it true, then, that the American Dream is beginning to fade? Is the majority correct in supposing that, for the first time in our history, children will not be able to achieve the same standard of living as their parents? Does life in the United States no longer bring rewards to those who work hard, obey the rules, and live within their means?

In fact, the picture is more complicated and, in all probability, less bleak than the pessimists would have us believe. There is little evidence to support Katherine Newman's claim that "the largest living generation of Americans is doing worse, enjoying less of the good life than those who came before, most notably its own parents." On the contrary, a recent study of baby boomers shows that both early boomers, aged thirty-five to forty-four, and late boomers, aged twenty-five to thirty-four, enjoy real incomes that are more than 50 percent higher than those of their parents' generation at a comparable age.[58] Even workers in the bottom quintile are earning considerably more than comparably situated members of their parents' generation.[59]

Prospects are especially favorable for college graduates. There is no reason to think that the economy will not keep growing, as it has at varying rates of speed over the past half-century. Jobs and earnings will continue to increase, even if the rate of growth is slower than it was during the golden decades after World War II. Moreover, opportunities are not solely a function of growth but result from changes in the mix of jobs. For some time, the occupations that have expanded the fastest are those that pay the most, offer the greatest challenge, and command the highest prestige.[60] Estimates for the next decade forecast a continuation of this trend: managerial, administrative, and professional jobs are expected to be among the most rapidly growing categories of employment.[61] As a result, there is every indication that college-educated Americans can look forward to a larger number of attractive jobs than ever before.

Granted, the prospects are not entirely favorable. As more young people go to college, the mounting supply of well-educated Americans may begin to dampen earnings increases for managers and profession-

als, and the premium for obtaining a bachelor's or professional degree—now at historically high levels—could easily fall. Unless the
economy starts to grow faster, white men will continue to feel the
effects of greater competition from college-educated women and minorities. As more well-trained candidates scramble for the best positions and as global competition continues to shrink the number of
stable, lifelong jobs, there may be greater uncertainty, anxiety, and
stress even among the best and brightest. Some college graduates will
lose their jobs in mid-career and have to settle for less desirable, lower-
paid positions. Still, such tensions do not negate the fact that the total
number of attractive career possibilities has been steadily increasing
and will very probably continue to grow for better-educated Americans. For the highly educated, it is important not to confuse competition and uncertainty with declining opportunity.

The outlook for those who do not seek a college degree is much
more mixed. For several decades after World War II, millions of young
men could go directly from high school to join the swelling ranks of
manufacturing workers enjoying good pay, excellent benefits, and the
prospect of moving comfortably into the middle class. Since 1970,
these jobs have been steadily declining, severely narrowing the most
promising path to a secure future for those with only a high school
degree.

Fortunately, there are many alternatives to blue-collar manufacturing jobs that promise reasonable wages and a good future. Some
young people who would have gone to work in a factory thirty years
ago will enter a community college to learn a useful skill. Others will
find ways to be trained for positions in expanding areas, such as health
services, envirotechnology, computing, or sales.

Only for the bottom quarter of the population are the prospects
truly bleak. Without a college degree, young people in this category
will find it difficult to find work at rates of pay sufficient to lift them
much above the poverty level. Many jobs will be temporary and of
uncertain duration. Most will not bring health and other benefits. Few
will offer much prospect for advancement.

One can always ask why young people from low-income families
do not go to college to better their chances. Undoubtedly, some of them
will. But family circumstances and community pressures seem to lower
the odds of advancing in this fashion. The cumulative weight of living
with parents who are not highly educated themselves, of having few if

any successful role models to emulate, and of being subjected to all manner of destructive neighborhood pressures appears to take its toll on a child's ambition. As a result, despite federal scholarship and loan programs, even the most talented students from poor families are much less likely to attend college (and more likely to drop out if they do) than students of comparable academic ability with well-to-do parents.

Bleakest of all are the prospects for offspring of single mothers on welfare. Such children are much more prone to drop out of school, be single parents themselves, and experience poverty and unemployment in later life. For them, the American Dream seems remote indeed. Unfortunately, their ranks are growing steadily. More than 30 percent of all children are now being born to unwed mothers, and the number is rising. In 1990, 45 percent of all first births in America were the babies of mothers who were either teenagers, unmarried, or lacked a high school diploma.[62] Without an expanding manufacturing sector offering good wages for semiskilled labor, these children are prime prospects for a permanent underclass with little hope of finding jobs sufficient to lift them significantly above the poverty line.

One can argue that this state of affairs is inevitable and that society has provided about as much opportunity as can be expected in an imperfect world. Certainly, many of the reasons that shrivel the prospects for poor children are rooted in private values and behavior patterns beyond the reach of government programs. Further obstacles result from deficiencies in talent or intelligence that are not amenable to the most enlightened public policies. Still, various possibilities remain by which to increase opportunities even for young people who grow up in the least promising circumstances. Providing prenatal care to expectant mothers and offering adequate nutrition to all infants who need it can lower the odds of retardation and other debilitating handicaps. Expanding preschool and enhancing its quality can increase the chances that children will enter school equipped to learn and advance without difficulty. Improving public education in poor communities would also help. Experience shows that well-constructed antidropout programs can keep many students from leaving school before they graduate. Improved school-to-work programs and better job training could prepare students for better jobs than those that currently await them. So could larger scholarships for high school graduates from poor families.

In short, notwithstanding all the progress made in expanding opportunity, the odds of success continue to be worse than they should be for those born into families with little income or education. America's programs for children are among the least generous and least comprehensive in the industrialized world. The schools that most poor children attend are much less amply funded than those in more prosperous communities. At present, the United States spends more than twice as much educating college students as it does training those who merely graduate from high school, and more than five times as much as it does on high school dropouts. So long as these conditions persist, one can hardly claim that society has done all it can to give every young person a reasonable opportunity to succeed. Rather, for Americans unlucky enough to be born poor, the future threatens to provide little more than intermittent unemployment and jobs that neither lift them out of poverty nor offer rates of pay close to the wages earned by the lowest-paid workers in other industrial democracies.

IV

PERSONAL SECURITY

11

Violent Crime

Much of the unease that pervades America today seems to result from a common perception that life has become more precarious, more unpredictable, even more dangerous. According to a Times Mirror survey conducted in late 1995, "anxiety may replace anger as the dominant voter emotion in 1996."[1] After traveling throughout the United States gathering impressions from people in all walks of life, Haynes Johnson reported that "nothing in my previous experience prepared me for the depth of feelings—the fear, the doubt, the anger, the *rage*—I encountered everywhere. Strongest of all was a feeling of bewilderment, a troubling sense that the assumptions of the old America were passing and that the uncertain new America promises to be far more unsettling."[2]

In such uncertain times, people yearn for greater stability in their lives and for a reasonable protection against life's principal hazards. Of course, it would be unwise as well as impossible to banish all fear from people's lives. Some dangers cause individuals to exercise care in preparing for the future and respecting the legal rights of others. Many risks are the inevitable result of essential transformations in society; the loss of jobs resulting from technological change is a familiar case in point. Some hazards, such as those of race-car driving or sky-diving, even bring excitement and pleasure to participants.

If some dangers are needed, however, others serve no useful purpose. Attempting to limit such risks and alleviate their harsh effects becomes especially important at times like the present, when people

217

are so apprehensive and insecure. Granted, some of their worries may come from problems that individuals can and should take care of by themselves. But other hazards call for collective action, because such a response is more efficient, or because some citizens lack the means to protect themselves adequately, or because society is somehow responsible for the danger involved, or because the consequences are not confined to those who do not protect themselves but will likely do harm to innocent bystanders as well. A major challenge for the modern State, therefore, is to help citizens protect themselves where appropriate without doing away with risks that serve a useful social purpose.

Of all the hazards that have no redeeming value, the most obvious is the threat of being victimized by violent crime. This danger casts an especially dark shadow over Americans, since the United States is the most violent of all the advanced industrial democracies. Almost 1.7 million violent crimes were carried out in this country during 1990.[3] One murder was committed every twenty-two minutes; one forcible rape every five minutes; one robbery every forty-nine seconds; one aggravated assault every thirty seconds.[4] Among those fifteen to twenty-four years of age, homicide is the third leading cause of death; it is now the principal cause of death for black men between the ages of fifteen and thirty-four. According to the Department of Justice, the risk of homicide at some point in one's life is 1 in 30 for black men, 1 in 132 for black women, 1 in 179 for white men, and 1 in 495 for white women.[5]

At current rates, so the Department of Justice tells us, five-sixths of all Americans will be victims of attempted or completed violent crimes in the course of their lifetimes.[6] Under such conditions, normal means of protection no longer suffice, and more and more people are taking matters into their own hands. Positions as private security guard are among the most rapidly growing forms of employment. By 1988, Americans were spending more money on private methods to protect themselves than the entire sum devoted to all public law enforcement, federal, state, and local.

Much of the mayhem occurs within the home, or in urban ghettos where most people rarely go. But violence is becoming a serious problem for every segment of society. More than 40 percent of all Americans report that there are places within a mile of their home where they are afraid to walk alone at night.[7] In 1990, a survey of high school seniors found that 88 percent worried about crime and violence "sometimes" or "often."[8] At Brown University, in Providence, Rhode Island, students take classes on how to defend themselves and receive instructions on which streets of the city to avoid. In Miami, visitors renting cars are advised not to leave their vehicle if they are hit from behind by another automobile; such collisions may simply be a ruse leading to a robbery, or worse. According to a woman studying law at Duke University, "It bothers me that my male friends can go running at night, and I can't do that . . . I remember never locking our doors as a child. That's just disappeared. It doesn't exist anymore."[9]

Much recent publicity about crime creates the impression that current rates of violence are unprecedented in modern times. Yet the situation today does not appear to be worse than at various periods in the past. Although homicide rates in 1955 were less than half of what they were in 1993, the 1993 rates were slightly below the levels of 1980 and 1933. The peak of 9.5 homicides per 100,000 people in the early 1930s was followed by a steady decline to less than 5 in the 1950s, but the rate rose rapidly to 10.4 in 1979–1981, declined in the early to mid-1980s, then returned to almost 10 per 100,000 in 1991, only to decline once again thereafter.[10]

Murder rates have not only fluctuated overall; there have been important shifts in the kinds of people who commit such acts and the circumstances in which murders occur. A growing percentage of homicides are carried out by teenage males, who continue to commit more murders even as rates for other age groups are dropping. As homicides within the family decline, more and more of them occur outside the home, often in connection with disputes involving gangs and drugs.

It is harder to ascertain the trends for other types of violent crime. Victimization surveys based on responses from a sample of American households indicate that violent crime (other than homicide) declined by 11 percent during the 1980s.[11] But crimes reported to the Federal Bureau of Investigation (FBI) show a level trend at best over the same period.[12] The most plausible explanation for this discrepancy is that rates of reporting violent acts to the FBI have been increasing as methods of data collection improve. If so, the rise in *reported* crime since the mid-1970s may give a distorted picture of the actual trends over the past twenty years.[13]

According to all known statistics, rates of violent crimes in America

Table 11.1. Murders committed annually by men aged 25–34, per
100,000 people, 1988–1991.

Country	Number of murders
Canada	1
France	1
West Germany	1–2
Japan	0–1
Sweden	1–2
United Kingdom	0–1
United States	38

Source: National Center for Health Statistics, *Health, United States* (1990); and World
Health Organization *Statistics Annual* (1990, 1991).

are *several times* greater than the levels recorded in other advanced
industrialized societies. The figures for murders by young men are especially telling (Table 11.1).

Although levels of violent crime in America have fluctuated widely
over the past seventy-five years, even at their lowest point they have
been far above the rates of other leading industrial democracies. Interestingly, however, the United States does not show higher rates of incidence for *all* types of crime, as Table 11.2 attests. In short, Americans
are no more disposed to commit crimes than the citizens of other industrialized countries. It is *violence* that sets us apart.

Table 11.2. Number of crimes per 100,000 people, 1984.

Country	Homicide	Rape	Robbery	Burglary	Auto theft
Canada	2.7	NA[a]	92.8	1,420.6	304.9
France	4.8[b]	5.2	105.6	809.8	483.4
West Germany	1.5	9.7	45.8	1,554.1	118.0
Japan	0.8	1.6	1.8	231.2	29.4
Sweden	1.4	11.9	44.1	1,708.8	460.0
United Kingdom	1.1[c]	2.7	44.6	1,639.7	658.6[c]
United States	7.9	35.7	205.4	1,263.7	437.1

Source: Interpol; cited in Erika Fairchild, *Comparative Criminal Justice Systems*, 8 (1993).
a. Not available.
b. Figure includes attempted homicides.
c. Figures are from 1983.

Searching for Solutions

Although politicians often declare that they will crack down on crime and restore law and order, it is extremely difficult to deliver on these promises. To quote David Farrington, James Q. Wilson, and Lloyd Ohlin: "Policymakers who wish to put in place new programs to reduce crime, or to expand the scope or effectiveness of programs already in place, will quickly discover that the knowledge necessary to do this responsibly does not exist except in fragmentary and unsatisfactory form."[14] Theories abound concerning the causes of crime. Yet we still know surprisingly little about how valid the theories actually are.

The principal strategy against crime has always been to apprehend the culprit and impose a suitable punishment. For those who commit acts of violence, the penalty in all societies has generally included some form of imprisonment, thus simultaneously deterring would-be criminals and protecting society by putting dangerous offenders behind bars. Unfortunately, however, such measures have never come close to eliminating violent crime in the United States. The fear of apprehension and punishment inevitably fails to deter some wrongdoers, either because they think that they can escape detection or because they act impulsively without considering the consequences. Moreover, deterrence will always be hampered by the fact that Americans not only insist on a criminal justice system that prevents crime; they want one that neither inflicts punishments so severe as to seem inhumane nor ignores procedural safeguards that minimize the risk of convicting innocent suspects.

Within these limits, some authorities have continued to emphasize deterrence as the primary means for curbing violence. According to these experts, much violent crime is a product of rational calculation. If the chances of getting caught are great enough, convictions swift enough, and penalties severe enough, the number of violent acts must surely fall. As Ernest Van den Haag puts it, "Our only hope of reducing the burgeoning crime rate lies in decreasing the expected net advantage of committing crimes . . . by increasing the costs through increasing the expected severity of punishments and the probability of receiving them."[15]

According to this theory, the first line of attack on violence should be to strengthen efforts to apprehend perpetrators and hand them over to the State for prosecution. For decades, police departments tried to improve their performance by insulating themselves from political influence and concentrating on the single objective of fighting crime. Organizing themselves tightly along hierarchical lines, modern police forces sought to exploit new technology to respond quickly to reports of crime and to locate and apprehend the perpetrator. Gradually, the automobile replaced the foot patrol, and computerized data banks, modern forensic laboratories, and sophisticated methods of communication came into common use.[16]

For a time in the 1940s and 1950s, as levels of reported crime drifted downward, these methods seemed to be working. By the late 1960s, however, violent crime was steadily rising once again. Examining the record, researchers began to publish findings casting doubt on the efficacy of many prized techniques of professional policing, such as motorized patrolling, rapid response, and sophisticated detective work.[17]

Meanwhile, several other countries with less advanced technology seemed to be having greater success than America at catching criminals. In 1985, based on lists of similar crimes in various countries, clearance rates (the percentage of reported crimes "cleared" by referring a suspect for prosecution) were 48 percent in Germany, 40 percent in France, 38 percent in England, and only 23 percent in the United States.[18] The contrast with Japan was especially striking (Table 11.3). As these findings accumulated and violent crime climbed to near-record levels, few knowledgeable observers retained much faith that strategies based heavily on technology could have much positive effect.

With the public growing increasingly concerned, pressure mounted

Table 11.3. Clearance rates for violent crimes, in percent, Japan (1987) and United States (1993).

Crime	Japan	United States
Homicide	98	66
Robbery	78	24
Rape	87	53
Aggravated assault	93	56

Source: Department of Justice, *Crime in the United States: Uniform Crime Reports*, 206, 207 (1994). Research and Training Institute, Ministry of Justice (Japan), *Summary of the White Paper on Crime*, Table 1, 4 (1991). See also David H. Bayley, *Forces of Order: Policing Modern Japan*, 138–139 (1991).

to crack down harder on convicted criminals. If methods of detection were imperfect, perhaps longer prison sentences could persuade would-be wrongdoers to refrain from acts of violence. Proponents of tougher penalties found their champion in President Reagan, who promised to wage war on crime by raising the "battle flag" instead of the "surrender flag." In a series of laws, mandatory sentences were imposed, penalties increased, jails enlarged, pretrial detention author-ized for dangerous defendants, and large sums disbursed to apprehend drug traffickers. The number of prisoners relative to the total popu-lation tripled from the mid-1970s to the mid-1990s, and the cost of prisons in California alone began to exceed the total budget of the entire University of California system.[19] Once again, however, the re-forms failed to satisfy critics. By the end of the 1980s, as rates of violent crime were rising again and prison populations swelled to overflowing, reports from the field alleged that the get-tough strategy was not suc-ceeding.[20]

Critics of a get-tough policy argue that comparisons with other countries show the futility of trying to reduce crime substantially by imposing harsher penalties. America has long had exceptionally high rates of incarceration. The fraction of the population behind bars in the United States is four to six times the level in other industrial nations (Table 11.4). The likelihood that someone arrested for serious crimes will actually be imprisoned seems to be approximately the same in the United States as it is in other advanced countries.[21] So is the amount of time that convicted criminals spend in prison.[22] Nevertheless, the incidence of violent crime in America remains, comparatively, very high.

Table 11.4. Comparative incarceration rates, 1990.

Country	Number of people in prison per 100,000 of population
Sweden	58
France	82
West Germany	78
United Kingdom	93
United States	398

Source: Warren Young and Mark Brown, "Cross-National Comparisons of Imprisonment," in Michael Tonry (ed.), 17 *Crime and Justice: A Review of Research*, 1, 5 (1993).

Comparisons of this kind have not dissuaded those who believe that toughening up the criminal justice system will lower the level of unlawful violence. Because the chances of escaping apprehension are greater in America, longer sentences are said to be needed to make crime sufficiently unattractive to deter potential wrongdoers. And whether or not prolonged incarceration actually deters much violent crime, it should still reduce it by keeping more criminals behind bars, where they cannot harm others. As John DiIulio asserts, the increased use of imprisonment saved Americans 66,000 rapes, 323,000 robberies, 380,000 assaults, and 3.3 million burglaries in 1989 alone.[23]

These arguments suggest that efforts to get tough on crime are not about to slacken. Even so, the policies of the 1980s have hardly had enough success to justify the hope that emphasizing detection, conviction, and incarceration will ever reduce serious crimes to levels close to those in other industrial democracies. Regardless of our views about deterrence, then, we must look further for other means of curbing violence in America.

It is here that the struggle against violent crime encounters one of the great ideological divides that generates disagreement on so many policy issues in America. Those who seek to increase criminal penalties tend to emphasize the criminal's personal responsibility for committing acts of violence. But others, while admitting that individuals are responsible for their acts, have been reluctant simply to blame criminals and have long sought other reasons to explain crime and other ways to prevent its occurrence.

For generations, penologists have pleaded the case of prevention by claiming that criminals could be rehabilitated through enlightened prison reform. Since a large proportion of violent crimes are committed by persons who have previously been convicted and imprisoned, efforts to reform criminals promised to reap large dividends. Inspired by this prospect, progressive officials tried various methods to induce offenders to give up their criminal ways. Low-security prisons, early parole, indeterminate sentences, education programs of all kinds—these and other reforms were introduced in one state or another. Sadly, the results have been profoundly disappointing. After repeated experiments, we still have not discovered any methods of treating prisoners that have much effect in persuading them to change their lives.

Other commentators emphasize that many criminals grow up under conditions of privation, discrimination, and limited opportunity.

For writers of this persuasion, crime is very much an outgrowth of poverty, unemployment, broken homes, and racial prejudice and will persist until we overcome these afflictions. As a presidential commission declared in 1967, "Warring on poverty, inadequate housing and unemployment is warring on crime." Accordingly, said the commission, "The great social programs" of the Johnson administration were "America's best hope of preventing crime and delinquency."[24]

Some observers go further and point out that criminal tendencies are especially likely in a country such as the United States, where competition and material success are considered so important. In the words of Robert K. Merton, "A cardinal American virtue, 'ambition,' promotes a cardinal American vice, 'deviant behavior.' "[25] Steven Messner and Richard Rosenfeld are even more explicit: "The American Dream itself exerts pressures toward crime by encouraging . . . an environment in which people are encouraged to adopt an 'anything goes' mentality in the pursuit of personal goals."[26]

Like theories of deterrence, an emphasis on social and cultural conditions seems intuitively plausible. If Americans are driven by a desire for material success and if opportunities to earn a living by lawful means are hard to find, many will presumably be tempted to follow a life of crime. Is it any wonder, then, that crime rates are far above average among those whose opportunities are least promising—poor people, minorities, the chronically unemployed, and the children of broken homes?

However appealing such theories seem, they do not have much hard evidence to support them. During the 1960s, the Kennedy and Johnson administrations did make substantial progress in reducing discrimination and poverty in America. Yet crime rates did not fall. Quite the contrary. From the early 1960s to the mid-1970s, as poverty, inequality, and discrimination all declined, the incidence of violent crime steadily rose. Conversely, during the 1930s, when unemployment and human suffering rose to exceptional levels, homicides actually fell. Numerous studies on possible links between unemployment rates, inequality, and crime reach conflicting conclusions and thus leave the issue unresolved.[27]

If economic conditions and the hungering for wealth were truly a major cause of deviant behavior in America, one would also expect the United States to have much higher rates of theft, burglary, and other property crimes than countries such as Sweden, where poverty, in-

equality, and the striving for material gain have been much less prominent. Yet the incidence of property crimes in Sweden is not much
below that in the United States; it is our rates of homicide, rape, armed
robbery, and assault that set America apart.[28] As a result, although
ambition, unemployment, and inequality may well contribute to our
high levels of crime, they do not seem to be a major cause. If we would
make serious inroads on murder, rape, and robbery, then, we need to
go beyond these economic and cultural forces and focus on factors in
the environment that tend not toward deviance in general but toward
violence in particular.

An obvious possibility is the widespread use of alcohol and drugs.
In 1989, surveys of criminals in jail established that 41 percent of the
convicts had been under the influence of liquor when they committed
the crime that led to their arrest.[29] If we could somehow restrict the
use of alcohol, therefore, could we not succeed in reducing acts of
violence?

On further examination, the link between liquor and violent crime
seems questionable, since other nations with higher rates of alcohol
consumption than ours do not have nearly as many murders and rapes.
It is not surprising, therefore, that researchers investigating the matter
have been unable to prove that liquor actually *causes* violent behavior.
Apparently, most of those who commit violent crimes while under the
influence exhibited a disposition to violence *before* they took to
drink.[30]

Much the same is true of narcotics. There is no clear proof that
drug use causes violent acts, even though a high proportion of criminals are involved with narcotics. Nor do homicide rates appear to be
greater in cities with unusually high cocaine use.[31]

More likely is the proposition that *criminalizing* drugs has contributed to the rise in violence. Battles within the narcotics trade often lead
to killing. The pressure on users to lay their hands on huge sums of
money required to support their illicit habit may also drive them on
occasion to acts of murder and armed robbery, not to mention forms
of nonviolent crime. At the same time, the drug trade does not appear
to be a *major* cause of violence, since other countries where drugs are
outlawed do not have nearly the rates of homicide and armed robbery
that exist in the United States. Moreover, even if the narcotics trade
does increase violent crime, there is no obvious remedy save to legalize

drugs, and that is a step which most Americans (and most experts on drugs) are unwilling to take.

Still another strategy for curbing the incidence of murders and assaults in this country would be to find some way of altering the "culture of violence" created by the constant beatings, shootings, and other acts of cruelty appearing in the media, especially in the movies and on television. Before finishing grade school, the average American child will have witnessed 8,000 TV murders and 100,000 acts of violence.[32] One study revealed that in 1988 children's weekend daytime programs averaged 15.5 violent acts per hour, while evening prime-time programs averaged 6.2 incidents per hour.[33] A Swedish survey in the 1980s reported that according to a specially devised scoring system for measuring the incidence of violence on TV, the United States scored 112.0; Britain, 58.0; Sweden, 51.6; and Norway, 30.9.[34]

Scores of studies have been carried out to determine what links might exist between the portrayal of violence in the media and the actual commission of violent acts. Many investigators have concluded that youngsters who spend more time watching violent episodes on the screen are in fact more likely to display aggression as children.[35] An especially interesting survey compared rates of violent crime in the United States and Canada, where television was introduced in the 1950s, with rates in South Africa, where TV did not make an appearance until 1975.[36] From 1945 to 1974, the homicide rate for whites in America rose by 93 percent, while Canada's rate rose by 92 percent. Over the same period, murders among white South Africans declined by 7 percent, only to rise significantly after television finally made its appearance. Similar studies have shown that homicide rates rose sharply after television was belatedly introduced in remote Canadian towns, whereas homicides in other communities where TV was available much earlier were already more common and did not increase over the time period studied.[37]

Spokespersons for television networks acknowledge that TV can affect children but argue that young people who watch a lot of television are only slightly more disposed to act violently than those who watch TV much less. Since relatively few people commit murder or robbery, however, even small differences are enough to have major effects on the rate of violent crime. All things considered, then, although the evidence is not conclusive, it does warrant a strong suspicion that television violence is at least one important cause of violent crime.[38]

Assuming this to be true, the problem remains of finding an acceptable way to limit media violence. Sweden has gone so far as to impose a limited form of censorship on media violence.[39] In the United States, however, such restrictions seem out of the question in view of the protection accorded to television under the First Amendment.

Fortunately, regulation is not the only way to curb TV violence. In this respect, Canada's experience is especially interesting. After a deranged man gunned down fourteen girls in a Montreal school, another young girl, Virginie Larivière, initiated a petition demanding legislation to outlaw TV violence. Eventually, the petition attracted 1.3 million signatures in a country barely one-tenth the size of the United States. A government commission, however, chose to try to make such violence socially unacceptable by voluntary means rather than prohibiting it by law. To this end, the prime minister urged the television industry to take appropriate action or face the possibility of government intervention. The commission brought industry leaders, parents, and teachers together in a series of meetings to discuss what might be done. Large conferences were held to air the subject with a wider audience.

Out of this process came a comprehensive agreement. The industry pledged not to show programs with gratuitous violence and to avoid all violence before 9 P.M. Companies agreed to prepare schedules with information about their programs, together with a self-administered rating system to help parents decide which programs their children could watch. Simultaneously, the commission initiated trials of a "V-chip" which would allow parents to block automatically any programs they did not want their children to see. Finally, the commission launched a $10 million public awareness campaign to educate families about the dangers of violent programming and the means available to guard against it.

The Canadian experience has attracted wide attention, not least in the United States. Congress has recently passed a law requiring manufacturers of television sets to begin installing V-chips in all new products. In February 1996, television producers agreed to devise a rating system to help parents decide which programs to allow their children to watch and which to block out with the aid of their V-chip. If enough parents succeed in blocking exceptionally violent programs, economic pressure may cause producers to take these shows off the air.

In addition to the concern over television violence, many people have pointed to the risks arising from the extraordinary number of firearms owned by private individuals in America. Some 5.5 million new guns are produced or imported into the United States every year, and experts estimate the total number in private hands at more than 200 million. According to the National Education Association, 100,000 *children* carry firearms to school on an average day.[40]

It is clear that guns are heavily implicated in the rise of violent crime in the United States. They are involved in roughly 60 percent of all homicides.[41] The principal reason for loss of life among teenagers in America, both black and white, is death from gunshot wounds.[42] Moreover, comparisons with other countries show that homicide rates in America where guns are *not* involved are much closer to rates in Europe.[43] It is firearms that make the differences so great. For example, in a study of Vancouver and Seattle—cities only 140 miles apart— crime rates were similar for the two communities in all respects save homicide, where the risk of death by homicide was 65 percent greater in Seattle.[44] This difference proved to be accounted for almost entirely by the use of handguns, which caused five times as many fatalities in Seattle as in Vancouver. In Canada, of course, guns are quite tightly controlled, whereas in Seattle and in most other American cities they are not.

Once again, however, the exact relationship between guns and homicide is still not clearly understood and often defies common sense. As the National Rifle Association is fond of pointing out, guns do not kill anyone—only people do; and killing need not result from the widespread possession of firearms. For example, the incidence of homicide by firearms is greatest by far in big cities, but gun ownership is much more prevalent in small towns and rural areas. In Switzerland, where all young men receive guns from the government for national defense purposes, homicide rates are very low. In Britain, guns are strictly controlled, but violent crimes were already much less frequent than in America generations *before* the passage of these restrictions.

These points are all legitimate. They remind us that guns are not the whole story of violent crime in this country, nor even, perhaps, the principal chapter. Still, as several researchers have shown, the mere possession of guns significantly increases the odds that arguments and fights will result in death. Hence, it does seem plausible that leaving so many lethal weapons in private hands in a society traditionally prone to violence and saturated by media murders and beatings will lead to many fatalities that might not otherwise occur.

The real problem, however, is to devise a practical means to reduce the number of firearms and bring their possession under strict control. It is true that most advanced nations control guns much more strictly than we do, and thereby keep them out of private hands. Yet the prospects for following suit in this country are far from promising. Counting all of the local ordinances and regulations, there are already approximately 20,000 gun laws in America, many of which contain the most obvious restrictions, such as prohibiting carrying a concealed weapon without a permit, requiring special permission to own automatic weapons, and prohibiting felons, drug addicts, and other dangerous people from owning guns.[45] At this late date, going further and trying to eliminate the millions of weapons now in private hands would be an exceptionally difficult task. It would also provoke determined opposition on the part of those who want to possess guns for hunting and self-defense and resent the thought of having to give them up just because other people act irresponsibly. As a result, only a minority of the public supports the sweeping controls on possessing guns that are in force in many other advanced industrial democracies.

Although drugs and guns and violence in the media may all contribute to violent crime, the remedies for these problems are hard to administer, highly controversial, and frequently expensive. Moreover, trying to move on any of these fronts would be all the more difficult because no one can say how much any single factor contributes to the levels of violent crime in this country. As a result, it is all too easy for opponents to argue effectively against an effort to legalize drugs, *or* forbid handguns, *or* limit violence on TV. How can one justify such drastic steps when the effects on crime are so difficult to predict?

It is quite likely that violence in America is the product of a complex mixture of many factors—guns, media violence, fixations on material success, inadequate deterrence, social conditions, and other forces not now wholly understood. If so, no effective campaign will ever be waged against violent crime by concentrating on one factor alone. Rather, success will require a coordinated assault on every significant front simultaneously. Yet the cost of such an ambitious program would be huge and the opposition overwhelming. Moreover, the well-coordinated, multifaceted initiative required is precisely the sort of effort that has proved so difficult for American officials in a variety of other settings—urban policy, job training, and poverty, to name only a few. For the time being, then, prospects for an effective campaign against violence seem decidedly remote.

Washington's Response

Hampered by insufficient knowledge about the causes of violent crime, how has Washington responded to the public outcry to do something to stop the mayhem? Throughout the 1980s and early 1990s, almost every Congress wrestled repeatedly with this problem. With little hard knowledge to guide them, however, lawmakers quickly became bogged down in ideological battles. Conservatives pressed for tough measures. They advocated extending the death penalty, imposing more mandatory sentences, and building more prisons, and urged the repeal of procedural rules excluding illegally seized evidence from criminal trials or allowing prisoners sentenced to death to delay their execution for years with repeated habeas corpus appeals. Liberals countered with proposals to emphasize crime prevention, drug rehabilitation, and restrictions on sales of firearms.

Faced with such conflicting approaches to the problem, members of Congress typically did nothing until the last moment before they adjourned to campaign for new elections. At this point, lawmakers would quickly agree on a compromise dealing with a small piece of the problem—financial fraud, child abuse, drugs, or some other issue currently in the news. As accounts of violent crime continued to saturate the media, however, pressure mounted for a much more comprehensive response.

With the election of President Clinton, liberals and conservatives again took up an omnibus crime bill. Again they clashed over their respective programs. In 1993, however, as crime became the number one problem in the eyes of the public, both houses of Congress agreed on the so-called Brady Bill requiring a five-day waiting period before the purchase of a handgun. One year later, after intense negotiations, Congress finally enacted a comprehensive bill including a variety of measures pushed by either side. For conservatives, the death penalty was extended to fifty-eight federal crimes, money was appropriated for new prisons, and rules were enacted requiring life sentences for criminals convicted three times for violent offenses. For liberals, there were preventive programs for job training, drug counseling, and treatment, and bans on nineteen makes of assault weapons. Democrats and Republicans alike rallied behind additional measures to help cities and towns pay for 100,000 more patrolmen to combat crime.

To lawmakers, the final bill was testimony to the government's unwavering commitment to fight crime, win back the streets, and preserve innocent people from violence. President Clinton described it as "the toughest and smartest crime bill in the history of the United States."[46] Most experts, however, were much more skeptical.[47] As many of them observed, banning nineteen types of assault weapons would hardly accomplish much when scores of other semiautomatic weapons were still perfectly legal. There was no conclusive evidence that extending the death penalty would reduce violent crime perceptibly. Even more suspect was the rule requiring life imprisonment for three-time felons. According to criminologists, the likelihood of committing violent crimes drops to very low levels after the age of thirty-five, so that continued imprisonment for decades more would simply result in large government expenditures for very little benefit. Finally, liberals had problems justifying their own proposals, for no one could make a convincing empirical showing that their preventive measures would have much effect in reducing crime. All in all, therefore, it was hard not to agree, at least in part, with Cynthia McKinney, a reluctant supporter of the legislation who described it as "an ounce of prevention, a pound of punishment, and a ton of politics."[48]

Fortunately, more promising approaches are also under way. Members of Congress are pressing the television networks to exercise greater restraint, while also requiring V chips in new television sets. Lawmakers have made funds available for much-needed improvements in police information systems. Police chiefs and mayors are evincing greater interest in training policemen to work more closely with communities and to seek ways of preventing crime rather than simply responding to violent acts that have already occurred. All these approaches are worth trying. How much they will accomplish, however, is still unknown, and even proponents consider their potential to be limited. At best, therefore, the results promise to be modest, albeit well worth pursuing.

Confronting Ignorance

Given the limits to current knowledge, one can fault politicians for their overblown rhetoric but scarcely blame them for failing to bring about major reductions in violent crime. What one *can* ask is whether the government is carrying on a sufficiently vigorous, imaginative program of research and experimentation to hasten the day when lawmakers know enough to proceed more effectively.

On this score, America's record is mixed. The United States government probably spends much more on research than any other industrial nation (as it should, since our problem is so much greater). Yet our record in investigating the causes and prevention of crime is far from ideal, according to the comprehensive report on violence published in 1993 by the National Academy of Sciences.[49] In this report, the panel details how much we still do not know about the subject and offers a long list of promising avenues for research. According to the study, the government ought to devote at least $70 million per year to pursuing lines of inquiry that offer a reasonable chance of contributing to our knowledge of how to reduce violence in the society. In fact, only $20 million per year was currently being spent. This sum amounted to $31 for every life ended by violence, an amount far below the $491 per life lost that the government was expending on heart and lung research, or the $697 per life lost to AIDS, let alone the $794 per life lost to cancer. As more than one critic has observed, we allocate less money to anticrime research than we do to anticavity research.

One can only speculate about why this country does not devote more money to investigating a problem as serious as violent crime. Apparently, there is widespread skepticism, especially in the legal profession, about the value and potential of social science research of this kind. But two students of the subject have also attached importance to another factor. In their view, "the policies intended to address crime and criminal justice are so strongly driven by fundamental ideological convictions that neither side wants to confront empirical reality that might undermine their deeply held beliefs."[50]

Whatever the reason, the limited funds for investigating violence are divided among a number of federal agencies—including the Department of Justice, the National Science Foundation, the National Institute for Mental Health, and the Center for Disease Control. Such dispersion undoubtedly promotes a diversity of research. What is lacking, however, is a coordinated view of what hypotheses most need testing, how programs in the field can be evaluated to add to our knowledge where greater knowledge is most needed, and which experiments might be launched to fill critical gaps in our understanding. Because such work has not been done systematically in the past, few of the many programs funded in the recent Crime Bill have been tested in a reliable way. The risks are great that the ample sums authorized by Congress will be doled out again without sufficient heed to evaluating funded programs for the future. If so, we will again postpone the day when it will be possible to develop a crime bill based on substantial knowledge and informed judgment rather than guesswork and ideology.

The inadequacies of the federal research program underscore the frustrations of trying to cope with violent crime in the United States. On the one hand, there is far more violence in America than in any other advanced industrial society. On the other hand, the causes of violence are not well understood and effective remedies thus elude our understanding. Without hard evidence to lean on, policies vacillate from emphasizing preventive measures of all kinds to enacting harsher penalties to deter potential offenders. As yet, neither approach seems to have been notably successful.

Amid all of the carnage and mayhem, perhaps the most striking aspect of our policy is that we have gone on so long allowing more violence to saturate the media and more guns to stay in private hands than any other nation on earth. There are reasons for this, of course. No one can be sure how much violent crime could be avoided by curbing media violence or imposing strict controls on guns. It is not even clear how measures of this kind could be implemented effectively. Still, the willingness to tolerate so much media violence and so many guns over all these years testifies to the strength of our commitment to individual rights and free enterprise even in the face of compelling provocation.

12

Health Care

In 1994, the administration mounted an unprecedented campaign to reform America's health care system. To dramatize the importance he attached to the issue, President Clinton put the First Lady, Hillary Rodham Clinton, in charge of the effort to design new legislation. Interest groups spent more than $100 million to promote their respective points of view. By the time the campaign ended, innumerable plans had been trotted out, costed out, and talked out along the corridors of power in Washington.

After all the reports were issued and all the speeches made, however, no legislation was passed, not even a compromise bill. All that remained was fading rhetoric, preserved in the *Congressional Record* to remind anyone interested in the subject just how differently people in power looked upon our health care system. According to President Clinton when he presented his plan to Congress, Americans are "choking on a health care system that is not working."[1] To Republican lawmakers, echoing former President Bush, our health care system, far from not working, was the finest in the world. In fact, Republicans repeated this encomium on several different occasions, as if to dramatize their concern that they might never be able to make the same statement again if the president's plan, or anything like it, were enacted into law.

Republicans and President Clinton could hardly be further apart in their views. But which side is nearer the truth? Is our health care system the best in the world or only an overpriced, broken down, jerry-built contraption in urgent need of repair?

Although every industrialized country has its own distinctive system for delivering health care, the goals are invariably the same. Each nation hopes to offer the best care it can provide for the money that the public is willing to invest. Since modern medicine is hugely expensive and becoming more so all the time, every nation seeks to provide its care in the most efficient manner possible. Finally, because health care is so important, each government wants to make high-quality medical care available to all people regardless of their financial means.*

In pursuing these objectives, industrialized nations face a strategic choice of great importance. Either they can treat health care like most other commodities and rely primarily on the market to determine the amount, quality, and type of medical services provided. Or their governments can intervene and take the lead in shaping the health care system. Of the nations we are considering, the United States is the only one that still looks primarily to the private market. In all the others, governments have chosen to play the principal role in determining the cost and supply of care. Amid many variations of method and approach, each of these nations has created a system in which all citizens are automatically eligible for health care, whether or not they are in the work force. The costs are largely paid for by taxes (either general revenues or a payroll levy); and the State exercises control, directly or indirectly, over the total amount expended on the system.

While all these countries have achieved universal access, they have chosen different ways to control costs.[2] Britain has opted to nationalize health care so that most doctors and nurses work for the State, and the government decides each year how much money to spend. France and Japan have hybrid systems in which some people are covered by State-run health plans and others by plans organized by semiautono-

---

*The last of these objectives is the only one that provokes serious differences of opinion. Inasmuch as good health is so essential to well-being, writers and political leaders often speak of the need to give everyone the same quality of care. This statement, however, cannot be taken literally. Hardly anyone would insist that poor people have full access to cosmetic surgery or to private hospital rooms, even though no one (at least in America) is prepared to deny these privileges to people wealthy enough to pay for them. What *is* desired is that poor people receive excellent medical services when they really need them, even if such care is extremely expensive. Thus, it seems fair to say that a basic goal of America's health care system is to ensure that high-quality medical services are available and affordable to everyone when truly needed.

mous sickness funds. In both countries, however, the government sets the fees for all physicians and retains enough other powers to influence profoundly the total amount of money spent on health care. Canada and Sweden delegate authority to regional units of government, allowing the regions to decide how much to spend on health care and to negotiate fees with associations of doctors, nurses, hospitals, and other providers. Germany convenes a national council of representatives, including doctors, hospital personnel, and members of other interested groups, to help the government decide each year on a total budget for health care. The government then delegates to sickness funds (organizations somewhat akin to insurance companies) the power to negotiate fees with providers and to levy payroll taxes on member employers and employees in amounts corresponding to the total budget agreed to by the national council. Whatever the method these nations use, however, the government retains some form of control that enables it to limit the total amount spent on health care.

Few nations control *all* of the health services available to their people. Even countries that have nationalized their health service typically allow some form of private practice for patients willing to pay for it. As Table 12.1 attests, however, the fraction of the population not covered by government health plans is nonexistent or small, compared with the majority of Americans who lie outside any publicly controlled system of health insurance.

On several occasions—in 1915, in the 1930s, and with greater conviction in the late 1940s—reformers in the United States felt that

Table 12.1. Percent of population covered by public health care system, 1991.

Country	Inpatient care	Ambulatory care	Pharmaceutical costs
Canada	100	100	34.0
France	99.0	98.0	98.0
West Germany	92.2	92.2	92.2
Japan	100	100	100
Sweden	100	100	100
United Kingdom	100	100	100
United States	44.0	44.0	12.0

Source: OECD Health System: Facts and Trends, 1960–1991, Volume 1, OECD Health Policy Studies no. 3, 267–269 (1993).

the time might be ripe for some form of universal government health insurance. Elaborate plans were drawn up to achieve this goal. In each case, however, the opposition proved too strong, and the plans came to naught.

There are many reasons for relying primarily on the marketplace.[3] American doctors have always fought against regulation by the State. Business has resisted government control, fearing that it might set a precedent for intrusion into other sectors of the economy. Opponents of all kinds have made their case by advancing the familiar arguments for free markets: their ability to stimulate innovation, to adapt quickly to shifting consumer needs, and to perform more efficiently than large government bureaucracies.

Yet the market for health care differs at least in degree from the market for most other goods and services. Medical services are indispensable for the seriously ill, but they are expensive—for some types of illness, prohibitively so. The sheer complexity of modern medicine, with its heavy use of sophisticated technology, keeps health costs high. The inability of most people to comprehend the intricacies of medicine is also a factor, since it keeps the average person from shopping around for less expensive but adequate care and hence weakens competition as a force for increasing efficiency and holding prices down. For these and other reasons, large segments of the population are at risk of needing medical care they cannot afford.

Those who support the market zealously argue that insurance can take care of this problem for the great majority of people and that charity will meet the needs of those too poor to insure themselves. For a long time, this view prevailed in the United States. As time went on, however, the number of poor people needing care put a strain on charitable resources that was increasingly hard to bear. Even those who could afford insurance often came to grief. Some had chronic conditions that led insurance companies to refuse to cover them. Others did not bother to buy a policy. Still others lost their insurance when they left their employer and were temporarily unprotected while they looked for another job. All these individuals faced severe financial problems when they fell seriously ill.

In 1965, Congress acted to take care of the worst of these problems. By passing Medicare, it offered basic protection to all persons over age sixty-five. With Medicaid, it undertook to share with participating states the cost of providing health care to the poor—at least to as many of the poor as each state chose to include within the program. Federal and state governments thus assumed a hefty portion of the nation's health care costs. As time went on, however, and medical expenses grew more rapidly than the total economy, government officials and corporations felt increasingly burdened by the costs they had agreed to pay.

In the 1970s, Congress enacted a series of cost-containment measures. Some of these initiatives favored the market, such as legislation to encourage the formation of health management organizations that competed with one another. Other measures brought more intrusive government planning, such as the requirement that hospitals obtain a certificate of need from public officials before embarking on new construction. In the end, however, none of the initiatives seemed to accomplish much to halt the rise in costs.

Toward the end of the 1980s, many companies felt compelled to cut back health care plans or give them up entirely as too expensive. Working and middle-class families grew increasingly anxious about losing medical benefits. Popular support for reforming the health care system rapidly mounted. In 1993, President Clinton launched a massive campaign to ensure universal coverage and restrain costs. Anticipating fierce opposition to any plan emphasizing government control, the president elected not to put forward a program, such as Canada's, that would require new taxes and give Washington the task of collecting and dispensing the funds to operate the entire health care system. Instead, he proposed a system of managed competition among large private health care organizations that would offer benefit packages subject to federal guidelines.[4] Under the plan, smaller insurance companies feared that they would be frozen out of the health market, and many small businesses faced the prospect of having to pay the cost of insuring their employees for the first time. Before long, insurance companies and small-business organizations launched massive campaigns to convince voters that Clinton's reforms might lower the quality of their health care. Meanwhile, more than a hundred members of Congress introduced a single-payer plan, similar to Canada's. Not to be outdone, Republicans introduced their own scheme, giving government a more modest role than the president envisaged. In the next few months, a flurry of new proposals appeared as lawmakers struggled to find a formula that could command majority support.

In the end, it proved impossible to muster the necessary congressional support for any of the rival schemes. Gradually, the public grew confused by all the complicated plans and became fearful that reform might simply mean higher taxes, bigger government, and greater restrictions on their choice of doctor. Eventually, opinion polls revealed that substantial majorities of the people had concluded that it would be best if Congress began all over again the following year to devise a better system. Wearily, Congress adjourned without taking any action.

The Quality of Care

With its unique approach to organizing health care, how does the United States compare with other industrialized countries in the quality, cost, and accessibility of its system? Of these criteria, quality is the hardest to measure. There is simply no yardstick that allows a precise, comprehensive comparison. All we can do is gather scraps of relevant information and try to make some rough judgments.

There is a broadly shared opinion that American health care at its best is at least equal if not superior to that of any other nation in the world. Certainly, the preparation of our doctors reaches a very high standard. No other nation attracts as many wealthy patients from abroad or as many foreign students seeking advanced training in its teaching hospitals. The amount and quality of research and innovation are likewise second to none. No country approaches the United States in the number of new discoveries it makes in the biomedical sciences or the patents it obtains for new technology.

Advanced techniques are also more readily available in the United States than in other nations (although this is by no means an unmixed blessing, as we will see). In many cases, the differences are startlingly large. For example, only six years after renal dialysis was approved for payment under Medicare, the United States was giving such treatment at a rate more than three times the average in thirty-two European countries.[5]

In terms of convenience, America has been comparatively free of the long waits for certain types of operations that plague several of the countries where there is greater government control. In Sweden, for example, 31,000 people were on waiting lists for surgery in 1989 in a nation with a population only one-thirtieth the size of that of the United States.[6] Although the Swedes have since made strenuous efforts to reduce this number, substantial delays still exist for certain types of treatment such as removing a cataract, replacing a hip, and carrying out a coronary bypass. Britain is even more noted for long delays, with more than 900,000 people on waiting lists in 1990.[7] Yet serious queuing is not inevitable when the State takes control. In Japan and Germany (at least prior to reunification), the demand for medical services seems to have stayed in reasonable balance with the supply.

One aspect of the health care system that matters especially to Americans is the freedom of patients to choose their own doctor. Some countries with State-run health care systems have not given their citizens that choice in the past. This has been true of Sweden, for example. In Britain, patients have been able to select their own family doctor but have had no opportunity to choose the physicians to whom they are assigned for surgery or other types of specialized care.

There is no intrinsic reason why a health care system organized by the State cannot allow patients to select their physician and their hospital. This opportunity already exists in Canada, Japan, and Germany. Sweden, too, is moving to allow individuals to choose their own general practitioner, and Britain acted in 1989 to give general practitioners greater freedom to select hospitals and specialists for their patients. Apparently, all advanced countries are converging on a system that gives patients a considerable role in selecting their physician.

Although most Americans have substantial freedom to choose their doctor and hospital, they do not seem to visit either as much as the citizens of several other countries. For example, the United States ranks below all the other countries discussed here except Sweden in the average number of visits per capita to a doctor.[8]

Such figures must be interpreted carefully. For example, Japanese patients visit a physician much more frequently than Americans do, but the average length of each visit in Japan is much shorter. Even taking such factors into account, however, William Hsiao of Harvard concludes that contact with doctors is somewhat more extensive in Britain, Japan, Germany, and Canada than in the United States.[9]

Survey data seem to confirm Hsiao's conclusion. According to a 1994 study, 12 percent of Americans reported that they "couldn't get needed medical care in [the preceding] year," compared with 8 percent in Canada and 6 percent in Germany. Despite reports that people in other countries must endure long waits before seeing physicians, 15 percent of Americans indicated that they had to wait more than a week to see a doctor, compared to 16 percent in Canada and only 6 percent in Germany.[10]

The ultimate test of quality is the effect of medical care on people's health. Here, alas, the indices are especially crude. The two most widely used criteria are life expectancy and infant mortality. On both scores, the United States has made steady improvement over the years (Table 12.2).

Medical care is not solely responsible for the length of one's life; personal habits, adequate nutrition, and many other factors also contribute. Thus, no one can be sure exactly how much our progress in medical science has contributed to the steady improvement in life expectancy recorded above. A recent study, however, estimates that clinical and preventive medicine have given approximately five years of added life to Americans in this century, chiefly from advances made since 1950.[11]

Despite its record of steady improvement, the United States ranks very low among advanced nations, both in life expectancy and in infant mortality (Table 12.3). One should not read too much into these comparisons. Both life expectancy and infant mortality are ambiguous measures of quality at best, because they are affected so much by the

Table 12.2. **Life expectancy and infant mortality in the United States, 1900–1995.**

Year	Life expectancy at birth			Infant mortality (deaths per 1,000 births)
	All	Men	Women	
1900	47.3	46.3	48.3	—
1910	50.0	48.4	51.8	—
1920	54.1	53.6	54.6	85.8
1930	59.1	58.1	61.6	64.6
1940	62.9	60.8	65.2	47.0
1950	68.2	65.6	71.1	29.2
1960	69.7	66.6	73.1	26.0
1970	70.8	67.1	74.7	20.0
1980	73.7	70.0	77.4	12.6
1990	75.4	71.8	78.8	9.2
1995	76.0	72.8[a]	79.7[a]	7.9

Source: Statistical Abstract of the United States, 1995, 86; U.S. Department of Commerce, *Historical Statistics of the United States: Colonial Times to 1970,* 55.

a. Figures are projected.

Table 12.3. Comparative life expectancy and infant mortality, 1995.

Country	Life expectancy (in years)	Infant mortality (deaths per 1,000 births)
Japan	79.4	4.3
Canada	78.3	6.8
France	78.4	6.5
Sweden	78.4	5.6
West Germany	76.6	6.3
England	77.0	7.0
United States	76.0	7.9

Source: Statistical Abstract of the United States, 1995, 849, 850.

amount of poverty, the lifestyles of the population, the extent of violent crime, and many other factors. But the quality and accessibility of health care are undoubtedly contributing causes. Moreover, America's ranking is not greatly different for other scattered measures of quality, such as the number of deaths due to medical complications or the incidence of adverse effects from doctors' prescriptions of medicines or licit drugs.[12]

A final test of quality is the opinion of the customer. How do residents of various industrialized nations feel about the quality of their health care? Of course, comparisons of this sort suffer from the fact that very few people have sampled the medical services of even two countries, let alone six or seven. For what it may be worth, however, Table 12.4 records the judgments of patients in several countries re-

Table 12.4. Comparative levels of satisfaction with health care, 1992.

Country	Percent of people saying they are somewhat or very satisfied
Canada	94
West Germany	92
Japan	67
Sweden	82
United Kingdom	87
United States	88

Source: William Hsiao, "Comparing Health Care Systems: What Nations Can Learn from One Another," 17 *Journal of Health Politics, Policy and Law*, 630 (1992).

garding *their own medical care.* According to a more recent survey, conducted in October 1994, 35 percent of Americans rated the quality and responsiveness of health services in their community as only fair or poor (rather than excellent or good).[13] This figure compares with 27 percent in Canada and 28 percent in Germany. Interestingly, despite the lack of a State-run comprehensive health care system, Americans report more administrative complications than Germans or Canadians. Eighty-three percent of Americans characterized their health care system as too bureaucratic, compared with 74 percent of Canadians and 58 percent of Germans.

In patient satisfaction, then, America appears to rank below the top, most probably somewhere in the middle of the six nations surveyed here. This result is generally consistent with the other criteria of quality previously noted, some of which put the United States in a very favorable light while others do not.

Cost

The evidence about cost is much more clear-cut than the indications of quality. In brief, Americans pay much more for their health care, both absolutely and in relation to the Gross Domestic Product, than citizens in any of the other countries discussed (Table 12.5). This has not always been the case. As late as 1960, the share of GDP devoted to health care in the United States was not seriously out of line with that in several of the other countries. Table 12.6 makes this clear. It is only fair to add that the figures in Table 12.6 are somewhat misleading,

Table 12.5. Comparative costs of health care, 1993.

Country	Health care expenditures per capita (in dollars)	Health care costs as share of GDP (in percent)
Canada	1,971	10.2
Japan	1,495	7.3
West Germany	1,814	8.6
Sweden	1,266	7.5
France	1,835	9.8
United Kingdom	1,213	7.1
United States	3,299	14.1

Source: Statistical Abstract of the United States, 1995, 853.

Table 12.6. Total expenditure on health care, as percent of GDP, 1960–1992.

Country	1960	1965	1970	1975	1980	1985	1990	1992 (preliminary)
Canada	5.5	6.0	7.1	7.2	7.4	8.5	9.4	10.3
France	4.2	5.2	5.8	7.0	7.6	8.5	8.9	9.4
West Germany	4.8	5.1	5.9	8.1	8.4	8.7	8.3	8.7
Japan	3.0	4.5	4.6	5.6	6.6	6.5	6.6	6.9
Sweden	4.7	5.6	7.2	7.9	9.4	8.9	8.6	7.9
United Kingdom	3.9	4.1	4.5	5.5	5.8	6.0	6.2	7.1
United States	5.3	5.9	7.4	8.4	9.3	10.8	12.6	13.6

Source: National Center for Health Statistics, *Health, United States, 1994*, 220 (1995).

since they reflect not only the growth in health expenditures but also the fact that America's population has grown faster and its per capita GDP has risen more slowly than has been true abroad. To compare the rate of increase of health care costs in America with increases in other advanced countries, it is more useful to examine the growth rates in real per capita health expenditures since 1960.

The figures in Table 12.7 show that costs have been rising everywhere, in part because of the aging of the population and even more because of improvements in health treatments and technologies that

Table 12.7. Average annual increase in real spending on health care, per person, 1960–1990.

Country	1960–1990 (in percent)	1980–1990 (in percent)
Canada	4.7	4.3
France	5.5	3.3
West Germany	4.4	1.4
Japan	8.2	3.7
United Kingdom	3.7	3.1
United States	4.8	4.4

Source: Joseph P. Newhouse, "Open Issues in Financing and Coverage," in Eli Ginzberg, ed., *Critical Issues in U.S. Health Reform*, 12, 16 (1994).

everyone wants to have. America's rate of increase over the past three decades has not been especially high by international standards. In recent years, to be sure, as all governments have begun to grapple more seriously with mounting health bills, other nations seem to have been more successful than America in controlling costs. What most distinguishes the United States, however, is not the rate of its expenditure growth but the unusually high cost of health care that has prevailed *throughout* the last several decades.

These expenditures might be understandable if they reflected a higher quality of care. But there is no evidence that Americans have gained better health or a better quality of life as a result of the vastly greater per capita outlays. Defenders of American medicine have advanced all manner of arguments to discredit other health care systems and to justify the higher costs in the United States. Reporters and critics have talked about long waiting lines abroad and streams of Canadians coming across the border for medical treatment. Commentators have pointed out that the United States carries the burden of medical research for the rest of the world and that various illnesses, notably AIDS, are more prevalent in this country. A careful look at the evidence, however, suggests that claims of this kind are inaccurate, misleading, or explain only a small part of the large disparities in spending that set America apart from other leading industrial democracies.[14]

Several factors seem to be responsible for our persistently high costs. By far the most important cause is the constant, uncontrolled spread of expensive new technology. Countries with more comprehensive, centralized health care systems find it easier to control the use of costly equipment. For example, once hospitals began using CAT scanners ("CAT" for computerized axial tomography), Britain took advantage of its control over the Health Service to limit the number of these machines to 1 for every million people in 1979. Sweden and West Germany, being more decentralized, did not achieve quite this degree of control but still kept the number of machines per million people to 1.7 and 2.6, respectively. In the United States, on the other hand, the relatively weak planning organizations (health systems agencies) quickly gave ground in the face of strong local pressures to install the machines. Installations per one million people reached 5.7 by 1979—almost six times the figure in England and more than three times the level in Sweden.

Spurred by decades of federally subsidized hospital construction, patient beds in the United States also exist in far greater numbers than the nation needs. According to OECD figures, while occupancy rates in American hospitals stood at 69.5 percent in 1990, they reached 86 percent in Germany, 84.9 percent in Canada, 84.2 percent in Sweden, and approximated 80 percent in most of the other countries examined here.[15] There are also substantially more hospital personnel per patient in America than in other countries. For example, one comparison of similar public hospitals in New York and Paris revealed that the New York hospital had 28 percent more direct-patient-care staff, 61 percent more functional department staff personnel, and 77 percent more employees engaged in finance and billing.[16] In addition, encouraged by a system that has traditionally paid most doctors according to the number and complexity of the services they render, physicians perform more surgical procedures in the United States than they do abroad (Table 12.8). These higher rates would not give cause for concern if they signified a higher level of health care in this country. Unfortunately, various studies of medical practice in the United States have concluded that as much as 15 to 25 percent of the most commonly prescribed tests and procedures are unnecessary, and another 20 percent are rated as questionable.[17]

A further reason for the high costs is the ability of American doctors to charge more for their services. As Milton Friedman and Simon Kuznets revealed years ago in a massive study, physicians earned substantially more for their services than the free-market price even in the

Table 12.8. **Admission rates for selected medical procedures (number of admissions per 100,000 population), 1980.**

Procedure	Canada	Japan	Sweden	United Kingdom	United States
Tonsillectomy	89	61	65	26	205
Coronary bypass	26	1	—	6	61
Cholecystectomy	219	2	140	78	203
Inguinal hernia repair	224	67	206	154	238
Prostatectomy	229	—	48	144	308
Hysterectomy	479	90	145	250	557
Operation on lens	139	35	—	98	294
Appendectomy	143	244	168	131	130

Source: OECD, *Health Care Systems in Transition: The Search for Efficiency,* 22 (March 1990).

Table 12.9. Physicians' earnings, in U.S. dollars, 1990.

Country	Average earnings
Canada	84,819
France	53,405
West Germany[a]	88,394
Sweden	39,991
Japan	45,021
United Kingdom	51,118
United States[b]	155,800

Source: OECD, *U.S. Health Care at the Cross-Roads, 1992*, Health Policy Studies No. 1, 89 (1992).

a. Figures are for 1986.

b. Figures are for 1989.

1930s, due to their power to limit entry to the profession.[18] Thereafter, the methods of payment provided under Medicare and private insurance plans enabled them to continue charging artificially high prices. As a result, physicians in the United States came to earn much more than physicians in other countries (Table 12.9).

Another possible cause of inflated health costs is the frequency of fraud and abuse on the part of health care providers. In 1992, the U.S. General Accounting Office (GAO) ventured a rough estimate that the total amount of money wasted in this way was $80 billion, or 10 percent of total health expenditures at that time.[19] According to the GAO, these abuses were more prevalent in private insurance plans than in federal programs, chiefly because most private plans did not invest much in fraud detection.

Finally, one of the principal advantages of free markets, efficient administration, has eluded the United States in the field of health care. With numerous competing health plans and insurance carriers, much money is spent on such items as advertising, disputes over which provider should bear the cost of care, and arguments over whether patients are eligible for reimbursement. Over the past two decades, as HMOs (health maintenance organizations) and other group plans have multiplied, overhead costs have risen sharply and now make up some 14 percent of the total costs of private health insurance. Though exact comparisons are not available for all the nations discussed here, an OECD report concludes that "overhead costs are far higher in the United States than in other OECD countries, owing to high administrative costs associated with the U.S. private-sector insurance industry."[20] Such costs in Canada reportedly amount to only $21 per person per year, less than one-fourth the corresponding figure for the private insurance market in the United States.[21]

Some analysts suggest that yet another reason for America's high health care costs has to do with the social pathologies of the poor, including widespread drug use, poor nutrition, violence, and the like. But cost increases are by no means confined to the poor. Moreover, any added expenses resulting from the behavior of the "underclass" are offset by the fact that many poor people are not covered by health insurance and hence get less care than they would under universal coverage.

Of all the possible causes mentioned here, the lavish use of technology is undoubtedly the most important in accounting for the higher level of health care costs in America. At the same time, the cumulative weight of other factors, such as overhead, high doctors' fees, fraud, and unnecessary procedures adds many billions of dollars more, helping to inflate costs in America far above those in other countries.

Quality Medical Care for All

The United States has made great progress toward the goal of giving everyone access to health care of high quality. After 1940, as more and more employers offered health insurance to their workers, the percentage of the total population lacking any form of health insurance declined steadily for three decades (Table 12.10). All age groups seem to have shared in this progress. From 1962 to 1992, the percentage of children under fifteen covered by hospital insurance rose from 68.7 to 88.3. The elderly have fared even better; thanks to Medicare, their coverage has risen from 54 percent in 1962 to an impressive 98.8 percent in 1992.

Despite these gains, over 15 percent of the total population—more than 40 million people—still lack medical insurance in the United States. This proportion has been rising at a rate of approximately one million persons per year since the mid-1970s and is far above that of the other countries in this study. In these nations, either everyone is covered, or those who remain outside are a small minority of well-to-do people who prefer to purchase their own health care in the private market.

Table 12.10. Percent of population uninsured, 1940–1992.

Year	Percent
1940	90.7
1950	49.3
1960	27.7
1970	13.6
1980	14.8
1990	13.9
1992	14.7

Source: U.S. Bureau of the Census, *Current Population Reports*, P60-184, "Money Income of U.S. Households, Families and Persons in the United States, 1992," xxiii, xxiv (1993), and earlier editions.

The uninsured in America are a varied lot. Some are young people who do not believe that they will be sick, some have preexisting medical problems that make them uninsurable, and some are between jobs and will remain uncovered for only a brief period of time. In contrast to the situation abroad, however, poor people in America are the least likely to be covered, despite the existence of Medicaid. One-third of the uninsured (private or public) have incomes below the official poverty line, and approximately two-thirds are either poor or nearly poor (receiving 100 to 200 percent of the official poverty income).[22] Among all people with incomes below the official poverty line, approximately 30 percent are neither privately insured nor covered by Medicaid.

The lack of universal coverage in the United States affects more people than the bare figures suggest. In 1993, Marc Roberts reported that one in four Americans would lose his health insurance during any two-year period.[23] One in twenty Americans had a health insurance policy which did not cover a preexisting medical problem.[24] One in four households had someone who could not leave his job for fear of losing health insurance coverage, and 60 percent of Americans worried in 1991 that they might not be adequately insured in the future.[25] Only in 1996 did Congress finally seem poised to enact legislation guaranteeing that workers could carry health insurance with them when they changed jobs without being barred from coverage because of a preexisting medical condition.

What does it mean not to be covered by insurance? Some accounts of our health care system leave the impression that individuals without coverage are cut off from all doctors and condemned to die untreated and alone. That is far from the truth. In fact, the emergency rooms of famous hospitals are filled with people who lack medical insurance but still receive treatment. It is now against the law for a hospital to refuse to accept a patient due to inability to pay.

At the same time, those who lack insurance are undoubtedly disadvantaged. If they have assets and income of their own, they can be forced to use them to pay for their medical care expenses until they are poor enough to qualify for Medicaid. They will probably not have a regular doctor. They are less likely to receive adequate preventive care, and will visit a hospital only when they fall ill or become injured and require immediate help. In 1986, a survey comparing the insured and uninsured populations found that the latter had 27 percent fewer physician visits per year (3.2) than those who were insured (4.4).[26] In addition, only 4.6 percent of the uninsured persons were hospitalized, compared with 5.7 percent of the insured—a difference of 19 percent.[27] In sum, the quality of health care for the uninsured appears to fall significantly below the standard implied by the national goal to give everyone in the society access to high-quality care. Ironically, caring for the uninsured turns out to involve much unnecessary expense for society, since emergency rooms are relatively expensive to operate. Furthermore, the costs involved are simply added to the bill of patients who can afford to pay—an arbitrary way of financing the care. All in all, therefore, the current way in which we care for the uninsured leaves much to be desired.

The Travails of Health Care Reform

After this comparison of America's health care system with the models in the other industrialized countries, what could President Bush have meant in calling our system the finest in the world? Presumably, he had in mind the research achievements of American scientists and the levels of technological sophistication and expertise in our great academic health centers. Perhaps he was pointing to the convenience of so many well-equipped hospitals in cities and suburbs throughout the United States. Conceivably, he was referring to the satisfaction expressed by most Americans with the quality of their own care (although several other countries record even higher levels of contentment).

Notwithstanding these achievements, anyone comparing this coun-

try with other advanced industrial democracies can only conclude that
the American health care system represents a problem of vast proportions. Making allowances for the greater size of our population, the
United States spends over $250 billion more each year than the next
most expensive system among the countries considered in this study.
Despite these huge outlays, the health of our citizens appears to be no
better than that of residents of other leading nations. Americans are
less satisfied with the quality of their care than Germans or Canadians,
and report encountering equal or greater delays in seeing physicians
and more bureaucracy in the system. Worst of all, the United States is
the only country considered here that leaves millions of its citizens
unprotected by any health care insurance and many millions more in
fear of finding themselves uninsured.

These deficiencies do not result from some perverse desire on the
part of Americans to ignore the health needs of the uninsured or to
spend record amounts on medical services. Quite the contrary. The
public is extremely dissatisfied with the current system. In a 1990 survey conducted by the Louis Harris organization and the Harvard
School of Public Health, respondents in ten countries were asked their
opinion on what kind of changes were needed in their health care
system. The results are highly revealing (Table 12.11). Among citizens
of the ten countries surveyed, Americans are the most likely to believe
that their health care system needs "fundamental changes" and the
least likely to feel that "minor changes" will suffice.[28]

Table 12.11. **Satisfaction with the health care system, 1990.**

Country	Percent of public believing that health care system works "pretty well"
United States	10
United Kingdom	27
Japan	29
Sweden	32
West Germany	41
Canada	56

Source: Robert J. Blendon et al., "Satisfaction with Health Systems in Ten Nations," 9
Health Affairs, 188 (Summer 1990).

Some critics blame the defects of our system on the powerful interests involved in American medicine. Yet these groups are no more pleased than the general public with the product that has emerged. Big business, which lobbied hard to preserve private company-sponsored health plans against the threat of national health insurance, now finds the cost excessive and a disadvantage in global competition. Physicians are even more upset. By the late 1980s, with proliferating regulations, intrusive supervision by insurance companies and health plans, malpractice suits, and other annoyances, almost 40 percent of all doctors in America declared that they would not go into medicine today if they had the choice to make all over again.[29] An equal number averred that they would not recommend a medical career to their own children. This is a remarkable result for a nation in which physicians receive much higher incomes than in any other industrialized nation in the world.

Just as government deserves credit for many of the brightest achievements of American medicine, so also must it bear much of the blame for the failings of our current system. Experience in other advanced democracies demonstrates that a nation does not have to leave millions of people without basic medical coverage. Nor does it need to overbuild its hospital network, allow excessive amounts of expensive equipment, permit its doctors to earn hundreds of thousands of dollars per year, or suffer from such massive paperwork and overhead costs.

The process that has led to these results is distinctive in several respects. As in many other fields of endeavor, the debate over health care policy in America has been accompanied by a persistent ideological battle over the appropriate role of the State in organizing and providing medical services. In 1918, the American Medical Association labeled "compulsory" social insurance a "dangerous device . . . announced by the German emperor from the throne the same year he started plotting to conquer the world."[30] By the 1930s, the designated culprit had changed from Kaiser Wilhelm to "social theory, even socialism and communism—inciting to Revolution," but the tone was equally shrill.[31] After World War II, the American Medical Association, with the support of business, continued to hammer away at the theme of socialism and Communism to defeat President Truman's proposals for national health insurance. And even in 1992, Loretta McLaughlin of the *Boston Globe* predicted—accurately, it turned out—that the fate of President Clinton's reforms would turn on whether voters eventually viewed them as "socialistic" and strengthening "bureaucracy."[32]

Observing this ideological debate is a deeply divided public. At times, Americans are relatively complacent about the state of their health care, and at times (as in the early 1990s), popular opinion moves strongly in favor of change. But even when the public seems united behind reform, agreement disappears as soon as one asks what changes should be introduced. One large bloc favors national health insurance, another supports improvements in private insurance, while a third embraces a series of health plans engaged in managed competition.[33]

Amid such differences of opinion, policy shifts have not come about through comprehensive system-wide reforms, as in Europe, but through a long series of incremental adjustments. The changes that have ensued have ranged from market-oriented schemes, such as the health maintenance organizations in the 1970s or the current proposals for managed competition, to efforts at direct regulation, such as prospective payment requirements for hospitals, resource-based fee schedules for doctors, and certificate-of-need legislation to restrain hospital growth.

In some fields of endeavor, incremental change can be a sound procedure that avoids risk of massive failure and allows policy to evolve wisely in the light of experience. But this has not been true for health care. Without a consistent, comprehensive vision of how medical services should be delivered in our society, piecemeal reforms have typically led to unanticipated problems that have made the system more costly and more difficult to fix than before.

For example, the 1946 decision to subsidize the building of new hospitals, taken without accompanying measures to restrain costs, led to vast construction programs which resulted in empty beds and redundant facilities once the country began seriously trying to make health care more efficient. Allowing hospitals to compete for doctors (and their patients) while underwriting the bills for large segments of the public only encouraged wholesale spending on expensive and redundant equipment and facilities, thus inflating health care costs substantially. Relying on unions to extend health care insurance by bargaining with employers yielded short-term gains in coverage. But union negotiations eventually produced a system in which large numbers of nonunion workers had no health plan at all while millions of employees who were covered were afraid to leave their jobs for fear of losing their insurance. Enacting Medicare undoubtedly helped the elderly, but in the absence of adequate controls on physicians' fees it quickly pushed up health care charges and allowed providers to dodge efforts to contain costs by shifting the burden to other, younger patients. Increasing the number of doctors in the late 1960s without any vision of an overall health care system helped produce even greater numbers of specialists and caused prices to rise still more.

The fruits of this process have not been without their ironies. Determined efforts to preserve the free market have resulted in many layers of regulation intended to restrain costs, expand access, and ensure fair competition among rival health care providers. The most appreciated program with the lowest administrative costs turns out to be the largest government-run program, Medicare.[34] Most curious of all, after decades of making concessions to satisfy all interested groups, Congress has managed to create a system of health care that appears to please virtually no one.

13

Regulating the Workplace

Work is an essential part of most people's lives. It is a means of live-lihood, but it is much more than that. It is a daily experience around which friendships form and valuable personal relationships revolve. It is a source of self-respect and personal growth, a means of fulfillment and self-expression. Because work serves so many important purposes, a job is critical for most people. Yet it can be threatened, invaded, or destroyed in many different ways.

Every year, several million employees are dismissed, usually for good reason but sometimes not. Millions more are laid off when companies go bankrupt, move, abandon product lines, or restructure their operations. Still others suffer accidents for reasons connected with their job. In principle, individual workers can protect themselves against such dangers by insisting on suitable safeguards when they take a job and quitting to find work elsewhere if their terms are not met. In practice, however, the thousands of wrongful discharges that occur every year, the unilateral terminations of employee benefits, the sudden plant closings without warning are all pointed reminders that most employees do not have the power to defend their vital interests in this fashion. Nor does the right to quit give much protection to an ordinary worker in a country where unemployment has exceeded 5 percent in nineteen of the past twenty years, and many employees have to forfeit valuable, seniority-based benefits if they leave to take a job elsewhere.

Because the lone employee is so vulnerable, governments everywhere have looked for ways to ensure that workers receive at least some basic protection from being injured on the job or treated unfairly by employers. But fashioning proper safeguards against these risks is a delicate business. A heavy-handed government can easily impose regulations that will restrict the flexibility of employers and limit their ability to compete, while forcing public officials to intervene in problems of employment they are not well-equipped to resolve. As a result, governments face a formidable challenge in trying to shield employees from genuine injustices and undeserved hardships without creating a cumbersome web of regulation that serves no one's interests well.

How has America responded to this challenge and how well has it succeeded? As we will see, the federal government has chosen a distinctive strategy for protecting employment interests with results quite different from those achieved by other industrial democracies.

Empowering the Individual Employee

Governments can protect workers in at least two ways. They can allow them to join together in a union so that they will have greater power to protect themselves. Or the State can intervene directly and fix the terms of employment by decree. Since the latter course would embroil public officials in a hopelessly complicated task, every advanced industrial democracy has chosen to empower workers by giving them the right to join unions and bargain collectively with employers.

While recognizing the right of employees to organize and negotiate, the United States has implemented this policy in a way different from the one adopted by most other nations.[1] On the continent of Europe, where most employers belonged to trade associations, unions formed and bargained on an industry-wide basis. The terms they arrived at were often observed voluntarily by other employers or extended by law to cover all firms in the industry. In the United States, however, employer associations were much weaker, and unions typically had to organize each company separately. Accordingly, when the federal government finally intervened in 1935 to enact a basic law of labor relations, it established machinery allowing employees at each work site to cast a secret ballot to decide whether to be represented by a union (which their employer was then obliged to recognize and negotiate with in good faith).*

---

*Unlike the laws of several European countries, American legislation stipulates that one

This policy was a natural response to the company-based traditions of union organization in the United States. At the same time, the new law had pronounced effects on the development of collective bargaining and labor-management relations. American employers were traditionally independent and inclined to resist collective efforts by employees to negotiate limits on management's freedom of action. The new legislation accentuated such feelings by confronting firms with the danger of being unionized while their competitors were not. In Europe, a company faced with a union could be reasonably certain that its competitors would have to observe the same collectively bargained wages and benefits. In the United States, a successful organizing drive could force a company to accept wage costs and work rules that were more burdensome than those of its business rivals. Obviously, employers did not take kindly to this possibility, and many opposed unionization in any way they could. This practice continues in full vigor to this day.

To keep from being organized, companies have used both blandishments and intimidation.[2] On the positive side, many firms have sought to match the wages and benefits provided in organized plants in order to remove any advantage to unionization. But employers have mounted vigorous negative campaigns as well. Not only have they talked to their workers about the disadvantages of union membership; they have often resorted to threats and even fired employees who are active in helping the union organize. Such coercive tactics, of course, are illegal. Nevertheless, the penalties imposed by the law are relatively mild, and are usually delayed for many months, even years, while cases wait to be heard by administrative authorities and, eventually, by the courts. As a result, incentives to comply with the law are extremely weak, and when the parties do manage to settle their differences voluntarily, the terms are usually influenced by the realization on both sides that the threat of legal penalties does not offer much of a deterrent.

Various studies have shown that strong employer resistance coupled with ineffective remedies has retarded unionization in the United States. One investigator made a careful statistical analysis to explain why rates of organization throughout America were only half as high

---

union shall be the exclusive representative of all workers in any unit designated by the National Labor Relations Board as appropriate for collective bargaining purposes.

as those in Canada.[3] After testing for several possibilities, the author concluded that greater employer hostility in the United States and less effective legal safeguards and procedures were the principal causes. The likelihood that a union will win representation elections declines sharply in America as companies resist more strongly. When employers go so far as to resort to threats and unfair labor practices, as they have done increasingly in recent years, the rate of union victories falls to very low levels indeed (4 to 10 percent).

Originally, policymakers hoped that adversarial tactics would subside as employers grew accustomed to unions and collective bargaining. Instead, employer opposition intensified steadily until the mid-1980s. Complaints charging employers with unfair electioneering rose from 3,000 in 1950 to 18,000 in 1980, and fell back to fewer than 12,000 in 1990 only after union organizing slackened and elections declined by 50 percent.[4] The number of workers illegally discharged for their union sympathies likewise increased to almost 3,000 per year in the mid-1980s, and declined to around 2,000 only when organizing efforts dropped off toward the end of the decade.[5] Over the same four decades, the frequency of illegal discharges rose from one in every twenty elections affecting one in every seven hundred union supporters to one in every four elections affecting one out of every fifty supporters.[6]

The fear of employer resistance may well have prevented many employees who would like to be represented by a union from having that opportunity. In a 1991 survey, 47 percent of the respondents indicated that "if a union did organize my workplace, I would be inclined to support it."[7] Yet 41 percent replied that it was likely that they would lose their job if they tried to join a union, and 79 percent thought that nonunion workers would be fired if they openly participated in trying to organize a union.[8] With so many workers anticipating employer retaliation, it is not surprising that unions have won few elections in recent years and that they have had much greater success organizing public sector employees.

It is important to add that employer opposition and weak statutory protection are by no means the only reasons unions have found it difficult to organize workers. Americans have traditionally been independent by nature, lacking the strong working-class culture common to many countries of western Europe. They are divided by ethnic and national differences that sometimes make it difficult for them to join

Table 13.1. Percent of wage and salary earners belonging to unions, 1970–1990.

Country	1970	1980	1990
Canada	31.0	36.1	35.8
West Germany	33.0	35.6	32.9
Japan	35.1	31.1	25.4
Sweden	67.7	79.7	82.5
United Kingdom	44.8	50.4	39.1
France	22.3	17.5	9.8
United States	23.2	22.3	15.6

Source: OECD, *Employment Outlook*, 184 (July 1994).

together. The periodic scandals and corruptions that have plagued the American labor movement have further dimmed the enthusiasm of many workers.

In the past few decades, the labor movement has suffered further blows that have weakened its position in the private sector. The manufacturing jobs that form the stronghold of industrial unions have declined with the growth of automation and global competition. The most rapidly increasing sectors of the work force have been white-collar service jobs, which have traditionally been hard to organize. Meanwhile, employers have grown more adept in figuring out how to satisfy employee needs in ways that make a union seem superfluous.

This long litany of problems has produced a level of unionization in the United States that is much lower and declining much faster than the level in most other industrialized countries (Table 13.1). By 1992, the union share of private sector wage and salary earners in America had sunk further, to 12 percent, and some analysts project additional declines by the year 2000.

Strengthening the Hand of Unorganized Workers

The existence of unions is not always enough to protect employee interests in the workplace. In most nations, a majority of employees are not union members. Even in countries where unions are strong nationally, they are often poorly organized on the shop floor. Yet employees have legitimate interests in making sure that companies observe health and safety requirements, talk over prospective changes in work rules, and refrain from harassing workers for reasons of race or gender. Once these needs become apparent, governments can simply do nothing, on the ground that workers are always free to protect their interests by joining a union. Alternatively, lawmakers may decide to create some other type of organization at the plant level that can consult with management on behalf of employees.

On the continent of Europe, governments have generally taken the latter course by mandating elected workers' committees, or works councils, in all companies with more than a minimum number of employees.[9] In Japan, the Ministry of Labor recommends the establishment of joint consultation committees. Such committees cannot strike and do not normally bargain over wages. Instead, they talk with employers about other issues in the workplace, such as health and safety matters, disciplinary questions, the introduction of new technology, and changes in work rules and methods of incentive pay. As a practical matter, works councils often fail to materialize in small companies even when required by law. Nevertheless, they do exist in the vast majority of large and medium-size enterprises employing the preponderance of all civilian workers.

Organizations of this kind have not been recognized by law in the United States or Britain and are authorized in Canada only to talk with employers about health and safety issues. In the past, few American employers wished to create works councils. Unions have also opposed them, fearing that they would become rivals and make it even harder to organize employees. The result is to leave American workers at a unique disadvantage. On the continent of Europe, three-quarters or more of all workers are covered by a collective bargaining agreement, and the vast majority are represented by a works council as well. In England, Sweden, and Canada, although there are, strictly speaking, no works councils, much higher proportions of employees are protected by collective agreements which provide for union representatives to protect worker interests on the shop floor. France, the only industrial nation with a level of union organization even lower than that of the United States, has an active set of councils and delegates to represent workers at the plant level. Only in America do employees lack both a strong labor movement and a legally mandated organization to represent their interests.

This state of affairs is not what most American employees would prefer. In a 1988 Gallup poll, 90 percent of all respondents (and even

82 percent of those who disapproved of unions) agreed that "employees should have an organization of co-workers to discuss and resolve legitimate concerns with their employers."[10]

Interestingly, over 90 percent of American executives and managers and over 95 percent of owners of businesses with two or more workers agreed in the same Gallup poll that employee associations were desirable.[11] Now that worker participation is widely perceived as helpful in boosting productivity, more and more firms are creating employee groups in the workplace, hoping to emulate the quality circles and other forms of shop floor involvement that Japanese employers have used so successfully. Yet associations of this kind have a doubtful status under American labor law, which prohibits employers from dealing with any employee organization other than a duly designated union on matters involving wages, hours, or working conditions. One can also question whether employer-sponsored associations without legal rights of any kind could be strong enough to allow genuine worker participation, let alone give meaningful protection to legitimate employee interests, in a nation where labor-management relations are as adversarial as they are in the United States.

Direct Regulation to Protect Workers

Even in countries with strong union movements, governments have concluded that certain matters are so important to individual workers or to society that special legal safeguards are required. The need for such laws is particularly obvious in the United States, where so few workers are covered by collective bargaining agreements. Over the years, Congress has enacted a long list of statutes to protect employees from discrimination, safeguard their pensions, or uphold some other employment interest. Other countries have passed similar kinds of legislation. Among the many safeguards enacted, three are especially common in advanced industrial democracies: (1) protection from arbitrary and unjustified dismissal; (2) advance warning, consultation, and temporary financial support in the event of plant closings and mass layoffs; (3) safeguards against unnecessary risks to health and safety on the job, with prompt compensation when job-related illnesses and injuries do occur.

Unjustified discharges. American employers terminate an estimated 3 million workers every year.[12] The tradition in the United States has been that employees in the private sector who are not covered by a collective bargaining agreement can be discharged at will, unless some provision to the contrary is included in the individual contract of employment. Clyde Summers has estimated that 75 percent or more of all employees in America fall into this unprotected category.[13]

Increasingly, American judges have found ways to intervene, especially in cases where the employer has discriminated on grounds of race, religion, gender, or age, or has acted in violation of some other public policy. By the 1990s, employees were filing some 10,000 suits per year in state courts alleging wrongful dismissal. Still, court proceedings, even in cases where judges will act, are an expensive means of redress for the average worker. In many instances, a lawyer will not take such a case, even for a contingent fee, because the payoff is too small to justify the effort and risk involved. As a result, most of those who do bring suit are relatively well-paid employees who can afford a lawyer. For the typical worker, going to court often remains only a theoretical possibility.

Most of the other countries surveyed in this study give much more protection against unwarranted discharges, although the remedies available often include compensation but not reinstatement. Several countries impose procedural obligations on employers seeking to dismiss a worker. For example, Sweden requires several months' advance notice, while in France the employer must give notice, meet with the employee involved, and provide written reasons for the discharge. In France, Germany, Great Britain, and Sweden, employees can appeal to special labor tribunals if they believe that they have been dismissed without just cause.[14] In Japan, workers can take such cases to the courts with relatively little expense.[15] Even Canada allows workers to arbitrate under legislation in three of its eleven jurisdictions, and courts throughout the country are much more willing than those in America to infer a right to early notice prior to discharge.[16] The net result is that all or almost all employees in Europe and Japan enjoy substantial safeguards against unjustified dismissal, whereas only a small proportion—perhaps 20 percent—of American employees are effectively protected.

Group layoffs. Companies in every country must occasionally lay off workers when business sags because of recession or other economic difficulties. In recent years, announcements of such layoffs have appeared more frequently as companies scramble to become more efficient in the face of mounting competition at home and abroad. In fact, however, there is considerable doubt whether the number of jobs lost through "downsizing" has actually increased.[17] What does seem to have occurred is that larger numbers of those let go in recent years have not been blue-collar workers, who have long endured hardships of this kind, but middle managers, engineers, and other professionals who tended to assume that they could have their jobs as long as they performed satisfactorily.[18] Suddenly, the human costs of competition have become more visible and vivid, leading political candidates and other interested parties to propose remedies ranging from import controls to the provision of tax benefits for "responsible" employers.

A glance at existing laws and practices in other leading democracies reveals a wide array of methods to minimize layoffs and spread their costs. Along this spectrum, the United States stands apart. No other nation accords such freedom to employers to lay off workers or puts the burdens of unemployment so squarely on the individuals who are let go.[19]

Germany offers an apt example of the markedly different approach to layoffs common in Europe.[20] German employers contemplating layoffs must notify their works council well in advance and discuss the reasons for such action, along with appropriate terms of settlement for the employees involved. Under German law, layoffs are permitted only as a last resort, after firms have considered other options, such as hiring freezes, attrition, transfers to other plants, early retirement, and reductions in working hours for all employees. Prevailing policies make these alternatives more attractive by allowing unemployment insurance to compensate employees for lost time if their hours of work are cut and by giving state pension benefits to older workers let go before the normal retirement age. If alternative measures are impractical and layoffs are required, the law compels the company to dismiss workers according to criteria that give priority to those who have dependents or who are otherwise vulnerable economically.

Further measures help ease the burden of workers who must be let go. Unemployment benefits replace more than 60 percent of prior wages and can be paid for at least a full year. Agreements between works councils and employers typically provide severance pay amounting to many weeks' earnings. Active labor market programs are available to assist in job searches, training, and relocation to help employees secure a new position. In all these ways, the cost of declining work opportunities is shared quite widely by the firm, the company's entire labor force, and the society as a whole.

Japan provides a somewhat different approach to the problem of layoffs.[21] In large and medium-size firms, regular employees are normally hired with an understanding that they will remain for their entire working lives. During periods of slack business, companies will do away with overtime, rely on attrition, reassign employees, put them through training programs, or even start a new business to keep them working rather than let them go. Through a program of employment insurance financed by worker and company premiums, the government defrays much of the cost of employer measures to avoid layoffs.

In the eyes of most Japanese executives, lifetime jobs are justified less as a matter of social responsibility than as a way of building loyalty and commitment to the firm. Whatever the motive, this practice spreads the burden of declining business well beyond the individual employee while minimizing the cost of unemployment benefits for the State. At the same time, the system is not universal. It does not extend either to workers in small firms or to temporary employees (accounting for less than 20 percent of the Japanese labor force) who are hired and let go to accommodate temporary shifts in the demand for a company's products.

According to the OECD, American employers have fewer restrictions in laying off workers than companies in Japan or any country in western Europe and North America. Until recently, the United States was virtually the only industrial nation that did not even require advance notice in the event of plant closings or layoffs. As the plight of displaced employees grew more visible in the early 1980s, however, Congress responded in 1988 with the Worker Adjustment and Retraining Notification Act (WARN). This legislation requires companies to give their employees sixty days' notice prior to layoffs, but the law covers only plants employing more than a hundred workers and applies only to layoffs involving at least fifty employees and more than one-third of the plant's work force.

Reports to date indicate that WARN has been less effective than was initially supposed. The General Accounting Office reported in 1993 that "half the mass layoffs involving more than 50 employees were not covered."[22] In addition, a GAO official testified that 54 percent of employers covered by the law had failed to give the required notice to state officials, and 29 percent had failed to notify their employees.[23] Compliance is also less than perfect in the other countries surveyed. Still, much higher proportions of workers abroad receive prior notification from their employer before being laid off, not to mention having the benefit of other procedural safeguards not provided for in America.

Once their jobs come to an end, workers in the United States, like their counterparts abroad, receive temporary help through unemployment compensation for a stipulated length of time (twenty-six weeks in the United States, unless extended by Congress). Employees must normally have worked for at least a minimum period in order to qualify for such funds, and must also accept training opportunities and make some reasonable effort to find work in order to stay eligible for support.

Of the seven countries surveyed here, the United States has been among the strictest in its eligibility requirements and among the least generous in its payments. Since 1980, the situation has grown worse. Many states have run into trouble funding their unemployment insurance programs, and have tried to hold down costs by tightening eligibility requirements and shortening the period for paying benefits. By 1990, unemployment insurance averaged 35 percent of prior wages. Because of eligibility requirements and limits on the length of time that benefits could be paid, insurance payments replaced only 13 percent of all wages lost through joblessness in the recession of 1991–1992. This figure was far below the level of most European countries, where benefits amounting to 60 percent or more of prior wages are the norm and benefits often last for more than a year.[24]

The United States is also unusual for the limited amounts it spends on job training and other active labor market policies that might help laid-off workers find a new job. Only Japan spends less, and meager public programs there are offset by the much larger training budgets of Japanese employers. In recent years, as America has liberalized trade policies and signed the North America Free Trade Agreement (NAFTA), Washington has provided extra unemployment benefits and special retraining funds for workers displaced by foreign competition. The government has had some success with efforts to assist such employees with job searches. By all accounts, however, the retraining has been so short-term and so poorly devised that recipients have not been able to find better jobs than those obtained by similar workers without special training.[25] As a result, all of the benefits provided by federal programs compensate for only a small fraction of the long-term losses suffered by employees displaced by foreign competition.[26] Moreover, these measures cover only a minority of all laid-off workers and do not fundamentally change the American practice of placing responsibility for training primarily on individual employees themselves.

The problem of mass layoffs thus affords a vivid illustration of the varying choices different nations have made in deciding how to distribute the burden of economic change among the individual employee, the firm, and society as a whole. Other countries have taken elaborate steps to protect workers from layoffs and to spread the cost of unemployment when it occurs. In the United States, the pattern has plainly been otherwise, either because organized labor is weak or because of America's longstanding tendency to look more to individual self-reliance than to government programs for solutions to the vicissitudes of ordinary life.

Protection against injury and illness. Places of work can be dangerous for employees. Whether they be miners afflicted with black-lung disease, factory hands maimed by the machinery they use, carpenters made ill by asbestos, or window washers falling from high places, workers have always been at risk in performing the tasks from which they earn their living. This was especially true in the early stages of the industrial revolution when new machines were everywhere and protective legislation nowhere to be found. By 1912, as many as 18,000 to 21,000 workers were dying from job-related causes every year, and several times that number were being injured.

In those early days, an injured employee could gain redress only by going to court and suing his employer. Such suits were costly, however, and complainants had to prove that their employer was negligent—no simple matter at the turn of the century. Because of these difficulties, states enacted Workmen's Compensation laws under which employees received automatic payment, regardless of whether the employer was at fault, for medical expenses and a portion of lost wages.

Although this new legislation was an improvement over the system it replaced, it did not succeed in causing employers to take enough preventive measures to reduce accidents substantially. Work-related injury and illness remained at high levels in the 1950s and rose sharply in the mid-1960s. From 1964 to 1975, more workers died from industrial illness and accidents than all the American soldiers killed in Vietnam. Spurred by these figures, unions and public interest groups began to press for new legislation to increase safety in the workplace.

Congress responded with the Occupational Safety and Health Act of 1970. Under this legislation, a new entity—the Occupational Safety and Health Administration (OSHA)—was established in the Department of Labor. It had the power to promulgate safety and health regulations, conduct workplace inspections, and levy fines on firms that did not comply with the rules.

The way in which OSHA went about its appointed task tells much about the special characteristics of the American workplace. Because few American firms are unionized and there are no works councils, OSHA could not approach companies by sitting down with management and labor groups to hammer out a suitable safety plan.* Instead, the new agency had to rely on promulgating rules and enforcing them through official inspections on a plant-by-plant basis.

The consequences of this approach were predictable.[27] OSHA took a great deal of time to develop rules for different types of workplace hazards, since it had to compile voluminous amounts of evidence, allow interested parties to comment, and build a record for its decisions that could withstand the almost certain appeals from employers, unions, public interest groups, and other aggrieved parties seeking redress from the courts, from Congress, or from higher levels of the federal government. In contrast to the practice in other countries, lawyers were heavily involved at all stages in the regulatory process. Because the agency had to promulgate general standards (often under strict, unrealistic timetables), the rules were frequently unsuited for the special conditions of individual firms and consequently seemed arbitrary and profoundly irritating to employers. Since it enforced its ill-fitting rules by issuing citations and levying fines, OSHA inevitably aroused ill-will and accentuated its adversarial relationship with companies under its jurisdiction.

OSHA soon bore the scars of all these conflicts and tensions. In the first two years, the agency tried to meet Congress' deadlines by issuing 4,000 safety and health standards that were already endorsed by independent groups familiar with the specific work hazards involved. This blizzard of rules antagonized many small employers by burdening

---

*By 1993, however, at least ten states had mandated some form of joint labor-management health and safety committees in some or all workplaces.

them with requirements that did not always fit the particular circumstances of their plant. When OSHA moved on and began to produce its own safety standards, the process proved to be incredibly slow. Ten years after its creation, the agency had managed to complete regulations covering only 17 of 110 known carcinogens and only 630 out of the thousands of potentially hazardous substances used in American workplaces.[28]

OSHA was also handicapped by having to enforce its rules with very limited resources. By the early 1990s, the agency had an investigative staff of only about a thousand people (supplemented by just over a thousand more investigators from various states) to cover more than 6.5 million workplaces.[29] A typical small firm could expect to be visited no oftener than once every two hundred years. According to a General Accounting Office report, "even employers in high-hazard targeted industries are rarely inspected."[30] It was not surprising, then, that GAO studies revealed that over half of all employers were out of compliance with key provisions of OSHA regulations and that many were not even aware the regulations existed.[31]

From the start, almost everyone was upset by OSHA's performance. Union representatives complained about the slow pace of the agency's work and criticized its rules for being too lax. Corporate executives were exercised by the arbitrariness of its rules and the high-handed ways of its inspectors. Virtually every rule that OSHA issued was attacked in court, and unions, employer associations, and public interest groups tried continually to reverse agency actions they did not like by appealing to Congress, the White House, or any other source that might give them relief.

The contentious history of OSHA differs sharply from the experience of similar entities created overseas to develop higher standards of health and safety in the workplace. These agencies have tended to use a markedly different strategy to carry out their mission.[32] The laws under which they act typically authorize the creation of joint employee-management committees on safety. Building on a tradition of powerful unions and active works councils, these new committees are often strong enough to carry on serious discussions with employers about improving safety. As a result, government officials rely much more on negotiation between the parties to produce safety measures tailored to the special conditions of each firm. In addition, with the help of the joint committees, the government has been able to emphasize training workers in safety methods rather than ordering employers to make changes in the workplace. The existence of active joint committees also helps ensure compliance. Although government agencies do conduct inspections, these visits tend to be less adversarial than those in the United States and more likely to result in negotiated solutions rather than fines.

By virtue of their more conciliatory strategy, agencies abroad are much less likely than OSHA to provoke the parties they regulate. Because there is rarely any possibility to appeal decisions to the courts or other independent authorities, agency actions in other countries are not subject to the delays that accompany OSHA regulations, and regulators abroad do not feel compelled to act defensively to build a record that will withstand attack. The effects can be striking. In the early 1980s, for example, Swedish officials promulgated *four times* as many health standards *in three years* as OSHA had produced in the previous thirteen.

The methods used abroad are not without disadvantages. They work considerably better in larger firms than in small enterprises, where there may not be enough employees to have effective, independent safety committees. They often restrict safety discussions to the immediate parties involved and hence are less open to outside views of the kind that public interest groups can offer so easily in the American regulatory system. Errors are less likely to be corrected, since judicial review is not freely allowed. Nevertheless, the process overseas is undoubtedly much less costly, more expeditious, and far less rancorous than regulation in the United States.

The bottom line for safety regulation, of course, is how many lives are preserved, how many injuries are prevented, and how many days away from work are saved through changes in behavior at the workplace. It is difficult to answer such questions definitively. Even official figures are far from reliable, since they are usually compiled by asking employers. The most cooperative employers are hard put to decide which injuries and ailments are truly related to the workplace, especially when illnesses occur that do not become visible for months or years.

The figures in Table 13.2 report the number of injuries and the number of workdays lost per hundred full-time workers in America from 1972 (just after the passage of OSHA) to 1990. Except for an initial decline in accidents, OSHA does not seem to have managed to

Table 13.2. Rates of occupational injury and illness, private industry, 1972–1990.

Year	Total cases (per 100 full-time workers)	Workdays lost (per 100 full-time workers)
1972	10.9	47.9
1975	9.1	56.1
1980	8.7	65.2
1985	7.9	64.9
1990	8.8	84.0

Source: Bureau of Labor Statistics, *Occupational Injuries in the United States by Industry, 1990*, 1 (1991).

diminish the rate or the severity of workplace injuries. The lack of any significant reduction since 1975 is especially remarkable in view of the steady shift of employment from manufacturing to services, where the likelihood of accidents tends to be lower.

Not all changes in the incidence of accidents result from government regulations. Hence, several economists have carried out studies to determine what effect OSHA has had in the reductions that have taken place in the number of job-related accidents and illnesses. The results are not encouraging. Although individual employers sometimes report that OSHA has improved their safety practices considerably, most investigators have concluded that the agency has had little or no effect, except perhaps in plants it has actually inspected.[33] Since OSHA visits such a small percentage of work sites every year, the overall impact of the law appears to be slight.

If it is hard to measure injury and illness rates within a single country, it is even harder to compare the records of several countries. The most careful effort to make such a comparison is the study of Richard Wokutch and Josetta McLaughlin, which contrasts the experience of America and Japan.[34] According to these authors, the frequency of work-related illness and injury was four times higher in Japan in 1952. By 1970, the rates in the two countries were almost identical. Fifteen years later, the Japanese had achieved a level of injuries and illnesses substantially below that of the United States. Although part of the difference may result from greater underreporting, Wokutch concludes that "there is no doubt that the Japanese rates have declined dramatically relative to those of the United States."[35] Interestingly, Wokutch believes that the greater success enjoyed by Japan comes about not so much because the law is administered more effectively but because the Japanese are much more likely to obey the rules and to respect government officials. As he points out, "The cynicism and bad habits that have developed over time in U.S. plants regarding occupational safety and health make it questionable whether a turnaround in attitudes and practices can be achieved."[36]

Because of differences in the methods of reporting and classifying workplace injuries, it is hard to compare national data. More helpful is an examination of trends among nations over time. On this score, the United States appears to lag behind most of the other countries discussed in this study. For example, since the mid-1960s to the end of the 1980s, the OECD reports that fatality rates declined by one-half to two-thirds in Germany, England, France, Sweden, and Japan but by only one-quarter to one-third in the United States.[37] Over the same period, the number of work-related injuries resulting in lost time from work rose by approximately 15 percent in America, while falling by 30 percent in Sweden and by roughly 50 percent in France, Germany, England, and Japan.[38] Only Canada's record seems to have been worse than America's according to these calculations.

Plagued by the inadequacies of existing methods, OSHA administrators have recently begun to experiment with more cooperative approaches to regulation. Rather than impose government rules, they have invited companies to formulate their own health and safety plans with the participation of their employees. Firms submitting plans that are deemed effective will be rewarded by having fewer and more limited inspections, relief from unnecessary rules, and reductions of up to 100 percent in fines for which they might otherwise be liable. In a pilot program involving the two hundred firms in Maine with the largest number of injuries, participating companies identified *over fourteen times* as many hazards as OSHA inspectors could find by themselves, and injury rates declined in over 60 percent of the firms involved.[39]

In addition to this initiative, OSHA has started to rewrite its regulations in plain English, eliminate outmoded or unnecessary rules, and find ways of communicating requirements more effectively to employers. Government regulators are also making greater efforts to negotiate proposed new rules in advance with interested parties, rather than announce them and invite written comments. Finally, OSHA is developing a comprehensive means of evaluating its own enforcement activities to focus on results in reducing illness and injury, instead of simply counting the numbers of inspections conducted and violations cited. These efforts are highly promising. But only time will tell how effective they will be and whether they presage a wholesale, permanent change in OSHA's regulatory strategy.

Evaluating the Record

Nowhere has America's long-standing preference for individual initiative and limited government left a more visible mark than in efforts to protect the basic interests of employees. Among leading nations, the United States has the smallest percentage of workers with any type of representative body to protect their interests, even though 90 percent of all employees say that they would like to have some form of organization to speak for them. In addition, American workers lack many of the protections commonly given to employees in other industrial democracies. They have very limited safeguards against being fired arbitrarily by their employer. They receive much less assistance when they are laid off for economic reasons. And they appear to experience greater risks of illness and injury in performing their work (although the data supporting this conclusion are hardly definitive).

Despite these modest results, the government has not hesitated to intervene in matters affecting employment relations. No less than twenty-six major pieces of legislation regulate the American workplace, and the corpus of federal regulations alone would fill many volumes. The process of enforcing these rules, however, takes a form rarely found in other industrialized nations. Efforts to regulate have typically proceeded in an atmosphere of considerable hostility, both between labor and management and between these parties and the government. The product of these labors is an intricate body of regulations that often seem to be written more for lawyers than for the workers and employers for whom they are ostensibly intended. The enforcement of the rules has been highly legalistic with adversary proceedings and frequent appeals. As always, such procedures consume much time and money and leave an ample residue of dissatisfaction. The final results—whether they are measured in industrial accidents or in time and money spent on litigation—have rarely been impressive by international standards.

It is only fair to add that other nations with less adversarial forms of regulation and more extensive safeguards for their workers have run into problems of their own. Several countries have paid a price by burdening management with restrictions onerous enough to hamper efficient operations. Some disability statutes appear to have been administered too loosely; some nations have layoff procedures that can be excessively time consuming and expensive; and some courts have undoubtedly construed protective laws so strictly that employers cannot terminate workers who deserve to be fired. Ironically, such overly zealous protection can harm the interests of workers by causing firms to restrict employment, hire part-time employees, or use independent contractors simply to escape employment regulations that have become too costly. As a result, some critics charge that employment laws are partly responsible for the high jobless rates that currently plague almost all European nations.

Although these criticisms must be taken seriously, they do not prove that governments should not try to protect employees from being fired arbitrarily or laid off unnecessarily; they merely suggest that such laws need to be constructed carefully and administered sensibly. Moreover, the criticisms themselves have not gone unchallenged. Careful recent studies have concluded that labor laws have not had significant adverse effects on economic growth or unemployment in Europe.[40] According to McKinsey investigators, "while many employers complained about inflexibility in interviews, the evidence showed that when companies were forced to react to dramatic changes in the marketplace, they were able to overcome these barriers."[41] Countries that have relaxed their restrictions on terminating workers in the hope of stimulating employment have found that jobless rates have not gone down. Moreover, the very fact that unemployment was lower and that productivity increased more rapidly in Japan and Europe through almost all of the past several decades suggests that claims about the heavy burden of employment restrictions abroad may well be exaggerated.

There is still too much disagreement to be certain where the proper balance lies between protecting workers and maintaining sufficient flexibility in employment practices. If Europe has moved too far in shielding employees, however, the United States seems to have erred in the opposite direction. It is hard to believe that basic safeguards such as protection from unwarranted dismissal, an effective early-warning law for mass layoffs, and more vigorous labor market programs for displaced workers would exact a significant toll on efficiency and growth. Nor is there any valid business reason why the government should have gone so long without finding a way to prevent laid-off employees from losing not only their job but their health insurance and their private pension as well. No other advanced industrial democracy offers such modest, loosely enforced safeguards for a set of rights and interests so important to working people. Neither productivity nor prosperity requires that employees remain in such a vulnerable condition.

14

The Burdens of Old Age

Old age is a peculiarly vulnerable time. Unable to obtain a job and sometimes infirm or even bedridden, many senior citizens are powerless to cope with the loss of their spouse, their health, or their income. As a result, they badly need some system of support that can at least assure them adequate medical care and the means to avoid a drastic fall in their living standards. Worry over whether such assistance will be available is common as individuals grow older. In advanced democratic societies, then, most people favor some sort of State program that will guarantee at least a reasonable level of protection against the common hazards of old age.

Until the mid-twentieth century, Americans could not look forward to much security in their later years. In the eighteenth and nineteenth centuries, fewer than 4 percent of the country's people even reached the age of sixty-five, and the average life expectancy hovered below fifty years. Those few who were long-lived and who were fortunate enough to have property and wealth could get along comfortably enough, although they might be eyed impatiently by heirs eager to inherit their possessions. Most elderly people lived with their children and continued to work if they could. Those who had no relatives to take them in went to the neighborhood almshouse if they resided in the community. The luckless few who had no town to call their own were turned away to wander and beg until they died.

As the twentieth century began, 60 percent of the elderly still lived with their children, but doubts about this practice were already beginning to grow. Grandparents worried about becoming a burden to their children. Their sons and daughters felt increasingly trapped between their obligations to their parents and their responsibilities to their children. Conscious of these sentiments, a growing minority of old people took advantage of the rising prosperity in America and managed to live by themselves.

Many older people, of course, were not so lucky. The least fortunate continued to go reluctantly to the almshouse, which increasingly came to symbolize the worst fears and tragedies of old age. In 1871 a poem on the cover of *Harper's Weekly* described all too eloquently the predicament of the elderly.[1]

> Over the hill to the poorhouse—my childr'n dear, good-bye
> Many a night I've watched you when only God was nigh
> And God'll judge between us; but I will al'ays pray
> That you shall never suffer the half I do today.

By the 1920s, more and more people were living to retirement age, and popular sentiment began to favor the creation of some form of public pension. One convert to this view was the governor of New York, Franklin D. Roosevelt. In 1929, he observed that "we can no longer be satisfied with the old method of putting [the elderly] away in dismal institutions with the loss of self-respect, personality, and interest in life."[2] By the end of the 1920s, many states had responded by enacting laws giving pensions to widows "who kept a suitable home." Even so, state officials had broad discretion to decide who was worthy of a pension, and many needy widows were excluded.

At this point, the Great Depression struck the country, wiping out the savings of millions of families, throwing millions more out of work, and forcing countless farmers to lose their land. Virtually overnight, whatever resources the elderly had accumulated for their old age disappeared. In the face of such a disaster, even skeptics had to acknowledge the need for some kind of public pension scheme. In 1935, responding to these sentiments, Congress agreed to pass President Roosevelt's plan to create a social security system for industrial workers.

As proposed by Roosevelt, the Social Security Act provided a system of pensions for rich and poor alike, financed entirely by equal contributions from workers and employers. Some critics complained that this was a regressive way to pay for a public program. But the president had his reasons: "We put those payroll contributions there so as to give the contributors a legal, moral, and political right to collect their pensions . . . With those taxes in there, no damn politician can ever scrap my social security program."[3]

Time vindicated Roosevelt's prediction. Social Security has proved to be the most secure of all social programs in America, largely because it is universal in scope and its benefits are thought to be "earned" by the taxes paid by the beneficiaries.

As Justice Benjamin Cardozo declared in upholding the constitutionality of the Social Security Act, "The hope behind this statute is to save men and women from the rigors of the poorhouse as well as from the haunting fear that such a lot awaits them when journey's end is near."[4] To reach this goal, the federal government had to accomplish two things. First, it needed to provide all elderly persons with a secure pension ample enough to avoid poverty. And second, it had to protect them from the risk that they would fall ill and be forced to choose between giving up all their savings or going without the medical care they required.

As originally enacted, the Social Security Act did not accomplish either objective. It covered only 60 percent of the work force and provided no help at all with medical bills. The fulfillment of these objectives would have to wait for many years, as popular support for such initiatives gradually developed.

Through a series of amendments, Congress steadily broadened the scope of the act until it covered virtually all members of the labor force except state and local employees (who normally had pension plans of their own). By 1990, more than 95 percent of all employees were included under the act, and 92 percent of all retired workers were receiving monthly checks. A succession of amendments also increased benefits to the point that someone retiring with an average earnings history would receive a pension equaling 44 percent of peak earnings if the individual was single and 66 percent if married. In 1972 and again in 1986, Congress took further steps to index benefits so that they would rise automatically with inflation.

By themselves, of course, Social Security payments were not large enough to prevent most workers from experiencing a serious drop in income when they retired. But Congress never envisaged government pensions as the sole source of income for a typical retired person. Instead, it sought to provide all employees with a basic floor of protection which they could supplement with savings and private pensions to maintain their standard of living after they retired. Recognizing that low-paid employees would have a harder time accumulating savings, Congress adjusted the floor so that workers with modest earnings would receive Social Security checks replacing a much greater share of their previous pay than that given to highly paid employees. Supplementary payments and food stamps were also available to bring the poorest of the aged up to a reasonable minimum standard.

Still remaining was the problem of protecting elderly persons from the threat of medical bills that could wipe out all their savings and reduce them to penury. Not until 1965, three decades after the passage of Social Security, did Washington address this problem seriously. By passing Medicare, Congress created a scheme that took care of most of the costs of acute care—hospitalization, doctors' bills, nursing expenses, and the like. By enacting Medicaid, the legislature provided a program for poor people—old and young alike—under which the government would assume almost all medical costs for those who were truly unable to pay for themselves.

By 1980, then, Congress had succeeded remarkably well in raising the living standards of the aged to a level comparable to that of younger adults. Total cash incomes of elderly people may have continued to fall below those of full-time workers. But counting the tax advantages of Social Security payments and the value of Medicare and other in-kind benefits, most experts agreed that older people enjoyed a standard of living which, on average, equaled that of younger working people. Poverty rates among the elderly, which exceeded 35 percent in 1959, steadily diminished to 12.2 percent in 1990—about the same level as that of the entire population and substantially below the poverty rates for young children.[5] And official poverty rates did not include important items, such as Medicare, which greatly enhanced the economic position of everyone older than sixty-five.

As the situation of the elderly improved, America's old-age policies came under attack, not for their inadequacies but for having succeeded too well. Some critics complained that social programs had benefited the old at the expense of the young.[6] Others warned darkly of a coming war between the generations, as fewer and fewer active workers were forced to support an ever-increasing number of retired people. Still gloomier predictions were widely expressed that the Social Security program was seriously underfinanced and would be bankrupt before long if nothing were done to put matters right.

The 1980s, therefore, proved to be a decade not of further growth but of consolidation and retrenchment. On the recommendation of a bipartisan commission, Congress acted in 1983 to raise payroll taxes and trim benefits to put the Social Security program on a sounder financial footing.[7] Faced with spiraling medical costs, the government revised Medicare to increase the copayments and deductibles, forcing the elderly to assume a larger share of their health care expenses. But these were relatively minor adjustments, so far as the aged were concerned. In the early 1990s, even after a decade or more of retrenchment, the elderly continued to enjoy incomes that, on average, equaled those of the rest of the population.

How Much Have We Accomplished?

Overall, the United States has come a long way in giving security to its senior citizens. Their standard of living compares well with that of younger age groups, and their health care burdens have been lightened significantly. Adjusting for family size, tax benefits, and the value of homes and other assets, people who are elderly tend to have considerably greater wealth than those who are still working. Poverty rates among the aged have been cut by almost two-thirds as a result of the government's social programs. By any measure, then, the economic position of the elderly is incomparably better than it was half a century ago.

A close look at the record, however, reveals several problems still remaining. The most obvious one is poverty. Granted, only 12.2 percent of the elderly are poor, and some of these have means beyond their reported incomes. But the aggregate figure for old-age poverty conceals the plight of several important groups.[8] Only 9.7 percent of persons aged sixty-five to seventy-four, and only 5 to 6 percent of all elderly couples, can be classified as poor. But more than 20 percent of all people over eighty-five are poor. Among single widows over sixty-five, the official poverty rate rises to 21.4 percent. More than half of all black women over the age of seventy-five are either poor or nearly so.

Of course, those officially classified as poor may be able to supplement their cash incomes with food stamps, housing assistance, and

Medicaid. But only about one-third of all elderly poor actually receive Medicaid benefits.[9] Fewer than one-fourth of the elderly poor have food stamps, because many do not know the program exists, because they cannot travel to the nearest food stamp office (and do not know that the application can be sent to them by mail), because they are confused by the complexities of applying, or because they do not wish to bear the stigma of receiving a government handout. Only 40 percent live in public housing or have vouchers to limit their rent.[10] In fact, no more than half received any kind of federal public assistance in 1990 (other than Social Security and Medicare).[11]

The standard of poverty used by the government has also been widely criticized as too restrictive. It is based on a food diet that even the Department of Agriculture does not consider adequate for permanent use. Moreover, the government's standard assumes that older people eat less than younger people without considering other expenses, such as medical costs, that tend to be higher than normal for the aged, even with Medicare.[12] According to a 1993 study by the Urban Institute, one-third of all elderly households with incomes below the poverty line reported that during the past few months they had gone without food or had to choose between buying food and paying their rent or medical bills.[13] All things considered, then, the problem of poverty among the elderly continues to be genuine for a substantial number.

It is true that poverty rates among senior citizens are no greater and may even be less severe than those of the population as a whole. Nevertheless, the two groups are not truly comparable. Whereas the public may restrict benefits to avoid malingering among younger beneficiaries, this is hardly much of a problem among the elderly. Almost 75 percent of all of the aged poor are women; the majority are widows, most of whom are older than seventy-five. One can fault them for not saving more for their retirement in their younger years, but that would be a harsh judgment indeed. Many elderly widows could not control how much their husbands saved, and many more had their savings depleted by the illness of their spouse. (More than three-fourths of all widows in poverty were not poor until their husbands died.) Even the toughest-minded critic would be hard-pressed to discover a reason for allowing such people to live the last years of their life in a state of penury.

Another major problem that casts a shadow over countless elderly people is the fear of needing long-term care, either at home or in an institution. Approximately 1.5 million elderly people are living in nursing homes. In 1992, the cost was more than $54 billion.[14] Such patients make up only 22 percent of all those needing long-term care; the rest typically remain in their homes, receiving help from professionals or, in most cases, from family members.[15] As the number of aged people needing care continues to grow, the combined cost of institutional and home care—estimated at approximately $75 billion per year in 1992—is projected to rise to $131 billion in constant dollars by the year 2000.[16]

Thus far, neither the private market nor the public sector has produced an effective method of guarding against the expense of protracted nursing-home care. Medicare does not cover such costs. Private insurance policies for long-term care do exist but are held by only a small percentage of the elderly; such policies are beyond the financial reach of almost all retired people and often have complicated exclusions and qualifications that limit their usefulness. The most important form of outside assistance widely available to the aged poor is Medicaid, which currently accounts for over 60 percent of all public spending for nursing homes and home care. But Medicaid covers only families that are officially poor. As a result, either families must spend their own resources down to a point that qualifies them to receive such assistance, or they must evade the law by transferring the patient's assets to other relatives who then refuse to support their bedridden member. In this way, the law-abiding must impoverish themselves to take care of their relatives while the unscrupulous escape responsibility.

The magnitude of this problem has now persuaded most people that some form of government program is required. In a recent survey, 85 percent of the public agreed that government action was needed, and 70 percent declared that they were prepared to pay more taxes to finance such an initiative.[17] The obvious remedy would be to place some kind of cap on the total amount of medical expense that any senior citizen is required to pay. For the moment, however, the price tag seems too great for a Congress struggling to keep the cost of Medicare and other entitlements within limits. Hence, this particular hole in the medical safety net remains unplugged.

Vulnerability to poverty is not limited to those who need long-term care or who are officially classified as poor. At present, approximately 20 percent of all elderly people have incomes just over the poverty line (between 100 and 150 percent of the official poverty line). Such people do not qualify for Medicaid or public housing or other means-tested programs, but still spend almost 20 percent of their own incomes on medical expenses and even higher percentages on housing. For aged persons in this category, clearly, the margin separating them from poverty is narrow, and a few mishaps can easily push them into serious economic difficulty.

One study has tried to estimate the percentages of poor and near-poor senior citizens who are exposed to one or more of the common risks of old age.[18] The authors identify five major predicaments.

1. Having to incur heavy acute-care expenses, among those who do not qualify for veterans benefits or Medicaid and do not have insurance from prior employment.
2. Having to cope with chronic health care expenses (two or more years in a nursing home), among those who lack the assets, including a home, to pay for such costs.
3. Having insufficient income to meet emergencies, among those who depend on Social Security for more than 65 percent of their income but do not qualify for Supplementary Social Insurance.
4. Having to spend excessive amounts of money (more than 33 percent of income) on housing.
5. Suffering from a serious disability, such as inability to get in and out of bed without help, to cook meals and do housework by oneself, or to look after one's personal needs unaided.

Among all senior citizens, 35.5 percent had at least two of these sources of insecurity, and 14.1 percent had three or more. The elderly poor were considerably more exposed to risk: 42 percent had two sources of insecurity, and 23.4 percent had three or more. But the group most subject to insecurity were the near-poor, with incomes of 100 to 200 percent of the poverty line. Within this group, 60.8 percent had at least two sources of insecurity, and 27.6 percent had three or more.

The last major issue arising from programs for the aged involves not the adequacy of benefits but their financing. Despite a major reform in 1983, some observers continue to fear that Social Security is underfunded and will give rise to serious difficulties during the next century unless taxes are raised or benefits are curtailed.[19] Such critics point out that current receipts from Social Security taxes will no longer be sufficient to cover pension payments by the year 2013. The consequences are often depicted in alarming terms. According to James Jones, head of Americans for Generational Equity, "It is self evident . . . that the expectations of [our] young people are going to be disappointed. And when that happens—if we do not use the intervening years to change our retirement policies, our investment habits, and, most importantly, our method of political decision-making, the social result may resemble the physical and destructive power of an unanticipated avalanche."[20]

To dramatize their point, such critics often observe that there were a hundred workers for every retired person in 1900 but that the ratio has steadily declined from ten-to-one in the early 1940s to three-to-one today, and may be below two-to-one when the baby boom generation eventually retires. Such ratios conjure up visions of a work force laboring longer and harder every year to support a growing army of "greedy geezers" protecting their swollen Social Security paychecks through the political power of the American Association of Retired People.

Alarmed by the prospect of runaway entitlements, various groups have advanced bold plans to restructure the Social Security system. One proposal would "privatize" the system by placing each employee's payroll taxes in an individual retirement account to be invested in the private market (where it might provide a better return to retirees on their investment).[21] Another scheme would dismantle the current program and provide government-administered pensions only for those meeting a means test.

There is reason to doubt whether such drastic changes are necessary to avoid insolvency. Current payroll taxes for Social Security are already high enough to be generating huge surpluses that should be used to offset the added expense when the baby boom retires. If this were done according to plan, current financing ought to be sufficient to fund Social Security benefits until approximately the year 2030. If Congress acted promptly, it could keep the system solvent for many additional decades either by raising payroll taxes by slightly more than 2 percent, or by combining a smaller increase with other measures, such as investing part of the current surpluses in equities rather than Treasury bills, or by increasing the retirement age by another year or two.[22] Regardless of what the government eventually decides to do, therefore, Congress can probably preserve the basic system that is now in place if it moves reasonably quickly to make the necessary adjustments.[23]

More serious difficulties beset Medicare, which is scheduled to go into deficit very soon and to experience rapidly rising shortfalls if nothing is done to correct matters. This problem is largely the result of an inability to control health costs, compounded by a steadily increasing elderly population. For policymakers, the challenge is to find a way of restraining costs while still ensuring quality care for all the elderly and shielding them from having to confront important choices about competing health plans that are too complicated for many of them to understand. Current proposals for reform range from modest cutbacks in the existing program to bolder changes such as issuing vouchers that will allow the elderly to select their own means of obtaining care, or encouraging senior citizens to choose among competing health plans with varying costs and deductibility provisions. As this book went to press, no decision had been made about which type of reform the government would adopt.

Comparisons with Other Nations

Since public pension schemes are one of the oldest bulwarks of the welfare state and since the needs involved seem so compelling, it is not surprising that all the nations surveyed here have well-developed systems to ensure adequate incomes for their retired population. The methods used, however, vary widely from one country to another.[24] Some countries pay a flat pension to everyone; others tie pensions to earnings; still others combine the two. A few countries, such as Denmark, fund the bulk of their pensions from general revenues; most others, such as Germany, Britain, and Sweden, pay one-fourth or one-third of the costs in this manner. Only the United States does not add a substantial amount of government funds to the sums contributed by employers and employees.

The benefits provided by America's Social Security system are not markedly greater than those of other countries. France and Sweden are both considerably more generous. Nevertheless, because older Americans are more likely to work or to receive asset income, the United States has succeeded better than any of the other countries in keeping

Table 14.1. Ratio of adjusted disposable household income (after cash transfers) among elderly relative to that among nonelderly people, ca. 1980.

Country	Aged 65–74	Aged 75 and above
Canada (1981)	.94	.81
West Germany (1981)	.85	.79
Sweden (1981)	.96	.78
United Kingdom (1979)	.76	.67
United States (1979)	.99	.84

Source: John Palmer, Timothy Smeeding, and Barbara Torrey, *The Vulnerable*, 93 (1988).

the aggregate incomes of its elderly population at or above those of the rest of society (Table 14.1).

At the same time, the United States has the greatest income inequality among the aged of all the countries surveyed (just as it has the greatest income inequality within the entire population).[25] For this reason, despite the overall prosperity of America's aged population, poverty rates among the elderly are higher than those of any other nation surveyed save Britain (Table 14.2). The poverty gap (measured by the total amount of money that would just suffice to lift all of the elderly poor out of poverty) is also unusually large in the United States (Table 14.3).

The relatively high burden of poverty among the elderly in America is chiefly the result of government transfer policies that are less generous to the poor than those of other advanced industrial democracies.

Table 14.2. Poverty rates among the elderly, 1978–1980.

Country	Percent of elderly living on less than 50% of median adjusted income	Percent of elderly with incomes below official U.S. poverty line[a]
Canada	17.2	4.8
West Germany	11.1	15.4
Sweden	0.8	2.1
United Kingdom	29.2	37.0
United States	23.9	16.1

Source: John Palmer, Timothy Smeeding, and Barbara Torrey, *The Vulnerable*, 96 (1988).
a. Incomes in other countries converted to dollars using purchasing power parities.

Table 14.3. Poverty gap for families older than 65, in percent, 1979–1982.

Country	Average poverty gap[a] (after taxes and transfers)
Canada	22.7
West Germany	26.5
Sweden	3.0
United Kingdom	16.4
United States	29.3

Source: John Palmer, Timothy Smeeding, and Barbara Torrey, *The Vulnerable,* 114 (1988).

a. The percentage by which the average elderly poor family in each nation falls below a poverty line, defined as half the median family income of the country in question. In computations of the poverty gap, the income of the average poor family includes certain in-kind transfers (such as food stamps) that have an easily calculable monetary value.

Table 14.4 compares the effects of official policies in the same group of countries in reducing poverty among the elderly (using as a measure of poverty one-half the median household income, standardized for varying sizes of households). It is immediately clear that America has one of the lowest rates of poverty among the aged *prior* to government transfers but the highest poverty rate *after* government programs have been taken into account.

Other countries have also done more than the United States to protect the aged from being impoverished by protracted health care problems. The majority of the nations in this study cover all or most of the cost of prescription drugs under their national health programs. Most of these countries have likewise provided reasonable ways of defraying the cost of long-term care.[26] Sweden has long included home care as well as nursing-home expenses in its national health plan. Germany has recently passed a measure to add the cost of long-term care to national health insurance by increasing the payroll tax on employers and employees. Eight of ten Canadian provinces share the expense of long-term care, charging individuals an amount graduated according to their income.

In sum, the picture of American policy that emerges from these comparisons is quite similar to the picture for the United States as a whole. Like all Americans, the average retired person in this country enjoys a standard of living which compares very well not just to that

Table 14.4. Percent of elderly living in poverty before and after income transfer programs, ca. 1980.[a]

Country	Before transfer	After transfer	Percent reduction in poverty rate
Canada			
Single	71.5	11.3	84
Couple	55.2	8.7	84
France			
Single	87.5	1.4	98
Couple	77.7	3.4	96
West Germany			
Single	85.8	10.4	88
Couple	70.6	8.8	88
Sweden			
Single	92.0	0.0	100
Couple	81.1	0.0	100
United Kingdom			
Single	86.2	15.6	82
Couple	70.1	17.8	75
United States			
Single	72.6	31.9	56
Couple	57.4	16.4	71

Source: Deborah Mitchell, *Income Transfers in Ten Welfare States*, 68 (1991).

a. Households living in "poverty" are defined as those living on less than 50 percent of the median family income of the country in question.

of the rest of the population but to that of elderly people in other countries. At the same time, not all of our senior citizens share in this good fortune. Despite our still unequaled prosperity, the United States has not succeeded as well as other nations in eliminating poverty among the aged, especially those eighty-five years of age or older. Nor has America managed to find ways of minimizing the most obvious risks that can eat up the incomes of elderly people at a time when they can no longer do much to help themselves. The fear of becoming poor in old age continues to be a major worry for younger Americans; according to one poll, it looms even larger than concerns over losing one's job or being victimized by crime.[27] As a result, notwithstanding all the progress made over the past sixty years, the United States still ranks low among the most advanced countries of the world in freeing its people from the greatest and more worrisome risks of old age.

The contrasts in old-age policy between the United States and other leading industrial democracies highlight a common theme that runs through all of the past four chapters. Without a doubt, the average American has been left more exposed to the major hazards of life than the average citizen in other leading countries of the world. The danger of being victimized by violent crime is much higher. The fear of being caught without health insurance remains a problem only in the United States. The protection given to workers against job-related injuries, arbitrary firing, or sudden layoffs is far weaker in America than it is elsewhere. And the risk of suffering a serious loss of income in old age is considerably greater in this country because there is so little public provision made for catastrophic illness and long-term care.

These risks are a source of growing anxiety for Americans. In November 1995, The Times Mirror Center for the People and the Press reported that 77 percent of the public were very concerned or somewhat concerned about not having enough money for their retirement; 81 percent were very or somewhat anxious about becoming a victim of crime; 83 percent were similarly worried about being unable to afford necessary health care; and 51 percent were troubled by the fear of losing their job or having to take a cut in pay.[28]

The dangers Americans face are not distributed evenly or randomly throughout the population. Poor people are far more likely to be victimized by crime than the well-to-do. Two-thirds of those without health insurance have incomes less than twice the poverty level. Job-related injuries and long layoffs have not struck managers and professionals as often as they have afflicted blue-collar workers. The likelihood of falling into poverty in old age is much greater for persons with modest incomes than for those more comfortably situated. In America the hazards of life are distributed almost as unequally as income.

To be sure, one can find cases in which Americans have arguably received *too much* protection from risk. Laws that allow individuals to declare bankruptcy and still retain lavish homes with servants and several automobiles fall into this category. So do offshore asset protection trusts. Savings-and-loan legislation in the 1980s that provided government guarantees against losses while imposing few restrictions on speculative investments proved to be another exceptionally costly example. In cases such as these, imposing greater risks might help ensure a reasonable degree of care and personal responsibility.

Can we use similar arguments to justify America's current programs for the elderly, the sick, the individual employee, and the citizen concerned about violence? Certainly, critics of the welfare system do worry that government assistance programs may protect so comprehensively against the hazards of life that people will cease to be self-reliant. Bit by bit, they claim, the society will grow slack and feeble. Yet this theory finds little support in the published research. Contrary to widespread belief, such studies as there are show no decline in the work ethic of Americans and little increase in the tendency of citizens to expect the government to solve their problems.[29]

In any case, the hazards studied here are not the kind that could conceivably do much to help society. The risk of being murdered or raped has no redeeming social value. There may be good reason to require the medically insured to share the cost of their health care in order to deter them from using more services than they need. But there is no great value in burdening the elderly with the risk of needing long-term care and having to suffer a severe loss of income in their declining years. These are not the sort of dangers we need to invigorate society or to spur people to live more wisely. Some might argue that the fear of indigence in old age will cause people to save more in their youth. As an empirical proposition, however, this point seems questionable, since personal savings rates in America are the lowest of all the other countries surveyed although the risks of falling into poverty in old age are among the highest. Moreover, it is unrealistic to expect poor working families to save adequately when their earnings barely equal the official poverty line, just as it is unfair to blame elderly widows because their husbands did not lay aside enough money for their retirement. There are better ways by which the government can encourage greater personal savings if it wishes to do so.

Granted, Americans have plenty of risks and uncertainties that the government cannot or should not remove. Global competition has increased the possibility of losing one's job as a result of corporate restructuring and downsizing. Familiar work skills and competencies are becoming obsolete at a more rapid rate. Marriages are no longer as stable as they once were. Crime rates have risen since 1960. With largely unavoidable dangers like these to contend with, Americans have all the more reason to want to alleviate hazards that could and should be controlled through wise government policies. Yet this is not what has been happening. Throughout the past twenty years, some avoidable risks—such as the threat of unjustified discharge, losing medical insurance, and suffering serious income loss during unemployment—have actually increased, while others that could have been substantially reduced still persist at unnecessarily high levels.

Why does America do less than other countries to protect citizens against dangers that have no redeeming social value? Not because we are unable to afford programs to alleviate these hazards. Taking full account of the amounts Americans already spend on prisons, police protection, Social Security, OSHA, and, above all, health care, we are probably paying a higher proportion of our gross domestic product to protect ourselves from basic risks than the citizens of other industrial democracies. Our problem, then, is not so much that we are unwilling to set aside the funds that are required to protect ourselves adequately. Our problem is that we are getting too little protection for the money we already spend.

VALUES

15

Individual Freedom
under Law

Individual freedom has always been at the center of the American experience. It was in search of freedom that the Pilgrims, Puritans, and Quakers first traveled to this continent. Similar motives inspired successive waves of immigrants to make the long, arduous journey to America in the generations that followed. The quest for freedom led the colonists to start a revolution to liberate themselves from British rule. The liberties they cherished were included in their state constitutions and were quickly added to the federal Constitution with the passage of the Bill of Rights. Over the years, these sentiments have endured. Ask any representative group of Americans what is truly important about the United States and most will reply that this is a country where people are free to say and do what they please.

The Growth of Constitutional Freedoms

Despite the long tradition of freedom in America, individual liberties, as we know them today, did not truly come into their own until relatively late in our history. For almost a century, the Bill of Rights coexisted with the widespread practice of slavery. Even for whites, it is only in the past seventy years that most important freedoms gained a solid basis of support in the Constitution.

Until well into this century, the Supreme Court refused to hold the First Amendment applicable to the states. As a result, freedoms of speech and press were dependent on the attitudes of local judges and legislatures. All too often, these officials were content to go along with popular pressures to silence abolitionists, pacifists, socialists, labor organizers, and others who advocated controversial policies or questioned the wisdom of going to war. Categories of expression, such as seditious utterances, blasphemy, private libel, and obscenity, were broadly defined and widely thought to fall outside the scope of rational discourse protected by the Constitution.

From the Reconstruction era to the Great Depression, the principal freedoms that the Supreme Court did uphold were the rights of property and contract. To the Justices of that age, the "liberty" of the Fifth and Fourteenth Amendments meant the right to run one's business without interference from a government seeking to protect the weak or to promote other social values. The Court was willing to uphold federal laws, such as the Sherman Act, that sought to protect competition. In principle, at least, it acknowledged the right of governments to legislate in behalf of "the health, good order, morals, peace and safety of the community."[1] More often than not, however, the Justices struck down laws that sought to regulate prices or to protect workers by establishing maximum hours of work, minimum wages, or the right to join a union.[2]

The shift toward the modern era of individual freedom began in the 1920s, with the trial of left-wing activists who had spoken out against America's entry into the First World War. Although most of these convictions were upheld, the cases gave dissenting Justices Oliver Wendell Holmes and Louis Brandeis an opportunity to present the doctrines of free speech that eventually persuaded a majority of the Court.[3] Equally important, the "Red Scare" cases offered an occasion for the Supreme Court to declare at last that the principles of the First Amendment did apply to the states. Henceforth, the Justices could announce rules that defined the scope of essential civil liberties for every level of government throughout the land. In 1938, the Court even declared that First Amendment freedoms would henceforth occupy a "preferred position," so that state actions allegedly interfering with these freedoms would be subject to special scrutiny by the federal judiciary.[4]

These opinions set the stage for an extraordinary growth of constitutionally guaranteed freedoms during the decades after World War II. The protection accorded to free speech and a free press expanded in all directions. Now government officials could prohibit speech that openly advocated the use of force or the violation of law only "where such advocacy is directed to inciting or producing *imminent* lawless action" (italics added).[5] The most provocative speech was protected, including expressive acts such as wearing signs insulting the United States or publicly burning an American flag.[6] In addition, the Court extended the reach of the First Amendment far beyond discourse on public affairs to include artistic expression, scholarly writings, and, to a limited extent, commercial advertising.

The Justices also interpreted the First Amendment to give broad protection to the press. As early as 1931, the Court had struck down a Minnesota law allowing judges to halt a publication if they concluded that it was "an obscene, lewd and lascivious newspaper, magazine or other periodical, or a malicious, scandalous and defamatory newspaper."[7] In 1971, when the federal government sued the *New York Times* for publishing a secret account of the Vietnam War, a majority of the Court refused to uphold the power of the executive branch to curb publication.[8] According to Justice Potter Stewart, such censorship was impermissible without proof that disclosure would "surely result in direct, immediate, and irreparable damage to our Nation or its people."[9]

The Justices were equally emphatic in protecting newspapers from libel suits over published comments on the performance of public figures. An Alabama jury had awarded damages against the *New York Times* for advertisements that allegedly gave an inaccurate account of civil rights demonstrations. Striking down this result, the Supreme Court declared that such a decision could not stand unless the complaining party proved that the newspaper in question had printed the disputed statements with knowledge that they were false or with reckless disregard of whether they were true or not. Merely printing false statements about public figures was not enough.[10]

The Justices were also active in enlarging political rights outside the scope of the First Amendment. For decades, many states had divided themselves in electoral districts of highly unequal populations to maintain the power of rural voters over cities and suburbs. In 1964, however, the Court ruled that states could not create districts of grossly disparate populations, because they deprived citizens of an equal vote.[11] With a single opinion, the Court altered the political balance in a large number of states and required their legislatures to draw a brand new electoral map. Further support for an equal right to vote arrived through a series of rulings forbidding all-white primary elections, poll taxes, and other devices to keep poor people and blacks from casting a meaningful ballot.

In addition to the voting cases, federal courts led the way to many equal rights for blacks. The pivotal case, of course, was *Brown v. Board of Education,* which prohibited the segregation of public schools.[12] More than a decade later, *Brown* was followed by court orders requiring cities to bus students from one neighborhood to another in order to integrate their schools.[13] With the aid of federal legislation, blacks were likewise granted protection from discrimination in the workplace, as well as in purchasing a residence, gaining admission to colleges and universities, and entering places of public accommodation. Quickly, these guarantees were extended to other ethnic minorities and to all nationalities, religious groups, and women.

Through the interpretations of the Supreme Court, the Constitution also came to protect a growing number of personal choices. Individuals could decide to send their children to private or parochial schools,[14] to travel freely among the states,[15] and to enter the occupation of their choice unhindered by unreasonable state restrictions.[16] Many of these personal rights emerged through the doctrine of "privacy"—a term not used specifically in the Constitution but championed by Justice Brandeis and eventually recognized by the entire Court as a citizen's right to be let alone by the State, to have "protection against intrusive observation and intimate decision, to autonomy with respect to the most personal of life choices."[17] Eventually, the Justices extended the meaning of "privacy" to include the right to use and sell contraceptives, to marry persons of a different race, and to view pornographic materials in one's home. Most controversial of all, the Court extended the privacy doctrine to uphold a woman's right to an abortion—an unrestricted right prior to the fetus' viability, and a right even after viability if the woman's life or health would be endangered by carrying her child to term.[18] Only when it came to sodomy did the Court draw back and uphold the power of states to impose prohibitions.[19]

Finally, the Supreme Court clarified and refined an extensive set of rights protecting those suspected or accused of committing a crime. The Bill of Rights includes requirements for a speedy trial by a jury of one's peers, a right to counsel, and protection against self-incrimination and unreasonable searches and seizures. A series of cases made these provisions binding on state courts as part of the "due process" required by the Fifth and Fourteenth Amendments.[20] Other cases strengthened the safeguards. Especially significant were rulings restricting the State from introducing illegally seized evidence in court and requiring the government to provide suitable counsel at public expense to all indigent persons accused of felonies or other important crimes.[21]

The Supreme Court opinions here described are only the most noteworthy in a long line of decisions during the 1950s, 1960s, and 1970s that defined an extraordinary array of individual freedoms. By drawing them from the Bill of Rights, the Supreme Court placed them beyond the reach of the executive and the legislative branches save through the long, exacting process of amending the Constitution. By incorporating them into the Fourteenth Amendment, the Justices extended the safeguards to protect Americans from official actions at every level of government.

Curiously, while the Supreme Court was enlarging all manner of personal liberties and freedoms, the opposite was happening to contract and property rights. Bit by bit, these economic rights were qualified and limited. Legislatures repeatedly passed laws to regulate private businesses in the interest of the environment, the consumer, and the individual employee. Courts voided contracts that offended public policy or took unreasonable advantage of weaker tenants and customers. No longer the most protected of rights under the Constitution, property and contract often seemed to be the most vulnerable. Even the right to just compensation on the part of owners deprived of their property was narrowed by rulings limiting the meaning of a "taking" (although the pendulum seems to be swinging back in recent Supreme Court decisions).[22]

It may seem odd that in a nation so dedicated to free enterprise, the courts would fail to give close scrutiny to government actions that allegedly infringed the rights of property and contract. Practical reasons probably dictated this result. In the realm of free speech and other civil liberties, the Court could extend broad protection and confine itself to reviewing cases in which the State pleaded exceptional and compelling reasons for interfering. With respect to the economy, however, it was clear by the 1930s that a modern State would have to intervene repeatedly to guard against market failures and protect other strong public interests. Having judges exercise strict scrutiny over property and contract rights, therefore, would force them to assess the reasonableness of countless forms of economic regulation—a complex task which the courts were singularly ill-equipped to perform.

With judges understandably reluctant to interfere, Americans have been subject to a growing body of regulations as more and more interests are deemed worthy of protection by the law. Most of these rules involve business enterprises, but some affect individuals through building codes, health and safety regulations, and the like. In one sense, such restrictions do not seem to diminish any freedom we should care about, since they merely prevent firms or individuals from committing acts that harm or endanger others. No one, after all, worries very much about homicide laws because they curtail the freedom of potential murderers. Nevertheless, as rules accumulate—each year, there are more than 60,000 additional pages of federal regulations—it is almost certain that more and more people will have to comply with general rules that make no sense in their particular situation, that more and more companies will be victims of laws mistakenly applied, that more and more organizations will be subject to restrictions of which they are not even aware. Already, these burdens have led large majorities of the public to conclude that the government is interfering too much with their lives. Such complaints reveal a problem that many consider the largest threat to freedom currently experienced in the United States.

Individual Rights Abroad

One cannot compare the amount of freedom in different countries as one can compare the purity of their air, the cost of their health care system, or the growth of their gross domestic product. There is simply no gauge with which to aggregate individual rights and measure the total amount of freedom. Nor are the degrees of freedom recognized by law necessarily the same as the extent of freedom that exists in fact. Custom, conformity, and economic circumstance may all qualify the liberties recognized by law. In Japanese schools, for example, students may seem to be as free as their counterparts in the United States, but domineering teachers and strong social pressures to conform often make the environment of a Japanese school much more constrained than most educational institutions in this country.[23] Conversely, citizens in both Japan and the United States have equal rights to walk as they choose in public places. Yet many more Americans feel restricted in exercising this right because of a fear of violent crime that forces them to avoid whole sections of American cities after dark.

Amid these complications, what generalizations can one make about the differences in the status of freedom in advanced industrial democracies? Interestingly, there is no indication that Americans believe in basic freedoms more strongly than residents of other leading industrial democracies. In fact, Americans may actually be *less* firmly committed to civil liberties than citizens in several major European countries (Tables 15.1 and 15.2). As these figures suggest, majorities in all industrialized democracies are committed to basic individual rights. In fact, the list of legally recognized freedoms is now so similar in most advanced countries that efforts to weigh the variations yield insubstantial results. For example, consider the findings by a New York City–based organization, Freedom House, which for the past twenty years has published an annual survey rating countries on a scale of 1 to 7, according to the protection they accord to political and civil rights

Table 15.1. Percent of people saying that various protest activities against the government should "definitely" or "probably" be allowed; survey conducted in 1989.

Activity	United States	Britain	Germany
Hold protest meetings	78	89	91
Issue protest pamphlets	69	86	73
Conduct marches and demonstrations	66	70	31
Engage in nationwide strikes	20	30	42

Source: Roger Jowell, Sharon Witherspoon, and Lindsay Brook, eds., *British Social Attitudes: Special International Report*, 46 (1989).

Table 15.2. Percent of people saying that those who want to overturn the government should "definitely" or "probably" be allowed to engage in various activities; survey conducted in 1989.

Activity	United States	Britain	Germany
To hold public meetings	55	54	77
To teach 15-year-olds in school	21	13	19
To publish books	57	68	74

Source: Roger Jowell, Sharon Witherspoon, and Lindsay Brook, eds., *British Social Attitudes: Special International Report*, 55 (1989).

(Table 15.3).[24] All of the countries listed in the table recognize the fundamental civil liberties of speech, press, and assembly. All respect personal freedoms, such as a limited right to an abortion or the right to attend private or religious schools. All acknowledge such basic procedural safeguards as the opportunity for a speedy, impartial trial, the right to counsel, and the freedom from unreasonable searches and seizures.[25] Although judges and lawmakers from these countries may de-

Table 15.3. "Freedom House" Comparative Survey of Freedom (1 is the highest rating), 1975–1990.

Country	1975	1980	1985	1990
Canada				
Political rights	1	1	1	1
Civil rights	1	1	1	1
France				
Political rights	1	1	1	1
Civil rights[a]	2	2	2	2
West Germany				
Political rights	1	1	1	1
Civil rights[b]	1	2	2	1
Japan				
Political rights	2	2	1	1
Civil rights	1	1	1	1
Sweden				
Political rights	1	1	1	1
Civil rights	1	1	1	1
United Kingdom				
Political rights	1	1	1	1
Civil rights	1	1	1	1
United States				
Political rights	1	1	1	1
Civil rights	1	1	1	1

Source: R. Bruce McColm et al., *Freedom Review: The Comparative Survey of Freedom, 1990* (1990), and similar surveys from earlier years.

a. Apparently, France is given a rating of 2 because of its more restrictive press laws and a persistent "authoritarian attitude in government-citizen relations."

b. Germany receives a rating of 2 in some years because of limitations on hate speech and other inflammatory literature and, perhaps, because of measures taken in response to terrorist activities.

scribe these rights in different ways and support them with different philosophical underpinnings, the results are much the same in the vast majority of concrete cases. What remains is a residue of contrasts that are not fundamental but still throw interesting light on prevailing practice in the various societies involved. Five differences seem especially worthy of mention.

Although each of the seven countries discussed here recognizes the importance of free speech, American courts tend to offer protection that is more far-reaching and uncompromising than the safeguards provided in the other nations.[26] For example, Swedish law permits the censorship of motion pictures that are considered excessively violent, although such powers are used very sparingly today.[27] Moreover, almost every country except the United States draws the line when it comes to "hate speech"—words that amount to a provocation of "discrimination, hatred, or violence toward any person or group of persons on the ground of their origin" (France) or that "threaten or express contempt for a group of a certain race, skin color, or national creed" (Sweden).[28] A 1990 French law even makes it a misdemeanor to deny the existence of certain crimes against humanity, with the result that Jean-Marie Le Pen, head of the right-wing Front National party, was found liable for having stated that the Holocaust was merely a "detail" of World War II.

These differences reflect a greater tendency in the United States than elsewhere to favor the rights of the individual over the interests of the community. As many commentators have pointed out, the language of human rights in America often seems predicated on the notion of a solitary person free of strong communal obligations and ties.[29] Even the family, closest of all human relationships, is often treated by the law as a collection of separate individuals. In the words of the Supreme Court, "The married couple is not an independent entity with a mind of its own, but an association of two individuals, each with separate intellectual and emotional make-up."[30] In Europe, on the other hand, to quote a German judge, "The concept of man in the Basic Law is not that of an isolated sovereign individual; rather the Basic Law has decided in favor of a relationship between individual and community in the sense of a person's dependence on and commitment to the community without infringing on a person's individual value."[31]

Although the judicial formulations just described may seem vague and abstract, they radiate through the law to affect the rulings in concrete cases. For example, residents of many states in America have an absolute right to divorce, and obligations to support the divorced spouse and children have tended to be relatively modest and loosely enforced. In Europe, divorcing fathers are required to pay considerably higher levels of child support, and there are even rules in some countries (rarely invoked, to be sure) that petitions for divorce can be denied if they threaten to cause exceptional hardship for either spouse or for children below the age of majority.[32] Most European countries make considerably greater efforts to establish paternity and to enforce child support.[33] Similarly, whereas parents in the United States have broad freedom to give away their money and to disinherit their children, such gifts may be disallowed in many European nations if they threaten to place other members of the family in difficult economic circumstances.

Judges in the United States are also more inclined to favor the individual when civil liberties come in conflict with the claims of the State. In France, for example, public officials have received more protection than ordinary people from libelous statements by the media, and French authorities during the Algerian War seized newspapers that published the writings of Algerian nationalists or that harshly criticized the conduct of the war.[34] More recently, the European Court of Human Rights (like the Supreme Court of Japan) has taken a position closer to that of American judges by recognizing that officials should have *less* protection than private citizens against publications attacking them on grounds related to their official duties.[35] In Britain, public bodies are likewise unable to sue a newspaper for libel because of the chilling effect such suits might have on free expression. But America still seems unusual in requiring a "reckless disregard" for the truth and not merely a false accusation to render a newspaper liable for attacking a public figure.

Another illustration of the differing balances struck between the individual and the State is the degree of protection given to newspapers to publish embarrassing or compromising government secrets. The Supreme Court has refused to curb such disclosures unless they would "surely result in direct, immediate, and irreparable damage to our Nation or its people."[36] In most other countries, judges are inclined to weigh the interests of the State more heavily and to give the government the benefit of the doubt. In Great Britain, for example, the Official Secrets Act makes it unlawful for newspapers or government officials to publish damaging government secrets involving security, defense, crime, foreign relations, and other specified categories if they know or have reason to know that the information is intended to be kept confidential.

In much the same way, few of the other countries discussed here go so far as the United States in protecting individuals from heavy-handed behavior by the police. By and large, police in these countries have much more latitude in holding suspects for questioning, warning them of their rights, and conducting searches. In France, for example, suspects can be held for up to twenty hours without seeing a lawyer and even thereafter can be interrogated without counsel being present. In most countries, judges are less willing than their counterparts in America to exclude illegally seized material from being introduced in a criminal trial. To the United States Supreme Court, admitting such evidence would invite improper searches and seizures and reward public officials for violating the Constitution (although the Supreme Court has recently seemed eager to find exceptions to the exclusionary rule). Judges in most other advanced democracies are more inclined to allow such evidence, fearing that excluding it could let a criminal go free merely because of a policeman's blunder. For similar reasons, American courts will not accept confessions from prisoners who have not been advised of their right to have a lawyer and to remain silent. Other countries rarely exclude confessions on these grounds.

The third difference that distinguishes the protection of individual freedoms in America is the central role given to the courts. In Britain, judges play a much less prominent part, since there is no written constitution with a bill of rights which the courts can uphold through judicial review. In France, a special court (the Conseil Constitutionnel) can judge a law's constitutionality, but the Conseil can act only at the request of the president, the premier, or presidents of the senate and the National Assembly, or on petition by members of Parliament and only before legislation comes into force. Even in Canada, which has a bill of rights with judicial review, the constitution allows the Parliament to make specific provision to override the constitution for a five-year period when the legislature considers it necessary to do so.

These differences in the role of the judiciary have undoubtedly narrowed as European courts have found ways to strike down administrative actions that interfere with basic individual rights and freedoms. The role of the courts in Europe has also expanded through the influence of the European Convention on Human Rights, passed by the

Council of Europe in 1950. With its comprehensive list of basic free-
doms, the Convention has now been ratified by most European coun-
tries. As interpreted by the European Commission and by the Court of
Human Rights, it forms a part of the domestic law of many nations.
The Convention is also taken into account in the interpretation of all
European Community law as applied by the Court of Justice of the
European Community.

Notwithstanding this convergence of legal doctrine, it is unlikely
that many other countries will allow their judges to assume wide-ranging powers to resolve such seemingly political questions as whether a
State has correctly drawn its voting districts or equitably financed its
public schools.[37] Even more remote is the possibility that other judicial
systems would undertake the wholesale reform of major institutions
or the detailed supervision of State functions that American judges
have carried out in order to be sure that individual rights are fully
respected. In 1835, Alexis de Tocqueville wrote that "a more imposing
judicial power was never constituted by any people."[38] More than 150
years later, Tocqueville's words ring truer than ever. As Archibald Cox
observed in describing Boston in the late 1970s, "Federal judges were,
at the same time, superintending public school administration, reforming the care of the retarded and emotionally disturbed young people,
and attempting to correct defects in prison administration by forcing
the construction of new facilities. Concurrently, a state court receiver
was supervising the Boston Housing Authority."[39] No other country in
the world has granted its judges such sweeping powers.

There is a link between the tendency in America to value individual
freedoms over the claims of the State and the willingness to give the
courts such a prominent role in resolving major social and political
questions. At bottom, both tendencies reflect a deep-seated distrust on
the part of Americans toward their government. There is no possible
way by which a citizenry can protect itself completely against the threat
of arbitrary actions by its officials. But surely a good way to begin is
to have a constitution with elaborate guarantees of personal liberty,
coupled with provisions for review by a body of jurists whose tenure
does not depend on the shifting sentiments of voters or the pressures
of factional interests. Although the American people may not have
recognized at the outset all the protection that our modern Constitution would eventually provide, they clearly appreciate it now. That is
why Americans continue to have such confidence in our system of

government despite their distrust of politicians, and why they resist so strongly efforts by presidents or by Congress to tamper with the independence of the Supreme Court.

The fourth distinguishing feature of America's treatment of freedom is the contrast between the elaborate protection given to political, intellectual, and artistic freedoms and the absence of any affirmative constitutional rights to such basic necessities as food, jobs, shelter, and health care. In other industrial democracies, such as Germany and Japan, constitutions make explicit mention of these material rights. For example, the Swedish constitution declares that "the personal, economic and cultural welfare of the individual shall be the fundamental aims of the activity of the community. In particular, it shall be incumbent on the community to secure the right to work, to housing and to education and to promote social care and security as well as favorable living experience."[40] Not only are there no similar guarantees in the U.S. Constitution; Chief Justice William Rehnquist has made it clear that the Fourteenth Amendment is "a limitation on the State's power to act, not a guarantee of certain minimum levels of safety and security."[41]

In fact, the contrast just described may be more apparent than real, for courts abroad have consistently declared that constitutional rights to food, shelter, and the like are statements of aspiration and not judicially enforceable obligations of the State.[42] One may legitimately ask whether it is wise to include in a constitution basic rights that have no binding effect. Yet their position in a national constitution doubtless endows these claims with a certain moral force—a force that may have something to do with the fact that other industrial democracies have gone to greater lengths than the United States to assure reasonable levels of food, health care, and affordable housing to all their citizens.

A related difference, which constitutes the fifth distinctive element in America's approach to freedom, is a tendency on the part of U.S. judges and lawmakers to be less concerned than lawmakers abroad with whether individuals have the economic means to exercise their legal rights under the Constitution. For example, the Supreme Court has made it clear for many decades that parents have a constitutional right to send their children to private or parochial schools. Yet despite the recent interest in voucher plans, almost no governments in this country make provision to reimburse families who choose to have their children educated outside the public school system. In contrast, parents in every other country in our survey receive at least partial support if they send their offspring to a church-related or private school.

In much the same way, other advanced democratic nations frequently have more elaborate legal aid systems than America's to enable low-income residents to obtain legal advice and assistance. Similarly, although the Supreme Court has interpreted the Constitution to give women greater freedom to terminate a pregnancy than in almost any industrial democracy, the Justices have also upheld the government's right to withhold public funding for abortions.[43] In practice, therefore, opportunities for poor women to have an abortion are considerably reduced in many areas of the country. In Europe, on the other hand, governments tend to restrict abortions more carefully, but they provide complete or partial funding to any woman who does have a legal abortion.

Still another illustration arises in the context of political campaigns. American judges have gone to great lengths to protect the right of free speech on the part of political candidates and to insist on equal rights for candidates and voters. At the same time, election campaigns have become increasingly expensive, especially when it comes to televised political advertisements and speeches. As a result, well-financed candidates have a distinct advantage over their less affluent rivals, so that equal rights in law threaten to become unequal opportunities in fact.

In Europe, governments have typically addressed this problem by making free television time available to all candidates. In some countries judges have gone further, demanding special efforts by broadcasters to ensure access to the media by all points of view. In Germany, for example, Article 5(1) of the constitution guarantees to everyone the right to express and disseminate an opinion and "to inform himself from generally accessible sources." Interpreting this provision, the German Constitutional Court has held that "broadcasting institutions must therefore be organized in such a way that all relevant interests have the opportunity to exert influence on the governing bodies and to express themselves in the overall program."[44] Similarly, the Conseil Constitutionnel in France has called for the establishment of rules guaranteeing the democratic expression of diverse ideas and opinions on television, together with rules to prevent political advertising from advantaging those who have more financial resources.[45]

In the United States, the closest approximation to the European position has been the "fairness doctrine," which required that television stations which allowed one candidate to appear must make equal time available on the same terms to rival candidates. But this doctrine was repealed on the grounds that the proliferation of new channels has made it much easier for all candidates to gain access to the public.[46] Proposals to give greater access to the media by granting free television time to candidates have not met with favor. Trying another tack, Congress enacted a campaign finance law in 1971 which sought to ensure greater equality in campaigning by limiting the amount of money that candidates could spend in an election. The Supreme Court, however, ruled that limitations on campaign spending were an unconstitutional infringement of the candidates' right of free speech.[47] Ironically, then, the First Amendment, which is supposed to promote a free marketplace of ideas, now helps bring about campaigns in which the ability of candidates to communicate depends on the size of their pocketbook.

Some writers emphasize one final difference in comparing degrees of freedom in the United States and other Western countries. In their view, taxation represents a serious loss of liberty, in that taxpayers must pay part of their income to the government and thus give up opportunities to purchase goods and engage in other pursuits that cost money.[48] By this calculation, citizens in the United States enjoy more freedom than Europeans or even Canadians, because prevailing levels of taxation in America are lower (Table 15.4).

Whether differing levels of taxation create differences in liberty is an argument that never ends. On the one hand, no one can deny that lower taxes do leave Americans with greater freedom to decide what to buy and consume. On the other, much of the money taken from

Table 15.4. Total taxes collected from all sources, as percent of GDP, 1992.

Country	Taxes
Canada	43.1
France	46.1
West Germany	45.3
Japan	34.4
Sweden	60.0
United Kingdom	38.8
United States	32.2

Source: OECD, *Statistics for Member Countries* (June–July 1994).

European and Canadian taxpayers pays for programs that open opportunities for many citizens which they would not otherwise possess.
For example, one reason Americans have lower taxes than Canadians
is that government in the United States pays a much smaller share of
the total health care bill. Under the Canadian health plan, however, all
Canadians can see any doctor they choose and change jobs without
fear of losing their medical benefits. In contrast, many Americans have
much more limited options when they fall ill because they lack insurance. Others who are insured have only a restricted choice of doctor
under the health plan selected by their employer. Still others are inhibited from leaving their job because they may become uninsured as a
result. Worst of all, Americans end up having to spend far more of
their money on medical care than Canadians are required to do, with
no demonstrable benefits in terms of better health. In view of all these
ramifications, it is far from clear that our health care system allows
greater freedom, notwithstanding the higher taxes that Canadians have
to pay.[49]

The Triumph of Freedom

Over the past forty years, the United States has not only maintained
but strengthened its historic commitment to individual freedom. Public
support for civil liberties has steadily grown. More important, the Supreme Court has added much to the corpus of individual rights, including important decisions upholding a woman's right to an abortion,
outlawing racially segregated schools, and requiring the creation of
election districts that allow greater equality among voters.

An even more remarkable development in the quest for individual
freedom, however, is the expansion of civil liberties in other advanced
industrial nations. In some countries, such as Britain and Canada,
judges have built upon long traditions of respect for liberty. Other
nations, notably Germany and Japan, have developed a full-blown system of individual rights following periods of extreme authoritarian
rule. In every case, it is interesting to observe that guarantees of personal freedom have continued to grow even though national governments have greatly expanded their role through the creation of a modern welfare state.

With each country following its own path for expanding freedom,
the striking result has been the convergence of all industrial democ-

racies on a common set of basic individual rights and procedural safeguards. In this process, American judges have played an important intellectual role. As a well-known British commentator, Anthony Lester, has observed: "When life is at stake, the landmark judgments of the Supreme Court of the United States, giving fresh meaning to the principles of the Bill of Rights, are studied with as much attention in New Delhi and Strasbourg as they are in Washington, D.C., or the state of Washington, or Springfield, Illinois."[50]

Observing the differences that remain, one would be hard-pressed to insist that any of the countries examined here, including the United States, is currently "more free" than the others. Perhaps the frontiers of individual rights have been pushed further in America than they have abroad. Surely there is no other nation where the nature of individual freedom has been elaborated in such detail, or any other society that is so well organized to ensure that essential liberties are defended and preserved. At the same time, freedom in the United States may be more limited by other forces than it is abroad. For example, the government in America often makes less effort than others to make sure that all or most Americans have the means to exercise important rights they formally possess. To choose but one example, it is impressive to grant everyone accused of a serious crime the right to qualified counsel, but the right may not be worth much in practice if the lawyers assigned turn out to have so little time that they can scarcely do more than hastily agree to exchange a guilty plea for a slightly reduced sentence.[51] Yet this is the situation that exists in many jurisdictions of this country.

It is likewise difficult to insist that the balances struck between the rights of the individual and the needs of the society are necessarily wiser or better in one country than in another. For example, there is much to admire about the determination of our judges to protect even the most outrageous and provocative speech. At the same time, one can also appreciate the historical reasons that have led countries in Europe to prohibit communications that sow hatred by deliberately insulting the members of a particular ethnic or religious group. Similarly, in a nation such as ours—with the highest homicide rate in the world and the largest number of television sets per family—it is hard to feel certain that we are right in refusing to review motion pictures to prevent scenes of excessive violence, whereas the Swedes are wrong to permit such a review.

Much the same is true in evaluating the differing roles played by judges in advanced democracies. Observing the momentous decisions of the Supreme Court that periodically reshape our political, social, and cultural lives, one has to marvel at the willingness of Americans and their elected leaders to accept the judgment of nine jurists with no funds or police at their disposal, and to abide by their decisions even in cases involving the most sensitive political and personal questions. Surely no nation exists in which respect for the judiciary has been so amply proven under such trying conditions and with such far-reaching results. Even so, there is also something troubling about a democracy in which the people rely so heavily on judges who are not elected yet who regularly resolve issues that are profoundly legislative and political in nature.

In the end, despite the difficulty of judging different approaches to individual freedom, we can all celebrate the remarkable progress that each of these countries has made toward securing the essential rights of their citizens. New circumstances will doubtless arise that will call for creative adaptations. New generations may perceive important gaps in the law that are not apparent to a contemporary observer. For the moment, however, the ideal of providing the maximum of individual freedom consistent with the legitimate interests of others seems closer to fulfillment in industrial democracies today than any of their other major goals.

16

Personal Responsibility

Few have explained more eloquently than Edmund Burke the link between freedom and responsibility: "Men are qualified for civil liberty in exact proportion to their disposition to put moral claims on their own appetites . . . Society cannot exist unless a controlling power upon will and appetite be placed somewhere; and the less of it there is within, the more there must be without. It is ordained in the external constitution of things that men of intemperate minds cannot be free. Their passions forge their fetters."[1]

Despite Burke's intimations to the contrary, personal responsibility is not merely an alternative to external rules as a means of curbing improper behavior. No set of rules, however elaborate, can fully reflect all of the obligations that human beings owe to one another, nor can laws ever be enforced effectively enough to put a stop to all the actions they prohibit. Thus, a shared sense of moral responsibility is an indispensable complement to the law in preserving a civilized society.

This lesson has particular relevance to a nation such as ours, which depends so heavily on a competitive striving for success to supply the motivation and energy that progress demands. The desire to get ahead can easily tempt participants to break the rules or evade them by subterfuge. As a result, whether in commerce and industry, scientific research, health care, politics, or legal proceedings, systems based on competition work well only if rules are backed by enough self-discipline and respect for basic standards of morality to keep the competition within reasonable bounds. For this reason, there is special cause

for anxiety whenever signs appear that personal responsibility is beginning to break down.

As tales of urban killing flood our television screens and reports of
increasing child abuse and teenage pregnancy fill our newspapers,
Americans have come to worry acutely about the moral condition of
our society. Their concerns go well beyond violence and crime to include a growing fear that standards of ethics and personal responsibility are eroding in many areas of life—in politics, in business, in our
local communities, and even in our families. William Bennett speaks
for many others when he says that "the most serious problems afflicting
our society today are manifestly moral, behavioral, and spiritual."[2]
Opinion surveys rank moral decline among the most important non-
economic problems facing the nation.[3] The percentage of adults who
say they trust other people has dropped by one-third since the 1960s.[4]
Over three-fourths of all Americans are "unhappy with the honesty
and ethical standards of other citizens."[5] More than 75 percent of respondents under twenty and 70 percent of those aged thirty to forty-
four believe that "most Americans try to avoid taking responsibility
for their actions."[6]

Although everyone can cite anecdotes to illustrate these concerns,
it would surely be a mistake to accept assertions of moral decay at face
value. Was there ever a time when the public believed that ethical standards were going up? Or that young people were behaving more responsibly than children of previous generations? There is a deep-seated
human tendency to suppose that virtue is on the wane. As a result, one
should be wary of such charges and look for evidence to test them.

Before searching for data, one must be clear about just what traits
of character are worthy of concern. Engaging in acts of disputed ethical
significance, such as abortion, cannot provide a convincing measure of
personal responsibility, because large segments of the population do
not regard such behavior as immoral. Nor can one include such laudable virtues as courage, courtesy, perseverance, and humility, for traits
of this kind are impossible to measure and are probably not the ones
that trouble people most about American society. What is of greatest
interest is the willingness of ordinary citizens to fulfill the most basic
and most widely accepted obligations to others, since these are the
duties and restraints that have the most profound effect on the functioning of society. This chapter, then, will deal with the disposition to

tell the truth, to obey the law, to keep commitments, to accept responsibility for those legitimately dependent on one's behavior, to avoid acts of violence, to respect other people's property, and to make some affirmative effort to help one's community. Although it is possible to quibble over details, these obligations make up the core of what most people have in mind in thinking of "personal responsibility."

Alas, it is one thing to specify the forms of personal responsibility and quite another to measure them in real life. What many people would like to know is whether character has changed over the past thirty to forty years, and specifically whether people have a greater or lesser inclination to restrain their selfish impulses out of respect for the interests of others. But there is no way of directly measuring the ebb and flow of character. Nor is there even a straightforward way of tracking the level of honesty or promise keeping in the society.

What *is* feasible is to search for evidence of behaviors that suggest how well people are fulfilling their duties to one another. Experience in other advanced nations should help determine whether changes occurring in the United States are unique to this country or whether they reflect broader trends affecting all industrial societies. Where possible, one can try to point out whether such changes signify shifts in values and attitudes or result from changes in external forces, such as stiffer penalties or greater efforts to enforce rules and detect violators. What will emerge from these efforts is not a precise index of individual responsibility over the past several decades but a catalogue of behavioral trends that should throw some light on how well or badly Americans are fulfilling their basic obligations to one another.

The information in this chapter comes from four broad domains of American life. The first is crime, both violent and nonviolent, since the prevalence of criminal acts provides one striking indication of how willing people are to respect the legitimate interests of others. The second includes violations of a variety of other rules, such as failing to pay taxes, cheating on exams, and drinking before the legal age. The third area involves family responsibilities, such as marital fidelity and willingness to pay child support. A final category of personal conduct comprises various forms of civic responsibility, including voting, community service, and charitable donations, which give a rough measure of how willing people are to sacrifice their immediate interests to serve the needs of others.

Crime

Chapter 11 dealt with the problem of violent crime in America. But violent acts, though regrettably frequent, are committed by only a small minority of Americans; they do not provide an especially revealing index of the state of personal responsibility in the society as a whole. As a result, it is more useful to widen the lens to include all forms of crime, including theft, robbery, and embezzlement, as well as homicide and rape.

At this point, a problem arises that cropped up earlier in the discussion of violence. There are two separate methods of measuring the incidence of crime, and they give sharply differing answers to the question whether criminal acts are increasing or decreasing in America. One of these measures is the annual survey that asks respondents whether they have been the victims of crime during the past twelve months. According to this index, the total number of crimes in 1973, when the first victimization survey took place, was slightly more than 200 per thousand people (roughly four times the number reported by the police to the FBI). Over the ensuing twenty years, the victimization reports record a gradual *decrease* in crime of roughly 25 percent.[7] In contrast, FBI figures based on police reports suggest a substantial *increase* in the total amount of crime during the 1970s, before eventually stabilizing in the 1980s. One reason for this discrepancy is that the rise in crime reported by police is inflated by the increasing success of the FBI in obtaining cooperation from local police in reporting crimes. In addition, the difference reflects the fact that victimization surveys do not include "victimless" crimes, notably drug offenses, which have risen rapidly in the past twenty years.

Is it possible to determine trends prior to 1973? Although police reports are not entirely reliable and victimization studies are unavailable, there is one type of crime—homicide—for which the data are reasonably accurate and extend back over many decades. It is unlikely that fluctuations in reporting will greatly affect the FBI figures on homicide, since murders are the most likely of crimes to be known by the police and reported to the FBI.

According to FBI reports, homicides in America declined gradually in the 1950s.[8] Thereafter, the number of murders rose rapidly and almost doubled, from 4.8 in 1961 to 9.4 in 1973 (while FBI reports showed that all other types of crime, such as robbery and motor vehicle thefts, more than doubled).[9] Although FBI reports may have overestimated the increases in overall crime, the more reliable homicide figures suggest that the total number of criminal acts did rise significantly and probably at least doubled between 1960 and 1973.

Despite the growth of crime since 1960, earlier figures on homicide suggest that current levels of criminal behavior are not unprecedented in America. Murder rates were almost as high in the early 1930s as they were in the peak year of 1980. Although one cannot be certain, there is no reason to suppose that rates for other types of crime were markedly different.

In the end, therefore, the trends seem somewhat more complicated than popular impressions might suggest. By all accounts, the incidence of crime did rise dramatically between the mid-1960s and the mid-1970s. Since then, rates appear to have fallen somewhat, in part because the proportion of young males in the population has declined for demographic reasons and in part because a growing fraction of the most dangerous offenders are now behind bars. Even with the recent decline, however, the incidence of crime has still not retreated to anything close to the low levels enjoyed in the late 1950s and early 1960s. The net result is that criminal behavior in the 1990s remains at relatively high levels historically, although it appears neither to be unprecedented nor to reflect a constant increase in lawlessness since the early years of this century.

How does America compare with other advanced nations in the prevalence of crime? The most reliable source of information is a recently completed international victimization survey covering several advanced countries during a five-year period ending in 1988.[10] As shown in Table 16.1, the United States has the unhappy distinction of leading all countries not only in total crime but in almost every specific category of criminal behavior. Yet for the most part, the differences in the rates of nonviolent crime are not dramatic. Moreover, America was not alone in experiencing rapid increases during the 1960s. In Britain, the number of murders and manslaughters more than doubled between 1960 and 1980, while rates for assaults and robberies seem to have jumped several-fold.[11] Reports from Sweden also reveal a doubling of robbery rates and increases of three or four times in the prevalence of theft.[12] Among the advanced industrialized nations, only Japan seems

Table 16.1. **Average number of crimes committed annually, per 1,000 people, 1983–1988.**

Type of crime	Britain	West Germany	France	Norway	Canada	United States
All crimes	46.0	51.3	52.0	38.9	53.0	57.6
Car theft	6.6	1.9	7.3	2.7	2.8	6.3
Car vandalism	17.3	22.1	19.6	11.2	18.8	21.7
Burglary	9.4	4.7	10.4	3.2	10.2	13.7
Personal theft	8.3	13.3	12.8	8.3	13.2	14.2
Sexual incidents	3.4	7.9	4.3	4.7	10.0	10.4
Assault	5.3	9.3	7.1	8.2	8.8	12.7

Source: J. M. van Dijk, Pat Mayhew, and Martin Killias, *Experiences of Crime across the World: Key Findings of the 1989 International Crime Survey*, 175 (1990).

to have escaped this upward trend. According to Japanese sources, rates for homicide and other crimes have actually dropped substantially since the decade following World War II.[13]

Obeying the Rules

Despite all the talk about a declining respect for authority, there is little hard data on the subject. The fragments of information that exist lend scant support to the common belief that Americans are increasingly unwilling to obey the rules. Instead, the picture that emerges is more complicated.

One interesting piece of evidence involves the willingness of citizens to pay their taxes. For many years, the federal government has compiled elaborate estimates to chart the extent of compliance. These figures show that the percentage of income taxes from individuals that is *not* paid (either because of underreporting or by not filing a return at all) rose from approximately 17 percent in 1973 to 21.8 percent in 1978, but declined to 16.8 percent in 1992.[14] There are no data on the levels of underpayment prior to 1973. But government records do show that the percentage of taxpayers who failed to file a return at all rose only slightly, from 7 percent in 1963 to 7.6 percent in 1973.[15]

Drunken driving also seems to have followed a downward course in the 1980s. Alcohol was a factor in 57.3 percent of all highway deaths in 1982, when the National Highway Traffic Safety Administration started to collect information on the subject. By 1993, the percentage of alcohol-related fatalities had dropped to 43.6 percent.[16] Arrests for driving under the influence have likewise been falling since 1983 after rising sharply in the early years of that decade.[17] Once again, however, the crude estimates available suggest that alcohol-related fatalities may have occurred significantly less often in the early 1960s than they did even in the 1990s.[18]

Other bits of information have to do with adolescent behavior, based on accounts that youngsters give of their own conduct. Several surveys have asked students whether they have cheated on examinations. Only one survey extends over several decades; it suggests that the proportion of high school students who admitted having ever cheated on tests rose steeply, from 34 percent in 1969 to 60 percent in 1979, and then grew slowly to 68 percent by 1989.[19] Several recent surveys of college students have also found high rates of cheating, ranging between 68 and 75 percent.[20] Yet Gallup surveys of high school students suggest that the percentage who admit having cheated peaked at 66 percent in 1981 and then declined to only 46 percent in 1992.[21]

Various scraps of evidence give further indication that standards of ethical behavior among young people tended to stabilize in the 1980s. For example, one survey shows that the percentage of high school students who admitted taking books or other valuable property from school increased sharply in the 1970s but leveled off in the 1980s.[22] Official government studies reveal that the percentage of high school seniors who admit having taken something from a store without paying rose only slightly, from 28.6 percent in 1981 to 30.7 percent in 1993.[23] Similarly, the proportion of seniors who acknowledged stealing another person's possession worth less than fifty dollars barely increased, from 31 percent in 1981 to 32.1 percent twelve years later.[24]

Department of Justice surveys actually suggest major *declines* in unlawful drug and alcohol use among young people in the 1980s. Among those aged twelve to seventeen, the percentage acknowledging drinking alcohol in the preceding month rose from 34 percent in 1974 to 37 percent in 1979, but then dropped steadily to only 18 percent in 1993.[25] The percentage admitting having ever used marijuana in the same age group followed a similar trajectory, rising from 14 percent in 1972 to 30.9 percent in 1979 but then dropping precipitously to only 11.7 percent in 1993.[26] The same patterns exist for the use of cocaine and hallucinogens.

All in all, therefore, there is little evidence of a continuing decline in the willingness of Americans to obey the rules. Rather, the evidence suggests a moderate to sharp deterioration in the 1960s and 1970s, followed by stabilization or improvement in the 1980s. As yet, however, the types of personal conduct for which reliable data exist are too few to draw firm conclusions.

Family Responsibilities

The family is an especially useful source to draw upon for evidence of personal responsibility, since few human relationships give rise to such basic obligations toward others. The decades from 1960 to the present are also an interesting time to observe changes in family responsibilities, because such major transformations have occurred in the institution of marriage. The 1950s were years of strong support for the nuclear family. Men and women married at historically high rates, while divorce grew gradually less frequent. Parents had more babies than they had in the previous four decades, and unusually large proportions of mothers stayed at home taking care of their children. Within the brief span of twenty years, however, the situation changed completely. Marriage rates declined, divorces skyrocketed, and women began to enter the work force at historically high levels.

What light can changes in the family shed on personal responsibility in our society? One frequently cited trend is the explosive growth in the number of failed marriages. From 1960 to 1980, the annual divorce rate more than doubled, before declining slightly in the ensuing decade.[27] Whereas 20 percent of young couples marrying in 1960 could expect to be divorced, the likelihood had increased to approximately 50 percent only three decades later. Although divorce rates have risen in most Western countries, they are much higher in the United States than in any other advanced industrial democracy. Some observers would interpret such trends as signifying a pronounced and growing tendency to value personal fulfillment over concern for the welfare of one's offspring, citing evidence of the adverse effects broken marriages often have on children.[28] Nevertheless, because divorce is not widely regarded as a breach of one's personal obligations toward others, it does not provide reliable evidence of declining moral standards.

Stronger indications of parental responsibility come from the behavior of fathers toward their children after a marriage is dissolved.

The results are troubling. The National Survey of Families and Households found that 21 percent of absentee fathers did not visit their children at all in the preceding year and that 27 percent saw them only once or several times.[29] Another study of one thousand teenage children of divorced parents revealed that more than 40 percent had not seen their father at all during the preceding year.[30]

Another indication of parental responsibility is the extent to which absent fathers help pay for the care and upbringing of their children. Again, the evidence is not reassuring. Only half of all divorced mothers have child support orders, and the vast preponderance of those without orders probably do not receive significant help from the absent fathers. Of all parents ordered to give support, barely half provide the full amount due, even though the payments required are typically far below what is normally needed to bring up a child.[31] Approximately one-fourth of the fathers under a court order pay only part of what they owe, and another fourth pay nothing at all. These figures undoubtedly help explain the findings of several studies showing that after divorce the income of a typical husband rises 10 to 15 percent, while the income of the wife and children declines by an average of 30 percent.[32]

In the past twenty years, federal and state officials have intensified their efforts to make fathers pay child support. The amounts expended on enforcement increased almost sixfold in nominal dollars from 1976 to 1986. Even so, the percentage of the total support due that fathers actually pay has increased only slightly since 1970, from 64.6 percent to 68.7 percent.[33] Moreover, the amounts of support awarded have fallen not only in real dollars but as a percent of men's income (from 18.2 percent in 1969 to 12.1 percent in 1984).[34] Some absent fathers are undoubtedly jobless and unable to provide financial support. Yet studies show that this is not normally the case. On the contrary, most analysts believe that absent fathers can usually afford much more than they are currently asked to pay. Moreover, awards in the United States are substantially below what is customarily required in most European countries.[35]

Still another revealing trend is the massive, continuing rise in the proportion of children born out of wedlock during the past several decades. In 1950, fewer than 4 percent of all births involved unmarried mothers. Ten years later, the figure had crept up only to 5 percent. In the 1960s, however, illegitimate births began to increase rapidly, and by 1990 the proportion had climbed to almost 30 percent.[36]

The United States is not alone in recording such increases. Most European nations have had the same experience, and some surpass America in the percentage of children born out of wedlock. In other countries, however, most of these births involve a mother and father who are living together in a more or less stable relationship. What distinguishes the United States is a higher percentage of families headed by single parents, and a much greater proportion of teenage girls who become pregnant and have children. The high incidence of teenage mothers undoubtedly reflects a large and rising number of brief sexual encounters with men who feel no lasting personal obligation toward the children they produce. One recent study revealed that half or more of the babies born to unwed mothers aged fifteen to seventeen are sired by men twenty years of age or older, who are at least technically violating the law (Table 16.2).[37]

Although these trends are disquieting, there are several reasons the rising rates of illegitimacy in America provide less dramatic evidence of declining personal responsibility than the preceding figures might suggest. Part of the explanation for the growing percentage of children born out of wedlock has to do with the declining birthrates for married women. Another reason is that fewer women are getting married. Because these trends cause the number of children born in wedlock to

Table 16.2. Incidence of out-of-wedlock childbearing and single-parent families, 1960 and 1990.

Country	Births to unmarried women, as percent of all births		Families headed by single parent, as percent of all families		Number of pregnancies per 1,000 girls aged 15–19
	1960	1990	1960	1990	1994
Canada	4	24	9	15	27
France	6	30	9	12	9
West Germany	6	11	8	14	13
Sweden	11	47	9	13	13
United Kingdom	5	28	6	13	33
United States	5	28	9	23	64

Source: Reynolds Farley, ed., *State of the Union: America in the 1990s*, vol. 2: *Social Trends*, 15 (1995); UNICEF, *The Progress of Nations*, 47 (1996).

fall, the fraction of all births that occur out of wedlock will rise even if the number of illegitimate births stays the same. Once one makes allowances for this fact and asks what has happened to the probability that a single woman will have a child, the trends look rather different. For example, the birthrate among unmarried black women has actually *declined,* from 98.3 births per thousand unmarried women in 1960 to 90.5 in 1990. Because of a rise in the rate for single white women, however, especially in the 1980s, the total number of out-of-wedlock babies per thousand unmarried women rose, from 21.6 in 1960 to 26.4 in 1970 to 29.4 in 1980, and then to 43.8 in 1990. These figures, which provide the best indication of changes in individual behavior, show a much more modest rate of increase than the commonly cited rise in the percentage of births occurring out of wedlock.

Unfaithfulness to one's spouse is another indication of personal responsibility. Unfortunately, evidence of marital infidelity is none too reliable, since no one can be sure how accurately people report their own sexual behavior. Based on nonrandom samples, Dr. Alfred Kinsey reported in 1948 and 1953 that approximately 50 percent of all married men and 26 percent of married women had been unfaithful.[38] In contrast, a more careful recent study of the subject estimates that only 25 percent of men and 15 percent of women have had extramarital affairs.[39] Survey data from the National Opinion Research Center show even lower levels of infidelity: 21 percent among married men and 11 percent among married women.[40] Since respondents over fifty report less infidelity than men and women in their forties, it is possible that unfaithfulness is increasing. Nevertheless, because of the obvious problem of getting reliable answers to questions about people's sexual lives, it would be hazardous to try to draw any firm conclusions from these materials.[41]

Finally, official figures on reported child abuse have also risen rapidly from 10.1 per thousand children in 1976 to 45.0 in 1992 (including neglect, physical abuse, and sexual abuse).[42] The rate of growth is doubtless inflated due to the growing sensitivity to child abuse and greater emphasis on making such behavior known. Nevertheless, since the federal government has reported a virtual quadrupling of the numbers of seriously injured children from 1986 to 1993, there can be little doubt that abuse has increased substantially.[43]

All in all, one can hardly look at the evidence of family responsibility without a sense of dismay. Nevertheless, there is evidence that attitudes toward family responsibility have grown stronger in the past fifteen years, following the declines of the 1960s and early 1970s. Disapproval of infidelity, which had dwindled from 1965 to the mid-1970s, has subsequently turned upward to regain approximately half of the ground lost in the earlier period.[44] The percentage of mothers affirming the value of parenthood also increased following earlier declines, as did the percentage of both sexes believing that parents should try to stay together for the sake of the children.[45]

It is hard to say what effect these opinion changes will have on behavior. Americans have consistently led other nations in the percentage of people asserting the importance of family values. Fewer Americans believe that marriage is outdated than do Canadians, French, Germans, Swedes, or British.[46] Higher percentages assert that family is "very important" and that "more emphasis on family would be good."[47] Fewer Americans approve of adultery, and larger numbers of them (exceeded only by the French) believe that "parents have to do their best for their children."[48] The link between attitudes and actual behavior, however, is not particularly close. As previously noted, Americans may profess to have stronger family values than citizens of other countries, but their actual behavior sometimes falls below the standards found abroad. It would be premature, therefore, to assume that changes in the attitudes of Americans toward marriage will lead to significantly lower rates of divorce, out-of-wedlock births, or marital infidelity.

Responsibility to the Community

Almost everyone would agree that no community can function well unless its members contribute something to the larger group, beyond meeting their basic obligations to obey the law, honor their commitments, and tell the truth. Among the many ways of fulfilling this civic responsibility are voting in elections, making charitable gifts, and contributing time to community organizations of various kinds.

Voting is the most elementary civic duty that citizens perform for the good of the community. Of course, it is not always a selfless act; many people cast their ballots in accordance with their private interests. Nevertheless, since no single vote can affect the outcome of an election, even acts of this kind represent a gesture on behalf of others with similar interests.

Voting trends in the United States give little comfort to anyone concerned about civic responsibility. Election turnouts have gradually declined over the past forty years, especially among the poor, the young, and those with less education. Whereas 63 percent of all potential voters cast their ballots in 1960, the percentage fell steadily to 50 percent in 1988, before rising to 55 percent in 1992.[49] In off-year congressional elections, voting rates declined from 46 percent in 1962 to 33 percent in 1990.[50] It is important to note, however, that current levels of voting are not unprecedented in this century. The turnout in the pivotal presidential election of 1932 was only 52 percent, and in 1948 it sank to 51 percent. Voting in off-years for members of Congress fell below 40 percent in 1930, 1942, and 1946.

Since young people have always voted less frequently than their elders, part of the decline after 1960 resulted from the fact that in 1971 the voting age was lowered from twenty-one to eighteen. Hopes arising from the 1992 election that younger citizens might be beginning to show greater interest soon evaporated, as voting among Americans aged eighteen to twenty-four sank to a historic low in the election of 1994. Still, the addition of a new cohort of young voters does not account for more than a small portion of the total slippage since 1960. The overall decline among all age groups is especially striking, since voter registration laws were gradually eased during this period, Southern blacks were able to vote much more heavily, and the adult population grew better educated. All of these trends should have helped raise the number of citizens going to the polls.

Voting rates have long been much higher in Europe than in the United States. Some of the difference in participation undoubtedly results from voter registration requirements in this country and other technical differences.[51] Some may be due to more frequent elections or weaker political parties in America. It is significant, however, that most European nations have experienced no more than a slight decline during recent decades in the percentage of eligible voters going to the polls.[52] According to a recent survey of eighteen European nations from 1945 to 1989, the average turnout from 1945 to 1949 was 83 percent; it rose to 85 percent in 1960–1965, and then declined, but only to 80 percent, in 1985–1989.[53]

Evidence regarding other forms of political participation is more mixed. According to surveys from the 1970s, 14 percent of American adults participated actively in election campaigns, compared with 8 percent of West Germans, 5 percent of Austrians, 4 percent of British, and only 3 percent of the Dutch.[54] In contrast to voting trends there is no evidence of a decline in the willingness of Americans to work in political campaigns (although changing methods of electioneering have put more emphasis on contributing money and less on ringing door-bells).

In the past thirty years, however, there have been substantial increases in the numbers of people engaging in other forms of political activity, such as signing petitions, contacting public officials, and participating in demonstrations and boycotts.[55] These increases have been especially marked throughout much of Europe. As a result, if one considers all forms of political action and not just working for political parties and election campaigns, large majorities of citizens both in the United States and in many European countries seem to be participating actively in one way or another.

With respect to charity, Americans are inclined to give more than are the citizens of most other advanced nations. Although a recent survey reports that higher proportions of Canadians and British than of Americans make charitable donations, the percentage of personal income that individuals donate to charity in the United States tends to be at least twice the level in Canada and three times the level in Great Britain.[56] (Citizens of both these countries, in turn, contribute more than those of continental Europe and Japan.)[57] The habit of giving in America is by no means concentrated among the rich. In fact, available data suggest that donors with earnings below $20,000 may give as large a share of their income to charity as donors with incomes up to $125,000.[58]

There is no evidence of a continuing long-term decline in the generosity of Americans. Measured as a percentage of personal income, donations by individuals did drop, from 2.48 in 1955 to 2.25 in 1960, 1.95 in 1970, and 1.80 in 1980.[59] Thereafter, however, gifts increased substantially to regain much of the lost ground by 1989 before falling back slightly in the 1990s.[60] The surge in giving during the 1980s is especially noteworthy, since government subsidies for gifts by wealthy individuals fell substantially when Congress drastically lowered marginal tax rates, especially for people in the top income brackets.

At least as meaningful as writing checks is the contribution of time and energy that citizens make to activities that improve their communities. Americans have long been noted for their willingness to volunteer to help their schools, their hospitals, their neighborhoods, and other worthwhile causes. From Little League to Girl Scouts, from museum volunteers to college students staffing homeless shelters, people from every walk of life have given generously of their time to help their communities grow stronger. In 1993, nearly half of all adult Americans engaged in some form of volunteer activity in amounts averaging 4.2 hours per week.[61] Such evidence as exists suggests that volunteer work is much more common in the United States than in Europe, though not quite as common as in Canada.[62]

Robert Putnam has recently stirred up much debate by citing evidence from many quarters that community service in America has been dwindling over the past decades.[63] Few of the standard community groups have escaped this trend. According to Putnam, membership in the League of Women Voters has dropped by 42 percent since 1969; Boy Scout volunteers have declined by 26 percent; Parent-Teachers Associations lost more than half of their members from 1964 to 1982, before recovering partially when school reform became prominent in the 1980s.[64] Some of this decline may be offset by a rising interest in new kinds of service organizations. Even so, the best available government surveys suggest that the percentage of adults volunteering for any form of community-based activity fell four percentage points from 1974 to 1989.[65]

No similar decline in group membership seems to have occurred in all or even most countries of Europe.[66] Nor do all scholars agree that membership has fallen in the United States. For example, one survey, administered in 1967 and 1987, asked Americans whether they had, during the past year, worked with others on local problems, been an active member of a community problem-solving organization, or formed a group to help solve a local problem. The results showed small increases over the twenty years in each type of activity.[67] Such findings as these make it difficult as yet to reach a definitive conclusion regarding trends in civic or community activities.

Making Sense of the Evidence

What light do all these facts and figures cast upon the frequent assertions that America's ethical standards and personal responsibility are eroding? To answer this question, it would be helpful to know the trends over a much longer span than the past thirty to forty years. Without such information, one cannot fully evaluate the claim, advanced by many who perceive a decline in ethical standards, that attitudes in the United States changed fundamentally in the 1960s. It was in that decade, according to Daniel Yankelovich, that large numbers of Americans began "rejecting the ethic of self-sacrifice for others, the ethic of self-denial, and replacing it with a focus on self—the 'me generation.' "[68]

Of all the figures available, unfortunately, the only ones that span several generations are those pertaining to murder, divorce, voting, and births out of wedlock. In two cases—divorce and out-of-wedlock births—the figures today are far above what they were in the early decades of the twentieth century. In the case of homicide, there is reason to believe that current levels may be slightly below what they were in the early 1930s, despite the rapid rise of crime rates in the 1960s. Voting turnouts have likewise deteriorated since 1960 but are still no worse than they were in the 1920s or even in 1948. Overall, therefore, the evidence is too mixed to support any sweeping claims that standards of personal responsibility in America have declined to levels unprecedented in this century.

Much more evidence exists for developments from 1960 to 1990. Table 16.3 sums up what is known of the behaviors cited in the preceding pages. It is striking that one can find no form of personal responsibility that has improved continuously over the past thirty years. In fact, no firm evidence exists that *any* form of personal responsibility is stronger today than it was in 1960, whereas there are many examples of behaviors that have deteriorated. On the brighter side, only a few types of responsibility have deteriorated more or less steadily. If there is a general tendency to be found, it is one of decline until the mid- or late 1970s, followed by stabilization or improvement.

Declines in personal responsibility do not appear to be confined to any particular segment of American society. To be sure, crime is much more prevalent in inner cities than it is in the suburbs, and black women are more likely than whites to have children out of wedlock. Nevertheless, since 1980 out-of-wedlock births have risen much faster among white women than among blacks. Crime rose substantially in the 1960s not only in the cities but in suburbs as well. The proportions of college students who admit having cheated on exams are approximately as high as the percentages of high school students who have done so. Failure to pay child support occurs frequently among husbands who are not classified as poor. Declines in voting and member-

Table 16.3. Trends in forms of personal responsibility, 1960–1990.

More or less steady deterioration	No significant deterioration or improvement	Deterioration followed by stabilization or improvement	Improvement followed by deterioration	More or less steady improvement
1. Out-of-wedlock births	1. Child support	1. Crime	—	—
2. Child abuse	2. Involvement in political campaigns	2. Attitudes toward family responsibility		
3. Voting		3. Marijuana use		
		4. Charitable giving		
		5. Paying taxes		
		6. Drunk driving		
		7. Cheating in school		

ship in civic organizations are evident among middle-class suburban-ites as well as among inner city residents. In short, the trends described in this chapter seem to reflect behavioral patterns that are quite widely shared throughout the American population.

How does the behavior of Americans compare with that of people in other advanced countries? Apparently, every leading Western nation has experienced rising levels of crime, divorce, out-of-wedlock births, and other behaviors indicative of a decline in personal responsibility. Observing these trends, most commentators would agree with David Popenoe: throughout the Western world "there has been a gradual shift from a 'collectivist' culture (a term I use with a cultural and not a political meaning) toward an individualistic culture. In the former, group goals take precedence over individual ones. 'Doing one's duty,' for example, is more important than 'self-fulfillment' . . . In individu-alistic cultures, the welfare of the group is secondary to such personal goals as self-expression, independence, and competitiveness."[69] Table

Table 16.4. Trends in personal responsibility: United States in
comparison to other countries.

Lower levels of responsibility than most countries	Higher levels of responsibility than some, lower than others	Higher levels of responsibility than most countries
1. Crime	1. Out-of-wedlock births	1. Charitable donations
2. Teenage pregnancy	2. Paying taxes	2. Community service
3. Drug use		3. Participation in election campaigns (other than voting)
4. Voting		

16.4 summarizes the available evidence on how trends in various forms
of behavior in the United States compare with those in other advanced
Western societies.

Overall, there is no convincing evidence that America's standards
of personal responsibility are consistently lower than those of other
Western societies. If any generalization is possible, it is that Americans
are unusually generous and active in their communities, but less inclined than Europeans to abide by rules or confining obligations. For
the most part, however, the differences between the United States and
other Western societies are not great and the trends seem remarkably
similar.

Searching for Causes

What lies behind these trends? Among the many theories on this subject, one of the most common is that rising affluence has led to widespread self-indulgence of a kind that undermines ethical standards.
Could it be, then, that there is a basic inconsistency between our desire
to achieve higher standards of living and our concern to maintain appropriate levels of personal responsibility? This is a question with deep
roots in religious thought, and it would be rash indeed to try to resolve
the matter here. All that one can safely do is contribute whatever scraps
of evidence can be gleaned from the record of the nations described in
these pages, in hopes of throwing additional light on the issue.

The most obvious point is that all of the countries considered here (except Japan) have had unprecedented economic growth over the past forty years, while also experiencing a sharp deterioration in most observable forms of personal responsibility. There are several reasons these two tendencies might be linked. The urbanization that accompanies growth has weakened many of the social inhibitions often present in small communities, where everyone's behavior is known to friends and neighbors. In addition, rising standards of living have allowed ordinary people to indulge their appetites and desires to an extent previously possible only for a limited class of privileged persons. Advertising and easy credit have exposed entire populations to constant temptations to satisfy their impulses even at the expense of prudence and self-restraint. Such lures arouse feelings of desire and envy that may occasionally lead people to break the rules when they cannot satisfy their desires by normal, ethical means. At the same time, the emphasis on competition and success that supplies such a powerful incentive for economic growth can cause people to ignore the legitimate interests of others when it seems necessary to do so in order to get ahead.

Taken together, these tendencies would appear to exert substantial pressure on the moral restraints of a society. At the same time, growth and prosperity do not work only to undermine moral behavior. Affluence also permits generosity. Business success typically demands a reputation for honesty, hard work, and reliability. Economic growth creates more opportunities to advance in socially acceptable ways and brings higher levels of education, which in turn appear to be linked to greater personal responsibility.

Because economic growth engenders so many different attitudes and pressures, it would be surprising to find a simple inverse relationship between prosperity and personal responsibility, as nations move from lower stages of development to the levels of affluence achieved by Western democracies. Poverty creates its own motives for cruelty and immorality, as the record of numerous primitive societies attests. When the Industrial Revolution developed in the nineteenth century, bringing greater prosperity to larger segments of the population, rates of divorce, crime, and out-of-wedlock births all appear to have declined in Britain and America.[70] Today, rates of crime and corruption are much higher in many underdeveloped countries than they are in the industrialized West. Even the much-cited levels of violence in the United States are exceeded by those of many Third World countries.

It is likewise clear that there are large differences in personal responsibility among the select list of highly developed societies featured
in this study. For example, the rate of out-of-wedlock births in 1990
was 28 percent for the United States and 47 percent for Sweden, but
only 11 percent for Germany. Homicides occur several times more
frequently in the United States than in western Europe. Still greater
differences appear if we contrast the West with Japan, where births
out of wedlock are almost unknown and crime is not only low but
below what it was in the late 1940s. Even within the United States,
there does not appear to be an unvarying relationship between prosperity and irresponsibility. From 1945 to 1960, when the economy
grew at an unusually rapid pace, rates of crime and divorce went down.
And whereas most forms of personal morality seemed to decline
sharply in the 1960s, many of them improved in the 1980s although
the economy grew throughout that decade to levels of affluence well
above those of the 1960s. If prosperity erodes individual responsibility,
then, it appears to be but one of many social and cultural forces at
work, and its corrosive effects seem to manifest themselves only in
combination with other social circumstances and conditions.

If rising living standards seem insufficient by themselves to account
for declining moral standards in the 1960s and 1970s, what other
factors could have helped bring about this result? No one can be certain. The following account is necessarily speculative but may throw
further light on what took place.

The changes in personal responsibility that emerged in the 1960s
were concentrated largely in the postwar baby boom generation. It is
here that, in the 1960s and early 1970s, most of the increases in crime,
drug use, infidelity, and cheating occurred. The generation was unusually large and was the first to come of age when economic growth
brought prosperity and discretionary income to large segments of the
population. As young people began to have money to spend, they became more venturesome and felt more empowered to do what they
wanted. To this extent, prosperity played a role in bringing about the
shift toward self-fulfillment so widely noted by commentators on the
1960s. But more than affluence was involved. For the first time, young
people became an attractive market for mass merchandisers to reach
through heavy advertising of clothing, footwear, fast foods, and other
goods designed to appeal to teenagers and cultivate their desire for
self-expression and gratification. Motion pictures, television programs,

and records also began to cater specially to teenagers. This massive marketing effort helped give baby boomers a greater sense of identity and importance and contributed to a distinctive youth culture emphasizing their separateness from older generations. Modern methods of communication served to spread this culture overseas and build a sense of solidarity among young people, not only in matters of taste and lifestyle but in their resistance to war, their belief in tolerance, and their concern for the environment.

These developments took place concurrently with a well documented, longer-term trend on the part of parents here and abroad to place diminishing importance on obedience as a desirable value in children, and to put much more emphasis on personal autonomy and self-expression.[71] Encouraged to think for themselves and often better educated than their parents, postwar generations were less inclined to take established rules and restraints on faith and more disposed to examine them critically. Events such as the Vietnam War, Watergate, the civil rights struggle, and similar instances of weakness and bad judgment in other countries seemed to confirm the doubts held by many young people about the wisdom and morality of those in positions of power.

This new skepticism was accompanied by much idealism in fighting against racism and war, and doubtless led to attacks on many outmoded policies and practices. But it was easier for young people to learn to question authority than it was for them to discover when to respect it, especially when forbearance interfered with personal desires or strong peer pressures. As drugs became widely available, they served all too often both as a means of self-fulfillment and as the cause of a further weakening of inhibitions and decline in moral standards. In the end, the price of independence was a gradual relaxation of many established rules and obligations. In combination with a youth culture stressing self-realization and an affluence that made people less cautious and less concerned over the results of their actions, this dwindling respect for authority led to a widespread erosion of personal responsibility which has not been reversed to this day.

17

Helping the Poor

Samuel Johnson once observed that "a decent provision for the poor is the true test of civilization."[1] Such help has long had an honored place in American life, and even today countless people contribute time and money to churches and other local organizations to aid the needy and shelter the homeless. Yet as Spinoza declared more than three centuries ago, "To give aid to every poor man is far beyond the reach and power of every man . . . Care of the poor is incumbent on society as a whole."[2] Over the years, therefore, the individual's duty toward others in need has expanded to become a general responsibility of the entire body politic.

Almost everyone would like to banish the scourge of poverty, or at least relieve its harsh effects. The controversy is over the causes, the cures, and how to pay the costs. Liberals often assert that poverty is the product of unemployment, discrimination, and other social ills that arguably create an obligation on the part of society to help the poor. Conservatives respond that the indigent are often responsible for their predicament and that measures to combat poverty should not reward sloth or weaken the resolve of poor people to go to work like everyone else.

These views are not as far apart as they might seem. Few liberals still deny the importance of encouraging the able-bodied poor to help themselves, and few conservatives hold small children or handicapped persons responsible for their penury. Even staunch conservatives, such as Milton Friedman, recognize the need to provide all people with some protection against privation.[3]

Among the general public, there is also broad support for helping the poor, at least so long as the aid given does not reward malingerers. In 1991, 65 percent of Americans believed that the country should be doing more for the poor.[4] Opposition rises sharply, however, when people are asked about increasing "welfare," since welfare has acquired connotations of freeloading and abuse which the public clearly opposes. These attitudes are not of recent origin; with minor fluctuations, they have endured for several decades at least. The ultimate questions, then, are how much support people are willing to give and how to distribute it to avoid malingering. The nation has long wrestled with these issues. After all this effort, how have government policies evolved and how effective have they been in helping the needy without undermining habits of work and personal responsibility that Americans value highly?

Definitions of Poverty

In absolute terms, America has made great progress in reducing poverty over past generations. In 1876, 67 percent of all families received an income of less than $3,000 in inflation-adjusted dollars. By 1918, the proportion had declined to 63 percent. It dropped to 51 percent in 1935–1936, to 30 percent in 1950, and to 20 percent in 1960.[5]

Almost no one would argue, however, that this type of measurement is sufficient, for the meaning of poverty is always influenced to a degree by changing conditions in society. What was genuine poverty in the Middle Ages could scarcely be an adequate measure today. Instead, several other definitions have been suggested.

The *official poverty index* in the United States was designed by Mollie Orshansky of the Social Security Administration during the 1960s. Pressed for some workable definition to buttress the War on Poverty, she observed that families of limited means spend roughly one-third of their income on food. She then took the cost of the minimum subsistence diet recommended by the Department of Agriculture and multiplied it by three to arrive at a suitable figure.

Many people have attacked this standard. Advocates for the poor dislike it because it is based on a meager diet that was never designed for long-term use; because it does not make adjustments for taxes paid or costs incurred as a result of holding a job; and because it does not take account of rising prosperity in America and accompanying changes in our sense of what a minimum standard of living ought to be.[6] Others reply that, on the contrary, *too many* people are classified as poor because of the way the government adjusts the poverty line for inflation and because official calculations do not include in-kind benefits such as food stamps and Medicaid.[7] These critics go further and observe that official figures completely overlook unreported earnings, gifts from relatives, and other undisclosed resources that actually give families much more to spend than their reported income. Amid the controversy, everyone agrees that the official standard is arbitrary. Still, the government's figures remain, providing a crude indication of trends rather than a close approximation of the actual situation of the most economically deprived Americans.

No other industrial nation has adopted America's definition of poverty. Instead, the method most often used for international comparisons is a standard that defines as poor anyone falling below a certain *percentage of the median income nationwide.* For example, the Japanese have adopted the figure of 60 percent of the median income as a guide to antipoverty policies. Other countries prefer 50 percent. Such standards, of course, are completely relative, moving automatically with changes in the gross domestic product. For this reason, some consider the standards more a measure of the degree of inequality in the distribution of income than a means of identifying persons in serious need.

Finally, a few scholars propose the use of surveys that try to measure *privation,* arguing that the reason for worrying about poverty in the first place is that we want to avoid having people suffer.[8] One way of accomplishing this result would be to base our definition of poverty on consumption rather than income. A more ambitious alternative would be to try to identify privation directly. Under this approach, having too little to eat might make up one element in a composite view of poverty. Inadequate access to health care, overcrowded living conditions, poor quality of housing, unemployment, and lack of other necessities of life would be others. This method is appealing, because it is increasingly clear that reported income gives a highly inaccurate measure of the resources actually available to poor people. Nevertheless, measuring privation has not gained wide acceptance, perhaps because no one can agree on how to combine all of the relevant evidence in a single, convincing index of poverty.

The only conclusion one can draw from these disputes is that the subject remains in a state of great confusion. The official index in the United States is highly questionable, not only because its definition of poverty is arbitrary but because it relies on measurements of reported income that bear little relation to what poor people actually have to spend. It is unlikely that any single standard will ever capture all that concerns us in thinking about poverty. But the definition currently in use contributes little to our understanding and probably remains only because no consensus has emerged on what should take its place.

The Evolution of Policies to Reduce Poverty

Until the New Deal, poverty in America was the responsibility of local governments and charitable organizations.[9] The extent of suffering and unemployment in the 1930s, however, led the federal government to initiate a number of important programs to help the needy. By establishing Social Security as a national pension system, Congress created a mechanism that gradually reduced the scope of poverty among the aged. Unemployment insurance gave some protection to those who lost their jobs. Almost as an afterthought, Congress added a provision to help dependent children who had no fathers to support them. By this network of laws, Congress extended support to most of the "deserving" poor who could not help themselves. Others, who were of working age, were left to find a job or make do with such meager support as local authorities or charitable organizations chose to provide.

The next great change in America's policies occurred in the 1960s, when Lyndon Johnson launched his Great Society programs representing, in his words, the nation's "commitment to eradicate poverty among its people."[10] The president's strategy for the Great Society included several components to aid the poor. One line of attack sought to remove a major hazard for persons of limited means by enacting Medicare and Medicaid to ensure adequate health care for the elderly and the indigent. A second addressed the housing needs of the poor by encouraging construction of hundreds of thousands of low-cost units. A third piece of the grand design was meant to help those in need help themselves by creating job training programs, while a fourth encouraged the formation of neighborhood organizations to give the poor greater political power. The ultimate safety net continued to be welfare, administered by social workers who tried to rehabilitate able-bodied mothers and help them become fully functioning members of society.

As the Great Society took shape, more and more children were being born out of wedlock; the typical welfare claimant was no longer a bereaved widow with small children but a young mother who had never been married. At the same time, moved by the civil rights revolution and the War on Poverty, poor people and their advocates began to press aggressively for "welfare rights."[11] The Supreme Court handed down rulings broadening access to welfare and affirming the rights of needy individuals under federal laws. Suddenly, the number of claimants seeking benefits under AFDC (Aid to Families with Dependent Children) began to rise at an accelerated pace.

As welfare claims increased, improper payments became more frequent, eventually reaching 16 percent by 1973. At the same time, economic growth had slowed and personal incomes were no longer rising steadily for the population as a whole. As working people had to tighten their belts and reports of fraud and abuse began to circulate freely, a backlash soon developed. The emphasis under AFDC shifted toward tightening eligibility requirements and checking carefully to ensure strict compliance with the rules. Social workers seeking rehabilitation of the poor were increasingly replaced by bureaucrats enforcing regulations. By the 1980s, improper payments had declined by half, and procedures were more complicated.

Complaints about fraud and abuse were augmented by mounting concern over what seemed to be a steadily rising flood of young women who gave birth to illegitimate children but showed no interest in earning a living. Middle-class families increasingly resented the use of tax dollars to support what they regarded as an irresponsible lifestyle. Critics began to write influential papers suggesting that programs for the poor were disrupting families, weakening incentives to work, and creating a growing class of people who were dependent on the State.[12]

The late 1970s and 1980s proved to be lean years for the poor. Welfare payments in an average state for a family of three without other income fell by 43 percent in real dollars between 1970 and 1992. To a large extent, this decline reflected the states' efforts to take advantage of the growth in the federal food stamp program by holding down their AFDC payments to avoid attracting poor people from other parts of the country. Although food stamps did much to offset the erosion of cash payments, the two benefits combined still declined substantially and appeared to be removing fewer families from penury by the end of the 1980s. Although 57 percent of all families who would otherwise have been classified as poor in 1979 had been lifted out of poverty by government assistance (cash and in-kind), fewer than half were being emancipated from penury by 1990.[13] Meanwhile, the number of people with incomes far below the federal poverty line also rose steadily. In 1975, only 30 percent of the poor had incomes less than half of the official level. By the late 1980s, the proportion had crept up to 40 percent.

Table 17.1 records the effects of U.S. policies over the years by showing the number and percentage of Americans falling below the official poverty line since 1959, according to several alternative measures. Although these varying measures show substantially different levels of poverty, especially in the past twenty years, all of them reveal the same basic trend: a decline until the early 1970s, and a moderate rise thereafter. No one of the measures seems ideal. If poverty is a concern chiefly for the hardships it causes, figures based on consumption would appear to be most useful, since it is what people can consume rather than what their reported income is that most accurately reflects their material well-being. At the same time, consumption-based

Table 17.1. Rates of poverty by various calculations (percent of total population living in poverty), 1959–1992.

Definition of poverty	1959	1967	1974	1981	1988	1992
Official poverty line	22.4	14.2	11.2	14.0	13.1	14.5
Properly adjusted for inflation	23.2	14.2	10.5	12.2	11.6	13.1
Including in-kind benefits	23.1	14.0	9.7	10.8	10.5	11.3
Poverty rates based on consumption	13.0[a]	—	6.2[b]	7.5[c]	8.6	—

Source: Christopher Jencks, "Is the American Underclass Growing?" in Christopher Jencks and Paul Peterson, eds., *The Urban Underclass*, 28, 33 (1991); David M. Cutler and Lawrence F. Katz, "Macroeconomic Performance and the Disadvantaged," 2 *Brookings Papers on Economic Activity*, 46 (1991).

a. Figure is for 1960–1961.
b. Figure is for 1972–1973.
c. Figure is for 1980.

figures must be taken with a grain of salt, since they rest on a definition of poverty which is widely considered to be too low.*

Characteristics of the Poor

Who are the poor? The notion of poverty in the United States often conjures up images of idle mothers cashing monthly welfare checks. Not all those classified as poor, however, are mothers, or even persons we would normally think of as able to work. The largest category are children under the age of eighteen, who made up 37.9 percent of the poor in 1990. Among adults officially classified as poor, slightly more than 20 percent are over the age of sixty-five, almost 15 percent are under sixty-five but disabled, and 7 to 8 percent are in school. In short, far fewer than half of all poor people are able-bodied adults of normal working age.

Many individuals who are classified as poor also have full- or part-time jobs. In fact, almost one-third of all men between the ages of twenty-five and thirty-four earn less than would be needed to keep a family of four out of poverty (although many of them are not officially poor, since they are single, childless, or have a wife who works). As Table 17.2 makes clear, the percentages of poor people who work full or half time have remained fairly constant through the years.

For a long time, the existence of so many workers who still do not earn enough to escape from poverty presented policymakers with a dilemma. As wages for low-skilled jobs declined in the 1970s and 1980s, many people could not earn enough to escape poverty even if they worked full time throughout the year. Although policymakers were sympathetic to their plight, the traditional remedy of raising the minimum wage seemed risky to many legislators because it threatened to reduce the numbers of low-skilled jobs available.

*According to the inventor of the official poverty standard, if the index had been adjusted to take account of changing consumption practices and nutrition standards, the number of officially poor people in 1975 would have risen from 26 million to 30 million or from 24 million to 37 million, depending on the census survey used. Mollie Orshansky, "Measuring Poverty: A Debate," 36 *Public Welfare*, 47 (Spring 1978). More recently, another author has created what she considers a more realistic, up-to-date poverty budget that would increase the numbers classified as poor by over 50 percent. Susan Einbinder, Paper presented at 16th Annual Research Conference of the Association for Public Policy Analysis and Management (October 26–29, 1994). See also Patricia Ruggles, *Drawing the Line: Alternative Poverty Measures and Their Implications for Public Policy* (1990).

Table 17.2. The working poor, 1966–1992.[a]

Year	Percent of poor over 16 who worked year-round	Percent of poor over 16 who worked full time year-round	Percent of poor who worked less than full time
1966	43.8	13.5	30.3
1970	39.6	9.6	30.0
1975	38.7	7.6	31.1
1980	40.6	8.7	31.9
1985	42.4	9.3	33.1
1990	41.0	9.8	31.2
1992	40.3	9.2	31.1

Source: U.S. Bureau of the Census, *Current Population Reports,* Series P60-181, *Poverty in the United States, 1992,* xvii, Table E (1993). Figures prior to 1980: Center on Budget and Policy Priorities, *Poverty Tables, 1991,* 69 (1993).

a. Between 1966 and 1978, workers included all those over fourteen years of age. Between 1979 and 1989, workers included only those older than fifteen. Since 1990, workers include only those aged sixteen and older.

To avoid this dilemma, the government eventually hit upon the strategy of offering substantial tax credits to low-paid workers. In this way, the government could provide additional funds to those who work without inhibiting job creation by raising the cost of hiring new employees. In 1993, a Democratic Congress increased the tax credits to a point that a family of four headed by a full-time worker earning the minimum wage could receive just enough income, supplemented by food stamps, to reach the official poverty line. One year later, a new Republican majority began to attack the credits as excessively costly and subject to widespread fraud and abuse. Caught up in this controversy, the future of the earned income tax credit seemed more uncertain than it had only twelve months before.

Among the able-bodied adults who are not employed, disabled, or still in school, by far the largest number are single mothers with dependent children. Just under half of those parents who receive benefits for the first time will remain on welfare for a cumulative total of three years or more during their lifetime. But those who stay longer use up the lion's share of the benefits, and it is they who arouse most of the resentment against welfare.

Single mothers who remain on welfare are often caught in a predicament more difficult than many people realize. Benefits in many states do not yield enough, even with food stamps, to bring a family close to the official poverty line. But taking a job may not offer a realistic alternative. Even with tax credits, many single mothers contemplating work lack the skills to earn enough at the prevailing unskilled wage to make it worthwhile to leave welfare, forfeit Medicaid protection, and perhaps pay for child care as well. According to field interviews by Christopher Jencks and Kathryn Edin, welfare mothers seeking enough money for their families frequently resolve this dilemma by finding part-time jobs and not reporting their earnings.[14] Others spend much of their time looking for free food from local churches and charities—food that they can often get only by concealing their government benefits. In this way, welfare policies can put single mothers in a position where they see no alternative but to break the rules in order to raise the living standard of their families closer to the poverty line.

How can one sum up America's record in attacking poverty? Although it is often said that antipoverty programs are a failure, the facts do not support this conclusion. Briefly put, America spends approximately $300 billion per year to alleviate poverty. Of this sum, the lion's share goes to six programs: Medicaid ($132 billion), food stamps ($26 billion), Supplemental Security Income to the elderly poor and disabled ($26 billion), Aid to Families with Dependent Children, or "welfare" ($25 billion), low-income housing subsidies ($20 billion), and preschool and compensatory (Title I) education ($10 billion). Although none of these programs has totally solved the problems it addresses, all have achieved positive results and would undoubtedly have accomplished more with greater funding. Medicaid has succeeded in allowing poor, sick people to visit doctors at the same rates as the rest of the population. Food stamps have reduced malnutrition and hunger. Housing subsidies have improved the quality and affordability of accommodations for those fortunate enough to receive them. Supplemental Security Income has surely played a key role in reducing poverty among the aged from 19 percent when the program was created in 1972 to 12 percent in 1992. Head Start and compensatory education appear to produce at least modest improvements in learning and other behavioral problems, and might do more if properly targeted funding were available in sufficient amounts to permit programs of uniformly high quality. Finally, even the much maligned AFDC undoubtedly helps keep many children from becoming destitute, and claims that it fosters widespread illegitimacy and divorce are not substantiated by most careful studies to date.[15]

Allegations that federal antipoverty programs have failed or actually made America's social problems worse, therefore, do not accord with the evidence. On the other hand, no one would argue that federal policies have been ideal either in design or in execution. Just how successful the United States has been and how much better it might perform are questions that invite comparisons with other leading nations.

International Comparisons

The other industrialized nations considered here deal with poverty in a very different way.[16] Most of them try to reduce it by relying much more heavily than the United States on programs covering the entire population. Child allowances are given automatically for all offspring regardless of a family's means; health insurance is available to everyone; eligibility for unemployment insurance is more liberal and the benefits greater than in this country. Even housing allowances in the European nations discussed here are normally given to persons of moderate income as well as to the poor. Because of the broader coverage of benefit programs in other countries and the higher levels of support, the proportion of the poor relying on means-tested assistance has tended to be smaller than in the United States.

Another way to compare America's policies with those in Europe is to contrast the varying approaches to helping single mothers with children. The central dilemma that policymakers everywhere face is how to keep such families from falling into poverty without providing benefits that encourage mothers to have more children and avoid going to work. In the United States, officials have responded to this challenge by keeping benefits low, both to discourage single women from having children and to induce them to take a job. Thus, total government assistance (excluding Medicaid) for single mothers with no earned income amounts to only 27 percent of median family income in America, compared with 38 percent in France, 47 percent in Germany, 60 percent in Britain, and 64 percent in Sweden.[17] As a result, poverty rates among single mothers have been several times higher in the United States than they have been in Scandinavia and Northern Europe. At the same time, despite the lower benefits provided in America, only 65 percent of single mothers have jobs, compared with rates of over 80 percent in France and Sweden.[18] Hence, each of these countries seems to have done better than the United States both in keeping single mothers out of poverty and in encouraging them to take a job.

Why have Sweden and France been so successful?[19] Essentially, they have succeeded by shaping their assistance programs in ways that create strong positive incentives for recipients to seek employment. For example, both the French and Swedish governments provide extensive job training along with heavily subsidized child care to make it easier for single mothers to work. Minimum wages are likewise much higher in both countries than in the United States. Thus, working becomes a more attractive alternative in these countries than it is in the United States, because it pays more and because single mothers need not incur onerous child-care expenses. In addition, single mothers in France and Sweden do not risk the loss of health care benefits if they take a job, and universal child allowances help defray other incidental expenses resulting from combining work with parenting.

Other countries, such as Britain and Canada, have not chosen to emphasize employment to the same extent as Sweden and France, so that job training and subsidized child care are not so widely available. At the same time, social assistance payments are higher than in the United States. As a result, poverty rates among single mothers are lower than in America, but employment rates are also lower, especially in Britain, and the system as a whole is costlier to maintain.

How do leading industrial nations compare in holding down their overall rates of poverty? The most careful attempt to answer this question was made in the mid-1980s in the so-called Luxembourg Income Survey, which covered ten countries, including all of the nations discussed here save Japan. Investigators went to great pains to arrive at reliable, consistent measures of poverty and to include most in-kind benefits as well as cash payments. Table 17.3 shows the results of the study: rates of poverty before and after government assistance (using a poverty standard set at 50 percent of median income). These statistics reveal that the United States has the highest percentage of poor families (after transfers) and the least effective government programs of all the countries surveyed. Moreover, this record does not simply result from social problems peculiar to the United States, such as the presence of a large minority population. Poverty rates for whites alone are likewise above the levels found elsewhere (Table 17.4).

Analysts have also made comparative surveys of the "poverty

Table 17.3. Effectiveness of transfer programs in various countries.

Country	Percent of families living in poverty before government transfers	Percent of families living in poverty after government transfers	Percent reduction in poverty due to government programs
Canada	24.9	12.5	50
France	36.4	7.9	78
West Germany	31.0	6.8	78
Sweden	36.5	5.6	85
United Kingdom	30.0	8.2	73
United States	27.1	17.0	37

Source: Deborah Mitchell, *Income Transfers in Ten Welfare States*, 47 (1991).

Table 17.4. Percent of population living in poverty after government transfers, mid-1980s.

Age group	United States (whites only)	Average for nine other nations in Luxembourg study
All	9.1	4.8
Children (under 18)	13.2	5.5
Adults (18–64)	7.4	5.2
Elderly (65 +)	8.0	1.8

Source: Timothy Smeeding, unpublished data from Luxembourg Income Study.

gap"—the total amount of money that would just suffice to lift all poor people out of poverty (defined as 50 percent of the median national income).[20] According to these studies, America falls well below other advanced nations in the percentage of the total aggregate poverty gap that the government removes by its programs of assistance. The figures in Table 17.5 tell us that the poverty gap in the United States is only third in relative size among the poverty gaps in the six nations listed *before* taking account of government antipoverty and social programs. Because America gives less aid to the poor than other countries, however, the poverty gap *after* government benefits are received is much greater relative to GDP than in any of the five other nations, especially the four European countries.

Table 17.5. **Effect of transfer programs on the poverty gap.**[a]

Country	Pretransfer poverty gap (as percent of GDP)	Post-transfer poverty gap (as percent of GDP)	Percent reduction in poverty gap as a result of government programs
Canada	4.2	1.3	70
France	6.7	1.0	85
West Germany	6.4	0.6	91
Sweden	4.1	0.4	91
United Kingdom	3.3	0.2	93
United States	5.6	2.3	60

Source: Deborah Mitchell, *Income Transfers in Ten Welfare States*, 57 (1991).

a. The "poverty gap" is the amount by which the average poor family in each nation falls below a poverty line set at half the median family income of the country in question.

The one country discussed here that is not shown in all these figures is Japan. It is doubtful, however, that including Japan would change the results materially. The Japanese government in the 1960s tacitly acknowledged that the nation should try to bring all people in need of welfare assistance to a level equal to 60 percent of the median income. By the mid-1970s, one study estimated the percentage of people falling below even that standard at only 5 percent.[21] If this estimate is even close to being correct, Japan ranks among the most successful nations in the world in reducing poverty—far more successful, certainly, than the United States. But comparisons with Japan are difficult. It is likely that only a minority of the poor apply for public assistance. The Japanese rely far more than Americans do on corporations and families to share the burden of meeting social needs. Large companies have not laid off their regular workers in times of recession; thus, they have reduced the need for unemployment benefits. And Japanese families are much more likely than American families to share an obligation to take care of needy relatives, thus reducing welfare rolls.

Although the figures cited in Table 17.5 provide the best comparative survey of poverty yet devised, they are relative measures and therefore do not tell us how many people in each country fall below the same absolute level of income. More recent findings from the Luxembourg Study throw light on this question. According to these reports, American children in families in the middle 20 percent of the income range are better off than comparable children from almost any other advanced country. In sharp contrast, however, American children in the *bottom* 20 percent grow up in families with incomes below comparable families in all of the eighteen nations in the survey except Israel and Ireland—both much poorer nations than the United States. Family incomes of American children in the bottom 20 percent are actually *70 percent* or more below those of comparable families in Switzerland and Sweden and 50 percent below those of Belgium, Finland, Denmark, and Norway.

Unfortunately, official *income* figures do not give an accurate account of the actual *expenditures* that poor people make. Needy citizens in all countries appear to spend more money than their reported incomes would suggest, but it is not always clear by how much. As a result, the fact that poor families in the United States have much lower incomes than families in most other Western nations does not necessarily prove that poor people in America are actually living more deprived lives.[22]

In fact, little is known about how well or badly Americans live compared to their counterparts abroad. There is no reliable way as yet to compare food consumption. Such comparisons as can be made look to ownership of particular items, such as cars, telephones, washing machines, and the like, as well as figures on the prevalence of various housing defects, such as inadequate wiring and plumbing. Using these crude measures, the most careful study yet made suggests that differences in income among nations are considerably larger than differences in the way poor people actually live.[23] The 10 or 20 percent of Americans with the lowest incomes appear to buy fewer consumer items than comparably poor Canadians, and poor blacks in America seem to have significantly less to spend on the items surveyed than needy people in other industrialized countries. At the same time, the poorest 10 to 20 percent of Americans as a whole appear to spend about the same amount on the survey items as the poorest 10 to 20 percent in Germany and Sweden. Since the United States is wealthier than both of these nations, critics can assail America for not doing better by its least advantaged citizens (assuming that these crude surveys of consumption are reliable). Still, there is some comfort in learning that the living conditions of America's poorest citizens may not compare as badly to conditions in other advanced industrial nations as surveys based on income might suggest.

Interpreting the Record

Despite America's high official poverty rate and the limited effects of
its antipoverty programs, two arguments are sometimes made to minimize the severity of the problem. The first is that most poor people
seem to spend much more than their reported income, suggesting that
their true condition is considerably better than one might otherwise
suppose. This argument appears to be correct. Nevertheless, the latest
careful estimates suggest that even if one calculates poverty rates on
the basis of consumption rather than income, at least 8 percent of
Americans remain poor. Although 8 percent is considerably less than
the official poverty rate, it still amounts to more than 20 million people.

The second argument is that mobility in the United States is sufficiently high that many people who are officially classified as poor at
any point in time will not remain so for very long. This point, too, is
partially valid; many people do move in and out of poverty quite
quickly. Even so, recent estimates reveal that more than 60 percent of
all individuals who were in the bottom income quintile during the
1970s and 1980s were still in the bottom quintile five years later.[24] For
most people with low incomes, then, poverty cannot be regarded
merely as a brief, unpleasant episode in an otherwise comfortable existence. The net result is that poverty may not be as severe a problem
as official statistics might suggest, but it does represent a serious and
prolonged condition for many millions of Americans, most of whom
cannot be expected to do a great deal to better their condition.

Since the early 1970s, America has been stalled in its efforts to help
the poor. Just as in the fields of housing, old age policy, education, and
early childhood programs, government efforts to deal with the problem
often appear half-hearted. What accounts for this seemingly inadequate record?

One is tempted to respond that Americans simply have a different
sense of how much help poor people deserve. But that explanation is
not entirely convincing. As previously noted, large majorities of the
public favor more generous policies for the needy. Moreover, it is hard
to believe that most Americans are satisfied to have rates of poverty
among children, especially children under three years old, that are well
above those of any other age group in the population. Rather, the root
problem that has bedeviled U.S. antipoverty efforts through the years

has been the difficulty of reconciling the desire of Americans to help the poor with their strong distaste for policies that reward antisocial habits or allow able-bodied adults to avoid work. This dilemma arises with special poignancy in the debates over what to do about single mothers with infants born out of wedlock. How can one protect innocent children without encouraging sloth and irresponsible lifestyles on the part of their parents?

One might suppose that lawmakers could overcome this problem by devising programs with incentives that encourage able-bodied welfare mothers to get a job. Yet even experts do not fully understand why chronically unemployed Americans do not work or what could induce them to do so.[25] Some emphasize how many of these jobless people lack the education and skills to perform work that could pay enough to remove them from poverty.[26] Others suspect that there are not enough jobs that poor people can fill, at least not enough jobs that poor people can reach with the transportation available to them.[27] Still others point out that there is no incentive for mothers to work for the low wages that unskilled jobs provide, in view of the Medicaid benefits they lose and the child-care costs they may have to incur if they go to work.[28] But there are analysts who believe that the problem cannot be adequately explained by these considerations. In their view, America has a culture of poverty which is not yet fully understood and does not appear to yield to normal economic incentives.[29] They point to a gradual rise in the number of able-bodied men who are no longer even looking for work, a phenomenon which appears to persist even in times of low unemployment.[30] To these observers, either the cultural problem is intractable or the amounts of money required to induce many of the poor to work are well beyond the capacity of society to pay.

One can appreciate the complexities of this issue. There is much that we still do not understand about the motivations of those who refuse to work even when jobs are plentiful. Sweden and France appear to have had success in attacking the problem of unwed mothers by combining relatively high earnings for low-skilled jobs with heavy investments in child care and job training. But this approach does not suit America's preference for keeping the wages of the unskilled low. Nor are costly investments in training and child care a likely prospect for this country even if they might succeed in putting many single mothers into jobs and removing them from the welfare rolls. The policy that seems to be gaining favor now is simply to cut benefits for welfare mothers and to require them to work. Disagreements remain over whether smaller benefits will lower the number of teenage pregnancies and whether work requirements can succeed without expensive government efforts to provide child care, preserve eligibility for Medicaid, and create jobs. For the moment, all that seems certain is that existing programs are not working and that exasperation over teenage pregnancy and rising welfare rolls has put reforms on the national agenda that would have been rejected as inhumane only a few years ago.

Stepping back from the current welfare debates, it is important to recognize that problems of chronic idleness and teenage mothers do not fully explain why there are so many poor people in America. For poverty rates are greater here than in other leading industrial nations even among categories of people whom we do *not* expect to work. More than half of all Americans officially designated as poor either are working full time or are elderly people, disabled persons, or others we would not normally expect to be employed.[31] Only a small minority of these people could presumably be classified as malingerers. The rest are not, yet they still receive too little assistance to escape from poverty. In part, this is because official benefit levels are often too low even to reach the meager standard set by the official poverty index. In addition, most government programs do not actually reach a large percentage of those they are meant to help. In some cases, potential beneficiaries simply do not wish to accept the government's help. More often, however, either Congress fails to appropriate enough funds to cover all those it purports to assist, or the intended beneficiaries do not know that help is available, or they cannot fathom the intricate application forms they must fill out or choose among the multiple overlapping programs that purport to aid them. Thus, housing benefits are available only for 30 percent of the poor families that are ostensibly eligible, nutritional supplements are provided to only two-thirds of all poor mothers with small children, and barely half of those in poverty receive food stamps.[32]

Despite the frustrating problem of malingering, then, there are steps that a government could take to reduce poverty levels without real risk of encouraging such behavior. Washington recently enacted one of these reforms by providing a much more substantial earned-income tax credit. By raising the credit a bit more or by combining it with modest increases in the minimum wage, Congress could lift up to two million workers and their families out of poverty. Higher minimum benefits for single elderly persons could further reduce the poverty rolls without encouraging indolence and shirking. The same could be done for single persons who are disabled (whose benefits under the Supplemental Security Income programs, even with in-kind benefits, amounted to less than the official poverty level in 1994).* Further inroads on deprivation and want could result from raising participation rates in existing programs such as food stamps, housing benefits, and unemployment insurance. More effective enforcement of child support payments from absent parents could also help in some cases. Universal health care might encourage at least some mothers with children to work, since they would no longer run the risk of losing medical benefits for their families. More effective training and job counseling might shrink the welfare rolls a bit further. Carefully administered public-sector jobs programs could reduce poverty even more, especially in times of high unemployment.

Implementing all of these reforms would still leave the nation with a substantial number of people below the official poverty line. Yet the point remains that options do exist which would bring America's poverty levels much closer to those of other nations without rewarding malingering. To this extent, current levels of poverty are not immutable but are the result of policy choices, choices that seem at odds with the stated desire of most Americans to do more for the deserving poor.[33]

Freedom and Responsibility

This inquiry into efforts to help the poor concludes the survey of progress made in the United States over several decades in a wide range of human endeavors. Before pulling these pieces together to evaluate America's record as a whole, we might pause for a moment to ask once again whether the goals of the society are truly compatible with one another. Earlier chapters considered to what extent the quest for personal security fits with the society's other basic aims and whether economic growth and widespread affluence can long coexist with high

---

*Raising disability payments is often resisted on the grounds that it will encourage malingerers to maneuver themselves into being declared disabled rather than looking for a job. The answer to this problem, however, should surely be to find a way of enforcing eligibility rules strictly rather than penalizing the great majority, who are legitimately disabled, by keeping their benefits below the poverty line.

standards of personal responsibility. In the same spirit, it is worth inquiring whether the government's efforts to protect individual freedom and provide for the needy are fully consistent with the private exercise of virtue and responsibility.

At first glance, this question may seem odd. Yet America's experience over the past forty years reveals a curious relationship between the evolution of the laws to secure people's liberties and relieve poverty, on the one hand, and the changes that have occurred in private behavior, on the other. Both Congress and the federal courts expanded programs for the poor and enlarged constitutional freedoms throughout the 1960s and early 1970s, before judges and lawmakers entered upon a period of consolidation—some would say retrenchment—during the 1980s. Conversely, by all visible signs, personal responsibility seemed to erode in the 1960s and early 1970s, then stabilized or improved in the 1980s. In much the same way, as federal efforts to reduce poverty grew dramatically in the 1960s and early 1970s, private charity moved in the opposite direction, only to rise again in the 1980s after the government's antipoverty programs began to contract.

To all intents and purposes, then, public policy and personal responsibility seemed to be engaged in some sort of elegant minuet: as one moved forward the other receded, and vice versa. Observing these trends, one might well ask whether some causal relationship exists between government initiatives and the spontaneous exercise of personal responsibility and civic duty. Could it be that more aggressive government efforts to achieve basic values necessarily lead to corresponding declines in private virtue? If so, why should this be?

Many critics charge that the federal government has corroded the moral and civic virtues of America by enacting programs for the poor that have altered incentives in socially harmful ways. On the one hand, it is said, welfare laws have led to out-of-wedlock births and discouraged marriage, hence increasing the number of single-parent families and aggravating the problems of poverty. On the other, government assistance has replaced private charity and thus removed much of the reason for individuals and communities to come to the aid of persons in need. In a single stroke, therefore, federal welfare policies have encouraged private vice and crowded out private virtue.

While these arguments may not be wholly without merit, neither one turns out to be especially convincing. Much careful research has shown that welfare payments of all kinds have at best relatively minor effects on the rates of divorce and out-of-wedlock childbearing.[34] The number of children born to single women who are *not* on welfare has been increasing about as fast as births to women receiving AFDC payments. Out-of-wedlock births continued to rise during the 1970s and 1980s in the face of declining welfare payments (including food stamps). Moreover, meager benefits in certain states do not seem to have led to lower levels of illegitimacy than in states with more liberal policies. In fact, the highest rates of illegitimacy tend to occur in states such as Mississippi that have the *lowest* AFDC payments. It is likely, then, that the continued increase in out-of-wedlock births owes more to factors such as the diminishing stigma attached to illegitimacy, the increasing number of women who enter the labor market and can support themselves, and the declining earnings in low-skilled occupations that may lead many men to conclude that they cannot afford the responsibilities of marriage and fatherhood.

If welfare policies have not done much to destroy the family and promote illegitimacy, could they have weakened civic virtue by displacing responsibilities previously felt by individuals and communities toward the poor? Politicians increasingly make this claim. Conservative lawmakers have even suggested that if the government cut its welfare programs drastically, private charity would rise to the occasion and fill the void through increased gifts to churches, social service organizations, and other neighborhood groups that could offer aid in a more efficient, humane, and responsive manner.

But is it true that the government's social programs discourage private charity? Obviously, if the State provided for all legitimate social needs, there would be little or nothing for community organizations and charities to do. Nevertheless, America is very far from reaching this point and has little prospect of getting there in the foreseeable future. With an abundance of unfilled needs, more government programs have not necessarily meant less private assistance to the needy, or even less giving to charity. True, individuals began to give less of their income to all forms of charity during the 1960s and early 1970s while the War on Poverty and other programs for the poor were getting started. Nevertheless, the figures show that real gifts for human services continued to rise in the 1960s and only fell sharply from 1974 to 1977 after the War on Poverty was over.[35] Thereafter, donations for human services began to rise again in 1977, well before President Reagan began to cut back federal programs for the poor.[36]

There is also reason to believe that just as legal rules can sometimes strengthen personal responsibility, so can government aid encourage private giving. The creation of the National Endowment for the Arts, followed by extraordinary growth in private funding for the arts, offers an apt example. Increased government spending in such fields as health and higher education has likewise been accompanied by major growth in private donations for universities, hospitals, and research.

In fact, the very notion that federal aid to the poor crowds out private charity seems misconceived, because it wrongly assumes that government programs and nonprofit organizations are alternative ways of addressing human needs.[37] Since the Massachusetts Bay Colony first began assisting Harvard College, however, governments have supported nonprofit institutions to help carry out public purposes. This has long been America's way of reconciling its need for public services with its distrust of government bureaucracies. Thus, far from giving way to the Great Society, the nonprofit sector grew strongly in the 1960s and 1970s just as federal appropriations for the poor were rising rapidly. Conversely, when Washington cut its programs for the needy in the early 1980s, charitable donations did not immediately increase to fill the gap. Although nonprofit social service agencies eventually managed to replace the federal cuts, only 35 percent of the shortfall was made up by increased donations; the rest came primarily from charging fees.[38] In short, history suggests that instead of crowding out charitable efforts for the needy, federal programs have actually expanded the opportunities of nonprofit organizations to serve the poor.

The other major argument linking government policies with declining standards of behavior charges the courts rather than Congress as the principal culprit. According to Mary Ann Glendon, the preoccupation of lawyers and judges with individual rights has deflected attention from questions of responsibility and civic virtue to a fixation on the self and its interests.[39] In her words, "Our overblown rights rhetoric and our vision of the rights-bearer as an autonomous individual channel our thoughts away from what we have in common and focus them on what separates us. They draw us away from participation in public life and point us toward the maximization of private satisfactions."[40]

There are certainly examples of judicial decisions in the 1960s that emphasize rights at the expense of responsibilities. For example, in *King v. Smith* the Supreme Court declared that a state could not deprive the poor of welfare payments in order to impose moral standards about "illicit sexual behaviors and illegitimacy" on recipients.[41] Other judicial rulings demanded that teachers observe due-process requirements before disciplining students and that tenants be accorded procedural safeguards before being evicted for drug dealing and other forms of antisocial behavior.[42] Many observers believe that any benefits achieved by protecting individual students and tenants from arbitrary treatment have been far outweighed by the tendency of such safeguards to weaken the authority of those charged with maintaining proper rules of conduct in classrooms and housing projects.[43]

Although these examples offer lessons worth considering, they hardly provide an explanation potent enough to account for the massive rise in crime and other forms of irresponsibility in the 1960s. Nor do they explain why similar deterioration in personal behavior took place in other Western societies beyond the reach of American judges. It is likely, therefore, that court decisions, in their emphasis on rights, were more a reflection than a cause of the broad cultural trend in the 1960s toward elevating self-fulfillment over social responsibility.

It would also be wrong to assume that judicial efforts to vindicate the rights of individuals and groups are always at odds with personal responsibility. One contribution of the "rights revolution" was to articulate a set of moral principles often ignored by many Americans. "For good or ill," Justice Brandeis said, "our government is the potent, the omnipresent teacher."[44] By recognizing the rights of blacks, women, and handicapped persons, the Supreme Court defined the responsibilities owed by the rest of society to these neglected groups, and thereby helped persuade the public to take such obligations more seriously. Survey results make clear that changes in the law were accompanied by corresponding shifts in opinion manifesting greater respect for the interests of blacks and other protected groups and diminished tolerance for acts of discrimination against them. For this reason, one can acknowledge the role of procedural safeguards in perpetuating certain forms of irresponsible behavior and still question whether the net effect of the rights revolution was to lessen the public's regard for the legitimate interests of others. In a heterogeneous, individualistic nation such as the United States, the creation of rights may actually be the only sure way to establish the obligations that different groups in the society owe to one another.

Nothing that has been said should be taken to deny the obvious tensions that exist between a strong commitment to individual freedom and the maintenance of high standards of personal responsibility toward others. But those who try to blame high rates of crime, out-of-wedlock births, or child abuse on specific government policies and court cases are confusing symptoms with underlying causes. Much as one may fault politicians and bureaucrats, the changes in behavior that took place beginning in the 1960s were far too massive and sudden to result primarily from particular federal programs or judicial opinions. The fact that similar shifts occurred not only in America but in many other parts of the Western world offers further proof that cultural forces were at work far deeper than the acts of any single government.

VI

WHAT IT ALL MEANS

18

Summing Up

Now that we have compiled America's record in many different fields of endeavor, it is time to assemble the fragments into a larger mosaic that depicts the overall progress of the society over the past several decades. Has America truly moved forward or has it entered a period of decline? Is the country going where its people want to go or, in the language of the pollsters, is it "headed in the wrong direction"?

Comparisons with the Past

The easiest way to determine whether the nation has been advancing or slipping back is to ascertain how consistently it has moved ahead toward the basic objectives favored by most Americans. Table 18.1 summarizes the findings on this score. On the whole, the results are considerably better than pessimists would have us believe. Since 1960, the nation has made tangible progress toward more than two-thirds of the seventy or more significant domestic goals discussed in this study. Contrary to views often expressed, there is no reliable evidence that American students are learning less in school, or that the American Dream is vanishing, or that the environment is more polluted. Only in approximately one-quarter of the cases—most notably unemployment, per capita health care costs, crime, and other forms of personal irresponsibility—has the record of the United States actually declined.

If life has gotten better in most ways since 1960, why are Americans so worried about their country? After all, as a nation, we are wealthier,

Table 18.1. Changes in various aspects of American life: the 1990s compared with the early 1960s.

Policy area	Improved	About the same	Worse
I. PROSPERITY			
A. *The economy*			
1. Per capita income	x		
2. Productivity per worker	x		
3. Controlling inflation		x	
4. Minimizing unemployment			x
5. Net investment in plant and equipment as percent of GDP	x		
B. *Research and technology*			
1. Number of scientists and engineers per 1,000 people	x		
2. Number of articles in refereed journals	x		
3. Number of patents issued to Americans		x	
4. Share of GDP devoted to civilian R&D	x		
5. Share of worldwide high technology exports			x
C. *Education*			
1. Percent graduating high school	x		
2. Percent graduating college	x		
3. Student achievement (reading)		x	
4. Student achievement (math and science)		x	
D. *Labor market policy*			
1. Percent of work force trained by employers	x		
2. Range of vocational courses available in high school and college	x		
3. Amount of training, public and private sectors	x		
II. QUALITY OF LIFE			
A. *Housing*			
1. Percent of dwellings with serious defects	x		
2. Percent of population owning home	x		
3. Affordability for renters[a]			x

Table 18.1 continued.

Policy area	Improved	About the same	Worse
B. *Neighborhoods*			
1. Concentration of poverty in urban neighborhoods			x
2. Degree of segregation by race	x		
3. Percent of population living in neighborhood of choice (city, suburb, exurb)	x		
4. Perception of personal safety in neighborhoods			x
C. *The environment*			
1. Degree of air pollution	x		
2. Extent of water pollution	x		
3. Percent of drinking water purified	x		
D. *The arts*			
1. Number of arts organizations	x		
2. Size of audience for plays, concerts, etc.	x		
3. Total support for arts, other than ticket sales	x		
4. Consumer spending on arts (as percent of disposable income)	x		

III. OPPORTUNITY

	Improved	About the same	Worse
A. *Children's well-being*			
1. Rate of infant mortality	x		
2. Availability of daycare	x		
3. Extent of prenatal care	x		
4. Percent of children living in poverty	x		
5. Parental-leave policy	x		
6. Percent of infants vaccinated	x		
B. *Racial equality*			
1. Voting rights	x		
2. Housing discrimination	x		
3. Segregation in schools	x		
4. Quality of education for blacks	x		
C. *Equality of opportunity*			
1. Access to preschool	x		
2. Access to universities	x		
3. Extent of racial discrimination in employment	x		

Table 18.1 continued.

Policy area	Improved	About the same	Worse
4. Extent of gender discrimination in employment	x		
5. Overall equality of opportunity	x		

IV. PERSONAL SECURITY

A. *Health care*

1. Technical quality	x		
2. Life expectancy	x		
3. Percent of population covered by health insurance	x		
4. Cost (percent of GDP)			x

B. *Job security*

1. Percent of work force with some form of legally sanctioned representation			x
2. Protection from arbitrary discharge[b]		?	
3. Percent of work force laid off per year			x
4. Retraining and other help in case of layoffs	x		
5. Unemployment insurance (percent of unemployed receiving)			x
6. Incidence of job-related illness and injury		x	

C. *Violent crime*

1. Incidence (per 100,000 people)			x
2. Success in solving crime (clearance rate)			x
3. Fear for personal safety			x

D. *Old age*

1. Retirement income (as percent of prior wages)	x		
2. Percent living in poverty	x		
3. Percent covered by health insurance	x		
4. Financial assistance for long-term care	x		

V. VALUES

A. *Personal freedom*

1. Degree of freedom guaranteed by law	x		

Table 18.1 continued.

Policy area	Improved	About the same	Worse
B. *Personal responsibility*			
1. Obeying the law (extent of crime)			x
2. Percent of children born out of wedlock			x
3. Cheating on exams			x
4. Percent of income given to charity			x
5. Community service			x
6. Percentage of eligibles voting			x
C. *Providing for the poor and disadvantaged*			
1. Incidence of poverty	x		
2. Severity of poverty (aggregate poverty gap as percent of GDP)	x		
3. Effectiveness of government transfer programs	x		

a. "Affordability" indicates the percentage of people paying more than 30 percent of their income for housing.

b. Statutes and court decisions have extended greater legal protection for certain types of arbitrary discharge, but these gains are offset by declines in the proportion of workers covered by bargaining agreements requiring just cause for discharge. It is not possible to determine which of these conflicting tendencies is the stronger.

our poverty rates are lower, our health care is better, our lives last longer, our old-age pensions are larger, and our air is cleaner than was the case in the optimistic 1950s. How is it that so many people are convinced that the nation is headed in the wrong direction?

Part of the answer may lie in the fact that the standards we use to judge our society have changed profoundly in the past forty years. A number of problems that vex us today, such as poverty, the environment, and gender discrimination, went largely unrecognized from World War II until the 1960s. In that more complacent time, the public simply ignored many social conditions that were far worse than they are today.

Our awareness of these and other social afflictions has been magnified by the growth of television and the rise of investigative reporting. John Steinbeck wrote vividly about dirt farmers in *The Grapes of Wrath,* and Margaret Bourke-White took arresting photographs of families ruined by the Depression. Nevertheless, only with the advent of TV did the great majority of Americans have the opportunity to witness so vividly the deprivations of the poor, the violence of the inner cities, the existence of toxic waste dumps, unsafe cars, and child abuse, not to mention such newer problems as the spread of drugs, the ravages of AIDS, and the plight of the homeless.

In recent years, reporting by newspapers and television alike has increasingly emphasized scandals, violence, failed public programs, and other misadventures. Today, negative items have come to outnumber favorable stories by a large margin. More and more articles impute self-serving motives to politicians and interpret every decision as a tactic in the constant struggle for reelection. According to some observers, this trend in reporting the news is one reason that the public's trust in government has declined since the 1960s, and that the opinions people hold of all sorts of institutions and groups which they know only through the media are invariably lower than their views of organizations and individuals they have experienced firsthand.[1] With such a visual diet, is it any wonder that the public's sense of what goes on in the United States has not only become more vivid but more pessimistic as well?

In trying to understand the current mood of the nation, one must also bear in mind that few people judge their society by comparing it with conditions half a century ago. Their frame of reference tends to be much shorter. Although America may have improved in many respects over what it was in the 1950s, it has not been advancing as rapidly or as uniformly in the past fifteen to twenty years as it did in earlier decades. The greatest postwar advances in freedom, prosperity, opportunity, and personal security took place from the early 1960s to the early 1970s—a time, ironically, when individual responsibility rapidly declined and the nation suffered from extreme turmoil and anguish. After 1975, rates of progress slowed in many important areas, and in a number of instances, the situation actually deteriorated.

The slowdown has been especially obvious in matters involving the economy and material welfare. Median incomes have virtually stopped growing since 1973, although they rose by close to 3 percent per year between 1950 and 1970. Productivity grew by almost 2.5 percent each year between 1947 and 1973 but climbed by less than 1 percent per year thereafter. Inequality of income has risen over the past fifteen years, while levels of unemployment continue to be higher than they were during most of the 1960s. Poverty is more prevalent today than it was two decades ago. Health care coverage has declined and unemployment insurance aids fewer jobless workers. Homeless people are more numerous and housing is less affordable for those with modest incomes.

Of course, there are other fields in which America's performance was *better* from 1975 to 1990 than it was in the preceding fifteen years. The quality of the environment, safety on the job, charitable contributions, and student test scores, among other measures, all improved after deteriorating during the earlier period. Apparently, however, these advances have been much less noticeable than the slowdown in the economy and the anxieties brought on by massive layoffs, persistently high crime rates, and cutbacks in private health care coverage.

Over the past two decades, many American families have hardly increased their incomes at all and some have actually witnessed a decline in their fortunes. As certain costs, such as college tuition and medical bills, continue to rise more rapidly than inflation, there is less and less money left over to spend on other things. Families have to tighten their belts and mothers must go to work. Meanwhile, the government feels compelled to curtail needed social programs. Opportunities for advancement also tend to increase less rapidly when the economy is sluggish. More and more, life becomes a tense, anxiety-ridden competition in which gains for some mean disappointment and defeat for others. In such an environment, anger and resentment tend to increase—toward immigrants, blacks, women, public officials, and anyone else who can be plausibly singled out for blame.

These difficulties tend to obscure signs of progress in other social domains. For unskilled workers whose incomes have dropped by 20 percent or more since 1975, for young couples who find that a new home is now beyond their means, for long-term employees who discover that they no longer have medical coverage, the advantages of cleaner streams, more arts festivals, even safer workplaces cannot overcome a mounting sense of dismay.

Finally one must view the nation's current difficulties against the very high expectations that most Americans have for their country and its political leaders. Eighty-four percent of the public believe that we have the finest system of government in the world.[2] In 1994, a majority agreed that "as Americans, we can always find a way to solve our problems and get what we want."[3] In 1979, with Russians invading

Afghanistan, America's competitiveness under assault, and inflation and unemployment both rising rapidly, 73 percent of the public asserted that "there is nothing wrong with this country that good leadership couldn't cure."[4]

From the 1930s to the early 1960s, these expectations were repeatedly vindicated by events. Americans may have ignored a number of serious problems, but the problems they did acknowledge they overcame with remarkable success. The Great Depression ended; Germany and Japan were vanquished; the post-war economy performed beyond expectations; the Marshall Plan saved Western Europe; anti-Semitism receded, and the Supreme Court called a halt to official segregation. With the rest of the world still recovering from war, the United States seemed invincible.

Since the early 1960s, our triumphs have been fewer and farther between. Americans have had to accept the assassination of several of their most popular leaders, the quagmire of Vietnam, the revelations of Watergate, the travails of the oil crisis, and a host of stubborn domestic problems. Having enjoyed such remarkable success and having such faith in their system of government and their country's potential, Americans are understandably frustrated when many problems they care about have barely improved and some have even grown worse.

Comparisons with Other Nations

Concern that the United States is not living up to expectations has been heightened by continuing signs that America is not performing as well as other industrial nations. Stories have repeatedly appeared describing the influx of Japanese cars and appliances, the falling dollar, persistent trade deficits. These accounts have been augmented by periodic reports that American students fare poorly on international tests of science and math, that poverty rates are higher in the United States than in other advanced nations, and that crime rates in this country are the highest in the industrialized world. After a steady diet of such news, many Americans must fear that something is seriously amiss in a nation that seemed so dominant in the world only a few short decades ago.

In the main, these fears seem well founded. True, growth rates since the early 1970s have faltered, not only in America but throughout the entire industrialized world. Citizens in most advanced nations have seen their productivity increase more slowly and unemployment rise.

All of the leading industrial democracies seem to be suffering from overextended government programs, and all are experiencing acute public distrust of politicians and bureaucrats. Allowing for these universal problems, however, there is reason to believe that America's progress in pursuing most of its important national goals has lagged behind that of other leading industrial nations for more than thirty years. This point is clearly revealed by Table 18.2. *Of more than sixty separate items compared, the record of the United States from 1960 to 1990 was below average in two-thirds of the cases (forty-three), and at or near the bottom of the list in more than half (thirty-three).*

What do these comparisons reveal about the nation's progress toward the goals to which most Americans subscribe? On the positive side, they confirm that the United States is still the richest industrial nation in the world, measured by what individuals of average income can actually purchase with their money. We also continue to lead the world in productivity, as it is typically measured. Our economy has shown a remarkable tendency to generate new jobs, while employment has been stagnating throughout most of western Europe. As a result, after decades in which unemployment in the United States was substantially higher than it was in countries such as France, Germany and Sweden, jobless rates in Europe have climbed in recent years to levels well above America's.

At the same time, the nation's economic superiority has diminished greatly since the 1950s. Living standards and productivity levels have clearly risen faster in Europe and Japan than in the United States during the past four decades. Despite all the talk of downsizing and the surge of new technology, output per worker in the U.S. economy has continued to rise at a very slow pace. There are even studies suggesting that German and French workers are now more productive than Americans on an hourly basis, although their shorter work weeks and longer vacations cause their *annual* productivity to lag well behind levels in this country.[5]

Of course, many of these nations owe their faster growth in output and productivity to the fact that they were able to copy America's techniques while catching up from the ravages of World War II. As William Baumol and other economists have argued, the most advanced economies may simply be following a natural path toward convergence around a common rate of growth.[6] Now that productivity increases have slowed in all highly industrialized economies and America still

Table 18.2. U.S. record in various areas, compared with that of six other industrial democracies (Canada, France, West Germany, Japan, Sweden, and the United Kingdom).

Policy area	At or near the top	Above average	Average	Below average	At or near the bottom
I. PROSPERITY					
A. *The economy*					
1. Per capita income	x				
2. Per capita productivity[a]	x				
3. Growth rate of per capita income (1960–1990)					x
4. Growth rate of productivity (1960–1990)					x
5. Controlling inflation (1960–1990)		x			
6. Minimizing unemployment (1960–1990)				x	
7. Minimizing unemployment (1980–1995)		x			
8. Net investment in plant and equipment as percent of GDP (1960–1990)					x
B. *Research and technology*					
1. Number of scientists and engineers (per 100,000 people)	x				
2. Percent of articles in refereed journals	x				
3. Number of citations per scientific article	x				
4. Percent of patents issued	x				
5. Share of world trade in high-tech goods	x				
C. *Education*					
1. Percent graduating high school			x		
2. Percent graduating college	x				
3. Student achievement (reading, 9- and 13-year-olds)		x			
4. Student achievement (math)					x
5. Student achievement (science)					x
D. *Labor market policy*					
1. Percent of GDP spent on training (public and private)					x

Table 18.2 continued.

Policy area	At or near the top	Above average	Average	Below average	At or near the bottom
2. Percent of work force receiving training					x
3. Effectiveness of employment service				x	
4. Effectiveness of school-to-work programs				x	

II. QUALITY OF LIFE

A. *Housing*

	At or near the top	Above average	Average	Below average	At or near the bottom
1. Quality of housing	x				
2. Percent of population owning home	x				
3. Affordability for entire population					x

B. *Neighborhoods*

	At or near the top	Above average	Average	Below average	At or near the bottom
1. Degree of segregation by income in cities					x
2. Degree of segregation by race in cities					x
3. Length of commute to work					x
4. Variety of choice in living environments	x				

C. *The environment*

	At or near the top	Above average	Average	Below average	At or near the bottom
1. Reduction in air pollution (1970–1990)				x	
2. Reduction in water pollution (1970–1990)			Impossible to compare		
3. Percent of population with waste-water treatment			x		
4. Percent of waste recycled					x

D. *The arts*

	At or near the top	Above average	Average	Below average	At or near the bottom
1. Total audience for performances and exhibitions				x	
2. Total support (public and private) other than ticket sales				x	
3. Rate of growth in total support for the arts (1960–1990)	x				

Table 18.2 continued.

Policy area	At or near the top	Above average	Average	Below average	At or near the bottom
III. OPPORTUNITY					
A. *Children's well-being*					
1. Infant mortality					x
2. Percent of children vaccinated				x	
3. Percent enrolled in preschool				x	
4. Percent in poverty					x
5. Parental-leave policy					x
B. *Race*		Impossible to compare			
C. *Career opportunities*					
1. Rate of upward mobility[b]			x		
2. Gender earnings gap				x	
3. Women in high-status jobs		x			
IV. PERSONAL SECURITY					
A. *Health care*					
1. Technical quality	x				
2. Life expectancy					x
3. Patients' evaluation of their own care			x		
4. Cost as percent of GDP					x
5. Coverage by health insurance					x
6. Public evaluation of system					x
B. *Job security*					
1. Percent of work force with some form of representation					x
2. Protection from arbitrary discharge					x
3. Assistance in case of layoffs					x
4. Reduction in job-related illness and injury (1970–1990)		-		x	
C. *Violent crime*					
1. Incidence (per 100,000 people)					x
2. Success in solving crime					x
3. Fear for personal safety					x
D. *Old age*					
1. Level of average retirement income after taxes (as percent of previous wages)	x				

Table 18.2 continued.

Policy area	At or near the top	Above average	Average	Below average	At or near the bottom
2. Percent in poverty					x
3. Access to affordable long-term care					x

V. VALUES

Policy area	At or near the top	Above average	Average	Below average	At or near the bottom
A. *Individual freedom*					
1. Extent of freedom under the law[c]			x		
B. *Personal responsibility*					
1. Violations of criminal laws					x
2. Percent of children born out of wedlock			x		
3. Incidence of teenage pregnancy					x
4. Voting rates					x
5. Charitable contributions	x				
6. Community service	x				
C. *Providing for the poor and disadvantaged*					
1. Percent of population with incomes below poverty line					x
2. Severity of poverty (aggregate poverty gap as percent of GDP)					x
3. Effectiveness of government transfer programs					x

a. The proper rating depends on whether one relies on hourly productivity or annual productivity. Hourly productivity reflects the skills of the work force and the methods of production, whereas annual productivity also includes the number of hours worked. Although American workers still lead the world in annual productivity, their advantage may depend on the fact that they work longer hours and receive shorter vacations than their counterparts in Germany and France.

b. There is dispute among scholars over whether mobility in the United States is above average or merely average. There does not seem to be a preponderance of expert opinion that the United States has unusually high rates of mobility for the countries herein compared.

c. This is admittedly an arbitrary judgment, but it is consistent with evaluations made annually by Freedom House.

maintains its margin of superiority over most of its leading rivals, has it not consolidated its position as the world's most successful economy? Perhaps. There is evidence, however, that this view may be too optimistic. The basic building blocks for long-term productivity growth are investments in new plant and equipment, educational achievement, and job training. In all these respects, the United States has tended to trail most of its principal competitors. Our investments in plant and equipment are comparatively low, our students perform less well in science and math than their counterparts in most other advanced democracies, and our job training efforts are widely reputed to fall well below those of Sweden, Japan, and Germany. Only in scientific research and technological innovation do we continue to excel, and even here we are gradually losing our lead in patents and high-tech trade to the Japanese (though not to the Europeans).

According to the most careful accounts, our continuing lead in productivity is chiefly due to our traditional preference for free markets, coupled with the greater tendency of other nations to shelter parts of their economy from foreign imports and domestic competition.[7] As trade barriers fall and global competition intensifies, these forms of protection seem to be diminishing. To the extent that they do, investment in plant and equipment along with education and job training should play a more decisive role. These are areas in which the United States has performed relatively poorly, and reform will be hard to bring about. All in all, therefore, it is unclear that America will be able to retain its competitive edge, let alone manage to grow more rapidly over a sustained period than other advanced nations.

As for other matters that affect our quality of life, the results are mixed at best. On the one hand, well-to-do and middle-class Americans have attained levels of homeownership and a quality of housing that compare well with those found abroad. Even the poor tend to occupy dwellings with physical conditions equal or superior to those of their counterparts in other leading countries. On the other hand, the problems of finding affordable housing or decent surroundings in which to live are probably greater for the poor in the United States than they are elsewhere. Many have to live in crime-ridden public projects, and others spend higher proportions of their income on rent than is common in most other nations discussed in this study.

Much the same can be said of the neighborhoods in which people live. Again, one finds prosperous suburbs for the well-to-do that compare favorably with living environments in any other country of the world. At the same time, the condition of cities in the United States is probably worse than it is in other advanced nations. Ghettos inhabited by the urban poor have been described by informed foreign observers as of a quality "to be expected in a poverty-stricken Third World country."[8]

In other matters that bear on the quality of life, such as the environment and the arts, the United States has made considerable progress over the past few decades. Both are areas in which we can justifiably take pride. Nevertheless, in neither case is our record outstanding by international standards. America's efforts to cope with pollution and waste are hugely expensive and highly inefficient, with results that fall below those of Japan and may well trail the achievements of several other nations surveyed here. As for the arts, although we have made much progress in developing world-class performers, expanding all manner of arts activities, and attracting a growing public, we have not attained the level of financial support or the number of arts organizations or the size of audiences to match those of most nations in western Europe.

What about efforts to increase opportunities for all Americans? Certainly, the progress made over the past thirty years in reducing artificial handicaps of race and gender has been among the most impressive achievements of the United States. For middle-class women and minorities with talent and ambition, the government has lowered barriers and has smoothed the path to a good education and a career in the most attractive occupations in America. The earnings gap for women and blacks has narrowed appreciably, and minority and female professionals can be found in growing numbers in the great corporations, law firms, hospitals and university faculties of the land.

Once again, however, our record in expanding opportunity is not exceptional by international standards. Contrary to the conventional wisdom, experts are not agreed that men have been able to climb the occupational ladder more rapidly in the United States than in Europe. Nor have women done better in closing the wage gap than their counterparts abroad. Meanwhile, racial discrimination probably remains a greater barrier in America than it is in Canada and most of western Europe.

Moreover, if opportunities for women and minorities have improved in the United States, the same cannot be said of the prospects for young people from families of limited means. Although American children may be less inhibited by subtle barriers of class than youngsters in some other industrial democracies, those who live in blighted neighborhoods face formidable obstacles of a different kind. Some of these children do manage to rise from poverty through luck, exceptional ability, and sheer determination. Yet relatively few are so fortunate. Boys and girls growing up in inner-city neighborhoods encounter constant risks of violence, along with temptations of drugs, criminal behavior, and unwanted pregnancy that are much greater here than they are in comparable areas abroad. They are also less likely to receive the parental attention, adequate nutrition, vaccination against disease, high-quality child care and preschool programs that will help them thrive and ensure that they arrive at school prepared to learn. When they begin their education, their schools are often inferior, hobbled by bureaucracy, low academic standards, and teachers who are less capable and less experienced than their counterparts in the typical American suburbs. Such deficiencies help explain why poor children at every level of academic ability are far less likely to attend college or graduate with a degree than young people of similar talent from well-to-do families. For those who do not go to college, the programs available to ease the transition from high school to work are widely considered less effective than those in other advanced nations such as Sweden, Japan, and Germany.

In a society that has long emphasized self-reliance, it is not surprising that the United States leaves its citizens more exposed than their counterparts abroad to the principal hazards of life, such as sickness, poverty in old age, violence, unemployment, and injury on the job. For those who fall ill, America's medical research is unmatched, and its university health centers offer a quality of medicine unequaled in the world. Nevertheless, the existence of 40 million people without health insurance, the threat many workers face of losing coverage if they leave their job, the red tape and financial burdens of paying for the costliest health care in the world combine to leave Americans more vulnerable in case of illness than ordinary people in other advanced industrial nations.

America's record in guarding against other basic risks is hardly any better. The threat of being victimized by violent crime is far greater in the United States than in any of the other countries surveyed in this study. Less progress has been made in reducing injuries on the job.

Workers in this country receive less government assistance if they are laid off and have weaker safeguards against being fired arbitrarily from their jobs than their counterparts in the other nations. Once retired, they run a greater risk than citizens abroad of having their assets depleted by long-term illness. Overall, therefore, Americans enjoy less security from the principal threats to their well-being than the citizens of any other highly industrialized country.

The final goal of great concern to most Americans is maintaining the fundamental values of our society. Among the most important of these values is individual freedom. On this score, the United States, having long set an example to the world, has continued to make good progress over the past few decades. American judges have been vigilant in upholding individual liberty against encroachments from the community and the State. In the areas of free speech, freedom of the press, race relations, political behavior, and many others, new rights have been recognized and old ones strengthened.

By now, however, our respect for freedom is no longer exceptional; almost all advanced industrial nations have come to recognize much the same list of basic rights. The extra degrees of freedom we enjoy over the citizens of other democratic countries tend to involve not fundamental matters of personal liberty but questions at the margin, where reasonable people can honestly differ. Moreover, the freedoms that our laws so generously provide are often offset by a tendency to grant choices without providing the means for everyone to exercise them, whether they be choices to attend a private or parochial school, to have competent counsel in a serious criminal case, or to obtain a legal abortion. For many people with limited incomes, then, several important options remain academic in the United States. Overall, therefore, one cannot confidently assert that Americans enjoy more freedom in a practical sense than the citizens of other advanced democracies.

It is commonplace to note that a firm commitment to individual freedom must be balanced by a strong sense of personal responsibility. In this regard, most Americans are concerned that standards of behavior in the United States have deteriorated over the past several decades. The scattered evidence available suggests that these fears are well founded. Whether one looks at stealing, cheating on exams, paying taxes, charitable giving, paying child support, voting, births out of wedlock, or community service, it is hard to find a single case in which our record today is as strong as it was in 1960. By almost any measure,

moreover, Americans appear to be somewhat less responsible than citizens of other advanced nations in respecting the rights of others and
fulfilling basic obligations.

At the same time, standards of behavior have declined since 1960
throughout the Western world. There is little indication that our levels
of personal responsibility are much lower today than those of other
advanced Western societies, and our levels of charitable giving and
community service are generally higher. Better yet, most forms of personal responsibility seem to have stopped deteriorating in the United
States, and some are actually improving.

With respect to collective responsibility, the ultimate test of a nation—as Samuel Johnson pointed out—is the concern it displays for
the plight of the poor and the disabled, especially those who cannot help
themselves. Large majorities of the American people acknowledge this
point and claim that they support efforts to assist those in genuine need.
Yet our record falls far short of these aspirations. Higher percentages of
Americans, white and black, remain officially poor than in the other
countries surveyed in this study. Even with food stamps and all other
types of in-kind benefits, the incomes of poor people in the United States
fall further below the average standard of living than those of needy
citizens in any of the other countries considered.

The America just summarized will seem very different depending on
the segment of the income scale in which one happens to fall. For those
fortunate enough to be in the upper quarter or third, it would be hard
to find a better society in which to live. With higher incomes and lower
taxes than those of well-to-do citizens in other industrial democracies,
prosperous Americans have enough money to protect themselves from
most problems described in this volume. They can live in a privately
guarded community or at least in a neighborhood relatively free of
crime, pay for a private school if the local alternatives seem mediocre,
find exceptionally good health care, and even afford a nursing home
if necessary. The sort of job that most of them hold typically includes
safe working conditions, ample severance pay, and a good pension to
supplement Social Security checks in old age.

As one moves down the income range to families close to the median, problems begin to mount. Although incomes are still somewhat
higher than those in western Europe, many costs and common risks
seem considerably greater. Private education is prohibitively expensive

if local schools are unsatisfactory. Health care insurance may require costly copayments, along with restrictions on the choice of a doctor and the type of treatment available for various conditions. Prolonged stays in a nursing home can deplete a family's savings. Quality child care is hard to afford for working mothers, yet it is difficult *not* to work if all the bills are to be paid. Dad's job seems less secure than it was, and losing it may put an end to medical benefits while yielding little, if any, severance pay. The neighborhood may be tolerably free of crime, but the high school is probably not as safe as it used to be. It is harder than it once was for young couples to buy a home, and harder still to save very much if the family expects to make the payments on the car and appliances, take a vacation, and keep the children from feeling inferior to their classmates at school.

At the bottom quarter of the income scale, life is often much more precarious and anxiety ridden than it normally is in other advanced democracies. Incomes no longer compare favorably with those of similar families abroad. Rental housing eats up a larger share of family income, unless one is not only very poor but lucky enough to qualify for a housing voucher or an apartment in one of the projects. Crime is likely to be much more of a threat, especially in cities; even walking alone at night often seems too dangerous, and watching the kids go off to school each morning is a constant source of worry. Families may have no health insurance for at least part of the year, nor any pension in later years to supplement Social Security checks. Quality child care is likely to be unaffordable even though mothers may have to work. Holding a full-time, year-round job may still not suffice to keep the family out of poverty. There are constant risks of being laid off or fired without much unemployment insurance to tide one over and without job training that is truly capable of providing a fresh start. For families in these circumstances, the American Dream will probably remain only a dream, except for a small minority that possess unusual ability or exceptional tenacity and ambition.

Economic and Social Strategies

Another way of evaluating our record during the past thirty-five years is to examine how we differ in the methods used to achieve the goals that all advanced industrial democracies hold in common. Over the years, we have chosen special ways of adapting our traditional laissez-faire approach to pursue this demanding set of national objectives. The United States has a particular style or strategy for promoting greater growth and prosperity and another for protecting society against pollution, industrial accidents, and other forms of undesirable economic behavior. Still another distinctive approach characterizes our efforts to achieve social welfare goals such as aiding the poor, enhancing opportunities for all, and providing adequate pensions for the elderly. Finally, America has a special way of combining individual freedom with personal responsibility and civic virtue. At the risk of implying more conscious planning than has actually taken place, one can refer to the first as our economic model, to the second as our regulatory model, to the third as our social model, and to the fourth as our model for promoting basic values. How well have these models performed, and why have they not helped us compile a better record in pursuing our most important national goals?

America's economic model has been marked by three tendencies. The first is to rely heavily on competition while avoiding State ownership, cartels, and import barriers to keep out foreign trade. A second, closely related tendency is to look primarily to the market rather than rely on planning, subsidies, public training programs, and other State efforts to guide the economy and stimulate its growth. The third tendency is to emphasize incentives to encourage growth and progress by giving high rewards to those who succeed in key positions, and low wages and low benefits to those who have limited skills or refuse to work.

How well has the model performed? Of the three guiding tendencies, the most successful by far has been our preference for competition. Competition is credited as the principal reason America still maintains higher levels of productivity than its principal economic rivals. If we have stabilized our lead over the past fifteen years, it is chiefly because we have not protected large segments of the economy or relied on government monopolies to run important industries. Increasingly, other industrial powers are moving in our direction by privatizing State-owned businesses and reducing barriers to trade and competition.

The effort to look primarily to the market to stimulate economic growth has had more mixed results. There is little reason to find fault with America's refusal to engage in sector-by-sector planning to guide the economy's development. Such efforts abroad have not shown convincingly that they work well; they could be even less effective in the United States, which lacks the powerful elite bureaucracies found in countries such as France and Japan. On the other hand, relying on the private market for training workers has yielded disappointing results. While the federal government has had but limited success in funding remedial programs to benefit the poor and hard-to-employ, private firms have underinvested in job training for fear of spending large sums preparing workers who will quickly leave them for employment elsewhere. In technology, Washington has been unable to resist a number of megaprojects which have often proved to be expensive flops. Meanwhile, the government has failed (at least until recently) to install programs to make new technology known and readily accessible to small and medium-size businesses. Neither the market nor the government has managed to produce adequate rates of saving. These problems suggest that the United States has not yet arrived at a successful, consistent policy on when to intervene to encourage growth and when to allow the economy to develop in its own way.

Finally, America's emphasis on incentives does not seem to have produced the hoped-for results. The United States has greater inequality of income than any other advanced industrial democracy. Such massive differences are hard to justify unless they provide incentives that lift the prosperity of the vast majority of Americans above the levels in countries that are more egalitarian. By and large, the United States does not appear to meet this test. Over the past four decades, leading industrial nations with greater equality of income than the United States have still managed to grow more rapidly. Germany and Japan have demonstrated that important sectors of their economy can achieve higher levels of productivity than America's without giving such large rewards to corporate leaders and entrepreneurs.[9] More important, the inequalities of income in the United States do not seem to have produced a rising tide of prosperity sufficient to lift nearly all Americans to levels of prosperity higher than those abroad. For example, recent studies demonstrate that poor Americans do not enjoy as high a standard of living as poor Canadians.[10] Almost 20 million American workers receive lower earnings than corresponding groups of employees in France.[11] The lowest-paid 10 percent of American's full-time workers earn *less than half* the wages given to the bottom tenth in Germany and 59 percent below those earned by the bottom tenth in Sweden.[12] By and large, therefore, stressing high rewards does not seem to be notably successful in securing prosperity for all.

Those who defend the distribution of income in this country will point to America's recent success in holding down unemployment. Over the past fifteen years, the United States has clearly outperformed Europe in creating new jobs. In contrast, the Swedish practice of expanding employment by enlarging the public sector has proved too expensive to maintain, leading to higher jobless rates in the 1990s. French and German efforts to shrink unemployment by encouraging early retirement have pushed up payroll taxes, inhibited hiring, and made it harder for women and young people to find decently paid, full-time positions. As a result, unemployment rates in Europe seem to be stuck at double-digit levels. Even in Canada and Britain, whose policies more closely resemble America's, jobless rates have risen well above those in the United States.

Although these comparisons seem to favor the American model, the ultimate verdict is still unclear. Experts are not agreed on the extent to which low wages are necessary to create jobs and keep down unemployment rates in this country. Nor do they agree that higher wages and benefits are the principal causes of the high jobless rates in Europe. Distinguished economists, such as Robert Solow and Olivier Blanchard, put more emphasis on restrictive monetary policies and argue that European governments could keep their benefits and still lower unemployment close to American levels by reducing interest rates.[13] Other economists point out that Germany has kept unemployment rates among unskilled workers at the same level as in the United States through better education and training, even though German wages for employees in this category are at least twice what they are in America.[14] McKinsey analysts ascribe joblessness abroad chiefly to restrictions on product competition, which have prevented many European companies from expanding as they might have in this country.[15]

Commentators will doubtless continue to debate this issue for many years to come. Regardless of the answer, one wonders whether high rates of unemployment (with generous benefits) are so much worse a fate than having wages fall so low that millions who work cannot escape poverty, while millions more on the welfare rolls cannot earn enough to make it worth their while to take a job. Perhaps the fairest verdict one can render at this point is that no advanced democracy, save conceivably Japan, has discovered a satisfactory way in today's global economy to consistently provide jobs at decent wages for all who want to work.

With respect to regulation, all countries must impose restrictions on business to protect the public from various forms of unwanted behavior. What distinguishes the United States is its reliance on rules enforced by fines and other coercive sanctions. This approach has proved to be a major source of aggravation. Every year, federal agencies produce a maze of rules (more than 60,000 pages annually of new regulations). Typically, these requirements do not fit the particular circumstances of many individual firms to which they apply. Often, a majority of small businessmen do not even know about important rules, let alone obey them. With millions of firms to monitor, government agencies frequently lack the resources to inspect often enough to ensure compliance. And when government agencies issue new rules or impose administrative sanctions, they typically encounter lengthy appeals and lawsuits that tie up agency personnel and consume much time and money. In such an adversary atmosphere, parties do not have a common stake in the regulations or feel a responsibility to make the system work. Instead, government regulation in America continues to generate great controversy and dissatisfaction among all of the parties concerned.[16]

Other governments are much more inclined to rely on voluntary cooperation and negotiated solutions. Fines and other forms of coercion are held in reserve as a seldom-used last resort. The danger in this approach, of course, is that officials will be coopted by those they seek to regulate, and may be insensitive to views that do not come to them from established parties to the regulatory process. Although these problems are real, the overall results of regulation abroad seem at least as successful as ours in achieving such objectives as curbing pollution or reducing the number of accidents in the workplace. At the same time, the costs, delays, and aggravations of the regulatory process are much less severe overseas than they are in the United States.

In the field of social welfare, there are several strategies to choose from, at least theoretically. Most countries of western Europe have chosen an ambitious role for the State in guaranteeing personal security and minimizing poverty. Japan has relied more on the family and on large corporations to assume some of the tasks that European governments perform. It is even possible to imagine alternative models in which some other form of private organization, such as the churches, takes responsibility for important social welfare functions.

In practice, however, all advanced democracies have moved in the direction of creating a modern welfare state. In Western societies, churches and other private organizations have not been able to raise sufficient resources to take primary responsibility for significant welfare functions, nor do they coordinate their activities well enough to render assistance to the needy without having many fall through the cracks. In Japan, there is doubt that families will remain sufficiently strong and cohesive to continue doing as much as they traditionally have to protect elderly, unemployed, or impoverished members. It is even questionable whether the large Japanese corporations can continue to provide such safeguards as lifetime employment, now that growth rates have declined substantially. As a result, Japan, too, has created a comprehensive health care system and a generous pension program for all its citizens.

The United States has likewise followed the path of developing a modern welfare state, but with three distinguishing tendencies. The first is to respond to social problems by limiting government subsidies to those who are truly in need and by keeping benefits relatively low. The second is to decentralize authority over many fields of social welfare, allowing cities and states to take primary responsibility for matters such as crime, education, and municipal services and to administer welfare and Medicaid programs created and partly funded by Washington. The third characteristic tendency is to emphasize equality of opportunity rather than equality of result, so that individuals can compete fairly without having the government use its social programs or its tax policies to bring about a major redistribution of income.

In practice, America's social model has worked badly by almost every comparative measure. Decentralizing authority to cities and towns has helped many prosperous communities keep out poor families and segregate them in neighborhoods with limited services and inferior schools. Targeting social programs to serve only the needy and sharing responsibility with the states have resulted in very low levels of support in many areas of the country, along with limited funding that restricts benefits under many programs to only a fraction of those whom they purport to serve. The overall effect has been to stigmatize the poor and isolate them from the rest of the society to a greater extent than in other leading industrial nations.

A compensating virtue of the American model would seem to be its low cost. And low it is, so far as expenditures by the State are concerned. But it is not at all clear that the model is especially economical for the entire society. If one counts the hundreds of billions of additional dollars expended on health care, not to mention the money needed for such items as private security guards, extra prisons, child care, and remedial training programs for employees, the European social model may not prove to be much more expensive after all.

The last distinctive American approach to an important national need involves the effort to protect and promote the values most important to the society. Central to this approach is a strong commitment to individual freedom, elaborated in the Bill of Rights and protected by a corps of vigilant federal judges. No nation has gone further than the United States in expanding the outer limits of freedom and in ensuring that no one's liberty will be infringed by the State without observing due process of law.

Within this framework of individual choice, the government makes little conscious effort to build character or a sense of moral responsibility in its citizens. Indeed, attempts to do so in the past fifty years have increasingly provoked complaints that Washington is interfering with the freedom of individuals to choose their own values. Even the public schools have come to play only a modest role in character formation and often stir up controversy among parents and community groups when they try to do more. What the State has done, therefore, is to put reasonable limits on free choice not by helping to strengthen the ethical standards of the people but almost entirely by *requiring* appropriate behavior through an elaborate body of laws and regulations backed by criminal and civil penalties.

Since World War II, the government has done even less to promote civic virtue. This was not always the case. For many years, all sorts of domestic issues—slavery, the growth of manufacturing, wage labor, even public parks—were debated in terms of their effect on the qualities needed for self-governing citizens. In recent times, as Michael Sandel has persuasively argued, this practice has fallen into disuse and the State no longer does much to try to build citizenship, except in the public schools through the teaching of civics and American history.[17]

Supplementing the work of the State, of course, is a vast array of churches, charitable groups, and other private organizations which involve their members in serving the community and assisting those in need. Originally, these organizations assumed most of the responsibility for helping the poor and providing a variety of other local services. When this task proved too great, the State took over much of the burden. More recently, however, federal officials have sought to utilize the talents of private social service and charitable agencies by inviting them to help administer public programs with the aid of government grants. The hope is that these institutions, which constitute America's civil society, can help develop civic virtue and nurture a responsibility for community problems, thus allowing the nation to avoid relying on the heavy hand of the State to perform these functions.

The system just described has many advantages. The emphasis on individual freedom is of the greatest importance to Americans; no other aspect of life in the United States is valued more highly by the people. The fact that government officials do not try to impose an official morality, religion, or orthodoxy of any kind is true to the traditions of a country that began as a haven for the persecuted and oppressed. Today, such neutrality continues to be well suited to a land comprised of many different faiths, nationalities, and ethnic groups. Finally, the reliance on civil society has helped produce an extraordinary growth of community organizations dedicated to charitable work and civic improvement, bringing valuable services and benefits to countless individuals and neighborhoods.

Like any attempt to address such a complicated enterprise, however, the approach just described is not without serious weaknesses. One of the most vexing problems is how to maintain appropriate standards of personal responsibility in a nation so dedicated to individual freedom and competitive markets. Any society that emphasizes individualism, competition, and material gain while granting large rewards for personal success is bound to generate intense pressure to break, bend, or evade the rules in order to get ahead. Because of these pressures, more and more laws are needed to keep behavior within reasonable bounds, and more and more resources must be devoted to apprehending violators. As this process continues, resentment eventually builds up over the sheer weight of the laws and regulations and the time and expense devoted to enforcing them.

At the same time, the most elaborate system of rules cannot preclude a continuing stream of violations. Many people are undeterred by laws; many forms of undesirable behavior are simply too hard to detect or prevent; and many regulations, however carefully devised, leave loopholes that clever people can exploit. It soon becomes clear, therefore, that a strong sense of individual responsibility widely shared throughout the population is essential to maintaining reasonable standards of behavior. Yet ethical norms of this kind do not come about automatically. On the contrary, they are constantly under siege from the pressures generated by competition, acquisitiveness, and commercial efforts to awaken new needs and desires. Conceivably, the resulting temptations could be held in reasonable check by a police force empowered to investigate freely, incarcerate summarily, and impose harsh punishments on anyone violating the rules. But methods of this kind are hardly permissible in a country strongly committed to individual liberty and due process. As a result, there is no obvious way of reinforcing standards of conduct once the commitment to responsible behavior in the society comes under heavy pressure from cultural and economic forces, as it did in the 1960s.

The United States also has difficulty fostering an adequate sense of civic virtue. The schools, which have primary responsibility for this task, are overwhelmed with other functions and, in any event, find it difficult to build a spirit of citizenship that goes beyond simply learning American history or studying the basic facts about governmental institutions. In countries with totalitarian regimes, the State itself often plays a major role in generating patriotism and national pride (usually unsuccessfully). But it is much more difficult for a democratic government to work directly at promoting such sentiments in a nation that favors a free and highly critical press, looks askance at all forms of official dogma, and prohibits any kind of State-supported religion.

Under these conditions, the firmest foundation on which to build civic loyalty is the system of government itself, with its elected legislature, its commitment to the rule of law, and its dedication to individual freedom. In this regard, American democracy has succeeded exceedingly well. No other country generates so much patriotism and pride. But what Americans are proudest of is a constitutional system that protects them *from* government and leaves them with great freedom to do what they please. Nothing in that system carries a strong message that citizens themselves need to contribute if they are to make their democracy work. As a result, the United States is constantly at risk of having its people regard their government merely as a service which they purchase with their taxes and which they are entitled to complain about loudly when it does not deliver good value for their money.

In America's defense, it must be emphasized that no Western nation has fully succeeded in combining individual freedom and an acquisitive, market-oriented society with a strong sense of civic virtue and personal responsibility. Of all the countries surveyed in this book, only Japan has social norms strong enough to preserve high standards of conduct while still maintaining a vigorous market economy and a respect for basic personal freedoms. Yet even the Japanese have not been able to avoid extensive political corruption and a deep popular distrust of politicians. Moreover, it is far from clear that the strong social pressures to conform, so characteristic of that country, will remain intact much longer or that the Japanese themselves are content even now to live under such strictures. In any event, the case of Japan seems academic for the West, since its culture does not appear to be readily transferable to other nations with radically different traditions.

For the United States, therefore, along with other Western societies, the problems of promoting basic values are still unresolved, with little prospect of a lasting, satisfactory solution. There is much interest of late in trying to strengthen families and reinvigorate civil society in order to restore a stronger sense of community and communal norms. But this is a vast and immensely complicated task, and there is no real understanding yet of just how such a transformation could take place. In the foreseeable future, it seems more likely that the United States will continue its current efforts to bolster personal responsibility by such measures as stiffening criminal penalties, placing greater limits on divorce, cracking down harder on welfare dependency and malingering, and enforcing child support orders more vigorously. It is even possible that lawmakers will be tempted to attack high rates of drugs, crime, and other forms of antisocial behavior by chipping away at the edges of freedom through such means as mandatory drug testing, broader wire-tapping powers, stricter gun control, and greater authority on the part of police in carrying out searches and seizures. Such efforts are bound to meet with strong opposition. Whatever the outcome, the conflicts that arise over such proposals will serve as pointed reminders of how far America still remains from fully reconciling all of the basic goals of modern democratic society.

America's Progress

Looking back over the entire record, then, what answer can one give to the debate over whether America is "in decline"? As is often the case, everything turns on how the question is phrased. If one means to ask whether the country is further from its most cherished goals than it was several decades ago, the answer is almost certainly no. Although progress may have slowed a bit in the past twenty years, only in a minority of fields has America lost ground absolutely.

This conclusion, though heartening, still amounts to faint praise. Even poor Third World countries are generally making *some* progress in their living standards, education, health care, and other important endeavors. It is not surprising, then, that most of the discussion about America's alleged decline has less to do with whether the United States has deteriorated than it does with whether we are losing ground to other advanced nations.

By this yardstick, there is little question about the verdict. Over the past several decades, America has moved ahead more slowly than most other leading countries in most areas of activity that matter to a majority of the people.* Moreover, in fields in which we used to set an

---

*This is not to say that other advanced democratic societies are better than ours. Such a conclusion would require a more exhaustive study than is contained in this volume. Moreover, regardless of how many fields of activity one compares, there is no sure way of determining their relative importance, so that no overall judgment can safely be made. Undaunted by these difficulties, several more limited surveys have attempted overall rankings. Although their conclusions are not truly comparable, they are not inconsistent with those of this study. As shown at the end of Chapter 7, in one ranking of twenty-two nations of varying levels of development based on economic, social, cultural, and political measures, *The Economist* placed the United States eighth—after Germany, Sweden, and Japan but ahead of Britain, France, and Canada. "Where to Live: Nirvana by Numbers," *The Economist*, 39 (December 25, 1944–January 7, 1995). A similar survey ranked America eighth out of twelve nations, behind the Scandinavian countries, Canada, and Germany but ahead of Luxembourg, Spain, and Israel (France and Britain were not ranked). Raoul Naroll, *The Moral Order: An Introduction to the Human Situation*, 73 (1983).

There have also been periodic surveys recording the degree of satisfaction with life expressed by residents of various countries. These studies are harder to interpret, since they are subjective and bear an uncertain relationship to objective circumstances of the kind described in this volume. For whatever they are worth, however, such surveys also tend to place the United States in the top half but well behind the leaders. Typically, the Scandinavian countries, Switzerland, the Netherlands, and Canada rank close to the top, with the United States and Britain relatively close together and France and Japan considerably further down the list. See for example, "Mirth on Earth," 28 *Psychology Today*, 48 (July–August 1995).

example for the rest of the world, such as individual freedom and universal education, other countries have now caught up. As a result, while we remain the most powerful nation militarily, our claim to be exceptional in a positive sense has grown steadily more tenuous. All too often, the areas in which we lead the industrial world are fields in which we would greatly prefer *not* to excel, such as rates of homicide and incarceration, percentages of the population in poverty, or per capita costs of health care.

Does it matter very much that we have not fared better in comparison with the Germans, the French, or the Japanese? After all, we are not engaged in a race. If our society continues to progress toward most of our important goals, should we care whether other countries have done a bit better in curbing pollution, keeping down health care costs, or lowering their infant mortality rates?

The answer is that it does matter, regardless of whether we consider ourselves in a contest with anyone. Because other leading democracies are at a similar stage in development and share our basic goals, their progress gives some tentative sign of what we can expect of ourselves. We may not be able to solve our problems by simply importing policies from abroad. Nevertheless, when we discover that other advanced nations have lower poverty rates, or fewer industrial accidents, or better provision for long-term health care, there is a strong possibility that we, too, should be able to find a way to improve our record.

Thus, comparisons with other countries give us further reason to suspect that our health care costs are far too high, that our poverty rates are greater than they need to be, and that our methods of regulation are more expensive and less effective than one might legitimately expect. Americans are suffering more anxiety than they should about such issues as whether they will be covered by medical insurance, how to pay for long-term care, or whether they will be fired arbitrarily, injured at work, or forced to choose between losing their job and devoting themselves to a newborn child. Conceivably, there may be special reasons for the fact that we cannot match the record of similar nations in one area or another in which we have fallen behind. But it is more than likely that we should be able to improve substantially in most of these fields.

Our performance as a nation, then, merits concern for reasons quite apart from whether we are in a race with other countries. Not only has progress seemed to slow down in the United States during the past twenty years; in many respects, this country appears to be much further than it should be from the kind of society most Americans desire. With such a record, one can readily understand why so many people feel dissatisfied with America and worried about its future.

19

Questioning the Verdict

Not everyone will agree with the assessment just made about America's performance. Some may feel that the account misses something essential about America in describing so many areas of activity, just as a musicologist analyzing individual notes will never convey the whole of Beethoven's Ninth Symphony. Other critics will claim that the decades from 1960 to 1990 are an atypical and misleading period for comparing advanced industrial democracies. Still others may quarrel with the criteria used for evaluating progress, arguing that they do not truly reflect what America is all about. These objections are all sufficiently plausible on the surface that each deserves careful consideration.

America the Promised Land

Although Americans may complain about their country and believe that it is going downhill, word of these troubles has apparently not spread to other parts of the globe. All around the world, hopeful people continue to flock to American embassies seeking visas to come to this country. If the United States remains the destination of choice for so many, must it not have special qualities that the tabulations in this book have failed to capture? Many observers have made this point in commenting on the pessimism so widely expressed throughout the land. On close examination, however, the message of immigration is not as reassuring as one might think.

To begin with, immigration to the United States comes chiefly from the developing world, not from the countries considered in this volume. In the 1980s, for example, more people emigrated to America from the Dominican Republic alone than from Sweden, Britain, France, and Germany *combined*. Total immigration from western Europe was already below its allotted quota in 1960, and it has dropped by half in the past three decades. In some years, the numbers emigrating from America to Sweden have even exceeded those coming the other way. The United States may still be especially attractive to talented Europeans who wish to play on a larger stage and reap the exceptional rewards that America grants to the successful. Overall, however, opinion polls suggest that the United States is not necessarily the first choice of those thinking of emigrating from countries such as Britain and France.[1]

Although many people continue to leave the Third World in order to come to America, this is hardly surprising. Compared with developing nations, the United States is an incredibly prosperous society. Even the wages of unskilled busboys at McDonald's are far above the average pay of workers in most countries of Africa, Latin America, and South Asia. To inhabitants of these regions, the United States must appear to be a country of unimaginable wealth and opportunity. America is not unique in this respect; other advanced nations are also proving to be an attractive destination. In fact, the percentage of immigrants is now higher in Canada and Germany than it is in the United States.[2]

It remains true, of course, that the United States is the preferred destination of the largest number of people seeking to emigrate from Third World countries. But this, too, is readily explained. Our popular culture dominates the world market, projecting powerful images of America's opulence, opportunity, and excitement. Our mother tongue is the most widely spoken second language in the world. Our immigration policies have long been much more open than those of other industrial nations. Our society is much more heterogeneous—virtually no nationality, race, or religious faith is unrepresented. Overall, therefore, America must seem especially accessible, welcoming, and inviting to people from many developing nations. While this openness is commendable, it does not negate the problems of our health care system, the blight of our central cities, the inadequacies of our social policies, or any of the other troubling comparisons made in this volume.

Can Countries Be Usefully Compared?

Is there really much practical use in comparing the progress of different nations? Even if countries share similar goals and find themselves at roughly the same stage of economic development, any differences that remain may well result from national characteristics of a kind quite beyond the power of human ingenuity to overcome. If so, the kinds of contrasts made in this book may turn out to be immutable and hence of only academic interest.

One can certainly not dismiss this possibility out of hand. Nevertheless, the variations identified in this study—variations in health care systems, affordable housing, pollution control, and the like—seem to be products of human choice rather than matters rooted in some fixed and unchangeable set of national characteristics. If intractable differences do exist among nations, differences of a kind that could affect a nation's progress toward its basic goals, one should not merely assume their existence. Rather, one must identify them and show how they limit a country's capacity to accomplish what its citizens want.

This is not an easy task. Several natural endowments that formerly made a difference to the progress of nations have clearly become much less important than they were a century ago. Geographic isolation once helped shield the United States from the destruction of foreign wars, but there is little reason to think that oceans continue to offer much protection from modern weaponry. Coal, iron, and oil used to provide another kind of natural advantage. Today, however, modern methods of transportation and production have made such materials much less of a boon than they once were. Japan, Hong Kong, and Singapore all demonstrate that growth and prosperity no longer depend on possessing ample natural resources or even owning large expanses of land.

There is one physical characteristic of nations, however, that might still affect a nation's ability to achieve widely shared objectives. Clearly, the United States is a much bigger country than its leading industrial competitors. In a nation so large, might it be harder to organize and administer the kinds of programs and collaborative efforts which are needed to attain the national goals that modern industrial democracies have in common?

If this were clearly the case, America should be doing a better job coping with local problems than it does confronting issues that are national in scope. Public education, crime, and urban development are the principal examples in this study that fall primarily within the purview of town and municipal authorities. From a comparative standpoint, however, the United States has scarcely had any greater success in addressing these problems than it has had in grappling with problems of national scale.

There are many other fields of endeavor in which the size of the country seems quite irrelevant to its problems. The vastness of America hardly explains the nation's failure to do more to defray the costs of long-term health care or its refusal to provide more generous parental leave or protect workers against being fired unjustifiably. Nor can size account for the inability to provide all Americans with health insurance or its poorer citizens with enough affordable housing. Small countries, such as Sweden, may find it easier to implement certain kinds of policies, such as job safety rules or environmental regulations. Still, it is far from obvious why the United States, with 260 million people, should necessarily have a harder time than Japan, with 125 million people, in reducing the number of industrial accidents or limiting the amount of pollution.

Finally, size is not always a disadvantage in today's world. If larger countries were truly handicapped, Europe would hardly have devoted such effort to creating a vast new federated community. Along with administrative headaches, larger countries have greater pools of talent to draw upon, bigger markets, more powerful research and technology, and added opportunities for local experimentation. Such benefits help explain why the idea of a united Europe has proved so attractive to generations of leaders and statesmen.

In the future, changes in the world may make size more of a handicap and give an advantage to smaller communities in solving certain kinds of problems. Cities and towns may demand more local control over public services that affect their welfare. Metropolitan regions may become decisive units in global competition. People may insist on decentralization to loosen up rigid bureaucracies or to achieve greater efficiency in delivering services. Tendencies of this kind are already evident in Sweden, France, and other European countries. They call for imagination and skill in devising ways of delegating more authority to smaller bodies, which can adapt their services more effectively to meet local needs. But they scarcely make large nations obsolete, or even put them at a substantial disadvantage in pursuing the entire range of goals that people in all advanced democracies seem to desire.

The Effects of Race

Another common response to unflattering comparisons between America and other industrial democracies is to suggest that these differences are largely a matter of race. Take away the blacks—so the argument goes (often uttered in muted tones, out of the hearing of strangers)—and the figures would look very different.

This point, of course, is not an argument against the data set forth in this volume. It is only a way of isolating America's problems and blaming them on southern planters long dead, so that they do not appear to cast a shadow on the rest of the society. Even for this limited purpose, however, the argument is flawed.

Of course, there is no denying that blacks as a group have substantially higher rates of violent crime, illegitimacy, poverty, and educational underachievement than the rest of the population. They clearly make America's record look worse than it otherwise would. Even so, only a brief look at the figures suffices to show that race alone cannot fully explain the unfavorable comparisons recorded in the preceding chapters.

Consider education, for example. Blacks undoubtedly score lower than whites on standardized tests (although the gap has narrowed substantially in recent decades). Nevertheless, if the performance of black students were responsible for America's disappointing showing in international tests of science and mathematics, one would expect to find the bottom 10 to 20 percent of our students performing especially poorly in comparison with the bottom 10 to 20 percent of students in the other participating nations. In fact, every decile of American thirteen-year-olds, from top to bottom, appears to score below their counterparts in most other advanced nations participating in the IAEP tests of math and science. Indeed, on some tests, American students in the fortieth and seventieth percentiles fall further below their counterparts abroad than students in the bottom 10 percent.[3] These figures suggest that our modest international record cannot be explained simply by the performance of a particular ethnic group but represents a problem shared by all segments of the student population.

As Table 19.1 makes clear, the same conclusion emerges from other fields in which one can readily compare white Americans with citizens of other industrial democracies. Although blacks may make some of our statistics look worse than they would otherwise, the United States

Table 19.1. International comparisons on a range of social problems.

Problem	Canada	France	West Germany	Japan	Sweden	United Kingdom	United States (whites only)
1. Infant mortality (per 1,000 births)	6.9	6.6	6.5	4.3	5.7	7.2	7.3
2. Life expectancy (in years)	78.1	78.2	76.3	79.3	78.3	76.8	76.5
3. Percent of children in poverty	9.3	4.6	2.8	NA	1.4	6.9	13.2
4. Health insurance coverage (percent of population that is covered)	100.0	99.0	99.0	100.0	100.0	100.0	86.4
5. Homicides (per 100,000 people)	2.0	1+	1+	0.5	1+	0.5	5.3
6. Teenage pregnancy (per 1,000 teens)	44	43	NA	NA	35	45	93

Source: Statistical Abstract of the United States, 1994, 87, 91, 119, 475, 855 (1994). Timothy M. Smeeding and Barbara Boyle Torrey, *Revisiting Poor Children in Rich Countries: The Evidence from LIS,* 7, 26 (1995). Andrew Hacker, *Two Nations,* 77 (1992).

does not fare well even if blacks are excluded from the calculations.

More important still, in most comparisons with other nations, race has little or nothing to do with America's record. It does not explain why our health care system is so expensive, why we lack adequate provisions for long-term care, or why our school-to-work programs are disorganized and ineffective. Whether one includes blacks in the calculations or leaves them out, our child-care system is still inadequate, our preschool programs remain underfunded, our job safety record is disappointing, and our workers continue to lack adequate forms of collective representation for dealing with their employers. In these respects and many others, America's performance is no better for whites than it is for blacks. It is simply not valid, then, to pretend that all or even a significant fraction of the unfavorable comparisons in this study will disappear by removing blacks from the calculations.

A Misleading Era for Comparisons?

Every period for comparing nations is arbitrary in the sense that every one has features that are abnormal or unlikely to persist. This is as true of the years since World War II as it is of other periods of human history. Yet there are several aspects of the past several decades that make their use especially questionable for the kinds of comparisons made in this study.

For one thing, Europe and Japan have spent a good part of the past thirty-five years catching up with the United States following the destruction of World War II. Although the war inflicted great damage, it allowed these nations to make rapid progress simply by emulating the best American practices and technologies. Meanwhile, Americans had the slower, harder task of having to progress by constant innovation. Was it surprising, then, to see these other countries outstrip the United States for several decades in their rates of economic growth? What is more revealing, according to several writers, is that America has held its lead during the past ten to fifteen years, after the period of catch-up was largely over.

This argument is valid as far as it goes. The problem is that it applies to only a few of the many troubling comparisons made in this volume. The ability to copy American practices may explain why Europe's economies could grow faster than ours from 1950 to 1970. It does not reveal much about our inadequacies in health care, education, regulatory policy, or social welfare programs. The postwar period may have given Europe and Japan a special opportunity to advance economically and close the gap with America, but it hardly explains why these countries could move ahead of the United States in providing so many of the benefits and protections desired by large majorities of people in all advanced democracies.

It is only fair to add that during almost all of this period, America had to bear the bulk of the costs and other burdens of containing Communism and protecting the free world. As Paul Kennedy has suggested, this responsibility may have pushed the United States to engage in "imperial overreach," a commitment of weapons and personnel around the globe that left the country with insufficient resources to manage its domestic agenda well.[4] While Washington was preoccupied with resisting Communist expansion in every corner of the globe, our allies could devote all of their energies and funds to strengthening their economies and improving their societies. Is it any wonder, then, that they could move ahead faster than the United States?

Plausible as this theory seems, it cannot adequately explain the difficulties chronicled in this study. In many of the fields reviewed—health care, environmental regulation, employment relations, job safety, and education—America's difficulties do not result from having too little money to spend. In each of these cases, either the funds required for effective performance are small, or the United States has consistently spent as much as other countries or even more. America's problem has not been too little money but a failure to gain as much from its expenditures as other leading democratic nations.

The one area of public policy in which most other countries have traditionally spent significantly more than America is the field of social welfare. One could hardly maintain, however, that higher defense costs have been the principal reason for this trend. The United States has undoubtedly had greater defense burdens than other leading industrial democracies. Nevertheless, the differences are not overwhelming; by and large, they are considerably smaller than the added burdens America has assumed simply by virtue of its exceptionally expensive health care system (Table 19.2).

The burdens of the Cold War might offer a more convincing explanation if America were taxing its people as highly as other leading industrial democracies. In this event, one could argue that extra defense expenditures are a critical factor in limiting the nation's capacity to create social programs on the scale commonly found in western Eu-

Table 19.2. **Military expenditures, as percent of GDP, 1970–1990.**

Country	1970	1980	1990
Canada	2.4	1.9	2.1
France	4.2	4.0	3.6
West Germany	3.3	3.3	3.0
Japan	0.8	0.9	1.0
Sweden	3.6	3.1	2.7
United Kingdom	4.7	5.0	4.0
United States	7.9	5.3	5.6

Source: United States Arms Control and Disarmament Agency, *World Military Expenditures and Arms Transfers, 1970–1979*; Ruth L. Sivard, *World Military and Social Expenditures* (1990).

rope. But the facts do not sustain this argument. By international standards, America is hardly straining the limits of its resources; its rates of taxation are unusually low, not exceptionally high. In 1990, the total tax burden in the United States was 29.8 percent of gross income, compared with 34 percent in Canada, 37.3 percent in Britain, 37.4 percent in Germany, 44.4 percent in France, and 55.3 percent in Sweden.[5] If we have failed to match Europe's commitment to social programs, then, it is not because we have diverted too many of our resources to defense but because our lawmakers have made a political judgment not to adopt such expensive policies and seek the taxes needed to pay for them.

There is a final, more substantial reason one might not wish to rely on comparisons from the past few decades in evaluating the performance of advanced industrial democracies. According to many observers, the economies of western Europe are no longer expanding fast enough to sustain the burden of generous welfare programs enacted during the postwar decades of rapid growth. What appear to be advantages today in these societies will increasingly be seen as disadvantages tomorrow. As a result, Europe's superiority in social programs could well disappear before many more years have elapsed.

One can readily point to signs in western Europe that support this thesis. Rates of economic growth have slowed perceptibly during the last twenty years, while deficits in several countries have risen to unsustainable levels. In the 1990s, Europe's unemployment rates have far surpassed America's; in some cases, one-third or more of those out of work have been jobless for more than a year. To some extent at least, this unhappy situation may have resulted from welfare state policies that cost exorbitant amounts while pushing up labor costs so high that companies cannot afford to hire full-time employees.

Serious as they are, however, these problems do not necessarily presage the end of the welfare state. Governments throughout Europe are beginning to introduce reforms to resolve their difficulties. In order to improve efficiency, several legislatures have voted to privatize state-owned industries and thus subject them to normal market competition. European lawmakers have also been adjusting benefit levels to cut expenses and provide a more sensible set of incentives. For example, Sweden has now instituted longer waiting periods before workers can begin to claim paid sick leave or seek unemployment benefits. Great Britain has reduced its pensions. France is trimming its health care system. Germany has cut back unemployment benefits moderately. The 1993 White Paper of the European Community calls for gradual reductions in payroll taxes over the next few years.[6]

While noting these adjustments, one should bear in mind what is *not* taking place. There is no sign that countries in Europe are seriously contemplating massive rollbacks in social benefits, let alone dismantling the welfare state. Certainly, the conservative regimes now in power in countries such as France and Germany are not considering changes of this kind, and there is every indication that drastic reforms would be strongly resisted by large majorities of their voters. Even Margaret Thatcher—whose feelings toward the welfare state paralleled those of Ronald Reagan, and who had impressive parliamentary majorities to boot—could not manage much more than a sharp cut in public housing and a moderate reduction in future pension benefits.[7]

It is possible that European governments are not doing enough and that their unwillingness to reduce benefits further will eventually doom their economies to sluggish growth and second-rate status. Whether or not the welfare state has put Europe at a serious disadvantage in competing with countries such as the United States, economic performance over the past several years has clearly been weak, and deficits seem far too high to continue. As a result, the future of Europe's social experiment remains in considerable doubt.

Yet Europe is not alone in having to worry about the future of its welfare policies. The United States has reasons of its own to question whether its social model can continue indefinitely without endangering prosperity. As global competition and technological advances call for a more educated, more highly trained work force, problems of poverty, drugs, crime, dysfunctional schools, blighted neighborhoods, and ineffective labor market programs may take a mounting toll on productivity and economic growth. Increasing inequalities in wealth and income, exacerbated by racial tensions and welfare cutbacks, could lead to mounting social unrest that will further weaken the economy. In the end, therefore, if European welfare programs put prosperity at risk by doing too much, America's social policies threaten to do the same by accomplishing too little. If overgenerous benefits in Europe prove difficult to roll back, America may have allowed its social problems to become so deeply rooted that they will be all but impossible to overcome.

It is idle to spend much more time speculating about which nations will prosper in the long run. By all accounts, Europe and America have entered an era filled with challenges quite unlike those they have known heretofore. New technologies are rapidly spreading that promise changes as profound as those that followed the invention of the printing press and the internal combustion engine. National economies face intensifying global competition and the emergence of formidable new industrial powers in Asia. Health care advances coupled with demographic trends create unprecedented problems of finding resources to care for elderly populations. These developments promise to create a world sufficiently different from the one we have known that efforts to extrapolate from past experience are likely to prove misleading.

Amid these uncertainties, however, a few conclusions seem reasonably firm. To begin with, even if European welfare states feel obliged in the future to trim their social programs substantially, America, too, is cutting back so that there is little prospect that benefits abroad will retreat to U.S. levels. In the longer run, it would be surprising if Europe's welfare states copied our example by allowing low-skilled wages to drop well below the poverty level. It would be astonishing if they tried to cut costs by arbitrarily limiting housing, early childhood, and health insurance programs to cover only a fraction of the needy population. Whatever happens to Europe's welfare state, therefore, the American model is unlikely to emerge fully vindicated as the preferred solution.[8]

In addition, although slower growth, massive unemployment, and global competition may force other welfare states to make substantial changes in their minimum wage levels, unemployment compensation, early retirement, and old-age pension programs, they are unlikely to have much effect on many other important achievements that the European experience invites one to consider. What the record of other leading democracies reveals is that it is possible to provide universal health care insurance at a total cost well below what Americans are paying; possible to do more to curb emissions, reduce job injuries, and make other regulatory gains without all the litigation and delay that exist in the United States; possible to achieve higher levels of student proficiency without spending more on education; possible to reduce poverty to levels well below America's, even for single-parent families; possible to prepare entire generations of youth for productive careers (and not just those who go to college); and possible to avoid severely blighted slums with heavy concentrations of poverty, unemployment, and crime. Moreover, experience elsewhere suggests that a society can achieve these results and still preserve essential personal freedoms and maintain standards of personal responsibility that are as high as or higher than those currently prevailing in the United States.

These are among the most important lessons that other advanced democratic nations have to offer us. There is little reason to suppose that they will have to be rewritten even if the welfare states of the 1980s are substantially modified to survive in an era of global competition and slower economic growth. Rather, these achievements are likely to endure as a sobering reminder that our society could not manage during the past several decades to make important advances that other nations made toward basic goals that Americans share with people throughout the industrialized world.

Do Americans Have Different Priorities?

Before one can arrive at a final verdict on America's performance, a final argument merits consideration. Examining the contrasts between this country and other leading nations, could one conclude that the United States has actually succeeded quite well in building the sort of society its citizens want? Perhaps we have developed differently from Europe, Japan, or even Canada because we have different priorities and different values. If we lag behind in reducing poverty, could it be that we attach less importance to helping the needy? If we are not as successful in containing violent crime, might it be because we value individual freedom so strongly? If our levels of pollution are higher, could we simply prefer to strike a different balance between encouraging free enterprise and protecting the environment?

This line of argument has a plausible ring, since distinctive values undoubtedly affect the policies of every society. There is also much evidence to suggest that Americans are more inclined than the citizens of most other industrial democracies to believe in the virtues of self-reliance, to be suspicious of the State, and to resist regulations that interfere with their independence. These sentiments may well affect the *way* in which Americans try to achieve their national goals and the role they assign to the government. They may also help explain why we have had such difficulty achieving several of our most basic goals. Nevertheless, it would be wishful thinking to try to rationalize our record over the past thirty to forty years by arguing that we have somehow achieved the *results* we really want. Just a glance at a few of the areas previously considered should suffice to dispel this beguiling notion.

In education, for example, the lackluster performance of American students in international tests of math and science does not stem from any desire on the part of Americans to spend less on schools in order to have more for other purposes. In total dollars, the United States already devotes *more* to education than most industrial democracies and spends far more than Japan, whose children do much better on international tests.[9] Surveys consistently show that Americans care about their schools and want to improve the quality of education. Indeed, there is evidence that substantial majorities would be willing to pay even more for this purpose. America's record, therefore, is not a reflection of public preference but a source of wide frustration.

Health care offers another illustration. At present, the United States spends at least half again as much as other advanced countries without having a demonstrably healthier population or even managing to offer medical insurance to nearly all of its people. Can it really be that the public prefers to arrange its health care in this fashion? Hardly. Polls reveal that Americans are more dissatisfied with their current system and more inclined to believe that it needs fundamental change than the citizens of any of the other countries considered in this book.[10]

Even the treatment of the poor in this country cannot be easily explained as a simple reflection of the public's indifference. Few Americans are pleased that so many children under six years of age remain in poverty. Nor does the public approve of the fact that millions of household heads work full time throughout the year without being able to escape from being poor. On the contrary, most Americans favor spending more for the needy. What they do not want is to give more money to current welfare programs.

The ultimate argument in defense of America's postwar record concedes that genuine problems exist in fields such as health care, education, and poverty but insists that these are the kinds of drawbacks that Americans accept to achieve greater freedom, opportunity, and prosperity. By limiting the role of the State and tolerating a greater measure of insecurity and inequality, the United States has become the wealthiest nation on earth with a degree of freedom and opportunity for all unparalleled throughout the world. There is a price for this success, no doubt, but it is a price that Americans willingly pay for the advantages they receive in return.

Arguments similar to these are often made, especially by those who benefit most from the current state of affairs in the United States. But repetition does not make the claim correct. In fact, the argument has such flaws that it cannot withstand serious examination.

To begin with, as previous chapters have shown, there is no convincing evidence that the United States does provide greater opportunities for advancement than other leading industrial democracies. Most recent studies show that individuals move upward and downward in income and occupational status about as often and as rapidly in other countries as in America. Much the same is true of freedom. By now, most advanced democracies guarantee much the same liberties as those enjoyed by American citizens, and analysts who try to compare the extent of freedom from one country to another find little to choose among the nations surveyed in this study.

What *is* incontestably true is that the United States remains the wealthiest, most productive nation in the world. It is far from obvious, however, that the problems described in this volume are a necessary price that Americans must pay to achieve this prosperity. No serious person could argue that our hugely expensive health care system, the inadequacies of our public schools, our lackluster job training programs, our high levels of violent crime, our continuing racial segregation, or our meager policies for children have done anything for our standard of living except drag it down. Nor would anyone make such an argument to justify the excessive costs imposed by our clumsy regulatory system in areas such as job safety and the environment. Our current productivity advantage was built decades ago and owes much to our good fortune in escaping the destruction of two world wars in this century. According to the most careful studies, our continued edge in efficiency during the last decade is principally a result of our willingness to expose all sectors of the economy to competition, not an advantage that requires the social policies developed in this country.

If there is a plausible defense of America's policies in the name of productivity and growth, it is limited to the narrow area of employment legislation. Here, one can make a stronger argument that efforts to guarantee all workers generous wages and safeguards against the hardships of unemployment have hampered European companies and dampened productivity and employment. As we have seen, however, even these arguments are questionable. Recent efforts by some countries to relax job restrictions have not led to increased growth or employment. Nor did the massive McKinsey study on productivity assign great weight to such regulations in explaining differences in efficiency between the United States and Europe.

Whatever one makes of this argument, the decisive point remains that virtually none of the shortcomings noted in this study are in any sense a necessary price that must be paid to attain America's superior wealth and productivity. As a result, one cannot claim that our overall record since 1960 simply reflects a peculiar American desire for greater wealth at the expense of other social objectives. On the contrary, if Americans were truly getting the results they wanted, large majorities would not believe that the country is headed in the wrong direction, nor would even larger majorities believe that the nation's leaders are performing badly. In the end, therefore, the record suggests that over the past thirty to forty years, the United States has not achieved nearly as much as one could reasonably have hoped in pursuit of the goals that most Americans hold dear. The question that remains is why the country has not been able to accomplish more.

20

The Role of Government

What part has government played in the various successes and frustrations our society has encountered in attempting to achieve its most cherished objectives? Americans have had a massive change of mind on this question. In the early 1960s, the achievements of the New Deal were still warmly remembered and public officials and pundits of all kinds were brimming with optimism over the potential of federal programs to alleviate poverty, curb racial discrimination, extend health insurance, and rebuild America's decaying cities. Over the years, however, the mood gradually shifted to dark pessimism about the government's capacity to accomplish anything worthwhile. By the early 1990s, almost 70 percent of the public expressed the view that "government creates more problems than it solves."[1]

A careful look at the record suggests that both the gloom and the euphoria have been greatly overdone. During the past thirty-five years, our society has made substantial progress in most of the fields surveyed in this volume. In almost all of these advances, government actions have played a prominent role, whether it be in cleaning up the environment, expanding personal freedom, extending health care to the poor and elderly, reducing poverty, or increasing opportunities for women and minorities. Federal policies have clearly had a hand in America's greatest domestic achievements: the preeminence of our scientific research, the surge in the arts after the mid-1960s, and the quality of American medicine at its best. Even our continuing lead in overall economic productivity, which one might be tempted to ascribe to the skills of our work force or to the dynamism of our entrepreneurs, turns out—according to a massive study by the McKinsey Institute—to result primarily from the greater willingness of our government to insist upon open competition rather than nationalized industries or protected markets.[2] In view of this record, it is hardly fair to say that "government creates more problems than it solves."

At the same time, it is also true that government has been implicated in almost all of the difficulties the country has experienced in striving to make even greater progress toward a better society. Only rarely are America's problems chiefly problems of the private sector. Almost invariably, they grow directly out of official policies or programs which have not dealt successfully with some issue of wide importance to the nation. That is true of each of the following ways in which the United States has fallen behind most other advanced industrial democracies.

1. The high cost and limited coverage of America's health care system.
2. The inability of many families to provide for adequate care in the event of chronic or long-term illness in old age.
3. The exceptional risks of being victimized by violent crime.
4. The difficulty employees have in establishing any form of organization to represent their interests to employers (such as unions or works councils).
5. The limited safeguards given to workers in case of layoff or unjustified discharge.
6. The relatively high risk of suffering a job-related illness or injury.
7. The failure to meet national goals for vaccinating infants or to do more to provide adequate nutrition to small children, make quality child care or preschool opportunities wideiy available, or guarantee parental leave following the birth of a baby.
8. The disappointing performance of American students in math and science.
9. The lack of effective job training, vocational education, or school-to-work programs.
10. The excessive burdens of rent borne by many low-income families.
11. The existence of urban neighborhoods marked by high concentrations of poverty, high rates of unemployment, and heavy incidence of crime, drug use, and teenage pregnancy.

12. The small proportion of families rescued from poverty by government programs, including families headed by full-time workers, persons who are disabled, and individuals too old to work.
13. America's comparatively modest performance in reducing pollution, and the excessive costs of many of its environmental programs.

In a few of these areas, notably crime prevention and education, multiple causes are at work, and it is impossible to know how much the State is responsible for America's disappointing record. But even in the case of crime and education, public policies and programs are certainly among the important factors that affect whatever results have been achieved. According to the best research, good schools and good teaching can account for up to 25 percent of variations among students in academic performance, and there are growing signs that effective police methods can bring significant results in reducing crime.

In other fields, officials are hampered in making policy because existing knowledge is inadequate. Eliminating poverty is one example; guaranteeing each child a reasonable start in life is another; halting urban decay, still another. In such cases, it would be unfair to fault the government for failing to achieve everything its citizens want. Yet even in these complicated areas, governments should be capable of making *some* progress. Otherwise, how can one explain the fact that other industrial democracies have accomplished so much more than the United States in attacking the same issues?

This is not to say that politicians and bureaucrats are necessarily responsible for all of the nation's troubles. In a democracy, we are all implicated in the functioning of our government. But whether the fault lies with short-sighted legislators, clumsy officials, interest group pressures, media distortions, public prejudices, or all of the above, the fact remains that in each of the diverse fields considered in this book, inadequate public policies and programs seem to have had a lot to do with America's inability to make as much progress as one might reasonably have expected.

The Failings of Government

If public policies have played such a significant role, both for better and for worse, how can one explain the government's record in trying to help America achieve its goals? How can one account for its successes as well as its failures in coping with the wide variety of problems that have concerned this country over the past forty years?

Looking first at the successes, one is immediately struck by a common pattern. Almost all of our notable achievements as a nation have occurred in areas where the classic American formula most obviously fits—where progress still depends primarily on individual talent and creativity, and where the government distributes funds to the ablest candidates or breaks down artificial barriers that interfere with competition and hinder capable people from succeeding on their merits. These are the conditions under which America's major universities, research scientists, and teaching hospitals have come to lead the world. They describe the circumstances in which American artists have risen to world prominence (not to mention the astonishing global success of American popular culture). They have provided a favorable environment for successful entrepreneurs, while helping the U.S. economy to remain more productive overall than any of its rivals. In all of these cases, able, enterprising individuals have received the opportunity, the backing, and the incentives they needed to allow their talents to flourish. And when this nation has not been able to produce all the talent it needs from within its own borders, it has managed to attract it from other lands using the lure of abundant opportunities, huge markets, and lavish rewards for the successful.

The fly in the ointment is that many of society's goals do not lend themselves so obviously to these techniques. Tasks such as alleviating poverty, improving the public schools, and protecting the environment have other characteristics and call for other skills—complex planning, building public consensus, coordinating many organizations and agencies, cooperating with community groups, creating efficient bureaucracies. Faced with challenges of this kind, the United States has not performed as well as other leading industrial nations. Like muddy footprints from a wayward child, certain failings have repeatedly cropped up in field after field of American public policy, hindering the country's efforts to achieve important national goals.

Interestingly, the telltale tracks that emerge from this study are not necessarily the ones that vex the public most. For example, almost 60 percent of Americans believe that "most members of Congress make a lot of money by using public office improperly."[3] Yet nothing in the recent experience of Congress or the executive branch either justifies this indictment or rivals the accounts of massive bribes and improper payments that have recently come to light in Japan, Italy, and France. Federal officials have subjected themselves to a body of rules against corruption that are more detailed than those of any other legislative body in the world. In virtually no other country can one find such aggressive investigative reporters or such thorough official procedures for inquiring into allegations of wrongdoing. Washington does have scandals, of course, but they typically involve the private lives of officials or rather minor transgressions, such as the overdrafts of congressmen on the House of Representatives bank.

Another widely shared complaint is that Congress is unresponsive to the will of the people. Almost 80 percent of Americans feel that after members of Congress are elected, they "lose touch with the people pretty quickly."[4] Most careful studies, however, reveal that Congress acts in response to changes in public opinion more than two-thirds of the time.[5] Indeed, where domestic policy is concerned, it is easier to think of cases in which Congress has overreacted to voter sentiments rather than the reverse. In situations involving highly charged subjects such as toxic waste, violent crime, and drugs, legislators have been so anxious to respond that they have passed laws and spent large sums on schemes such as establishing Superfund, intercepting drug shipments, and throwing thrice-convicted felons into jail for life—schemes that seem unlikely to produce benefits equal to their cost.

Such few comparative studies as there are suggest that Congress is as responsive as the legislatures of other leading democracies.[6] More than one seasoned observer has expressed the view that Congress is actually the *most* responsive of any legislative body in a major country.[7] Certainly, few lawmakers abroad go to as much effort as members of Congress in dealing with constituent complaints, studying opinion polls and correspondence from their districts, and traveling home to talk to supporters and hold town meetings. If the results that emerge are not always to everyone's liking, that is usually due to the fact that voters are more divided on most issues than many of us care to admit.

Americans are also convinced that Congress is controlled by powerful lobbies representing industries, banks, and other influential groups. Large majorities of the public affirm that "government is run for the benefit of a few big interests."[8] This belief is not so much wrong as it is exaggerated. Interest groups have considerable political influence in America, as they do in every democratic nation. The tax code is littered with provisions to help one special interest or another. At the same time, studies of the legislative process have repeatedly found that the efforts lobbyists make to influence lawmakers and the money given to political campaigns have less impact on policy than popular opinion supposes.[9] Most students of Congress also believe that private interests do not have as much influence today as they did even a generation ago, although the trends in public opinion would suggest the contrary.[10] More important, there are many indications that interest groups frequently have less effect in the United States than they do in other industrialized countries, especially in affecting large issues of broad importance to the nation. For example, industries have not been as successful in America as they have often been abroad in obtaining protection through import restrictions and tariff barriers. American farmers have not fared as well in gaining subsidies and other benefits as their counterparts in Europe and Japan. Environmental laws are tougher on business in the United States than they are in most of Europe. In addition, Congress and the courts have long been more assiduous in enforcing antitrust laws and less inclined to shelter retailers and other businesses from competition than their counterparts in western Europe and Japan.

Finally, it is far from clear that the United States is as paralyzed by gridlock as many people seem to believe. Of course, the separation of powers, the weakness of our political parties, and the tendency for Republicans and Democrats to control different branches of the government all help produce stalemate on occasion. In most cases, however, such logjams reflect deep divisions in American public opinion, with the machinery of government helping to block official action much as the founding fathers intended. Moreover, despite the government's cumbersome qualities, comparative studies have found that the party that wins presidential elections in the United States manages to put its platform into effect about as successfully as in other democracies, including parliamentary systems with clear party majorities, such as Britain's.[11] Simply as a matter of common sense, there is something odd about leveling charges of gridlock against a nation that can produce more than 160 different programs of job training and 200 different programs of housing and urban development, not to mention more than 7,000 pages of legislation *every year* plus a staggering 60,000 pages of federal regulations. There may be serious questions about the *quality* of the legislation, but insufficient *quantity* does not appear to be a serious shortcoming.

Ironically, the problems that do weigh most heavily on the work of government often bear the imprint of the very tendencies Americans have traditionally used to good effect in developing the economy—our preference for individualism, self-reliance, and competition and our distrust of a large and active government. As these traditional values collide with public desires to do more in fields such as health care, poverty, and aid to children, lawmakers quickly bog down in arguments over the proper role of the State. Debates grind on over whether the public or the private sector should be relied upon to supply the housing, job training, medical services, and even the education that the nation requires. Although Americans like to think of themselves as a pragmatic people, free of the ideological struggles for which Europe is renowned, arguments over the respective merits of the government and the market take on an almost religious intensity in which reasoned discourse is soon overtaken by doctrinal fervor.

These arguments would be perfectly understandable, even useful, if they resulted in viable compromises or clear-cut victories for either side. More often, however, they produce erratic, vacillating policies that end by satisfying no one. Lawmakers announce ambitious housing goals, but the funds appropriated are too small to achieve their objectives or even to maintain the buildings properly. Congress makes bold claims for cleaning up the environment and improving job safety, but the machinery devised to implement these programs is so convoluted and the staffing so inadequate for the task that results fall below expectations.

No area of public policy offers more telling examples than the field of health care. Continuing disagreements over the proper role of government have led Congress to veer from market-oriented remedies, such as encouraging health maintenance organizations, to regulatory solutions, such as mandatory fee schedules for doctors under Medicare or certificates of need for building new hospitals. The result is hardly a coherent whole. What has emerged instead is enough of a free-market system to leave more than 40 million Americans without health insurance but enough government intervention to push up physicians' fees, create much burdensome paperwork, underwrite our excessive use of technology, and overexpand our hospital capacity.

Other ideological conflicts persist over who is responsible for many of the social ills that afflict the nation. To what extent is crime the fault of the criminal and to what extent is it a product of unfortunate social conditions? Are blighted neighborhoods attributable to irresponsible residents or to poverty, racial discrimination, and global competition? Is unemployment the result of shiftlessness and sloth or an outgrowth of the economy's failure to produce enough suitable jobs? These questions quickly turn from simple arguments over facts and logic into disputes that arouse strong moral passions. In the eyes of liberals, decisions to cut welfare, limit food stamps, and eliminate affirmative action are heartless and inhumane. To opponents, the existing programs are deeply immoral because they encourage dependency, malingering, and even perverse lifestyles. Tales of cheating by a small minority of participants are enough to ignite heated debates attacking the legitimacy of entire programs (just as grants to a few artists who exhibit lewd works are enough to call in question the entire National Endowment for the Arts).

These partisan differences over where to place responsibility for society's problems are neither recent nor temporary. Although their intensity has waxed and waned over the years, they have been evident throughout the six decades or more since the federal government first began to play a prominent role in social and economic affairs. They have repeatedly complicated efforts to cope with important social issues. As lawmakers with competing ideological views struggle to gain the upper hand, policies shift back and forth. Crime legislation moves from emphasizing counseling and teenage prevention programs to mandating stiffer jail sentences and tougher parole policies. Assistance to mothers with dependent children veers from heavy doses of counseling, to bureaucratic efforts to avoid fraud, to strong requirements that recipients go to work.

Once again, congressional arguments over these issues rarely end, even temporarily, with a clear-cut resolution. More often, programs are passed but with insufficient funds to accomplish their intended purpose. For understandable reasons, the limited resources available are then allocated almost entirely to the most desperate cases. Since these cases are typically the hardest to help—whether they be the poorest families needing shelter or chronically unemployed dropouts seeking job training—the programs often fail. At this point, the only saving grace is that each side can continue to blame the other for the disappointing results.

Nowhere are these tendencies so apparent as in the perennial debate over how best to provide for the poor. In principle, at least, Americans have long been strongly in favor of helping people in poverty. Through most of the period from 1960 to the early 1990s, a majority of the public has felt that the government should be doing more to alleviate poverty, while only a small minority has believed that aid should be cut. For decades, however, heated arguments have continued in Congress over whether the poor are responsible for their own problems and whether government assistance will make them more dependent.

As one side or the other gains the advantage, shifts periodically occur in all the policies that affect the needy—housing assistance, Medicaid, welfare, job training. Whichever side wins, however, the debate has tended to produce unsatisfactory compromises. Congress has enacted sweeping measures to aid the poor, only to restrict the coverage and thus exclude important segments of the needy population. Ambitious programs have been voted into law, but funding has been limited so as to reach only a minority of those in need. Lawmakers have voted impressive programs of aid but have given the states wide powers to limit the size and scope of the benefits. Assistance has been provided, but only with confusing administrative requirements that either discourage deserving applicants or keep them ignorant of the programs involved. The net result is that poor people in America live in the most blighted neighborhoods, enjoy the least adequate health care, attend the worst schools, and have the highest poverty rates to be found in any advanced industrialized nation. As best one can determine, their relative privations have not helped them to become more moral, more self-reliant, or more personally responsible than poor people in any other industrial democracy.

Only slightly more muted are the perennial debates over which level of government should perform the various tasks of the public sector. If conservatives must accept government intervention, they generally prefer to devolve as much responsibility as possible to the state or local level. Liberals, on the other hand, are usually more inclined to expand the federal role. Arguments over this question have persisted in such fields as urban development, education, Medicaid, and welfare.

Too often, discussions proceed not by carefully analyzing the evidence but by exchanging tired generalizations about the need for uniform standards or the importance of keeping government "close to the people." Decades of this sort of debate have not moved the country to an effective, comprehensible division of labor. Rather, they have produced a shifting tangle of shared responsibilities that few careful students of the subject can even explain, let alone justify.

One advantage of our federal system, of course, is the scope it offers for experimentation and innovation. With its great size, decentralization, and respect for individual effort, America offers fertile ground for new ideas. No nation is better at devising ingenious solutions to problems, whether they involve new products and inventions in the private economy or innovative grassroots approaches to pressing public issues. In field after field of social concern, one can find outstanding programs in Denver, Duluth, Dubuque, or some other region or community. The trouble comes in taking these initiatives and expanding them to make an impact nationwide. With thousands of separate initiatives scattered across the country, there is no moral equivalent of competition to induce government agencies and public service organizations to adopt the best practices of others. As a result, good ideas spread slowly, and officials rarely manage to build on successful initiatives to fashion comprehensive national programs. In the process, one of the great potential advantages of federalism and decentralization fails to fulfill its promise.

Quite apart from persistent ideological differences over federalism, individual responsibility, and the proper role of the State lies another pervasive problem, involving relations between public officials and the communities they seek to govern. Quite simply, government agencies in the United States have great difficulty cooperating effectively with the private sector. In recent years, this tendency has become more costly because it is increasingly clear in many different fields of endeavor that public officials need the active participation of interested parties to implement their programs successfully. School reform moves faster by involving parents, community leaders, and corporate employers. Crime control works better with grassroots cooperation from the community. Job training requires assistance from companies to identify future employment needs and from community groups to join in screening applicants.

Whatever their merits in helping to secure productivity gains, individualism, competition, and suspicion of the State do not nurture the kinds of cooperation needed to solve many of these problems. Efforts to regulate business offer a host of instructive examples. In many industrialized countries, where companies, unions, and other interested parties participate in establishing the rules, regulations are more likely to take account of the circumstances of individual companies and be accepted by them in turn. Yet cooperation of this kind is rare in the United States. Instead, the competition of the private economy and its counterpart, the adversary system in the field of law, have been joined by a similarly abrasive *modus operandi* in the regulatory sphere. Rather than seek a negotiated solution, the government almost invariably acts through formal proceedings in which all of the interested parties vie with one another in expressing views and arguments to public officials (and in protesting the decisions that result).

This procedure shifts decision making from the parties to officials who are not intimately familiar with the conditions of the firms they seek to regulate. With millions of different companies subject to their jurisdiction, federal agencies have little choice but to promulgate broad rules that cannot possibly fit the special circumstances of all the plants to which they apply. Government inspectors then have the unenviable task of trying to gain compliance from many recalcitrant firms that feel they have no stake in the rules and resent requirements they regard as unnecessary or perverse. In such an atmosphere, compliance is frequently spotty at best, rule making is highly contentious, and much time and expense go into legalistic efforts to exhaust every avenue for appeal.[12] Predictably, such a process generates widespread dissatisfaction, while costing so much money that the government can attend to only a fraction of the problems subject to its jurisdiction. The results in fields such as environmental protection and job safety are typically less impressive than in other countries that proceed in a more cooperative manner.

Problems of cooperation also crop up repeatedly within the government itself and cause substantial waste and inefficiency. Striking examples arise from the uniquely individualistic, entrepreneurial style of America's lawmakers. Unwilling to accept much direction from their party, members of Congress find it hard to cooperate in distributing public funds so that the money will do the most good. Instead, they compete in trying to bring as many tangible benefits as possible to their own districts. The best-known examples are the dams, roads, research facilities, and other tax-funded projects that are sometimes allocated so as to satisfy influential legislators and local interest groups rather than to maximize public benefits. Greater waste may result from spreading public money over a broader area than the problem at hand actually demands, in order to allow more lawmakers to provide their constituents with some of the government's bounty. In the case of programs for purposes such as rebuilding blighted cities or giving extra educational help to disadvantaged children, funds have been sprinkled so lightly over so many communities and school districts that their effectiveness has been seriously impaired.

Other forms of waste and inefficiency come about through enacting multiple programs to address a single problem, as individual lawmakers and committee chairs try to attach their names to their own special bill. At present, scores of separate job training programs serve the same purpose, many different funding initiatives exist for housing construction and rehabilitation, dozens of legislative schemes address the problem of child abuse, and multitudes of bills attend to food inspection and other kinds of consumer protection. Such proliferation causes much confusion, duplication, and administrative waste. In the case of business regulation, the government's own surveys reveal that companies are often confused, misinformed, or unaware of important legal requirements. In the field of social legislation, many eligible beneficiaries are either ignorant of programs designed to help them or discouraged and frustrated in trying to figure out which of several programs covers them and how they can apply.

While new government initiatives continue to emerge, old programs are much slower to disappear even when they are not working well.[13] In ways that are all too familiar, bureaucrats guard their turf tenaciously, vested interests fight to preserve familiar sources of support, and congressional subcommittees protect whatever lies within their jurisdiction. These tendencies add to the confusion and duplication of government activities, while squandering resources by perpetuating outmoded programs.

The federal government also wastes money by failing to coordinate programs well within the executive branch. Different agencies find it hard to subordinate their special priorities and procedures in favor of a larger, integrated effort. Job training offers a telling example, with its multitude of separate programs, each with its own special requirements, that fail to fit together in a sensibly organized system. Urban programs offer another illustration, as separate agencies work independently at law enforcement, housing, job training, health care, and early child development even though the problems involved are highly interrelated and badly need close coordination. Even within a single agency, such as the Environmental Protection Agency, different bureaus continue to deal with solid waste, toxic chemicals, and water pollution without managing to work together to find more effective solutions to environmental problems. As time goes on, the cost of poorly integrated programs has steadily increased as we become more aware of how interdependent the different problems are that affect our schools, our neighborhoods, our ecological systems, and our health care programs.

Further waste arises simply through poor administration. Part of the problem stems from the low prestige traditionally accorded to government careers and the tendency to staff higher levels of the executive branch with short-term political appointees drawn from outside the government. Under these conditions, the United States has been unable to create a permanent civil service of the quality found in France, Japan, and other leading democracies.

Another source of inefficiency is the persistent tendency on the part of high officials to place greater value on creating new policies than on trying to make existing programs function more effectively. Delays, rigidities, and red tape often result, but they are not the gravest administrative problems. Reports from the General Accounting Office repeatedly document more serious failings, such as an inability to set clear agency goals and priorities, hold officials accountable for results, create adequate information systems, or monitor outside contractors closely through auditing and performance reviews. Because of these shortcomings, writes the Comptroller General, "Important program objectives are not being met, funds are wasted, major programs are over budget and behind schedule, and moneys due are not collected. These problems have existed for many years and efforts to correct them have resulted in incremental improvements . . . But in too many cases, management problems persist long after they have been brought to light and long after agencies have agreed to correct them."[14]

Looking back on all these defects of government helps focus attention more clearly on where the greatest difficulties lie. Familiar forms of waste of the kind celebrated by tales of $500 screwdrivers and

$2,000 toilet seats are doubtless important enough to merit careful attention. Reinventing government to reduce red tape and increase efficiency is definitely a worthwhile task. Yet shortcomings of this kind account for only a small part of the ineffectiveness and waste of government activities. Badly designed programs represent a much more important problem. To some degree, poorly crafted laws result from entrepreneurial legislators jockeying to further their own ambitions and help their own constituencies. But much greater damage occurs through persistent partisan differences that too often result in awkward compromises and flawed programs. In the field of health care alone, a hybrid system of public and private care leads the United States to spend some $250 billion more each year than the next most expensive national program and still not provide insurance to 15 percent of the population.

Totting up all forms of unnecessary expense would surely produce an aggregate annual figure running into the hundreds of billions of dollars. In this sense, the public may be more nearly correct than experts have imagined. For years, pundits have criticized voters for wanting to keep all their benefits without being willing to raise taxes. Yet a careful look at the record suggests that it might be possible to have our cake and eat it too if only we could find a way to keep so many morsels from falling off the table. Had we designed our health care system more wisely, targeted our spending more precisely to accord with genuine needs, developed more cost-effective methods of regulation, and cut back farm subsidies and other unjustified benefits, we could have saved enough not only to keep from running deficits but to provide universal medical coverage, create better programs for long-term health care, build more affordable housing, and attend to many other needs in which we lag behind other leading industrial democracies.

Understanding America's Problem

Although Americans have correctly identified government as the principal source of their frustrations, it is not at all clear that citizens understand the depth and complexity of the problems they face. By huge margins, the public believes that the United States has the finest government in the world. If the nation's accomplishments fall short, people assume that the wrong individuals must have somehow been elected to Congress and the White House. Since the system is fundamentally sound; the problem must be that there are unscrupulous, ambitious public officials in Washington. The solution, then, is to replace them. Thus, 79 percent of the public in a Times Mirror poll say that "it is time for Washington politicians to step aside and make room for new leaders."[15] Sixty percent go so far as to assert that "we need new people in Washington even if they are not as effective as experienced politicians."[16]

This response is hardly adequate. Voters have now expressed acute dissatisfaction with government through seven consecutive presidencies and massive turnover in Congress. At some point, one has to ask whether so many elected officials can be unsuitable or whether deeper causes are responsible for the public's frustrations. Further doubts creep in when one notes how much more satisfied voters are with their own representatives than they are with Congress as a whole. That is one reason why, despite the widespread disaffection, more than 90 percent of incumbents are regularly reelected to the House of Representatives. Even in 1994, that banner year for the angry voter, 90 percent of all sitting House members and 92 percent of all incumbent senators won reelection. If voters believe that almost all of their elected representatives are doing a good job, there must be something wrong with supposing that the cure for America's problems lies in turning all the rascals out.

Politicians do not do much better than the people in providing an adequate diagnosis of what ails the public sector. For example, liberal Democrats have offered no major plan for improving government other than a commitment to "reinvent" executive agencies so as to incorporate sound management practices and modern technological sophistication. What this amounts to in practice is more contracting out of public services, more attention to "customers," more computerization, fewer bureaucrats, and greater scope for line officials to act on their own initiative.

There is nothing particularly wrong with any of these measures. Taken together, however, they fall far short of addressing most of the problems identified in this study. They do little or nothing to remedy the deficiencies and waste in our health care system, our persistently high rates of poverty, the inadequacies of our policies for small children, or the deterioration of our inner cities, to name just four of our pressing problems. Few Democrats would deny this statement. Asked how they mean to improve upon the deficiencies of past government policies, however, they seem to agree on little beyond a need to make government leaner while continuing to meet a variety of public needs. "The era of big government is over," President Clinton proclaimed in his 1996 State of the Union message. "But we cannot go back to the time when our citizens were left to fend for themselves."[17]

If liberals seem vague and indecisive, conservatives are just the opposite. In their view, government is inherently ineffective. As a result, public officials are bound to fail when they try to intervene directly to guide the economy or to enact ambitious programs to achieve large social goals. As Ronald Reagan observed in his first inaugural address, "Government is not the solution to our problems; government *is* the problem." Rather than look to Washington, conservatives advocate dismantling the welfare state along with many other government activities and returning to the qualities of private initiative, self-reliance, and free competitive markets that have served America so well in the past.[18]

One problem with this solution is that no industrial democracy has yet had much success pursuing the basic goals supported by most Americans without the help of a strong and active government. If the public sector is drastically cut back, how do conservatives propose to achieve the clean environment, equality of opportunity, old-age benefits, and other aims that large majorities seem to desire? To this, there are only two possible answers. Either Americans must be persuaded to abandon some of their basic goals, or conservatives must demonstrate that a large government is not essential for their achievement. The first approach would require giving up objectives which Americans have favored for over half a century. The second alternative may have support from intellectuals such as Friedrich von Hayek and Milton Friedman, but it rests on theories that have scarcely been tested by practice anywhere in the world. Thus, conservatives must choose between trying to transform the public's most basic aspirations for America and launching us on a course that amounts to little more than Samuel Johnson's well-known description of second marriages—"a triumph of hope over experience."

So far, put to the test of practical politics, Republicans have not seriously attempted either of these alternatives. Instead, most of their proposals seek to shrink the federal government moderately by cutting its funds and delegating some of its functions to states and local communities. This strategy does not solve any of the underlying problems of the public sector. It merely shifts authority from one level of government to others that command only a bit more confidence than Washington in the eyes of the public. Despite the rhetorical appeal of moving power "closer to the people," long experience with city officials in such fields as law enforcement, public education, and urban affairs hardly permits much optimism that state and local governments will perform a great deal better than federal agencies.

In sum, neither the people nor liberal Democrats nor conservative Republicans seem to have fully come to grips with the problems America is facing. Conservatives speak only about the failures of the State and talk as if it were capable of little else than making the country secure from enemies at home and abroad. Liberals seem demoralized by the attack on government and cannot explain convincingly how it might play a more positive role in the society. The public trivializes the nation's problems by supposing that they can be set right simply by putting new people into office.

None of these responses acknowledges how indispensable government has become to the progress of America and how important it is to find a way of strengthening it to function more effectively. Over the past forty years, the quality of government in the United States has almost invariably been decisive to our advances and our disappointments as a nation. Experience holds forth little hope that we will ever achieve the important goals of our society without learning to create wiser policies and execute them more effectively than we have in the past.

This conclusion holds not only for social welfare programs and law enforcement efforts, but even for the functioning of the economy and the quest for greater prosperity. Competitive markets may be the key to rising productivity, but effective competition calls for a great deal more than private initiative. The maintenance of free markets demands a continuing effort by lawmakers to withstand the pressures for protection that constantly arise from one industry or another. Successful markets also require a network of laws and courts to enforce agreements, prevent anticompetitive behavior, and protect the public against a host of undesirable practices. A private securities market can function effectively only so long as extensive regulations guard investors against fraud and manipulation. A food manufacturer must comply with rules that protect consumers against impurities and guarantee them accurate information about the contents of the goods they purchase. All companies have to obey a variety of laws to ensure truthful advertising, prevent discrimination in hiring, and maintain reasonable safeguards for the safety of employees. Each of these rules needs to be wisely conceived and skillfully administered to protect important public concerns without hobbling corporate managers or burdening them with unnecessary costs.

The same conclusions are even more obvious in the pursuit of other fundamental goals of American society. The maintenance of freedom depends upon an extensive system of judges and courts. Improving the environment and the safety of employees requires the development and enforcement of appropriate standards and rules. The reduction of poverty calls for programs to redistribute money, goods, and services to the needy without engendering excessive fraud or creating other kinds of perverse incentives. Providing all citizens with quality health care at reasonable prices, adequate retirement income, and protection from the ruinous costs of long-term care are all functions that have led to elaborate government programs in every country that has managed to provide such benefits.

To say that the government's role is vital is not to suggest that all programs should be carried out at the national level. It is entirely possible that more responsibility in certain policy areas should be allocated to the states. There is likewise no reason to suppose that the government must grow ever larger and more powerful. Many functions may lend themselves to privatization or deregulation and enjoy greater success as a result. Yet the point remains that deciding what should be privatized and deregulated and determining how these steps should be accomplished are themselves acts requiring considerable political wisdom and initiative. Moreover, deregulation and privatization must be carried out within a framework of rules and safeguards to be sure that public money is well spent and that essential public interests are protected. These tasks can be performed well or badly. As the case of military procurement makes clear, one can rely heavily on private enterprise to achieve important public purposes and still end up with a large and cumbersome bureaucracy and a lot of wasted money.

Much the same is true of newer schemes to use competition and market forces in carrying out public functions. Congress can replace direct regulation of the environment by creating a market of tradable permits that will determine how much waste companies can discharge into the air or water. But public officials are still needed to organize the market for permits, make sure that it operates fairly, decide how much polluting material can be discharged, and check to see that each participating firm emits no more of the regulated matter than it is authorized to do by the permits it holds. Experience to date suggests that these functions are much more extensive and difficult to execute than many enthusiasts anticipated when they first proposed such schemes. Similar lessons emerge from other attempts to introduce competition to the public sector. Thus, efforts to bring charter schools and voucher systems to the field of public education will require careful government supervision not only to ensure that parents have adequate information about the options available but to guarantee minimum standards in a wide variety of matters ranging from health and safety of children to curriculum and teacher competence.

It is not fashionable in the United States, nor has it ever been, to ascribe such importance to the State. Americans have looked to other sources for our salvation and found other reasons for our successes. In times past, many observers emphasized America's geographic isolation and its abundance of national resources to explain its rise to world importance. Even today, one still hears references to the character, initiative, and resourcefulness of the American people as the key to the nation's success. With the growing prominence of global competition, there is increasing talk about the vision of America's entrepreneurs and the decisiveness of its executives in restructuring giant corporations as the critical ingredients for meeting the challenges of a highly technological, information-based economy.

A cold look at the evidence gives little reason to suppose that the United States can gain much advantage from any of the sources just mentioned. Geography no longer protects the country much from foreign wars, and raw materials have ceased to give it a significant national advantage. Knowledge has become the most important determinant of progress. Unlike raw materials, knowledge travels anywhere at very little cost. No nation comes uniquely equipped with a superior supply. Rather, the creation, acquisition, and application of knowledge all depend on ingredients for which governments are heavily responsible—research organizations supported with public funds, schools and universities, job training programs, and other labor market policies.

As for the innate quality of the American people, there may have been a time when the rigors of traveling all the way to the United States meant that only the hardiest, bravest, and most enterprising souls made it to these shores. But this is hardly as true as it once was. Nor does immigration confer special benefits on the United States; Canada, Germany, and other countries have also become much more culturally diverse by welcoming foreigners into their midst. On both sides of the Atlantic, lively debates are in progress over the advantages and disadvantages of continuing to admit so many foreigners. In America, as in Canada and Europe, whether immigration turns out to be a boon or a blessing will depend on government policies and programs that determine who will be admitted, how many can enter, and how well they will be educated and assimilated after they arrive.

Finally, it is misleading to suppose that superior management and entrepreneurial skill can assure a nation's welfare and prosperity, or that America is especially blessed by people with these enterprising talents. There was a time after World War II when our executives seemed to be all-powerful, causing foreign observers, such as Jacques Servan-Schreiber, to muse about the long-term dominance of the American economy. With the rise of Japanese manufacturing and our persistent trade imbalances, such talk has largely disappeared. More realistic is the assessment of the McKinsey Institute, based on decades of management consulting around the world: "There are no general inherent differences among management abilities or natural talents across the countries we are looking at . . . Managers in the U.S. are not inherently 'better' or more talented than those in Western Europe or Japan, and vice versa."[19]

As the McKinsey study points out in explaining productivity differences among nations, it is the wisdom of policy choices, the skill with which legislation is crafted, and the effectiveness with which laws are carried out that differentiate advanced nations most clearly from one another. Advancing technology and global competition may be the primary forces that transform the world, but public policies will determine which nations (and regions within nations) can cope with these changes best and use them to greatest effect in furthering social goals. As a result, President Reagan was only half right. As he correctly perceived, government *is* the problem in the United States. But government must also be the solution, because there is no way out of our difficulties without more enlightened public policies and more effective public administration than we have had in the past.

In light of this conclusion, it is disturbing to hear so many prominent figures dismissing government as "hopelessly" inefficient, "incurably" dysfunctional, or "inherently" ineffective. Such fatalistic attitudes are not in keeping with the traditional optimism and enterprising spirit of Americans. They promise to cost us much more dearly than the euphoria that pervaded Washington in the salad days of Camelot and the Great Society. Today, any nation that accepts such dire conclusions is destined to experience endless frustrations and disappointments in trying to build the kind of society that its citizens desire.

In the end, therefore, we must be realistic about the pervasive role of the State in modern society and look much harder for ways to help our own government function better. This is a formidable task, but its importance can scarcely be overestimated. Until we recognize that global competition has as much to do with the quality of our government as it does with the efficiency of our corporations, we are likely to continue lagging behind other democracies in pursuing the goals that matter most. Accepting this challenge and reaching across ideological barriers to confront it represents the critical task that faces us, now that the Cold War has ended and we begin the next stage in America's remarkable history.

Notes

Introduction

1. Times Mirror Center for the People and the Press, *Voter Anxiety Dividing GOP; Energized Democrats Backing Clinton,* 72 (November 14, 1995).
2. New York Times–CBS Poll, *New York Times,* A-28 (November 3, 1994).
3. See Eric M. Uslaner, *The Decline of Comity in Congress,* 76 (1993).
4. Humphrey Taylor, "Harris Alienation Index Unchanged from Last Year's Very High Number," *Harris Poll* (January 17, 1994).
5. Quoted in Joseph C. Goulden, *The Best Years: 1945–50,* 426 (1976).
6. Quoted in Richard N. Goodwin, *Promises to Keep: A Call for a New American Revolution,* 3–4 (1992).
7. *Better Homes and Gardens* (April 1955), quoted in David Halberstam, *The Fifties,* 591–592 (1993).
8. Quoted in Halberstam, *The Fifties,* 243.
9. Lloyd A. Free and Hadley Cantril, *The Political Beliefs of Americans: A Study of Public Opinion* (1968).
10. Everett C. Ladd, "Big Swings in the National Mood Are a Staple of Contemporary Politics," *Public Perspective,* 3 (January–February 1992).
11. Quoted in Michael Wines, "At the Capitol, Selling Health Plans Like Snake Oil," *New York Times,* A-24 (October 28, 1993).
12. Quoted in Richard N. Goodwin, *Promises to Keep,* 57 (1992).
13. Ibid., 146.
14. Stanley Elam, Lowell Rose, and Alec Gallup, "The 26th Annual *Phi Delta Kappan* Gallup Poll of the Public's Attitudes toward Public Schools," *Phi Delta Kappan,* 41 (September 1994).
15. Albert Gore, *Earth in the Balance: Ecology and the Human Spirit,* 269 (1992).
16. Gregg Easterbrook, *A Moment on the Earth: The Coming Age of Environmental Optimism,* 648 (1995).

17. Jennifer Hochschild, *Facing Up to the American Dream: Race, Class and the Soul of the Nation,* 61 (1995).
18. Ibid.
19. E.g., Paul M. Kennedy, *The Rise and Fall of the Great Powers: Economic Change and Military Conflict from 1500 to 2000* (1987); David P. Calleo, *Beyond American Hegemony: The Future of the Western Alliance* (1987); Peter G. Peterson, "The Morning After," *Atlantic Monthly,* 43 (October 1987).
20. Paul M. Kennedy, *Preparing for the Twenty-First Century,* 324 (1993).
21. Samuel P. Huntington, "The U.S.—Decline or Renewal?" 67 *Foreign Affairs,* 95 (Winter 1989); Joseph S. Nye, Jr., *Bound to Lead: The Changing Nature of American Power* (1990).
22. Joseph S. Nye, *Bound to Lead,* 261.
23. William G. Mayer, *The Changing American Mind: How and Why American Public Opinion Changed between 1960 and 1988,* 343 (1992); Everett C. Ladd, "Generation Gap? What Generation Gap?" *Wall Street Journal,* A-16 (December 9, 1994); Times Mirror Center for the People and the Press, *The New Political Landscape,* 24 (1994).
24. ABC News poll, September 1994, Roper Center at the University of Connecticut, *Public Opinion Online,* Accession number 0232474.
25. According to Sidney Verba, the United States, both in de Tocqueville's era and today, is a society where fundamental inequalities in economic status are tolerated, even encouraged, as long as they are based on achievement. *Elites and the Idea of Equality,* 43 (1987); see also Everett C. Ladd, *The American Ideology: An Explanation of the Origins, Meaning, and Role of American Values,* A22 (February 1992).
26. Times Mirror Center, *The New Political Landscape,* 152.
27. See, e.g., "People for the American Way," *Democracy's Next Generation: A Study of Youth and Teachers,* 67 (1989).
28. Times Mirror Center, *Voter Anxiety,* 180. For a discussion of these attitudes, see Everett Ladd, "The Myth of Moral Decline," *The Responsive Community,* 52 (Winter 1993–1994).
29. Everett C. Ladd, *The American Ideology: An Explanation of the Origins, Meaning, and Role of American Values,* 34 (February 1992).
30. See, generally, Fay Lomax Cook and Edith J. Barrett, *Support for the American Welfare State: The Views of Congress and the Public* (1992).
31. In part, the decision not to include such a discussion stems from the necessity of imposing some limits on what is already a large undertaking. But the decision also reflects the difficulty of determining what constitutes "progress" in international affairs, let alone comparing the progress made by different countries having rather different objectives.

1. The Economy

1. John Maynard Keynes, *Essays in Persuasion: Economic Possibilities for Our Grandchildren,* 365–368 (1932).
2. See, e.g., John Zysman, *Governments, Markets and Growth: Financial Systems and the Politics of Industrial Change,* 234 (1983); Ira Magaziner and Thomas Hout, *Japanese Industrial Policy* (1981).
3. Zysman, *Governments, Markets and Growth,* 251; Peter Katzenstein, *Policy and Politics in West Germany: The Growth of a Semi-Sovereign State* (1987).
4. Klaus Misgeld, Karl Molin, and Klas Amark, *Creating Social Democracy: A Century of the Social Democratic Labor Party in Sweden* (Rev. English ed., 1992); Hugh Heclo and Henrik Madsen, *Policy and Politics in Sweden: Principled Pragmatism* (1987).
5. See Assar Lindbeck et al., *Turning Sweden Around* (1994).
6. See, e.g., Paul R. Krugman, "The Myth of Asia's Miracle," 73 *Foreign Affairs,* 62 (1994); Francis Fukuyama, *Trust: Social Virtues and the Creation of Prosperity,* 53 (1995).
7. McKinsey Global Institute, *Manufacturing Productivity,* Exhibit S-1 (1993).
8. Richard B. Freeman and Lawrence F. Katz, "Rising Wage Inequality: The United States vs. Other Advanced Countries," in Richard B. Freeman (ed.), *Working under Different Rules* (1994).
9. McKinsey Global Institute, *Service Sector Productivity,* Exhibit 1-3 (1992).
10. One recent study reports that approximately two-thirds of those in the lowest income quintile in a given year in the 1970s and 1980s were still in the bottom quintile five years later. Richard V. Burkhauser, Douglas Holz-Eakin, and Stephen E. Rhody, "Labor Earnings Mobility and Inequality in the United States and Germany during the Growth Years of the 1980s," Unpublished paper (February 1996).
11. Freeman and Katz, "Rising Wage Inequality," 39.
12. David Henderson, "The Europeanization of the U.S. Labor Market," *The Public Interest,* 66 (Fall 1993).
13. Robert M. Solow, "Is All That European Unemployment Necessary?" Robbins Lecture (1994); Olivier J. Blanchard, "How to Decrease Unemployment," remarks delivered at Mondragone seminar on Politics, Economics and the Slump of the 1990s (June 1993).
14. William J. Baumol, Sue Anne Batey Blackman, and Edward N. Wolff, *Productivity and American Leadership: The Long View* (1989).
15. McKinsey Global Institute, *Manufacturing Productivity* (1993); idem, *Service Sector Productivity;* idem, *Sweden's Economic Performance* (1995).
16. Baumol, Blackman, and Wolff, *Productivity and American Leadership.*

17. OECD, *Economic Outlook: Historical Statistics/Statistiques Retrospectives, 1960–1990*, 69 (1992).

18. E.g., Lester C. Thurow, *Head to Head: The Coming Economic Battle among Japan, Europe, and America* (1992). Gross savings declined from 17 percent of GDP in the 1970s to 12.5 percent in the early 1990s; personal savings declined from 5.5 percent to 3.5 percent over the same period; business savings were essentially unchanged; and net savings declined from 6 percent in the 1960s to 5.8 percent in the 1970s, 4 percent in the 1980s, and 2 percent in 1990–1993. *Economic Report of the President*, Chapter 3 (1995).

19. McKinsey Global Institute, *Capital Productivity* (1996).

2. Scientific Research and Technology

1. See, e.g., Robert M. Solow, "Technological Change and the Aggregate Production Function," 39 *Review of Economics and Statistics*, 312 (1957); Edward Fulton Denison, *Accounting for United States Economic Growth, 1929–1969* (1974).

2. See, generally, Bruce L. R. Smith, *American Science Policy since World War II* (1990).

3. Lewis M. Branscomb (ed.), *Empowering Technology: Implementing a U.S. Strategy* (1993). For a critical review of President Clinton's technology policy, see Murray Weidenbaum, "A New Technology Policy for the United States," paper presented for the Cato Conference on Technology Policy (April 22, 1993).

4. See, generally, Richard R. Nelson (ed.), *National Innovation Systems: A Comparative Analysis* (1993).

5. The percentage of total R&D devoted to basic research in six major industrialized nations is as follows:

	U.S.	Japan	Germany	France	U.K.	Sweden
1975–1978	13	15	25	21	13	18
1985–1988	14	13	19	21	13	22

Source: National Science Board, *Science and Engineering Indicators, 1991*, 344.

6. In 1992, the percentage of government R&D appropriations for each of five major industrialized nations, by objective, was as follows:

	France	Germany	Japan	U.K.	U.S.
Industrial development	12.6	13.3	3.9	7.9	.3
Health	.7	3.6	.5	1.6	14.7
Defense	37.4	10.5	5.9	46.2	59.4

Source: National Science Board, *Science and Engineering Indicators, 1993*, 379.

7. Henry Ergas, "Does Technology Matter?" in Harvey Brooks and Bruce Guile (eds.), *Technology and Global Industry: Companies and Nations in the World Economy,* 192 (1987); Richard R. Nelson (ed.), *National Innovation Systems: A Comparative Analysis* (1993).

8. National Science Board, *Science and Engineering Indicators, 1992* (1992).

9. From 1965 to 1989, the number of scientists and engineers (in thousands) engaged in R&D in five major industrialized nations was as follows:

	U.S.	Japan	Germany	France	U.K.
1965	494.2	117.6	61.0	42.8	49.9
1970	543.8	172.0	82.5	58.5	—
1975	527.4	255.2	103.7	65.3	80.5
1980	651.1	302.6	120.7	74.9	95.4
1985	841.2	381.3	143.6	102.3	97.8
1989	949.3	461.6	176.4	120.7	102.6

Source: National Science Foundation, *National Patterns of R&D Resources: 1992,* 67. The "1980" figure for the U.K. is actually for 1981, and the "1989" figure is actually for 1988.

10. Robert M. Rosenzweig, with Barbara Turlington, *The Research Universities and Their Patrons,* 84 (1982).

11. *Budget of the United States Government, Fiscal Year 1993,* 139, part 1.

12. See, e.g., "Europe Flunks the Graduate Course," *The Economist,* 48 (February 4, 1995).

13. Justin L. Bloom, *Japan as a Scientific and Technological Superpower,* U.S. Department of Commerce, National Technical Information Service, 65 (1990).

14. Interestingly, however, the United States is the only major country that receives far more in receipts from patent royalties and licenses than it pays for similar rights from abroad. In fact, over the past thirty years, its favorable balance of trade in this respect has remained at about the same ratio (receipts for sales of patents and know-how are approximately five times expenditures). How much this margin reflects our technological superiority and how much it reflects the rewards of innovations made many years before is hard to say. It is also hard to estimate the extent to which our modest payments to other countries for patents and know-how are due to a parochial inability of American scientists and engineers to keep abreast of technological developments abroad.

15. See *Science and Engineering Indicators, 1993,* 160–161 (1993).

16. See, generally, Linda R. Cohen and Roger G. Noll (eds.), *The Technology Pork Barrel* (1991).

17. See, generally, National Academy of Engineering, *Mastering a New Role: Shaping Technology Policy for National Economic Performance* (1993); Michael L. Dertouzos, Richard A. Lester, and Robert M. Solow, *Made in America: Regaining the Productive Edge* (1989).

18. Edwin Mansfield, "Industrial R&D in Japan and the United States: A Comparative Study," 78 *American Economic Review,* 223 (Papers and Proceedings, 1987).

19. National Academy of Science, National Academy of Engineering, National Research Council, Institute of Medicine, *Allocating Federal Funds for Science and Technology,* 17 (1995).

20. Quoted in Murray L. Weidenbaum, *Business, Government and the Public,* 249 (3rd ed., 1986).

3. Education

1. Peter F. Drucker, "The New Society of Organizations," 70 *Harvard Business Review,* 95 (September–October 1992).

2. For a discussion of this subject, see *Economic Report of the President,* 196–202 (1996).

3. National Center for Education Statistics, *Digest of Education Statistics, 1994,* 17 (1994). Additional students who take a high school General Equivalency Degree (GED) bring the total percentage to 87 by age twenty-nine. Figures showing graduation rates for seventeen-year-olds from 1870 to 1992 are provided in National Center for Education Statistics, *120 Years of American Education: A Statistical Portrait,* Table 19, 55 (1993).

4. Jeffrey R. Henig, *Rethinking School Choice: Limits of the Market Metaphor,* 3 (1994).

5. Ibid.

6. Ibid., 30.

7. Mortimer J. Adler, *The Paideia Proposal: An Educational Manifesto,* 26 (1982).

8. See National Education Goals Panel, *National Education Goals Report: Building a Nation of Learners,* xi (1992).

9. E.g., Gerald W. Bracey, "The Fourth Bracey Report on the Condition of Public Education," *Phi Delta Kappan,* 115 (October 1994).

10. Congressional Budget Office, *The Federal Role in Improving Elementary and Secondary Education* (1993).

11. Bracey, "The Fourth Bracey Report," *Phi Delta Kappan.*

12. National Center for Education Statistics, *Trends in Academic Progress: Achievement of American Students in Science, 1970–90, Mathematics, 1973–90, Reading, 1971–90, and Writing, 1984–90* (1991); Ina V. S. Mullis, et al., *Trends in Academic Progress: Achievement of U.S. Students in*

Science, 1969–70 to 1990, Mathematics 1973–90, Reading 1971–90, Writing, 1984–90 (1991).

13. Cited in David C. Berliner, *Educational Reform in an Age of Disinformation,* paper presented at the Meeting of the American Association of Colleges on Teacher Education, San Antonio, Texas (February 1992).

14. Ibid.

15. Dale Whittington, "What Have 17-Year-Olds Known in the Past?" 28 *American Educational Research Journal,* 759 (Winter 1991); Lawrence C. Stedman and Carl F. Kaestle, "Literacy and Reading Performance in the United States from 1880 to the Present," 22 *Reading Research Quarterly,* 46 (1987).

16. Eric A. Hanushek, *Making Schools Work: Improving Performance and Controlling Costs,* 27 (1994).

17. Ibid. A recent report suggests that most of the funding increase did not go to benefit the large majority of students but was used instead for a variety of special programs, such as education for the learning disabled, bilingual education, school lunches, and antidropout programs. Economic Policy Institute, *Where's the Money Gone?* (1995).

18. OECD, *Literacy, Economy and Society: Results of the First International Adult Literacy Study* (1995).

19. David F. Robitaille and R. A. Garden (eds.), *The International Association for the Evaluation of Educational Achievement (IEA) Study of Mathematics II: Contexts and Outcomes of School Mathematics* (1989).

20. Archie Lapointe, Nancy A. Mead, and Janice M. Askew, *Learning Science,* Educational Testing Service Report 22-CAEP-02 (1992); Lapointe, Mead, and Askew, *Learning Mathematics,* ETS Report 22-CAEP-01 (1992).

21. Ibid.

22. The scores for various percentiles of students on the IAEP tests were specially compiled for me by the Educational Testing Service. My special thanks go to Archie Lapointe for providing me with these results.

23. Richard M. Jaeger, " 'World Class' Standards, Choice and Privatization: Weak Measurement Serving Presumptive Policy," paper presented at 1992 Annual Meeting of the American Educational Research Association, San Francisco (April 20–24, 1992).

24. Harold W. Stevenson and James W. Stigler, *The Learning Gap: Why Our Schools Are Failing and What We Can Learn from Japanese and Chinese Education* (1992).

25. Charles Teddlie and Sam Stringfield, *Schools Make a Difference: Lessons Learned from a Ten-Year Study of School Effects* (1993).

26. See, generally, J. R. Hough, *Educational Policy: An International Survey* (1984).

27. Richard Elmore, "Innovation in Education Policy," Paper prepared for presentation at the Conference on Fundamental Questions of Innovation, Duke University, 42–43 (May 3–5, 1991).

28. See, e.g., Denis P. Doyle, Bruce S. Cooper, and Roberta Trachtman, *Taking Charge: State Action on School Reform in the 1980s* (1991).

29. Whether school choice can actually improve student learning is still a matter of dispute. See Henig, *Rethinking School Choice.* Several writers have claimed that Catholic schools obtain better results than public schools in graduating students and improving their performance on standardized tests. Anthony S. Bryk, Valerie E. Lee, and Peter B. Holland, *Catholic Schools and the Common Good* (1993).

30. See, e.g., Derek C. Bok, *The Cost of Talent: How Executives and Professionals Are Paid and How It Affects America,* 178–200 (1993).

31. National Education Goals Panel, *National Education Goals Report: Executive Summary,* 6–7 (1995).

4. Labor Market Policies

1. See, generally, Ray Marshall and Mark Tucker, *Thinking for a Living* (1992).

2. Helen Ginsburg, *Full Employment and Public Policy: The United States and Sweden* (1983).

3. Bernard Casey, "The Dual Apprenticeship System and the Recruitment and Retention of Young Persons in West Germany," 24 *British Journal of Industrial Relations,* 63 (1986).

4. France and England also have national systems of apprenticeship training, but they are newer and far less highly developed than those of Sweden and Germany. See William H. Kolberg and Foster C. Smith, *Rebuilding America's Workforce,* 59–63 (1992).

5. Thomas Kochan and Paul Osterman, *Human Resource Development and Utilization: Is There Too Little in the United States?* Paper prepared for Time Horizons Project of the Council on Competitiveness (February 1991).

6. David Cairncross and Ronald Dore, *Employee Training in Japan* (1989).

7. See Paul Osterman, *Employment Futures: Reorganization, Dislocation, and Public Policy,* 99–100 (1988).

8. Margaret Weir, *Politics and Jobs: The Boundaries of Employment Policy in the United States,* 4 (1992): "For a nation that claims the work ethic as a central feature of its political identity, the United States has been remarkably lax in introducing and sustaining policies that actively promote employment."

9. Donna Mertens, Douglas McElwain, et al., *The Effects of Participating in Vocational Education: Summary of Studies Reported since 1968* (1988).

10. Gus Haggstrom, *After High School, Then What? A Look at the Post-Secondary Sorting-Out Process for American Youth* (1991).

11. General Accounting Office, *Job Training Partnership Act: Services and Out-*

comes for Participants with Differing Needs, GAO-HRD 89-52 (June 1989); Osterman, *Employment Futures*, 92 et seq.

12. General Accounting Office, *Multiple Employment Training Programs: Most Federal Agencies Do Not Know If Their Programs Are Working Effectively*, Report HEHS 94-88 (March 1994).

13. "It is hard to exaggerate the consistency with which employers complain that the Service fails to screen workers and, whenever they list a vacancy, sends them large numbers of unqualified applicants." Osterman, *Employment Futures*, 99–100.

14. John Wirt, Lara Muraskin, David Goodwin, and Robert Meyer, *National Assessment of Vocational Education: Summary of Findings and Recommendations* (1989); Gareth Hoachlander, Philip Kaufman, and Karen Levesque, *Vocational Education in the United States: 1969–90* (1992).

15. Donna Mertens, Douglas McElwain, Gonzalo Garcia, and Mark Whitman, *The Effects of Participating in Vocational Education: Summary of Studies Reported since 1968* (1988); Hoachlander et al., *Vocational Education in the United States*.

16. Osterman, *Employment Futures*, 94–99.

17. Lisa Lynch, "Payoffs to Alternative Training Strategies at Work," in Richard Freeman (ed.), *Working under Different Rules*, 63 (1994). See, generally, Steven Brint and J. Karabel, *The Diverted Dream: Community Colleges and the Promise of Educational Opportunity in America, 1900–1985* (1989).

18. Statement of Clarence C. Crawford, General Accounting Office, *Multiple Employment Training Programs*, GAO HEHS 94-109 (March 2, 1994).

19. See, e.g., John Donahue, *Shortchanging the Workforce: The Job Training Partnership Act and the Overselling of Privatized Training* (1989); General Accounting Office, *Job Training Partnership Act: Services and Outcomes for Participants with Differing Needs*, GAO-HRD 89-52 (June 1989).

20. See, generally, U.S. Department of Labor, *What's Working (and What's Not): A Summary of Research on the Economic Impacts of Employment and Training Programs*, 29 (1995).

21. Ibid., 14

22. Lynch, "Payoffs to Alternative Training Strategies at Work," 64.

23. Office of Technology Assessment, *Worker Training: Competing in the New International Economy* (1990).

24. OECD, *Industrial Training in Australia, Sweden and the United States* (1993).

25. Lynch, "Payoffs and Alternative Training Strategies at Work," 71. These figures are all the more remarkable since the United States counts all workers who have ever received formal company training, whereas the other countries count only employees who received training *during the preceding year*.

26. Lynch, "Payoffs to Alternative Training Strategies at Work." See also OECD,

Industrial Training in Australia, Sweden and the United States, 9, 80–81 (1993), reporting that employers in America have to devote up to one-fourth of their training budgets to basic-skills instruction.

27. The United States is one of the very few industrial countries that does not have generally recognized occupational-skill standards. One reason that employers often cite is the time, effort, and expense required to produce such standards. A more important reason may be the lack of strong industry associations and the absence of any firm tradition of cooperation among employers in most industries.

28. Thomas Kochan and Paul Osterman, *Human Resource Development and Utilization: Is There Too Little in the United States?* Paper prepared for the Time Horizons Project of the Council on Competitiveness (February 26, 1991).

29. Paul Osterman, "Is There a Problem with the Youth Labor Market and If So How Should We Fix It?" *Lessons for the United States from the American and European Experience,* Mimeo, Sloan School, MIT, 12 (February 1992).

30. Ibid.

31. OECD, *Jobs Study,* Part 2, *The Adjustment Potential of the Labor Market,* 138 (1994).

32. Lawrence F. Katz, "Active Labor Market Policies to Expand Employment and Opportunity," *Reducing Unemployment: Current Issues and Policy Options,* Symposium sponsored by the Federal Reserve Bank of Kansas, Jackson Hole, Wyoming, 239, 272–273 (August 25–27, 1994).

33. Lynch, "Payoffs to Alternative Training Strategies," 64.

34. Commission on the Skills of the American Workforce, *America's Choice: High Skills or Low Wages!* (1990).

35. James Heckman, "Is Job Training Oversold?" *The Public Interest,* 94 (Spring 1994).

36. Dan Hull and Dale Parnell, *Tech Prep Associate Degree: A Win/Win Experience* (1991).

37. Paul Osterman and Rosemary Batt, *Employer-Centered Training for International Competitiveness* (1992).

5. Living Conditions

1. Quoted in Lyle Woodyatt, "The Origins and Evolution of New Deal Housing Programs," 102 (Diss., Washington University, 1968).

2. See Kenneth T. Jackson, *Crabgrass Frontier: The Suburbanization of the United States,* 116–138 (1985).

3. U.S. Bureau of the Census, *Decennial Census of Population: United States Summary,* and *1980 Census of Housing, General Housing Characteristics: United States Summary* (1983).

4. Census of Housing, 1940, 1950, 1960, 1970; American Housing Survey (1989).

5. Susan E. Mayer, "Measuring Income, Employment, and the Support of Children," draft paper for Conference on Indicators of Children's Well-Being, Table 6 (November 17–18, 1994). See also copies of the American Housing Survey for 1974–1990.

6. Arnold J. Heidenheimer, Hugh Heclo, and Carolyn T. Adams, *Comparative Public Policy: The Politics of Social Choice in America, Europe and Japan* (3rd ed., 1990); Bruce W. Headey, *Housing Policy in the Developed Economy: The United Kingdom, Sweden, and the United States* (1978); Martin Wynn (ed.), *Housing in Europe* (1984).

7. Van Vliet (ed.), *Housing Markets and Policies under Fiscal Austerity* (1987).

8. Rent supplements also proved to be a more efficient way of helping the needy, since governments were not sure that families living in subsidized units would continue to be poor enough to qualify for housing assistance. By 1970, an estimated 20–50 percent of subsidized housing in Europe was occupied by families that no longer met the criteria for state support.

9. United Nations, *Housing in the World: Graphical Presentation of Statistical Data*, 53, 74, 99, 143, 145 (1993).

10. Denise Di Pasquale and Langley C. Keyes, *Building Foundations: Housing and Federal Policy* (1990).

11. Joint Center for Housing Studies, Harvard University, *The State of the Nation's Housing, 1988–1991*; see also Sandra J. Newman and Ann B. Schnare, *Beyond Bricks and Mortar: Reexamining the Purpose and Effects of Housing Assistance*, 48–49 (1992).

12. See, e.g., Susan E. Mayer and Christopher Jencks, "Has Poverty Really Increased among Children since 1970?" Center for Urban Affairs and Policy Research, Northwestern University, Working Paper 94-14, Table 3 (1994); Mayer, "Measuring Income."

13. Susan E. Mayer, *A Comparison of Poverty and Living Conditions in Five Countries*, Institute for Research on Poverty, University of Wisconsin at Madison, Discussion Paper 987-982, 20 (1992).

14. See, generally, Christopher Jencks, *The Homeless* (1994).

15. Ibid.

16. Jackson, *Crabgrass Frontier*.

17. Anthony Downs, *New Visions for Metropolitan Development*, 8 (1994). For a detailed analysis of commuting by automobile, see Anthony Downs, *Stuck in Traffic: Coping with Peak-Hour Traffic Congestion* (1992). Estimates of average commuting time per commuting trip in 1980 are given on page 16.

18. Quoted in Alan Ehrenhalt, *The Lost City: Discovering the Forgotten Virtues of Community in the Chicago of the 1950s*, 212 (1995).

19. NBC-Newsweek poll (July 14, 1991), "Public Opinion On-line," Roper Center, University of Connecticut at Storrs.

20. See, generally, Henry G. Cisneros (ed.), *Interwoven Destinies: Cities and the Nation* (1993).

21. Nancy McArdle and Kelly S. Mikelson, "The New Immigrants: Demographic and Housing Characteristics," Working Paper W94-1, Joint Center for Housing Studies, Harvard University (1994).

22. Jackson, *Crabgrass Frontier.*

23. On the other hand, owners of rental properties received generous tax breaks of their own, which may have been passed on to the tenants, at least in part, by virtue of competition among landlords.

24. See Lawrence B. Lindsey, "More Opportunity through Deregulation," remarks to Financial Institutions Joint Housing Conference, Detroit, Michigan (October 29, 1994).

25. The urban problems previously described have generally been less severe in the South and West, because sunbelt cities have been able to annex vast expanses of land, thereby gaining control over the suburbs and their richer tax base. See David Rusk, *Cities without Suburbs* (1993). Levels of segregation by race and income are lower in these large metropolitan areas than they are in the older, more geographically restricted cities of the Northeast and Midwest. As sunbelt cities experience mounting problems of race, immigration, poverty, and crime, however, they too are beginning to encounter opposition to their efforts to absorb outlying areas.

26. See, generally, R. Allen Hays, *The Federal Government and Urban Housing: Ideology and Change in Public Policy* (1985).

27. Daniel P. Moynihan, *Maximum Feasible Misunderstanding: Community Action in the War against Poverty* (1969).

28. See, e.g., Hays, *The Federal Government and Urban Housing.*

29. Department of Housing and Urban Development, *National Urban Policy Report* (1980).

30. See, e.g., Helen F. Ladd and John Yinger, *America's Ailing Cities: Fiscal Health and the Design of Urban Policy* (1989).

31. Nicholas Lemann, "The Myth of Community Development," *New York Times Magazine,* 29 (January 9, 1994).

32. Andrew Cuomo, Statement before the Subcommittee on Select Revenue Measures and Subcommittee on Human Resources, Committee on Ways and Means, U.S. House of Representatives (March 22, 1994).

33. E.g., Robert Halpern, *Rebuilding the Inner City: A History of Neighborhood Initiatives to Address Poverty in the United States* (1995).

34. E.g., Peter Medoff and Holly Sklar, *Streets of Hope: The Fall and Rise of an Urban Neighborhood* (1994).

35. See, e.g., Jurgen Friedrichs, "Urban-Renewal Policies and Back-to-the-City

Migration," *American Planning Association Journal,* 70 (Winter 1987); Michael Hebbert, "Urban Sprawl and Urban Planning in Japan," 57 *The Planning Review,* 141 (1986).

36. See Michael Keating, *Comparative Urban Politics: Power and the City: The United States, Canada, Britain, and France* (1991); Heidenheimer, Heclo, and Adams, *Comparative Public Policy.*

37. In 1989, the population density in metropolitan areas, as measured by the number of persons per hectare (2.471 acres), was as follows:

	Inner area	Outer area (suburbs)	Metropolitan area
New York	107	13	20
United States	45	11	14
Toronto	57	34	40
Europe	91	43	54
Tokyo	153	58	105

Source: Peter Newman and Jeffrey Kenworthy, *Cities and Automobile Dependence: A Sourcebook,* 42 (1989).

38. Loic Wacquant, "The Comparative Structure and Experience of Racial Exclusion: Race, Class, and Space in Chicago and Paris," in Katherine McFate, Roger Lawson, and William Julius Wilson, *Poverty, Inequality and the Future of Social Policy: Western States in the New World Order,* 543, 561 (1995).

39. Margaret Weir, *Race and Urban Poverty: Comparing Europe and America,* Center for American Political Studies, Harvard University, Occasional Paper 93-9 (1993); Peter Willmott and Alan Murie, *Polarisation and Social Housing* (1988).

40. See, e.g., Heidenheimer, Heclo, and Adams, *Comparative Public Policy;* Keating, *Comparative Urban Politics.*

41. Somewhat similar requirements are now in place in a small number of American states, such as Florida and Oregon.

42. A similar arrangement exists in Minneapolis–St. Paul, where all municipalities share part of the total tax revenues of the region, and all contribute 40 percent of the revenues from appreciated land valuations to a common pool.

43. Americans in metropolitan areas spend an average of 309.9 hours per passenger per year in transporting themselves. Europeans on average spend 234.6 hours, and Japanese spend 286.4 hours. In European cities, residents make 25 percent of their trips by public transit, compared with less than 1 percent in many American cities, such as Phoenix, Houston, and Detroit. In Europe, people make 21.3 percent of their trips to work by foot or bicycle, compared with 15.8 percent in Tokyo, 5.8 percent in Toronto, and 5.3 per-

cent in the United States. Newman and Kenworthy, *Cities and Automobile Dependence*, 36–38.

44. Neil R. Peirce, *Citistates: How Urban America Can Prosper in a Competitive World*, 300 (1993).

45. "The lower class forms of all problems are at bottom a single problem: the existence of an outlook and style of life which is radically present-oriented and which therefore attaches no value to work, sacrifice, self-improvement, or service to family friends or community." Edward C. Banfield, *The Unheavenly City Revisited*, 235 (1974).

6. The Environment

1. Rachel Carson, *Silent Spring* (1962).

2. Robert C. Mitchell, "Public Opinion and the Green Lobby: Poised for the 1990s?" in Norman J. Vig and Michael E. Kraft, *Environmental Policies in the 1990s: Toward a New Agenda*, 85 (1990). See also Riley E. Dunlap and Rik Scarce, "The Polls-Poll Trends: Environmental Problems and Protection," 55 *Public Opinion Quarterly*, 651 (1991).

3. Gregg Easterbrook, *A Moment on the Earth: The Coming Age of Environmental Optimism*, xv (1995).

4. See Debra S. Knopman and Richard A. Smith, "20 Years of the Clean Water Act," *Environment*, 19 (January–February 1993).

5. OECD, *The State of the Environment*, Figure 13, 59 (1991); idem, *Environmental Performance Reviews, United States*, 79 (1996).

6. Richard A. Smith, Richard A. Alexander, and M. Gordon Wolfman, "Water Quality Trends in the Nation's Rivers," 235 *Science*, 1605 (1987).

7. Knopman and Smith, "20 Years of the Clean Water Act," 38.

8. OECD, *Environmental Performance Reviews, United States*, 65 (1996).

9. Ibid., 66.

10. General Accounting Office, Report to the Chairman of the Environment, Energy, and Natural Resources Subcommittee, Committee on Government Operations, U.S. House of Representatives, *Water Pollution: Stronger Efforts Needed by EPA to Control Toxic Water Pollution* (July 1991).

11. OECD, *Environmental Indicators*, 47 (1994).

12. See Table 6-3.

13. Katherine N. Probst, *Footing the Bill for Superfund Cleanup: Who Pays and How?* 14–15 (1995).

14. Ibid., 18.

15. OECD, *Environmental Performance Reviews: United States*, 132 (1996); idem, *Japan*, 184 (1994); idem, *Germany*, 207 (1993); idem, *United Kingdom*, 101 (1993); idem, *Canada*, 113 (1995).

16. According to the OECD, "While the United States to some extent has de-

coupled economic growth and air pollution over the past twenty-five years, the trend has not been as strong as in most other large OECD countries. Today, the United States still has some of the highest emission rates per capita and per unit among OECD countries for SO_2 and NO_x, and is the world's largest contributor of CO_2." *Environmental Performance Reviews, United States,* 121 (1996). Susan Rose-Ackerman presents reasonably detailed data describing the results in Germany and the United States from 1970 to 1988. During this period, Germany was more successful in reducing sulfur dioxide, suspended particulates, carbon monoxide, and carbon dioxide, while the United States made greater progress in reducing nitrous oxides and hydrocarbons. *Controlling Environmental Policy: The Limits of Public Law in Germany and the United States,* 21 (1995). It is also worth noting that the United States has the highest per capita emission of greenhouse gases of any of the countries surveyed. United Nations Development Program, *Human Development Report 1995,* 211 (1995). For listings of per capita emissions of several pollutants, see OECD, *Environmental Performance Reviews: United Kingdom,* 82 (1994).

17. OECD, *The State of the Environment,* 37 (1991).
18. Ibid.
19. Ibid., 41.
20. Ibid., 23.
21. Ibid., 39.
22. James DeLong, "Of Mountains and Molehills: The Municipal Solid Waste 'Crisis,'" 12 *The Brookings Review,* 34 (Spring 1994).
23. Richard B. Stewart, "Economics, Environment, and the Limits of Legal Control," 9 *Harvard Environmental Law Review,* 1, 7 (1985).
24. The ratio of actual cost to least cost for selected air quality projects is as follows:

Year of study	Pollutant	Area	Ratio of actual cost to least cost
1974	Particulates	St. Louis	6.00
1981	Sulfur dioxide	Four Corners	4.25
1982	Sulfates	Los Angeles	1.07
1983	Nitrogen dioxide	Baltimore	5.96
1983	Nitrogen dioxide	Chicago	14.40
1984	Particulates	Baltimore	4.18
1984	Sulfur dioxide	Delaware Valley	1.78
1984	Hydrocarbons	DuPont Plants	4.15

Source: T. H. Tietenberg, *Emissions Trading: An Exercise in Reforming Pollution Policy,* Table 4, 42 (1985). "Four Corners" means the junction of Virginia, West Virginia, Maryland, and Pennsylvania.

25. The ratio of actual cost to least cost for selected water quality projects is as follows:

Year of study	Area	Ratio of actual cost to least cost
1967	Delaware Estuary	1.43–3.13
1980	Lower Fox River (Wisconsin)	1.38–2.29
1983	Willamette River	1.12–1.19
1983	Upper Hudson	1.54–1.62
1983	Mohawk River	1.22

Source: Tietenberg, *Emissions Trading,* Table 5, 46.

26. Bruce T. Ackerman and William T. Hassler, *Clean Coal/Dirty Air* (1981).

27. See, e.g., Paul Faeth, *Growing Green: Enhancing the Economic and Environmental Performance of U.S. Agriculture,* 41 (1995).

28. E.g., Robert Stavins, "Harnessing Market Forces to Protect the Environment," 31 *Environment,* 6 (January–February 1989).

29. See Steven Kelman, *What Price Incentives? Economics and the Environment* (1981).

30. See David Vogel, *National Styles of Regulation* (1986). See, more generally, Ronald Brickman, Sheila Jasanoff, and Thomas Ilgen, *Controlling Chemicals: The Politics of Regulation in Europe and the United States* (1985).

31. Rose-Ackerman, *Controlling Environmental Policy.*

32. E.g., A. Myrick Freeman III, *Air and Water Pollution Regulation: A Benefit-Cost Assessment* (1982). A more recent estimate of the costs and benefits of implementing the Clean Air Act of 1990 put the benefits at $6–25 billion (in 1989 dollars) and the costs from $29–36 billion. See General Accounting Office, *Environmental Protection: Meeting Public Expectations with Limited Resources,* GAD/RCED, 91–97 (June 1991).

33. See, e.g., A. Myrick Freeman III, "Water Pollution Policy," in Paul Portney (ed.), *Public Policies for Environmental Protection* (1990).

34. See Environmental Protection Agency, *Reducing Risk: Setting Priorities and Strategies for Environmental Protection* (1990); Steven Breyer, *Breaking the Vicious Circle: Toward Effective Risk Regulation* (1993).

35. Quoted in John Hird, "Environmental Policy and Equity: The Case of Superfund," 12 *Journal of Policy Analysis and Management,* 323, 326 (1993).

36. The EPA has also been plagued by administrative problems in implementing Superfund efficiently. As of September 30, 1992, the agency had collected only 10 percent of the $5.7 billion classified as recoverable from parties responsible for polluting the sites. Because the agency's data were so poor, it could not account for the failure to collect the missing 90 percent. Additional waste resulted from the practice of using cost-reimbursement contracts with private companies, failing to estimate costs properly, and failing to carefully monitor the charges submitted.

37. Tammy Tengs and John Graham, "The Opportunity Costs of Haphazard Societal Investments in Life-Saving," in Robert H. Hahn (ed.), *Risk Management: From Theory to Practice* (forthcoming).
38. Remarks before the Environmental Law Institute (October 18, 1995).

7. Encouraging the Arts

1. Quoted in Russell Lynes, *The Lively Audience: A Social History of the Visual and Performing Arts in America, 1890–1950,* 357 (1985).
2. Quoted in "Origins of the National Endowment for the Arts," Independent Commission Report, 20 *Journal of Arts Management and Law,* 19 (1990).
3. Quoted in Russell B. Nye, *The Cultural Life of the New Nation, 1776–1830,* 263 (1960).
4. Milton C. Cummings, Jr., "Government and the Arts: An Overview," in Stephen Benedict (ed.), *Public Money and the Muse: Essays on Government Funding for the Arts,* 31, 34 (1991).
5. Ibid., 34–37.
6. *Congressional Record,* 75th Congress, 3rd Sess., 9491-92 (1938).
7. Quoted in Jerre G. Mangione, *The Dream and the Deal: The Federal Writers' Project, 1935–1943,* 321–322 (1972).
8. Quoted in Gary O. Larson, *The Reluctant Patron: The United States Government and the Arts, 1943–1965,* 103 (1983).
9. Ibid., 34.
10. President's Commission on National Goals, *Goals for Americans* (1960).
11. Dick Netzer, *The Subsidized Muse: Public Support for the Arts in the United States* (1978).
12. American Council for the Arts, *Americans and the Arts, VI: Highlights from a Nationwide Survey of Public Opinion* (1992).
13. James Heilbrun and Charles M. Gray, *The Economics of Art and Culture: An American Perspective,* 228–229 (1993).
14. National Endowment for the Arts, *Arts in America,* 9 (1990).
15. Total numbers of people (in millions) attending exhibits and performances are as follows:

Activity	1982	1992	Percent change
Art museums	36.2	49.6	+ 37.0
Plays	19.5	25.1	+ 28.7
Classical music	21.3	23.2	+ 8.9
Ballet	6.9	8.7	+ 26.1
Opera	4.5	6.1	+ 35.6

Source: John P. Robinson, *Arts Participation in America: 1982–1992,* 7 (National Endowment for the Arts, 1993).

16. Ibid., 10. Even more recent studies, however, claim to detect a marked fall-ing-off in attendance by younger generations when it comes to symphony concerts, opera, and ballet, but not for museums. Edward Rothstein, "The Tribulations of the Not-so-living Arts," *New York Times*, Week in Review, 1 (February 18, 1995).

17. E.g., Alvin Toffler, *The Culture Consumers* (1964).

18. William J. Baumol and William G. Bowen, *Performing Arts: The Economic Dilemma*, 35–69 (1966).

19. Heilbrun and Gray, *The Economics of Art and Culture*, 253.

20. Ibid.

21. Ibid., p. 252.

22. Joseph Zeigler, *Arts in Crisis: The National Endowment for the Arts versus America*, 62 (1994); see also Kevin V. Mulcahy, "The NEA as Public Patron of the Arts," in Judith H. Balfe (ed.), *Art, Ideology and Politics*, 333 (1985).

23. Quoted in Andrew Buchwalter (ed.), *Culture and Democracy: Social and Ethical Issues in Public Support for the Arts and Humanities*, 41 (1992).

24. 135 *Congressional Record* 58806 (July 6, 1989), 135 *Congressional Record* 512, 967-01 (October 7, 1989).

25. *Belle Lewitsky Dance Foundation v. John E. Frohnmayer*, 754 F. Supp. 774 (1991).

26. See, generally, J. Mark Davidson Schuster, *Supporting the Arts: An International Comparative Study* (1985).

27. See Marianne Andrault and Phillippe Dressayre, "Government and the Arts in France," in Milton C. Cummings, Jr., and Richard S. Katz, *The Patron State: Government and the Arts in Europe, North America, and Japan*, 17 (1987); see, generally, Andrew Feist and Robert Hutchinson (eds.), *Cultural Trends in the Eighties* (1990).

28. See F. F. Ridley, "Tradition, Change and Crisis in Great Britain," in Cummings and Katz, *The Patron State*, 225; John Meisel and Jean van Loon, "Cultivating the Bushgarden: Cultural Policy in Canada," ibid., 276.

29. Thomas R. H. Havens, "Government and the Arts in Contemporary Japan," ibid., 333.

30. Tibor Scitovsky, "Arts in the Affluent Society," reprinted in Scitovsky, *Human Desire and Economic Satisfaction: Essays on the Frontiers of Economics*, 37–45, Table 4 (1986).

31. Alice G. Marquis, *Art Lessons: Learning from the Rise and Fall of Public Arts Funding*, 243 (1995).

32. Ibid., 116.

33. Ibid., 135.

34. See, e.g., Robert S. Brustein, *Dumbocracy in America: Studies in the Theatre of Guilt, 1987–1994*, 26 (1994).

35. Quoted in Marquis, *Art Lessons*, 248.

36. Ibid., 244–245.
37. Raoul Naroll, *The Moral Order: An Introduction to the Human Situation*, 73 (1983).
38. David G. Myers and Edward Diener, "Who Is Happy?" 6 *Psychological Science*, 10, 13 (1995).
39. Figures supplied to me by Edward Diener, University of Illinois. See, generally, Myers and Diener, "Who Is Happy?" See also, Robert Lane, "Does Money Buy Happiness?" 58 *The Public Interest* (Fall 1993).
40. General Social Surveys, 1974 to 1994, National Opinion Research Corporation, Chicago; Richard Easterlin, "Does Economic Growth Improve the Human Lot?" in Paul A. David and Melvin W. Reder, *Essays in Honor of Moses Abramovitz* (1974).

8. Child Policies

1. Everett Ladd, *The American Ideology: An Exploration of the Origins, Meaning, and Role of American Political Ideas*, Occasional Papers and Monographs, Series 1, Roper Center for Public Opinion Research, Appendix 5A, 75 (1994).
2. Times Mirror Center for the People and the Press, *The People, the Press and Politics: The New Political Landscape*, 152 (October 1994).
3. Reported figures of child abuse (including neglect, physical abuse, and sexual abuse) more than quadrupled from 1976 to 1992. Although there is general agreement that abuse has become more frequent, there has probably also been a growing tendency to report such cases. As a result, it is hard to know precisely to what extent abuse has actually increased. Figures on reported child abuse were compiled by Marc Miringoff, director of the Institute for Innovation in Social Policy, Fordham Graduate Center, based on figures collected by the American Association for Protecting Children and, after 1985, by the National Committee for the Prevention of Child Abuse.
4. National Education Goals Panel, *Data Volume for the National Education Goals Report*, 32 (1995).
5. George Miller (ed.), *Giving Children a Chance: The Case for More Effective National Policies* (1990).
6. Ibid.
7. David A. Hamburg, *Today's Children: Creating a Future for a Generation in Crisis*, 55 (1992). According to the National Commission on Children, "While there is debate over the prevalence of childhood hunger in America, there is no doubt that the problem has increased over the past decade. Recent estimates of the number of children who experience hunger range from 2 million to 5.5 million." Final Report of the National Commission on Chil-

dren, *Beyond Rhetoric: A New American Agenda for Children and Families,* 124 (1991).

8. Carnegie Task Force on Meeting the Needs of Young Children, *Starting Points: Meeting the Needs of Our Youngest Children,* 66 (1994), hereafter cited as Carnegie Task Force.

9. Gopal K. Singh and Stella M. Yu, "Infant Mortality in the United States: Trends, Differentials, and Projections, 1950 through 2010," 85 *American Journal of Public Health,* 957 (1995).

10. United Nations Children's Fund (UNICEF), *The State of the World's Children,* 73 (1992). Although this ranking may be influenced by differences in measurement and reporting practices, such factors seem to have only a modest effect on America's relative standing. See Urban Institute, "Research Notes: International Infant Mortality Rankings," *Policy and Research Report,* 29 (Winter–Spring 1993).

11. Children's Defense Fund, *Maternal and Child Health Book,* Table 5 (1992).

12. United Nations Children's Fund (UNICEF), *The State of the World's Children,* 83 (1992).

13. Ibid., 83.

14. Hamburg, *Today's Children,* 52. This conclusion has been disputed. For an article criticizing the studies on the effectiveness of prenatal care, see Jane Huntington and Frederick Connell, "For Every Dollar Spent: The Cost-Savings Argument for Prenatal Care," 331 *New England Journal of Medicine,* 1303 (November 10, 1994).

15. See, e.g., C. Arden Miller, "Prenatal Care Outreach: An International Perspective," Appendix B, in Sarah S. Brown (ed.), *Prenatal Care: Reaching Mothers, Reaching Infants* (1988).

16. Ibid., 210–223.

17. Pierre Buekens, et al., "A Comparison of Prenatal Care Use in the United States and Europe," 83 *American Journal of Public Health,* 31 (1993).

18. Carnegie Task Force, 32–36.

19. Ibid.

20. Department of Health and Human Services, Center for Disease Control and Prevention, *Morbidity and Mortality Weekly Report,* 705–709 (October 7, 1994).

21. Carnegie Task Force, 65.

22. Warren E. Leary, "Survey Raises Estimate on Toddler Vaccinations," *New York Times,* A14 (August 25, 1995).

23. Hamburg, *Today's Children,* 45.

24. Eugene M. Lewit and Linda Schuurmann Baker, "Health Insurance Coverage," 5 *The Future of Children,* 192 (Winter 1995); Howard L. Freeman, Robert J. Blendon, et al., "Americans Report on Their Access to Health Care," *Health Affairs,* 6 (Spring 1987).

25. Lewit and Baker, "Health Insurance Coverage," 201–202.
26. Carnegie Task Force, 44–45. See also Edward Zigler and Meryl Frank (eds.), *The Parental Leave Crisis: Toward a National Policy* (1988).
27. National Commission on Children, *Beyond Rhetoric*, 251.
28. Sandra L. Hofferth, April Brayfield, Sharon Deich, and Pamela Holcomb, *National Child Care Survey, 1990*, 21 (1991); Carnegie Task Force, 45.
29. Carnegie Task Force, 9, 12.
30. Ibid., 49.
31. Ibid.
32. Ibid., 14; National Child Care Staffing Study, *Who Cares?: Child Care Teachers and the Quality of Care in America: Final Report* (1989).
33. See statement of Jane Ross, General Accounting Office, before the Subcommittee on Human Resources, Committee on Education and Labor, U.S. House of Representatives, *Child Care: Current System Could Undermine Goals of Welfare Reform*, GAO/T-HEHS-94-238 (September 1994).
34. B. Willer, *The Demand and Supply of Child Care in 1990* (1991); Carnegie Task Force, 56.
35. OECD, *Employment Outlook* (July 1990).
36. Swedish Institute, *Fact Sheets on Sweden: Child Care in Sweden* (May 1992); Steven Greenhouse, "If the French Can Do It, Why Can't We?" *New York Times Magazine*, 59 (November 14, 1993).
37. Valerie Lee, Jeanne Brooks-Gunn, et al., "Are Head Start Effects Sustained? A Longitudinal Follow-up Comparison of Disadvantaged Children Attending Head Start, No Preschool, and Other Preschool Programs," 61 *Child Development*, 405 (1990). A recent study concludes that Head Start does have long-term positive effects on test scores for white children but not for blacks. Janet Currie and Duncan Thomas, "Does Head Start Make a Difference?" 85 *American Economic Review*, 341 (June 1995); see also W. Steven Barnett, "Long Term Effects of Early Childhood Programs on Cognitive and School Outcomes," 5 *The Future of Children*, 25 (Winter 1995).
38. Lawrence J. Schweinhart, Helen V. Burnes, and David P. Weikart, *Significant Benefits: The High/Scope Perry Preschool Study through Age 27*, xv, 55, 92 (1993); Edward Zigler and Susan Muenchow, *Head Start: The Inside Story of America's Most Successful Educational Experiment* (1992).
39. Douglas Besharov, "Why Head Start Needs a ReStart," *Washington Post*, C1 (February 2, 1992).
40. Ernest L. Boyer, *Ready to Learn: A Mandate for the Nation*, 7 (1991).
41. Ibid., 8.
42. Lee Rainwater and Timothy Smeeding, "Doing Poorly: The Real Income of American Children in a Comparative Perspective," Luxembourg Income Study, Working Paper 127 (1995).
43. Ibid., Table 1.

44. Lisbeth B. Schorr and Daniel Schorr, *Within Our Reach: Breaking the Cycle of Disadvantage* (1988).

9. Race

1. See, generally, Chandler Davidson and Bernard Grofman (eds.), *Quiet Revolution in the South: The Impact of the Voting Rights Act, 1965–1990* (1994).
2. Raymond E. Wolfinger and Steven J. Rosenstone, *Who Votes?* 13–36 (1980).
3. Davidson and Grofman, *Quiet Revolution in the South*, 336, 345.
4. *Statistical Abstract of the United States, 1994*, 281, Table 437 (1994).
5. See Davidson and Grofman, *Quiet Revolution in the South*, 335.
6. *Miller v. Johnson*, 115 S. Ct. 2475 (1995).
7. Lani Guinier, *The Tyranny of the Majority: Fundamental Fairness in Representative Democracy* (1994).
8. William A. Clark, "Causes of Housing Segregation," in *Issues of Housing Discrimination: Consultation/Hearing of the United States Commission on Civil Rights*, 11 (1986).
9. Douglas Massey and Nancy Denton, *American Apartheid: Segregation and the Making of the Underclass*, 49 (1993).
10. Ibid.
11. *Index to International Public Opinion, 1994–95*, 443 (1995).
12. William A. Clark, "Causes of Housing Segregation," 23.
13. See, e.g., Reynolds Farley and William H. Frey, "Changes in the Segregation of Whites from Blacks during the 1980s: Small Steps toward an Integrated Society," 59 *American Sociological Review*, 23–45 (1994).
14. William Frey, "Minority Suburbanization and Continued 'White Flight' in U.S. Metropolitan Areas: Assessing Findings from the 1990 Census," 4 *Research in Community Sociology*, 20 (1994).
15. Massey and Denton, *American Apartheid*, 67–74; Richard Alba and John Logan, "Variations on Two Themes: Racial and Ethnic Patterns of Suburban Residence," 28 *Demography*, 411 (1991).
16. Charles Lamb, "Equal Housing Opportunity," in Charles Bullock III and Charles Lamb (eds.), *Implementation of Civil Rights Policy*, 159 (1984).
17. Massey and Denton, *American Apartheid*, 195–205.
18. See John Yinger, "Access Denied, Access Constrained: Results and Implications of the 1989 Housing Discrimination Study," in M. Fix and R. Struyk (eds.), *Clear and Convincing Evidence: Measurement of Discrimination in America* (1993).
19. Massey and Denton, *American Apartheid*, 92–93.
20. Clark, "Causes of Housing Segregation," 11.

21. Gerald D. Jaynes and Robin M. Williams, Jr. (eds.), *A Common Destiny: Blacks and American Society,* 331 (1989).
22. *Brown v. Board of Education,* 347 U.S. 483 (1954).
23. *Green v. New Kent County School Board,* 391 U.S. 430 (1968).
24. *Swann v. Charlotte-Mecklenburg Board of Education,* 402 U.S. 1 (1971).
25. See, e.g., *Milliken v. Bradley,* 418 U.S. 717 (1974).
26. Gary Orfield, *The Growth of Segregation in American Schools: Changing Patterns of Separation and Poverty since 1968* (December 1993).
27. Ibid.
28. *Statistical Abstract of the United States,* 141 (1991).
29. See, e.g., Jomills Braddock and James McPartland, "The Social and Academic Consequences of School Desegregation," 4 *Equity and Choice,* 5 (1988).
30. Ibid., 7.
31. Robert Crain and Rita Mahard, "School Racial Composition and Black College Attendance and Achievement Test Performance," 51 *Sociology of Education,* 81 (1978). See, generally, Amy Wells, "Reexamining Social Science Research on School Desegregation: Long versus Short-term Effects," 96 *Teachers College Record,* 691 (1995).
32. For a review of the literature on this point, see W. Steven Barnett, "Benefits of Compensatory Preschool Education," 27 *Journal of Human Resources,* 279 (Spring 1992).
33. Launor Carter, "The Sustaining Effects Study of Compensatory and Elementary Education," 13 *Educational Researcher,* 4 (1984).
34. Jeffrey R. Henig, *Rethinking School Choice: Limits of the Market Metaphor,* 249 (1994), as calculated by the author from National Center for Education Statistics, *Trends in Academic Progress,* Summary Report, Figures 2–4.
35. Ibid.
36. See, generally, Jennifer Hochschild, *Facing Up to the American Dream: Race, Class and the Soul of the Nation* (1995).
37. E.g., Richard G. Niemi, John Mueller, and Tom W. Smith, *Trends in Public Opinion: A Compendium of Survey Data,* 167–186 (1989); George Gallup, Jr., *The Gallup Poll: Public Opinion, 1990,* 64 (1991).
38. Paul Sniderman and Thomas Piazza, *The Scar of Race* (1993).
39. Jaynes and Williams, *A Common Destiny,* 130.
40. See, generally, Ellis Cose, *The Rage of a Privileged Class* (1993).

10. Career Opportunities

1. Seymour Martin Lipset and Reinhard Bendix, *Social Mobility in Industrial Society* (1959).
2. E.g., Robert Erikson and John H. Goldthorpe, "Are American Rates of Social

Mobility Exceptionally High? New Evidence on an Old Issue," 1 *European Sociological Review,* 1 (1985).

3. Richard V. Burkhauser, Douglas Holtz-Eakin, and Stephen E. Rhody, "Labor Earnings Mobility and Inequality in the United States and Germany during the Growth Years of the 1980s," Unpublished paper (February 1996).

4. E.g., Raymond Sin-Kwok Wong, "Understanding Cross-National Variation in Occupational Mobility," 55 *American Sociological Review,* 560 (1990).

5. Gerald Jaynes and Robin Williams, Jr. (eds.), *A Common Destiny: Blacks and American Society,* 272 (1989).

6. Ibid., 295.

7. U.S. Census Bureau, *Current Population Reports,* 20-471, 14 (March, 1992).

8. Jaynes and Williams, *A Common Destiny,* 334.

9. Robert M. Hauser, "Trends in College Entry among Whites, Blacks, and Hispanics, 1972–1988," Paper prepared for the Conference on the Economics of Higher Education (May 1991); Robert M. Hauser and Hanam Samuel Phang, *Trends in High School Dropout among White, Black and Hispanic Youth, 1973 to 1979,* University of Wisconsin, Institute for Research on Poverty, Discussion Paper 1007-93 (1993).

10. Christopher Jencks, *Rethinking Social Policy: Race, Poverty and the Underclass,* 37–38 (1992).

11. U.S. Census Bureau, *Current Population Reports,* 60-184, Table 29, 123, 127 (1993). These comparisons are for all women workers. Black women who worked full time and year-round earned slightly less than their white counterparts.

12. U.S. Census Bureau, *Current Population Reports,* P60-174, 198 (1993).

13. Richard G. Niemi, John Mueller, and Tom W. Smith, *Trends in Public Opinion: A Compendium of Survey Data,* 171 (1989).

14. Thomas DiPrete and David Grusky, "Structure and Stratification for American Men and Women," 96 *American Journal of Sociology,* 107 (1990).

15. *Adarand Constructors, Inc. v. Pena,* 115 S. Ct. 2097 (1995).

16. Jonathan S. Leonard, "The Impact of Affirmative Action Regulation and Equal Employment Law on Black Employment," 4 *Journal of Economic Perspectives,* 47 (1990).

17. James Smith, "Affirmative Action and the Racial Wage Gap," 83 *American Economic Review: Papers and Proceedings,* 80 (May 1993).

18. Ibid.

19. John Bound and Richard B. Freeman, "What Went Wrong? The Erosion of Relative Earnings and Employment among Young Black Men in the 1980s," 107 *Quarterly Journal of Economics,* 201 (1992).

20. Christopher Jencks, "Affirmative Action or Quotas?" in Jencks, *Rethinking Social Policy,* 54–56.

21. U.S. Census Bureau, *Current Population Reports,* 20-471, 52 (March 1992). Even annual earnings figures do not fully capture the economic predicament of blacks, because they do not include individuals who drop out of the work force entirely. In this respect, the situation seems to have deteriorated over the past half-century. In 1940, over a 45-year work career, black men spent about the same amount of time in the work force as whites. By 1985, according to the prevailing patterns of work, white men could expect to be employed for an average of 35.6 years out of the next 45, whereas blacks would work full time for an average of only 29.4 years. Jaynes and Williams, *A Common Destiny,* 306.

22. Barbara Reskin and Patricia Roos, *Job Queues, Gender Queues: Explaining Women's Inroads into Male Occupations* (1990).

23. Cynthia Costello and Anne J. Stone (eds.), *The American Woman, 1994–95: Where We Stand, Women and Health,* Table 3-10 (1994).

24. Bureau of Labor Statistics, U.S. Department of Labor, 19 *Employment and Earnings,* 134 (January 1973).

25. Bureau of Labor Statistics, U.S. Department of Labor, 42 *Employment and Earnings,* 175 (January 1995).

26. See, e.g., June O'Neill, "Women and Wages," 1 *The American Enterprise,* 24–33 (November–December 1990).

27. Ibid.; Jane Waldfogel, "Women Working for Less: Family Status and Women's Pay in the U.S. and U.K." (Ph.D. diss., Harvard University, 1994).

28. Francine D. Blau and Lawrence M. Kahn, *The Gender Earnings Gap: Some International Evidence,* National Bureau of Economic Research (September 1991; revised, November 1992), Figure 1.

29. Ibid.

30. Pamela J. Loprest, "Gender Differences in Wage Growth and Job Mobility," 82 *American Economic Review,* Supp., 526 (May 1992).

31. See Reskin and Roos, *Job Queues, Gender Queues.*

32. Waldfogel, "Women Working for Less"; Victor R. Fuchs, *Women's Quest for Economic Equality,* 62 (1988).

33. Ibid.

34. E.g., Robert Hauser et al., "Structural Changes in Occupational Mobility among Men in the United States," 40 *American Sociological Review,* 279 (1975).

35. Michael Hout, "More Universalism, Less Structural Mobility: The American Occupational Structure in the 1980s," 93 *American Journal of Sociology,* 1358 (1988).

36. William Julius Wilson, *The Truly Disadvantaged* (1987).

37. Lawrence Mead, *The New Politics of Poverty,* 137 (1992).

38. Thomas Sowell, *Race and Economics* (1975); Sowell, *Markets and Minorities* (1981); Sowell, *The Economics and Politics of Race* (1983).

39. For a thorough review of the literature, see Christopher Jencks and Susan Mayer, "The Social Consequences of Growing Up in a Poor Neighborhood," in Laurence E. Lynn and Michael G. H. McGeary (eds.), *Inner-City Poverty in the United States,* 111 (1990).

40. See James E. Rosenbaum, "Housing Mobility Strategies for Changing the Geography of Opportunity," unpublished paper (March 9, 1994).

41. See, e.g., Linda Datcher, "Effects of Community and Family Background on Achievement," 64 *Review of Economics and Statistics,* 32 (1982); Mary Corcoran, Roger Gordon, Deborah Laren, and Gary Solon, "Effects of Family and Community Background on Economic Status," 80 *American Economic Review* (Papers and Proceedings), 362 (May 1990).

42. Ronald Ferguson, "Paying for Public Education: New Evidence on How and Why Money Matters," 28 *Harvard Journal on Legislation,* 465 (1991).

43. Roderick J. Harrison and Claudette E. Bennett, "Racial and Ethnic Diversity," in Reynolds Farley (ed.), *State of the Union,* vol. 2: *Social Trends,* 141, 199 (1995).

44. Hout, "More Universalism, Less Structural Mobility," 1389.

45. Hauser and Phang, "Trends in High School Dropout among White, Black and Hispanic Youth."

46. William Sewell and Vimal Shah, "Socioeconomic Status, Intelligence, and the Attainment of Higher Education," in Jerome Karabel and A. H. Halsey (eds.), *Power and Ideology in Education,* 197 (1977).

47. Hauser and Phang, "Trends in High School Dropout among White, Black, and Hispanic Youth."

48. Sewell and Shah, *Power and Ideology in Education.*

49. Hout, "More Universalism, Less Structural Mobility."

50. See Thomas G. Mortenson and Zhijun Wu, *High School Graduation and College Participation of Young Adults by Family Income Backgrounds, 1970 to 1989* (1990).

51. Ibid., xxiii, 79.

52. DiPrete and Grusky, "Structure and Stratification for American Men and Women."

53. Katherine Newman, *Declining Fortunes: The Withering of the American Dream* (1993).

54. Ibid.

55. "How Fares the American Dream?" 6 *The Public Perspective,* 57 (June–July 1995).

56. Ibid.

57. "Mobility in America: Up, Down and Standing Still," *The Economist,* 30, 33 (February 24, 1996).

58. John Sabelhaus and Joyce Manchester, "Baby Boomers and Their Parents:

How Does Their Economic Well-Being Compare in Middle Age?" 30 *Journal of Human Resources,* 791 (1995).

59. Ibid., 795.

60. From 1983 to 1993, the greatest amount of job growth in the economy (29.1 percent of all new positions) took place in occupations with earnings in the highest quartile. Behind these figures lie above-average growth in some of the most desirable, lucrative callings, including managers and administrators (up 28.8 percent), lawyers, doctors, and other professionals (up 34.7 percent), and technicians (up 27.3 percent). Because of the "hollowing out" of the economy, however, the next largest increase in jobs took place among occupations in the fourth or bottom quartile of earnings, where 28 percent of total job growth occurred. The third quartile grew the least—only 18.3 percent of total job growth—reflecting the decline of manufacturing jobs. Neal H. Rosenthal, "The Nature of Occupational Employment Growth, 1983–1993," *BNA Daily Labor Report* (July 6, 1995).

61. George T. Silvestri, "Occupational Employment: Wide Variations in Growth," in Bureau of Labor Statistics, *The American Work Force, 1992–2005,* 56 (1994).

62. Nicholas Zill and Christine Nord, *Running in Place,* 26 (1994).

11. Violent Crime

1. Times Mirror Center for the People and the Press, *Voter Anxiety Dividing GOP; Energized Democrats Backing Clinton,* 1 (November 14, 1995).

2. Haynes Johnson, *Divided We Fall: Gambling with History in the Nineties,* 17–18 (1995).

3. Department of Justice, Federal Bureau of Investigation, *Crime in the United States, 1991: Uniform Crime Reports* (1992).

4. U.S. Department of Justice, Federal Bureau of Investigation, *Crime in the United States, 1990: Uniform Crime Reports,* 7 (1991).

5. Department of Justice, *Report to the Nation on Crime and Justice,* 28 (1988).

6. Department of Justice, *Report to the Nation on Crime and Justice,* 29 (1988).

7. George Gallup, Jr., *The Gallup Poll: Public Opinion, 1993,* 207 (1994). The percentage of people expressing such fear rose from 34 percent in 1965 to 42 percent in 1972, and has fluctuated between 40 and 45 percent ever since.

8. Jerald G. Bachman, Lloyd D. Johnston, and Patrick M. O'Malley, *Monitoring the Future, 1990* (1991).

9. Johnson, *Divided We Fall,* 300.

10. National Research Council, Albert Reiss, Jr., and Jeffrey A. Roth (eds.),

Understanding and Preventing Violence, 50 (1993); Steven F. Messner and Richard Rosenfeld, *Crime and the American Dream*, 27–28 (1994).

11. Bureau of Justice Statistics, *Criminal Victimization in the United States, 1991*, 4 (1991).

12. Department of Justice, Federal Bureau of Investigation, *Crime in the United States, 1990: Uniform Crime Reports*, Table 1, 50 (1991).

13. See, e.g., Cheryl Russell, "True Crime," 17 *American Demographics*, 22 (1995).

14. David Farrington, James Q. Wilson, and Lloyd Ohlin, *Understanding and Controlling Crime: Toward a New Research Strategy*, 1 (1986).

15. Quoted in Elliott Currie, *Confronting Crime: An American Challenge*, 27 (1985).

16. Samuel Walker, *A Critical History of Police Reform: The Emergence of Professionalism* (1977).

17. George L. Kelling and Mark H. Moore, "The Evolving Strategy of Policing," *Perspectives on Policing*, 4 (November 1988).

18. Ted D. Westerman and James W. Burfeind, *Crime and Justice in Two Societies: Japan and the United States* (1991).

19. See Alfred Blumstein, "Prisons," in James Q. Wilson and Joan Petersilia (eds.), *Crime*, 387–389 (1995).

20. See, e.g., Joseph W. Rogers, "The Greatest Correctional Myth: Winning the War on Crime through Incarceration," 53 *Federal Probation*, 21 (September 1989); Kenneth F. Schoen, "Will Tougher Prison Terms Make Us Safer?" 22 *Focus*, 3 (February 1994); see, generally, Currie, *Confronting Crime*, 52–101.

21. In 1993, the percentage of persons arrested who were incarcerated was as follows:

	U.S.	Canada	England	Germany
Robbery	49	52	48	23–58
Burglary	35	23	30	sc
Theft	18	14	14	4–9

Source: Erika Fairchild, *Comparative Criminal Justice Systems*, 200 (1993). See also James Lynch, "Crime in International Perspective," in Wilson and Petersilia (eds.), *Crime*, 32–33 (1995).

22. See Lynch, "Crime in International Perspective," 33–35.

23. John DiIulio, "Arresting Ideas: Tougher Law Enforcement Is Driving Down Urban Crime," 74 *Policy Review*, 12, 14 (Fall 1995).

24. National Commission on the Causes and Prevention of Violence, *To Establish Justice, To Insure Domestic Tranquility: Final Report*, 44–45 (1969).

25. Robert K. Merton, "Social Structure and Anomie," 3 *American Sociological Review*, 672 (1938).

26. Steven Messner and Richard Rosenfeld, *Crime and the American Dream*, 68 (1994).

27. Many of these studies are discussed by Richard B. Freeman, "The Labor Market," in Wilson and Petersilia (eds.), *Crime*, 171 (1995). See also Philip J. Cook and Gary A. Zarkin, "Crime and the Business Cycle," 14 *Journal of Legal Studies*, 115 (1985); Richard B. Freeman, "Crime and Unemployment," in James Q. Wilson (ed.), *Crime and Public Policy* 90 (1983).

28. Jan van Dijk, Pat Mayhew, and Martin Killias, *Experiences of Crime across the World: Key Findings of the 1989 International Crime Survey* (1990).

29. Kathleen Maguire and Timothy Flanagan (eds.), Department of Justice, *Sourcebook of Criminal Justice: Statistics, 1990*, 2 (1991).

30. See, e.g., Jeffrey Fagan, "Intoxication and Aggression," in Michael Tonry and James Q. Wilson (eds.), *Drugs and Crime*, 241 (1990).

31. See, e.g., Jan Chaiken and Marcia Chaiken, "Drugs and Predatory Crime," in Tonry and Wilson (eds.), *Drugs and Crime*, 203 (1990).

32. David Hamburg, *Today's Children: Creating a Future for a Generation in Crisis*, 192 (1992).

33. American Psychological Association, *Violence and Youth: Psychology's Response*, 32 (1993); Sissela Bok, *TV Violence, Children and the Press: Eight Rationales Inhibiting Public Policy Debates*, 2 (1994).

34. Reported in Nic Nilsson, "Children and the Commercial Exploitation of Violence in Sweden," Svenska Institutet, *Current Sweden*, 6 (October 1991).

35. L. Heath, L. B. Bresolin, and R. C. Rinaldi, "Effects of Media Violence on Children," 46 *Archives of General Psychiatry*, 376 (1989); L. R. Huesmann and L. S. Miller, "Long Term Effects of Repeated Exposure to Media Violence in Childhood," in G. Comstock (ed.), 3 *Public Communication and Behavior* (1986).

36. Brandon S. Centerwall, "Television and Violent Crime," 111 *The Public Interest*, 56 (Spring 1993).

37. Ibid.

38. See, generally, Edward Donnerstein and Daniel Linz, "The Media," in Wilson and Petersilia (eds.), *Crime*, 237 (1995).

39. See, e.g., Nilsson, "Children and the Commercial Exploitation of Violence in Sweden."

40. National Rifle Association, *Firearms Fact Card, 1990* (1990).

41. See Lynch, "Crime in International Perspective," 11, 22–23.

42. Nancy Gibbs, "Shameful Bequests to the Next Generation," *Time*, 42 (October 8, 1990).

43. See Lynch, "Crime in International Perspective," 11, 22–23.

44. John H. Sloan, Arthur L. Kellerman, Donald T. Rey, et al., "Handgun Reg-

ulations, Crimes, Assaults and Homicide: A Tale of Two Cities," 319 *New England Journal of Medicine,* 1256 (1988).

45. James D. Wright, "Second Thoughts about Gun Control," 91 *Public Interest,* 23, 26 (Spring 1988).

46. President Bill Clinton, 30 *Compilation of Presidential Documents,* 1697 (August 21, 1994).

47. See, e.g., Steven Duke, "Clinton and Crime," 10 *Yale Journal on Regulation,* 575 (Summer 1993), discussing many of the proposals in the Crime Bill; Wendy Kaminer, "Federal Offense," *Atlantic Monthly,* 102 (June 1994).

48. Cynthia McKinney, *USA Today,* 10A (August 23, 1994).

49. National Research Council, Albert Reiss, Jr., and Jeffrey A. Roth (eds.), *Understanding and Preventing Violence,* 345–352 (1993).

50. Alfred Blumstein and Joan Petersilia, "Investing in Criminal Justice Research," in Wilson and Petersilia (eds.), *Crime,* 465 (1995).

12. Health Care

1. Quoted in Michael Wines, "At the Capitol, Selling Health Plans Like Snake Oil," *New York Times,* A24 (October 28, 1993).

2. William C. Hsiao, "Comparing Health Care Systems: What Nations Can Learn from One Another," 17 *Journal of Health Politics, Policy and Law,* 613 (1992); OECD, *The Reform of Health Care: A Comparative Analysis of Seven OECD Countries* (1992).

3. For a history of the development of American health care policy, see Paul Starr, *The Social Transformation of Medicine* (1982).

4. *The President's Health Security Plan* (1993).

5. OECD, *Health Care Systems in Transition: The Search for Efficiency,* 96 (1990).

6. Goran Berleen, Clas Rehnberg, and Gunnar Wenstrom, *The Reform of Health Care in Sweden,* 37 (1993).

7. OECD, *The Reform of Health Care: A Comparative Analysis of Seven OECD Countries,* 120 (1992).

8. OECD, *OECD Health Systems: Facts and Trends, 1960–1991,* vol. 1, 194 (1993); Hsiao, "Comparing Health Care Systems," 613.

9. Hsiao, "Comparing Health Care Systems," 630–632.

10. Robert J. Blendon et al., "Who Has the Best Health Care System? A Second Look," unpublished paper (1995).

11. John P. Bunker, Howard S. Frazier, and Frederick Mosteller, "Improving Health: Measuring Effects of Medical Care," 72 *Milbank Quarterly,* 225 (1994).

12. *OECD Health Systems: Facts and Trends, 1960–1991,* 76 (1993).

13. Blendon et al., "Who Has the Best Health Care System?"

14. See, e.g., Joseph White, *Competing Solutions: American Health Care Proposals and International Experience* (1995).

15. OECD, Health Policy Studies 1, *U.S. Health Care at the Cross-Roads*, 94 (1992).

16. Victor G. Rodwin et al., "Louis Mourier and Coney Island Hospital: A Comparative Analysis of Hospital Staffing and Performance," in Victor G. Rodwin et al. (eds.), *Public Hospital Systems in New York and Paris*, 38 (1992).

17. Mark R. Chassin et al., "Does Inappropriate Use Explain Variations in the Use of Health Care Services?" 258 *Journal of the American Medical Association*, 2533 (November 13, 1987); Ritt Brook and M. E. Vaina, *Appropriateness of Care: A Chartbook* (1989). Malpractice suits and the costs of defensive medicine are often cited as a further cause of high health care expenditures. According to the General Accounting Office, however, malpractice premiums add only 1 percent to total U.S. health costs. At the same time, the American Medical Association has estimated that an additional $20 billion is expended in unnecessary (or defensive) tests and procedures designed to minimize the risk of malpractice suits.

18. Simon Kuznets and Milton Friedman, *Income from Independent Professional Practice* (1945).

19. General Accounting Office, Report to the Chairman, Subcommittee on Human Resources and Intergovernmental Relations, House of Representatives, *Vulnerable Payers Lose Billions to Fraud and Abuse* (May 1992).

20. OECD, *U.S. Health Care at the Cross-Roads*, 33 (1992).

21. Regina E. Herzlinger, "Healthy Competition," *Atlantic Monthly*, 69 (August 1991).

22. See Kaiser Commission on the Future of Medicaid, *Medicaid at the Crossroads* (1992).

23. Marc Roberts, *Your Money or Your Life: The Health Care Crisis Explained*, 4 (1993).

24. Ibid., 5.

25. Ibid., 6.

26. Howard E. Freeman, et al., "Americans Report on Their Access to Health Care," *Health Affairs*, 6, 10 (Spring 1987).

27. Ibid., 13.

28. Robert J. Blendon et al., "Satisfaction with Health Systems in Ten Nations," 9 *Health Affairs*, 185, 188 (Summer 1990).

29. L. K. Harvey and S. C. Shubert, AMA Surveys of *Physician and Public Opinion on Health Care Issues, 1990* (1990); C. E. Lewis, D. M. Prout, E. P. Chalmers, and B. Lecke, "How Satisfying Is the Practice of Internal Medicine? A National Survey," 114 *Annals of Internal Medicine*, 1 (1991).

30. Quoted in James A. Morone, *The Democratic Wish: Popular Participation and the Limits of American Government*, 256–257 (1990).

31. Ibid.

32. Loretta McLaughlin, "The Real Debate about Health Care Is about the Most Basic Principles," *Boston Globe* (May 30, 1993).

33. See, e.g., Robert J. Blendon, "The Gridlock Is Us," *New York Times* (May 22, 1994); "The American Public and the Critical Choices for Health System Reform," 271 *Journal of the American Medical Association,* 1539 (1994).

34. Nationwide poll conducted September 7–8, 1993 by KRC Communications, Inc., for the *Boston Globe* and the Harvard School of Public Health, "Health Insurance Report Card," *Boston Sunday Globe,* 14 (September 13, 1993).

13. Regulating the Workplace

1. Derek C. Bok, "Reflections on the Distinctive Character of American Labor Laws," 84 *Harvard Law Review,* 1394 (1971); T. Hanami and R. Blanpain (eds.), *Industrial Conflict Resolution in Market Economies: A Study of Canada, Great Britain and Sweden* (1987).

2. Derek Bok, "The Regulation of Campaign Tactics In Representation Elections under the National Labor Relations Act," 78 *Harvard Law Review,* 38 (1964).

3. Craig Riddell, "Unionization in Canada and the United States: A Tale of Two Countries," unpublished paper prepared for the U.S. and Canada Labor Markets Project (October 1992).

4. U.S. Department of Labor and U.S. Department of Commerce, *Fact Finding Report of Commission on the Future of Worker-Management Relations,* Exhibit III-4 (May 1994).

5. Ibid., Exhibit III-4.

6. Ibid., 70.

7. Fingerhut-Powers National Labor Poll, reported in Richard Freeman and Joel Rogers, *Who Speaks for Us? Employee Representation in a Non-Union Labor Market,* 12 (October 1992).

8. 1991 Fingerhut-Powers National Labor Poll, reported in Freeman and Rogers, *Who Speaks for Us?*

9. See, e.g., Freeman and Rogers, *Who Speaks for Us?* 21–28.

10. 1988 Gallup Study of Public Knowledge and Opinion Concerning the Labor Movement, quoted in Freeman and Rogers, *Who Speaks for Us?* Exhibit 4.

11. Freeman and Rogers, *Who Speaks for Us?* Exhibit 6.

12. Jack Stieber, "Employment-at-Will: An Issue for the 1980s," Bureau of National Affairs, 2 *Daily Labor Report,* D-1 (January 5, 1984).

13. Clyde W. Summers, "An American Perspective of the German Model of Worker Participation," 8 *Comparative Labor Law Journal,* 333, 334 (1987). See also Hoyt N. Wheeler and Jacques Rojot (eds.), *Workplace Justice: Employment Obligations in International Perspective* (1992).

14. See B. Hepple, *Industrial Tribunals* (1987).
15. Fumito Komiya, "Dismissal Procedures and Termination Benefits in Japan," 12 *Comparative Labor Law Journal,* 151 (1991).
16. Howard A. Levitt, *The Law of Dismissal in Canada* (2nd ed., 1990).
17. New York Times reporters published estimates suggesting that the number of employees laid off had increased substantially in the 1990s, but these estimates have been heavily criticized and should not be considered reliable. Louis Uchitelle and N. R. Kleinfield, "On the Battlefield of Business, Numerous Casualties," *New York Times,* 1, 27 (March 3, 1996).
18. Ibid., 27.
19. A ranking compiled by OECD from four different international studies places the United States as the least strict in employment protection regulations among twenty-one nations. *The OECD Jobs Study,* Part 2: *The Adjustment Potential of the Labour Market,* Table 6.7, 74 (1994).
20. Katherine G. Abraham and Susan N. Houseman, *Job Security in America: Lessons from Germany* (1993).
21. Tadashi A. Hanami, "Japan," in Edward Yemin (ed.), *Workforce Reductions in Undertakings: Policies and Measures for the Protection of Redundant Workers in Seven Industrialized Market Economy Countries,* 169 (1982); Koji Taira and Solomon B. Levine, "Employment Flexibility and Joblessness in Low-Growth, Restructured Japan," 544 *Annals of AAPSS,* 140 (March 1996).
22. See, e.g., Sylvia Nasar, "Layoff Law Is Almost Nil," *New York Times,* D1 (August 9, 1993).
23. Committee on Labor and Human Resources, United States Senate, Subcommittee on Labor, *Hearing Examining; The Coverage, Compliance and Enforcement of the WARN Act, February 23, 1993* (1993).
24. General Accounting Office, *Unemployment Insurance Program's Ability to Meet Objectives Jeopardized,* 43 GAO/GHRD 93-107 (September 1993). The following summary of unemployment benefits, prepared by the Congressional Research Service in 1992, makes these differences clear.

Country	Total weekly benefit in dollars (family of 4)	Duration	Percent of wages replaced	Percent of all unemployed workers assisted
Canada	360	35–50 wks.	60	80
France	420	8 mos.	40	55–72
Germany	620	12 mos.	63–68	39–68
Japan	390	6 mos.	60–80	—
Sweden	—	15 mos.	80	—
U.K.	370	12 mos.	36	32–90
U.S.	150–380	6 mos.		34

In column 1, the figure for the United States varies according to the state. In column 2, the duration of benefits in France, Germany, Japan, and Sweden was extended for older workers; in the United States, it was extended when unemployment exceeded a stipulated level. In column 4, unemployed workers may not have received assistance because they were ineligible, because they had exhausted their benefits, because they did not realize that they were eligible, or because they did not choose to claim benefits. In the case of France, Germany, and the United Kingdom, the higher figure includes employees claiming unemployment assistance—a lower sum given typically to workers who have exhausted their unemployment insurance benefits. See Congressional Research Service, *Unemployment Compensation in the Group of Seven Nations: An International Comparison* (April 1992).

25. Paul T. Decker and Walter Corson, "International Trade and Worker Displacement: Evaluation of the Trade Adjustment Assistance Program," 48 *Industrial and Labor Relations Review* (July 1995).

26. Louis Jacobson, Robert J. Lalonde, and Daniel Sullivan, *The Costs of Worker Dislocation* (1993).

27. Terry Moe, "The Politics of Bureaucratic Structure," in John Chubb and Paul Peterson (eds.), *Can the Government Govern?* (1989).

28. Thomas O. McGarity and Sidney A. Shapiro, *Workers at Risk: The Failed Promise of the Occupational Health and Safety Administration* (1993).

29. Commission on the Future of Worker-Management Relations, *Report and Recommendations*, 44, 54 (December 1994).

30. General Accounting Office, *Options for Improving Safety and Health in the Workplace*, GAO/HRD 90-66BR, 2 (August 1990).

31. General Accounting Office, *Occupational Safety and Health: OSHA Action Needed to Improve Compliance with Hazard Communication Standard*, 3, GAO/HRD, 92-88 (November 1991).

32. See, e.g., Steven Kelman, *Regulating America, Regulating Sweden: A Comparative Study of Occupational Safety and Health Policy* (1981).

33. The various studies are reviewed in McGarity and Shapiro, *Workers at Risk*. A somewhat more favorable account is provided by Wayne B. Gray and John T. Scholz, "Does Regulatory Enforcement Work? A Panel Analysis of OSHA Enforcement," 27 *Law and Society Review*, 177 (1993). For an overall assessment of OSHA, see Charles Noble, *Liberalism at Work: The Rise and Fall of OSHA* (1986).

34. Richard Wokutch and Josetta McLaughlin, "The U.S. and Japanese Work Injury and Illness Experience," *Monthly Labor Review*, 3 (April 1992).

35. Richard Wokutch, *Worker Protection, Japanese Style*, 208 (1992).

36. Ibid., 230.

37. OECD, "Occupational Illness in OECD Countries," in *Employment Outlook*, 105 (1990); see also OECD, *Employment Outlook* (1989), "Occu-

pational Accidents in OECD Countries," ch. 4. The National Safe Workplace Institute has sought to estimate the difference in fatality rates between the United States and several other industrial countries. Their results are reproduced below, although it is hard to know how reliable these figures are. The fatality rates are expressed as a percent of the U.S. rate.

Country	Fatality Rates
France	70.4
Germany	76.2
Japan	28.5
Sweden	17.1
United Kingdom	32.4

Source: Figures compiled by National Safe Workplace Institute and reproduced in McGarity and Shapiro, *Workers at Risk,* 5.

38. OECD, *Employment Outlook,* 143–146 (1989). Figures for the United States in these calculations go back only to the early 1970s, but this is unlikely to disadvantage America, since accident rates appear to have risen in this country throughout the 1960s.
39. President Bill Clinton and Vice-President Al Gore, *The New OSHA: Reinventing Worker Safety and Health,* B-1 (May 1995).
40. See, e.g., Rebecca Blank, "Does a Larger Social Safety Net Mean Less Economic Flexibility," in Richard B. Freeman (ed.), *Working under Different Rules,* 57 (1994); Abraham and Houseman, *Job Security in America.* McKinsey Global Institute, *Employment Performance,* ch. 2 (1994). The McKinsey study found that high minimum wages did retard employment in traditionally lower-paid industries, such as retailing, but that severance pay and other restrictions on terminating workers were not a significant factor in accounting for high unemployment and sluggish job creation in Europe.
41. McKinsey Global Institute, *Employment Performance,* ch. 2, p. 15.

14. The Burdens of Old Age

1. Quoted in Carole Haber and Brian Gratten, *Old Age and the Search for Security: An American Social History,* 128 (1994).
2. Ibid., 137.
3. Quoted in Martha Derthick, *Policymaking for Social Security,* 230 (1979).
4. *Helvering v. Davis,* 301 U.S. 619, 641 (1937).
5. Frank Schick and Renee Schick (eds.), *Statistical Handbook on Aging Americans, 1994 Edition,* Table E4-9, 250 (1994).

6. See, e.g., Samuel Preston, "Children and the Elderly: Divergent Paths for America's Dependents," 21 *Demography,* 435 (1984).
7. See Congressional Quarterly, Inc., *Social Security and Retirement: Private Goals, Public Policy* (1983).
8. See, e.g., General Accounting Office, "Elderly Americans, Health, Housing, and Nutrition Gaps between the Poor and Nonpoor," Report to the Chairman, House Select Committee on Aging, GAO-PEMD 92-29, 17–18 (1992).
9. Jack Meyer and Marilyn Moon, "Health Care Spending on Children and the Elderly," in John L. Palmer, Timothy Smeeding, and Barbara Boyle Torrey (eds.), *The Vulnerable,* 184–185 (1988).
10. General Accounting Office, "Elderly Americans," 30.
11. Ibid., 7.
12. According to the General Accounting Office, the elderly poor were spending 20 percent of their own income for medical care in the late 1980s, compared with 13 percent for older people who were not poor. "Elderly Americans," GAO-PEMD 92-29.
13. Urban Institute, "Hunger and Food Insecurity among the Elderly," *Policy and Research Report,* 4–5 (Fall 1993). A figure of 24.9 percent is given for 1984 in Christopher Jencks and Barbara Torrey, "Beyond Income and Poverty: Trends in Social Welfare among Children and Elderly since 1960," in Palmer, Smeeding, and Torrey (eds.), *The Vulnerable,* 229, 233. According to the General Accounting Office, "There is wide consensus that poor elderly persons are at risk for having inadequate nutritional intake. Data from national surveys corroborate this view by confirming that poor elderly persons consume less of some essential nutrients than nonpoor elderly persons and also are likely to consume less than RDA (recommended daily allowance). However, these data are limited in numerous ways and improvements in the scope of elderly nutritional data are needed before definitive conclusions can be drawn." "Elderly Americans," 37.
14. Joshua Wiener, Laurel H. Hixon, and Raymond J. Hanly, *Sharing the Burden: Strategies for Public and Private Long-Term Care Insurance,* 6 (1994); C. Eugene Steuerle and Jon M. Bakija, *Retooling Social Security for the 21st Century: Right and Wrong Approaches to Reform* (1994).
15. Joshua Wiener and Laurel H. Hixon, "Long-Term Care Reform in the 1990s: A Perspective from the United States," paper prepared for OECD conference, 6 (July 5–6, 1994).
16. Ibid., 7; see also Steuerle and Bakija, *Retooling Social Security for the 21st Century.*
17. Congressional Quarterly, Inc., *Aging in America: The Federal Government's Role,* 81 (1989).
18. Karen Holden and Timothy Smeeding, "The Poor, the Rich, and the Insecure Elderly Caught in Between," 68 *Milbank Quarterly,* 191, 195–196 (1990).

19. See, e.g., Peter Peterson, *Facing Up: Paying Our Nation's Debt and Saving Our Children's Future,* 90, 122–125 (1994). Such concerns are not unique to the United States. See World Bank Study, *Averting the Old Age Crisis: Policies to Protect the Old and Promote Growth* (1994).
20. James Jones, "Aging and Generational Equity: An American Perspective," paper given in Paris for seminar on aging (1988).
21. E.g., Caroline Weaver, "Social Security Reform after the 1983 Amendments: What Remains To Be Done?" paper delivered at meetings of the Eastern Economic Association, Boston, Massachusetts (March 18–20, 1994).
22. E.g., Robert Myers, "Social Security: It Ain't Broke Badly, So Adjust It," *Contingencies* (January–February 1995); Peter Diamond, "The Future of Social Security," Nemmers Prize Professorship Inaugural Lecture (April 19, 1995).
23. Henry Aaron, Barry Bosworth, and Gary Burtless, *Can America Afford to Grow Old? Paying for Social Security* (1989).
24. See, e.g., John B. Williamson and Fred C. Pampel, *Old-Age Security in Comparative Perspective* (1993).
25. Timothy Smeeding and Barbara Boyle Torrey, "An International Perspective on the Income and Poverty Status of the U.S. Aged," *Economic Outlook USA,* 13, 19 (1988).
26. OECD, *Caring for Frail Elderly People: New Direction in Care* (1994).
27. See 18 *World Opinion Update,* Issue 5, 57 (May 1994).
28. Times Mirror Center for the People and the Press, *Voter Anxiety Dividing GOP; Energized Democrats Backing Clinton,* 94 (November 14, 1995).
29. E.g., Paul Sniderman and R. A. Brody, "Coping: The Ethics of Self-Reliance," 21 *American Journal of Political Science,* 501 (1977); Daniel Yankelovich, *Putting the Work Ethic to Work: A Public Agenda Report on Restoring America's Competitive Vitality,* 19–24 (1993). Based on extensive surveys, Yankelovich finds that commitment to work remains strong in America, stronger than in other advanced Western democracies, but that managers have not succeeded in drawing on that commitment as effectively as they might.

15. Individual Freedom under Law

1. *Slaughter-House Cases,* 83 U.S. 36, 87 (1873) (dissenting opinion of Justice Field).
2. For example, *Lochner v. New York,* 198 U.S. 45 (1905).
3. E.g., *Debs v. United States,* 249 U.S. 211 (1919); *Whitney v. California,* 274 U.S. 357 (1927).
4. *United States v. Carolene Products Co.,* 304 U.S. 142, 152, note 4 (1938).
5. *Chaplinsky v. New Hampshire,* 315 U.S. 568 (1942).

6. E.g., *Rosenfeld v. New Jersey,* 408 U.S. 901 (1972); *Cohen v. California,* 403 U.S. 15 (1971).

7. *Near v. Minnesota,* 283 U.S. 697, 702 (1931).

8. *New York Times Co. v. United States,* 403 U.S. 713 (1971).

9. Ibid., 730.

10. *New York Times Co. v. Sullivan,* 376 U.S. 254 (1964).

11. *Baker v. Carr,* 369 U.S. 186 (1962); *Reynolds v. Sims,* 377 U.S. 533 (1964).

12. *Brown v. Board of Education,* 347 U.S. 483 (1954).

13. *Swann v. Charlotte-Mecklenburg Board of Education,* 402 U.S. 1 (1971).

14. *Pierce v. Society of Sisters,* 268 U.S. 510 (1925).

15. *Shapiro v. Thompson,* 394 U.S. 618 (1969).

16. *Schware v. Board of Bar Examiners of New Mexico,* 353 U.S. 232 (1957).

17. *Olmstead v. United States,* 277 U.S. 438, 478 (1928).

18. *Roe v. Wade,* 410 U.S. 113 (1973).

19. *Bowers v. Hardwick,* 478 U.S. 186 (1980).

20. *Gideon v. Wainwright,* 372 U.S. 355 (1963).

21. *Griffin v. California,* 380 U.S. 609 (1965); *Miranda v. Arizona,* 384 U.S. 346 (1966).

22. Recently, the Supreme Court has begun to limit the right of governments to issue regulations that diminish the value of land without paying compensation to the owners. See "Doland v. Tigard, Oregon," 62 *Law Week,* 4576 (June 21, 1994).

23. See V. Lee Hamilton and Joseph Sanders, *Everyday Justice: Responsibility and the Individual in Japan and the United States,* 61 (1992).

24. Another survey from 1991 lists the ratings of the countries as follows:

Country	Political-rights index	Civil-rights index
Canada	1.0	1.0
France	1.0	1.7
Japan	2.0	1.0
Sweden	1.1	1.0
United Kingdom	1.0	1.0
United States	1.0	1.0

Source: George Thomas Kurian, *The New Book of World Rankings,* 50–52 (3rd ed., 1991). Still another ranking, the Human Freedom Index of 1992 (on a 1–40 scale) gives Sweden, 38; France, 35; Germany, 35; Canada, 34; the United States, 33; and Japan and the United Kingdom, both 32. Michael Wolff, Peter Ruttan, and Albert F. Bayers III, *Where We Stand: Can America Make It in the Global Race for Wealth, Health and Happiness?* (1992). Both these rankings suffer from a failure to give details as to how the scores were computed.

25. Acknowledging the right to a speedy trial is not the same as actually providing such a trial. For example, in France suspected criminals sometimes

languish for many months in prison while the *juge d'instruction* gathers evidence.

26. With respect to matters of privacy, however, it is worth noting that the European Court of Human Rights has extended protection to private, consensual acts of sodomy, unlike the U.S. Supreme Court. See *Dudgeon v. United Kingdom*, 45-II Eur. Ct. of Hum. Rts. (Series A) (1981).

27. Nic Nilsson, "Children and the Commercial Exploitation of Violence in Sweden," Svenska Institutet, *Current Sweden* (October 1991).

28. Roger Errera, "Press Law in France," in Pnina Lahav (ed.), *Press Law in Modern Democracies* 137, 173–174 (1985); Håkon Strömberg, "Press Law in Sweden," ibid., 229, 240. See also Kent Greenawalt, "Free Speech in the United States and Canada," 55 *Law and Contemporary Problems,* 5 (1992).

29. See Mary Ann Glendon, *Rights Talk: The Impoverishment of Political Discourse* (1991).

30. *Eisenstadt v. Baird,* 405 U.S. 438, 453 (1972).

31. Quoted in Mary Ann Glendon, *Abortion and Divorce in Western Law,* 134 (1987).

32. Ibid., 70, 72, 74, 81–91 (1987).

33. Mary Ann Glendon, *Rights Talk: The Impoverishment of Political Discourse* (1991), 106–108.

34. Until a new Penal Code was enacted in 1994, it was actually a criminal offense in France to insult the president of the republic or a foreign head of state. See, generally, Roger Errera, "Press Law in France," in Pnina Lahav (ed.), *Press Law in Modern Democracies,* 137, 158 (1985).

35. See also Kyu Ho Youm, "Libel Law and the Press in Japan," 67 *Journalism Quarterly,* 1103 (Winter 1990).

36. *New York Times Co. v. United States,* 403 U.S. 713, 730 (1971).

37. The Supreme Court of Japan has declared unconstitutional legislative districts for election to the lower house of parliament in which there were very wide deviations in the number of voters per district. Hidenori Tomatsu, "Equal Protection of the Law," 53 *Law and Contemporary Problems,* 109 (Spring 1990).

38. Alexis de Tocqueville, *Democracy in America,* Vintage Classics Edition, vol. 1, 150 (1990).

39. Archibald Cox, *The Court and the Constitution,* 375 (1987).

40. A. P. Blaustein and G. H. Flanz (eds.), *Constitutions of the Countries of the World: Sweden,* 11 (1985).

41. *DeShaney v. Winnebago County Department of Social Services,* 489 U.S. 189, 195 (1989); see also *San Antonio Independent School District v. Rodriguez,* 411 U.S. 1 (1973).

42. See, e.g., Akira Osuka, "Welfare Rights," 53 *Law and Contemporary Problems,* 13 (Spring 1990).

43. *Webster v. Reproductive Health Services,* 492 U.S. 490 (1989). See also

"Resolving the Abortion Debate: Compromise Legislation, an Analysis of the Abortion Policies of the United States, France, and Germany," 16 *Suffolk Transnational Law Review,* 513 (1993).

44. Cass Sunstein, *Democracy and the Problem of Free Speech,* 70 (1993).
45. Decision of September 18, 1986, Conseil Constitutionnel Rec. C.C. 141, 1987 Actualité Juridique du Droit Administratif (ADAJ), 102 (Note Wachsmann).
46. Sunstein, *Democracy and the Problem of Free Speech,* 58.
47. *Buckley v. Valeo,* 424 U.S. 1 (1976).
48. See, e.g., Milton Friedman, *Capitalism and Freedom* (1962).
49. See, e.g., Robert E. Goodin, "Freedom and the Welfare State: Theoretical Foundations," 11 *Journal of Society and Politics,* 149 (1983).
50. Anthony Lester, "The Overseas Trade in the American Bill of Rights," 88 *Columbia Law Review,* 537, 541 (1988).
51. See, e.g., Margulies, "Resource Deprivation and the Right to Counsel," 80 *Journal of Criminal Law and Criminology,* 673, 679 (1989).

16. Personal Responsibility

1. Quoted in Digby Anderson (ed.), *The Loss of Virtue: Moral Confusion and Social Disorder in Britain and America,* xiii (1992).
2. William Bennett, "America at Midnight: Reflections on the Moynihan Report," *The American Enterprise,* 29, 32 (January–February 1995).
3. See, e.g., *The Gallup Poll: Public Opinion, 1993,* 168 (1993).
4. Eric Uslaner, *The Decline of Comity in Congress,* 79 (1993); *General Social Survey* (1993).
5. *The Public Perspective* (July–August 1993).
6. Roper Center for Public Opinion Research, *How Boomers' Opinions Differ from the Norm* (October–November 1994).
7. Department of Justice, *Criminal Victimization in the United States: 1973–92 Trends,* 9 (1993).
8. See Paul Holinger, *Violent Deaths in the United States: An Epidemiologic Study of Suicide, Homicide and Accidents* (1987).
9. Department of Justice, Federal Bureau of Investigation, *Uniform Crime Reports* (1960 to 1973).
10. Jan Van Dijk, Pat Mayhew, and Martin Killias, *Experiences of Crime across the World: Key Findings of the 1989 International Crime Survey,* 175 (1990).
11. A. H. Halsey (ed.), *British Social Trends since 1900,* 637 (1988); Dane Archer and Rosemary Gartner, *Violence and Crime in Cross-National Perspective* (1984).
12. Archer and Gartner, *Violence and Crime in Cross-National Perspective.* See

also National Council for Crime Prevention in Sweden, *Crime Trends in Sweden, 1988* (1990).

13. Archer and Gartner, *Violence and Crime in Cross-National Perspective;* Ted D. Westerman and James W. Burfeind, *Crime and Justice in Two Societies: Japan and the United States* (1991).

14. Internal Revenue Service, *Income Tax Compliance Research: Net Tax Gap and Remittance Gap Estimates,* 2 (1990).

15. Charles Christian, "Voluntary Compliance with the Individual Income Tax: Results from the 1988 TCMP Study," *IRS Research Bulletin, 1993–1994,* 35, 36.

16. National Highway Traffic Safety Administration, *Traffic Safety Facts, 1993,* 32 (1994).

17. Bureau of Justice Statistics, Special Report, "Drunk Driving," 2 (September 1992).

18. See Leonard Evans, "Alcohol's Rate in Traffic Crashes," in Evans, *Traffic Safety and the Driver,* 162, 182 (1991).

19. Fred Schab, "Schooling without Learning: Thirty Years of Cheating in High School," 26 *Adolescence,* 839, 843 (Winter 1991).

20. E.g., Donald McCabe, "The Influence of Situational Ethics on Cheating among College Students," 62 *Sociological Inquiry,* 365 (1992); John Baird, "Current Trends in College Cheating," 17 *Psychology in Schools,* 512 (1980).

21. Everett Ladd, The Myth of Moral Decline, *The Responsive Community,* 52, 62 (Winter 1993–1994).

22. Kathleen Maguire and Ann Pastore (eds.), Bureau of Justice Statistics, *Sourcebook of General Statistics, 1993,* 309.

23. Ibid., 308.

24. Ibid.

25. Ibid., 340.

26. Ibid., 338.

27. *Statistical Abstract of the United States* (1991); William J. Bennett, *Index of Leading Cultural Indicators,* 13 (1993).

28. E.g., Judith Wallerstein, "Children of Divorce: A Preliminary Report of a Ten Year Follow Up of Young Children," 54 *American Journal of Orthopsychiatry,* 444 (1994).

29. Cited in William J. Bennett, *Index of Leading Cultural Indicators,* 13 (1993).

30. Frank Furstenberg et al., "The Life Course of Children of Divorce: Marital Disruption and Parental Contact," 48 *American Sociological Review,* 667 (1983); William Mattox, "The Family Time Famine," 3 *Family Policy,* 90–91 (1990).

31. Gordon H. Lester, "Child Support and Alimony, 1989," *Current Population Reports,* Series P-60, no. 173, 3–4, 9 (1991).

32. See Sylvia Hewlett, *When the Bough Breaks: The Cost of Neglecting Our Children,* 73 (1991); Leonore Weitzmann, *The Divorce Revolution: The Unexpected Social and Economic Consequences for Women and Children in America* (1985); Sara McLanahan, "The Consequences of Single Motherhood," 18 *The American Prospect,* 48 (Summer 1994).

33. Lester, "Child Support and Alimony," 9.

34. Ibid.

35. Weitzmann, *The Divorce Revolution,* 295.

36. See Daniel Patrick Moynihan, "The Summer of '65: The Great Transformation," *The American Enterprise,* 38 (January–February 1995).

37. "Study Cites Adult Males for Most Teen-Age Births," *New York Times,* A-10 (August 2, 1995).

38. Alfred Kinsey, Wendell Pomeroy, and Clyde Martin, *Sexual Behavior in the Human Female,* ch. 10 (1953).

39. Edward Laumann, John Gagnon, Robert Michael, and Stuart Michaels, *The Social Organization of Sexuality: Sexual Practices in the United States,* 216 (1994).

40. Andrew Greeley, "Marital Infidelity," *Society,* 9 (May–June 1994). The survey includes persons currently or previously married.

41. Surveys show quite similar reported rates in Britain, France, and Denmark. Greeley, "Marital Infidelity," 10. Another investigator reports that Swedes probably have fewer extramarital affairs than Americans. Reiss, "Sexual Customs and Gender Roles in Sweden and America," in Helen Lopata (ed.), *The Interweave of Social Roles: Women and Men, A Research Annual,* vol. 1, 205–208 (1980).

42. Data compiled for me by Marc Miringoff, director of the Institute for Innovation in Social Policy, Fordham Graduate Center, based on figures collected by the American Association for Protecting Children and, after 1985, the National Committee for the Prevention of Child Abuse. The results are contained in a letter to me from Mr. Miringoff dated February 21, 1995.

43. Robert Pear, "Many States Fail to Meet Mandates on Child Welfare," *New York Times,* 1 (March 17, 1996).

44. Arland Thornton, "Changing Attitudes toward Family Issues in the United States," 51 *Journal of Marriage and the Family,* 873, 886 (1989); Peter Ester, Loek Hilman, and Ruud de Moor, *The Individualizing Society: Value Change in Europe and North America,* 103 (1993).

45. Thornton, "Changing Attitudes toward Family Issues in the United States," 881.

46. Ester, Holman, and de Moor, *The Individualizing Society,* 103.

47. Ibid.

48. Ibid.

49. *Statistical Abstract of the United States,* Table 455 (1993).
50. Ibid.
51. On the impact of registration laws on voting, see Ruy Teixeira, *The Disappearing American Voter* (1992).
52. G. Bingham Powell, Jr., "American Voting in Comparative Perspective," 80 *American Political Science Review,* 23 (1986).
53. See Richard Topf, "Electoral Participation," in Hans-Dieter Klingemann and Dieter Fuchs, *Citizens and the State,* 27 (1995).
54. Samuel Barnes, Max Kaase, et al., *Political Action: Mass Participation in Five Western Democracies,* 541–542 (1979).
55. Richard Topf, "Beyond Electoral Participation," in Hans-Dieter Klingemann and Dieter Fuchs (eds.), *Citizens and the State,* 52 (1995).
56. See Peter Halfpenny, "The 1991 International Survey of Giving," Susan K. E. Saxon-Harrold and Jeremy Kendall (eds.), *Researching the Voluntary Sector,* 207 (1993).
57. Virginia Hodgkinson et al., *Nonprofit Almanac, 1992–1993: Dimensions of the Independent Sector,* 50–52 (1992).
58. In fact, different studies report varying results for the percentage of income donated by different income groups. The findings are discussed by Christopher Jencks, "Who Gives What?" in Walter Powell (ed.), *The Nonprofit Sector,* 321 (1987).
59. Virginia Hodgkinson and Murray Weitzman, *Dimensions of the Independent Sector: A Statistical Profile,* 54 (1986); Virginia Hodgkinson et al., *Dimensions of the Independent Sector* (1992).
60. *Giving USA: The Annual Report on Philanthropy for the Year 1990,* 44 (1991); *Giving USA: The Annual Report on Philanthropy for the Year 1994,* 48 (1995); Hodgkinson et al., *Dimensions of the Independent Sector,* 61. There are numerous small discrepancies in the figures reported in the various sources, but the overall trends are clear.
61. Virginia Hodgkinson, Murray Weitzman, et al., *Giving and Volunteering in the United States,* 1994 (1994); see also Howard Hayghe, "Volunteers in the U.S.: Who Donates the Time?" *Monthly Labor Review,* 17–23 (February 1991).
62. Although international comparisons are scarce, recent reports find that Americans perform voluntary service at rates substantially greater than those of the British, French, or Spanish. Virginia Hodgkinson, Murray Weitzman, Christopher Topoe, and Stephen Noga, *Nonprofit America, 1992–93: Dimensions of the Independent Sector* (1992). See also Halfpenny, "The 1991 International Survey of Giving," 207, 215.
63. Robert Putnam, "Bowling Alone: America's Declining Social Capital," 6 *Journal of Democracy,* 65 (1995).

64. Ibid.
65. Hayghe, "Volunteers in the U.S."; see also Jeffrey Brudney, "The Availability of Volunteers," 21 *Administration and Society,* 413 (1990).
66. See Kees Aarts, "Intermediate Organizations and Interest Representation," in Klingemann and Fuchs, *Citizens and the State,* 227. Aarts finds that in some countries membership increases, in others it declines, and in still others it fluctuates without a clear trend.
67. Sidney Verba, Kay L. Schlozman, and Henry E. Brady, *Voice and Equality, Civic Voluntarism in American Politics,* 72 (1995); see, generally, 7 *The Public Perspective* 1–46 (June–July 1996).
68. Daniel Yankelovich, interviewed by Robert C. Welson, "America's Values Are Changing," in David L. Bender (ed.), *American Values: Opposing Viewpoints,* 110, 111 (1989).
69. David Popenoe, in Roper Center for Public Opinion Research, *The Public Perspective,* 22 (September–October 1992).
70. See Gertrude Himmelfarb, *The De-Moralization of Society From Victorian Virtues to Modern Values* (1995).
71. See, e.g., Duane Alwin, "From Obedience to Autonomy: Changes in Traits Desired in Children, 1924–1978," 52 *Public Opinion Quarterly,* 33 (1988). Alwin reports that the percentage of American mothers choosing "strict obedience" as one of three most desired traits in their children declined from 45.4 in 1924 to 16.8 in 1978, while the percentage choosing "independence" rose from 24.8 to 75.8.

17. Helping the Poor

1. *Bartlett's Familiar Quotations,* Justin Kaplan (ed.), 316 (16th ed., 1992).
2. Benedict (Baruch) Spinoza, *Ethics,* Appendix, 17 (1677).
3. Milton Friedman, *Capitalism and Freedom* (1962).
4. Everett Carll Ladd, *The American Ideology: An Exploration of the Origins, Meaning, and Role of "American Values",* 34 (1992); see also Hugh Heclo, "The Political Foundations of Antipoverty Policy," in Sheldon H. Danziger and Daniel H. Weinberg (eds.), *Fighting Poverty: What Works and What Doesn't,* 312 (1986).
5. James T. Patterson, *America's Struggle against Poverty, 1900–1980* (1981).
6. See, for example, National Research Council, *Measuring Poverty: A New Approach* (1995); Patricia Ruggles, *Drawing the Line: Alternative Poverty Measures and Their Implications for Public Policy* (1990). On page 167, Ruggles concludes that "poverty standards today, to be comparable in terms of their consumption implications to the original Orshansky thresholds, would have to be at least 50 percent higher than the official thresholds."
7. E.g., Susan E. Mayer, "Measuring Income: Employment and the Support of

Children," draft paper for Conference on Indicators of Children's Well-Being, Rockville, Md. (November 17–18, 1994).

8. Susan E. Mayer and Christopher Jencks, "Poverty and the Distribution of Material Hardship," 24 *Journal of Human Resources,* 88 (1989).

9. See Patterson, *America's Struggle against Poverty.*

10. For a succinct account of the evolution of federal antipoverty policies in the 1960s, 1970s and 1980s, see Mary Jo Bane and David T. Ellwood, *Welfare Realities: From Rhetoric to Reform* (1994).

11. See e.g., *Shapiro v. Thompson,* 394 U.S. 618 (1969).

12. Charles Murray, *Losing Ground: American Social Policy, 1950–1980* (1984).

13. Sheldon H. Danziger, Gary D. Sandefur, and Daniel H. Weinberg, *Confronting Poverty: Prescriptions for Change,* 49 (1994).

14. Christopher Jencks and Kathryn Edin, "Reforming Welfare," in Jencks, *Rethinking Social Policy: Race, Poverty, and the Underclass,* 204 (1992).

15. Robert Moffitt, "Incentive Effects of the U.S. Welfare System: A Review," 30 *Journal of Economic Literature,* 1 (1992).

16. Katherine McFate, Roger Lawson, and William Julius Wilson (eds.), *Poverty, Inequality, and the Future of Social Policy: Western States in the New World Order* (1995). See also Alfred J. Kahn and Sheila B. Kamerman, *Income Transfers for Families with Children: An Eight Country Study* (1983).

17. Greg J. Duncan et al., "Poverty and Social Assistance Dynamics in the United States, Canada, and Europe," in McFate, Lawson, and Wilson (eds.), *Poverty, Inequality, and the Future of Social Policy,* 84.

18. Constance Sorrentino, "The Changing Family in International Perspective," *Monthly Labor Review,* 53 (March 1990).

19. See Nadine Lefaucheur, "French Policies toward Lone Parents: Social Categories and Social Policies," in McFate, Lawson, and Wilson (eds.), *Poverty, Inequality and the Future of Social Policy,* 257, 278; Sid Gustaffson, "Single Mothers in Sweden: Why Is Poverty Less Severe?" in McFate, Lawson, and Wilson (eds.), *Poverty, Inequality and the Future of Social Policy,* 291, 306.

20. See e.g., Deborah Mitchell, *Income Transfers in Ten Welfare States* (1991); Timothy Smeeding, Michael O'Higgins, and Lee Rainwater (eds.), *Poverty, Inequality and Income Distribution in Comparative Perspective: The Luxembourg Income Study* (1990).

21. Tushiyuki Mizozuchi and Noriyuki Takayama, *Equity and Poverty under Rapid Economic Growth: The Japanese Experience,* 125 (1984).

22. The Luxembourg Study does take account of some items—notably food stamps and earned income tax credits—not included in the usual compilations of income. Nevertheless, it does not include other items—such as accumulated savings, gifts, and unreported income—that cause expenditures among poor families to be well above their official incomes.

23. Susan E. Mayer, "A Comparison of Poverty and Living Conditions in the United States, Canada, Sweden, and Germany," in McFate, Lawson, and Wilson (eds.), *Poverty, Inequality and the Future of Social Policy*, 109.
24. Richard V. Burkhauser, Douglas Holtz-Eakin, and Stephen E. Rhody, "Labor Earnings, Mobility and Inequality in the United States and Germany during the Growth Years of the 1980s," Unpublished paper (February 1996).
25. The various studies of the effect of welfare on work suggest that AFDC payments and other means-tested benefits may reduce the hours per week worked by recipients between 10 and 50 percent—that is, between 1 and 9.8 hours per week. Since few recipients could rise above the AFDC eligibility cutoff even if they worked an additional 10 hours per week, current welfare disincentives do not appear to add significantly to the total AFDC caseload. See Robert Moffitt, "Incentive Effects of the U.S. Welfare System: A Review," 30 *Journal of Economic Literature*, 1, 16–17 (1992).
26. E.g., Gordon Berlin and Andrew Sum, *Toward a More Perfect Union: Basic Skills, Poor Families, and Our Economic Future* (1988).
27. William Julius Wilson, *The Truly Disadvantaged: The Inner City, the Underclass, and Public Policy* (1987).
28. Christopher Jencks and Kathryn Edin, "Do Poor Women Have a Right to Bear Children?" *The American Prospect*, 43 (Winter 1995).
29. Lawrence Mead, *The New Politics of Poverty: The Nonworking Poor in America* (1992); Myron Magnet, *The Dream and the Nightmare: The Sixties' Legacy to the Underclass* (1993).
30. See Mead, *The New Politics of Poverty*. For a contrary view, see Richard Freeman, "Employment and Earnings of Disadvantaged Young Men in a Labor Shortage Economy," in Christopher Jencks and Paul Peterson (eds.), *The Urban Underclass*, 119 (1991).
31. Christopher Jencks, "Is the American Underclass Growing?" in Jencks and Peterson (eds.), *The Urban Underclass*, 28, 37 (1991).
32. In interpreting this figure one should bear in mind that according to a GAO study, 38.2 percent of those not receiving food stamps in 1987 indicated that they did not need such assistance. But 36.8 percent said that they did not know about food stamps or did not think they were eligible, while 25 percent were deterred by "administrative hassles," complications in applying, or because they were erroneously told that they were not eligible. General Accounting Office, *Food Stamp Program: A Demographic Analysis of Participation and Non-Participation*, GAO-PEMD 90-8, 16 (January 1990).
33. As Mary Jo Bane and David T. Ellwood have observed: "If we had an effective child support enforcement and insurance system, if we ensured that people got medical protection, if we made work pay, there would be far less need for welfare." *Welfare Realities: From Rhetoric to Reform*, 157 (1994).

34. See, e.g., Robert Moffitt, "Incentive Effects of the U.S. Welfare System: A Review," 30 *Journal of Economic Literature*, 1 (1992); Sharon Parrott and Robert Greenstein, *Welfare, Out-of-Wedlock Childbearing, and Poverty: What Is the Connection?* Center on Budget and Policy Priorities (1995). The latter study quotes a statement by seventy-six researchers on the subject: "Most research examining the effect of higher welfare benefits on out-of-wedlock childbearing and teen pregnancy finds that benefit levels have no significant effect on the likelihood that black women and girls will have children outside of marriage and either no significant effect, or only a small effect, on the likelihood that whites will have such births." Ibid., 17.
35. Nathan Weber (ed.), *Giving USA: The Annual Report on Philanthropy for the Year 1990*, 148 (1991).
36. Ibid.
37. Lester M. Salamon, *Partners in Public Service: Government-Nonprofit Relations in the Modern Welfare State* (1995).
38. Ibid., 163–165.
39. Mary Ann Glendon, *Rights Talk: The Impoverishment of Political Discourse* (1991).
40. Ibid., 143.
41. *King v. Smith*, 392 U.S. 309, 320 (1968).
42. See, e.g., Michael J. Horowitz, "Law and the Welfare State," in Peter L. Berger and John Neuhaus (eds.), *To Empower People: From State to Civil Society* (2nd ed.), 67 (1996).
43. Ibid.
44. *Olmstead v. United States*, 277 U.S. 438, 485 (1928).

18. Summing Up

1. See, e.g., Michael T. Robinson, "Public Affairs Television and the Growth of Political Malaise: The Case of 'The Selling of the Pentagon.' " 70 *American Political Science Review*, 409 (March 1976). See also Thomas Patterson, *Out of Order* (1994).
2. ABC News poll, September 1994, Roper Center at the University of Connecticut, *Public Opinion Online*, Accession number 0232474.
3. Times Mirror Center for the People and the Press, *The People, the Press and Politics: The New Political Landscape*, 27 (1994).
4. ABC News–Harris Poll, September 1979, quoted in Seymour Martin Lipset and William Schneider, *The Confidence Gap: Business, Labor, and Government in the Public Mind*, 390 (1983).
5. Richard B. Freeman (ed.), *Working under Different Rules*, 9 (1994).
6. William J. Baumol, Sue Anne Batey Blackman, and Edward N. Wolff, *Productivity and American Leadership: The Long View* (1989).

7. McKinsey Global Institute, *Manufacturing Productivity,* Executive Summary (October 1993), and *Service Sector Productivity,* Introduction and Summary, 3; ch. 4, 7 (October 1992).

8. Neal R. Peirce, *Citistates: How Urban America Can Prosper in a Competitive World,* 300 (1993).

9. Derek C. Bok, *The Cost of Talent: How Executives and Professionals Are Paid and How It Affects America,* 70–71 (1993).

10. E.g., McKinley Blackburn and David Bloom, "The Distribution of Family Income: Measuring and Explaining Changes in the 1980s for Canada and the United States," in David Card and Richard Freeman (eds.), *Small Differences That Matter: Labor Market and Income Maintenance in Canada and the United States,* 233 (1993).

11. McKinsey Global Institute, *Employment Performance,* ch. 2, 14; ch. 4, 12 (November 1994).

12. Richard B. Freeman, "Jobs in the USA: America Creates More Jobs than Europe but Are They Worth Having?" *New Economy,* 20 (1994).

13. Robert M. Solow, "Is All That European Unemployment Necessary?" Robbins Lecture, mimeo (1994).

14. Nickell and Bell, "Changes in the Distribution of Wages and Unemployment," 86 *American Economic Review (Papers and Proceedings),* 302 (1996).

15. McKinsey Global Institute, *Employment Performance* (1994).

16. See, e.g., Philip K. Howard, *The Death of Common Sense* (1994).

17. Michael J. Sandel, *Democracy's Discontent* (1996).

19. *Questioning the Verdict*

1. E.g., Elizabeth Hann Hastings and Philip K. Hastings, *Index to International Public Opinion, 1992–1993,* 202 (1994), and *1986–1987,* 224 (1988); but see idem, *1993–1994,* 198 (1995).

2. *OECD Jobs Study,* part 1: *Labour Market Trends and Underlying Forces of Change,* 27 (1995).

3. Data supplied to me by Archie LaPointe of the Educational Testing Service, Princeton, New Jersey.

4. Paul Kennedy, *The Rise and Fall of the Great Powers: Economic Change and Military Conflict from 1500 to 2000* (1987).

5. OECD, *Strategies for Member Countries* (June–July 1994).

6. Commission of the European Communities, *White Paper: Growth, Competitiveness, Employment—The Challenges and Ways Forward into the 21st Century,* Bulletin of the European Communities, 130 (1993).

7. See Paul Pierson, *Dismantling the Welfare State? Reagan, Thatcher and the Politics of Retrenchment* (1994).

8. See Christopher Pierson, *Beyond the Welfare State: The New Political Economy of Welfare* (1991).

9. See, e.g., M. Edith Rasell and Lawrence Mishel, "Shortchanging Education: How U.S. Spending on Grades K–12 Lags Behind Other Industrial Nations," Briefing paper, 1. See also Harold W. Stevenson and James W. Stigler, *The Learning Gap: Why Our Schools Are Failing and What We Can Learn from Japanese and Chinese Education* (1992).

10. Robert Blendon et al., "Satisfaction with Health Systems in Ten Nations," *Health Affairs* 185, 188 (Summer 1990).

20. The Role of Government

1. Karl Zinmeister, "Indicators," *The American Enterprise,* 16 (March–April 1995).

2. McKinsey Global Institute, *Manufacturing Productivity* (1993), Executive Summary; McKinsey Global Institute, *Service Sector Productivity,* Introduction and Summary, 3; ch. 4, 7 (1992).

3. Thomas E. Mann and Norman J. Ornstein, *Congress, the Press and the Public,* 34 (1994).

4. Ibid., 51.

5. Benjamin I. Page and Robert Y. Shapiro, "Effects of Public Opinion on Policy," 77 *American Political Science Review,* 75 (1983); Alan D. Monroe, "Consistency between Public Preferences and National Policy," 7 *American Politics Quarterly,* 3 (1985).

6. E.g., Joel E. Brooks, "Democratic Frustration in the Anglo-American Polities," 38 *Western Political Quarterly,* 250 (1985); Joel E. Brooks, "The Opinion-Policy Nexus in Germany," 54 *Public Opinion Quarterly,* 508 (1990).

7. E.g., Norman J. Ornstein, *The New Congress,* 382 (1981); George Will, *Restoration* (1992).

8. Seymour Martin Lipset and William Schneider, *The Confidence Gap: Business, Labor, and Government in the Public Mind,* 17 (1983).

9. E.g., Janet Grenske, "Shopping in the Congressional Supermarket: The Currency Is Complex," 33 *American Journal of Political Science,* 1 (1989); Gary Mucciaroni, *Reversals of Fortune: Public Policy and Private Interests* (1995); John P. Heinz et al., *The Hollow Core: Private Interests in National Policy Making* (1993).

10. Morris Fiorina, *Divided Government,* 105 (1992).

11. Hans-Dieter Klingemann, Richard L. Hofferbert, and Ian Budge, *Parties, Policies, and Democracy,* 153 (1994).

12. For innumerable examples, see Philip K. Howard, *The Death of Common Sense: How Law Is Suffocating America* (1994).

13. Jonathan Rauch, *Demosclerosis: The Silent Killer of American Government* (1994).

14. Charles Bowsher, "Government Management: Report on 17 High-Risk Areas," testimony before the Committee on Government Affairs, U.S. Senate, 19 (January 8, 1993).

15. Times Mirror Center for the People and the Press, *The New Political Landscape: The People, the Press and Politics,* 23 (1994).

16. Ibid.

17. *New York Times,* A-10 (January 24, 1996).

18. E.g., Massachusetts' governor, William Weld: "Government should do only what the private sector cannot, and we have ample evidence that the private sector does almost everything better." *Boston Globe,* 22 (August 4, 1995).

19. McKinsey Global Institute, *Service Sector Productivity,* ch. 3, 14–15.

Index

128, 132; and government policies, 411, 422–423. *See also* Pollution
Environmental Protection Agency (EPA), 116, 118, 119–120, 125, 126, 127, 128, 129, 417; Superfund program of, 121, 130, 131, 409, 442n36
Equality, 10, 11, 157. *See also* Race
European Community, 306, 399
European Convention on Human Rights, 305, 306
European Court of Human Rights, 304, 306, 465n26
European Economic Community, 90

Fair Housing Act: of 1968, 181; of 1989, 181
Farrington, David, 221
Federal Bureau of Investigation (FBI), 219, 316–317
Federal Housing Administration (FHA), 97, 101, 107, 180
Ford Foundation, 137, 143
Freedom, individual, 10–11, 295–312, 362, 383; and personal responsibility, 11, 14–15, 352, 356, 384, 386; international comparisons, 300–310, 312, 371, 375, 388, 401, 402–403, 404; and community, 303; and family, 303–304; and the courts, 305–312, 354, 375, 422; and taxation, 309–310
Freedom House, 301
Friedman, Milton, 247, 335, 420

General Accounting Office (GAO), 248, 265, 269, 417, 457n17, 462n13, 472n32
General Agreement on Tariffs and Trade (GATT), 90
Gingrich, Newt, 157
Glendon, Mary Ann, 354
Goldthorpe, John, 193
Goodwin, Richard, 5
Gore, Albert, 5
Government: distrust of, 7, 8, 11; role of, 8–9, 16, 74, 76, 91, 159, 172, 189, 299–300, 405–425; and scientific research, 46–47; reinventing, 81, 418, 419; and the arts, 135–138, 149–150, 408; and health care, 236, 411; and funding for abortion, 308; and private charity, 353–354; and rights, 354; opinions of, 365, 418–419, 424, 476n18; and civic loyalty, 385–386;

failings of, 407–418; successes of, 408; and gridlock, 410–411; waste and inefficiency in, 416–417; liberal vs. conservative views on, 419–421, 424; and deregulation, 422; and privatization, 422; and knowledge, 423; and global competition, 424, 425; and immigration, 424
Government regulations, 300, 378, 381, 384–385, 388, 401, 415, 464n22; international comparisons, 381
Great Depression, 1, 12, 56, 77, 277, 296, 364, 366
Great Society, 337, 338, 354, 425
Greenough, Horatio, 136
Gross Domestic Product (GDP), 19, 25–27, 33, 43, 44, 121

Hamburg, David, 161
Harris alienation index, 1
Harvard School of Public Health, 252
Hayek, Friedrich von, 420
Head Start, 169, 170, 173, 185, 186, 342, 447n37
Health and Human Services, Department of (HHS), 109
Health care, 4, 10, 235–255, 359, 362, 363, 365; quality of, 13, 14, 240–244; for children, 160–164; and prenatal care, 161–162, 213, 361, 446n14; international comparisons in, 236–237, 240–249, 252, 310, 344, 370, 383, 388, 393, 397, 402, 418; and free markets, 238; cost of, 244–249, 254, 290, 291, 362, 370, 388, 395, 406, 418, 457n17; for elderly, 281–283, 287, 289, 337, 400; universal, 351; and government policy, 411, 418, 422. *See also* Infant mortality; Life expectancy
Health insurance, 33, 164, 249–250, 252, 254–255, 289, 310, 411; international comparisons in, 343, 370, 374, 377, 393, 395, 400, 418; and income, 377
Health maintenance organizations (HMOs), 248, 254
Helms, Jesse, 143, 144
Herrnstein, Richard, 58
Hitchcock, Henry-Russell, 135
Holmes, Oliver Wendell, 296
Hoover, Herbert, 95
House Un-American Activities Committee, 137